D0073477

ENTREPRENEURSHIP

AND

VENTURE

MANAGEMENT

ENTREPRENEURSHIP

AND

VENTURE

MANAGEMENT

CLIFFORD M. BAUMBACK

JOSEPH R. MANCUSO

Prentice-Hall, Inc., Englewood Cliffs, N.J.

Library of Congress Cataloging in Publication Data

Baumback, Clifford Mason, comp.
   Entrepreneurship and venture management.
   Bibliography: p.
   1. Small business—Management—Addresses, essays,
lectures. 2. New business enterprises—
Addresses, essays, lectures. I. Mancuso, Joseph, joint comp.
II. Title.
HD69.S6B374   658'.022   74-13348
ISBN 0-13-283119-8

HD
69
, S6
B374

Printed in the United States of America

10 9 8 7 6 5 4 3 2 1

Prentice-Hall International, Inc., London
Prentice-Hall of Australia, Pty. Ltd., Sydney
Prentice-Hall of Canada, Ltd. Toronto
Prentice-Hall of India Private Limited, New Delhi
Prentice-Hall of Japan, Inc., Tokyo

980327

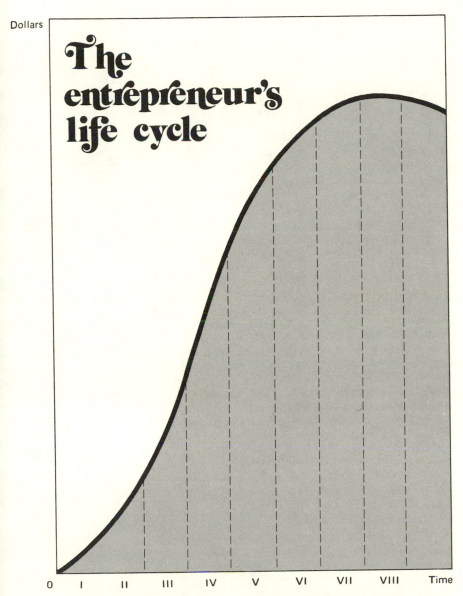

The chapters in this book are arranged in chronological sequence to correspond to the classic life cycle of the small business—and of the entrepreneur's business life. (Numbers indicate the appropriate chapter.)

Contents

VII

ADDENDUM

APPENDIX A

APPENDIX B

APPENDIX C

APPENDIX D

SUBJECT INDEX

NAME INDEX

Preface

This book is intended for college or adult extension courses in entrepreneurship and small business management. It may be used either as a companion volume to a standard text on small business management or as the principal text in courses oriented largely toward entrepreneurship and new business formation. It may also be used for independent reading by those who plan to go into business for themselves, and by those who already own and operate their own business ventures.

Entrepreneurship and Venture Management contains 35 carefully selected articles by well-known, authoritative writers in the field, appearing in over 20 professional journals. Its initial focus—on *Entrepreneurship*—is on the type of person best fitted to be "his own boss," to run his own business. Attention is then directed to the question as to why a new business venture "takes" or fails to "take," why some succeed and others fail—i.e., on *Venture Management.* The articles are grouped into eight chapters, plus an Addendum on "Minority Business Enterprise." Each chapter is preceded by a summary of the major ideas presented in the articles and by the authors' own thoughts on the subject.

The outstanding feature of the book lies in its organization. The chapters are arranged in chronological sequence to correspond to the classic life cycle of the business—and of the entrepreneur's business life. By looking at the field of entrepreneurship and independent venture management in this way, the reader is presented with a logical, integrated framework.

Though the bias of our book is toward technical entrepreneurship, or on the forming of new, technologically-based manufacturing ventures, the principles and ideas expressed herein are relevant to any type of business enterprise at any stage of its life cycle.

We are directly indebted to the contributors to this book as well as to the publications in which their articles appeared. We express our gratitude also to the following graduate students who have, in some important way, been of help to us in the preparation of this volume: Donald Gorsuch, Kaye Henry, John Dodge, Lyle Mumm, and Charles Hicks.

Clifford M. Baumback

Joseph R. Mancuso

ENTREPRENEURSHIP

AND

VENTURE

MANAGEMENT

ONE

Who is the Entrepreneur?

What attributes characterize the entrepreneur? What environmental factors and experiences have influenced his personality development and motivational drives? What makes him willing to bring a vision into reality? These are obviously difficult questions to answer. Some information has become available in the past ten years from an increasing number of psychological studies of entrepreneurial behavior, and these studies have offered insight into the entrepreneur's role in economic development. It is through these studies that we gain an insight into, and understanding of, the characteristics common to those we call "entrepreneurs."

Essentially, the technical entrepreneur is an innovator, combining different technologies to produce a marketable product or service. He fills in the people, financing, production, and marketing gaps by acquiring and assembling the necessary resources into a newly created firm. But foremost, he is able to recognize potentially profitable opportunities, to conceptualize the venture strategy, and to become the key force in successfully moving the idea from the laboratory to the marketplace.

He is usually the first child in a family having a self-employed father, whose successes result in the entrepreneur's high need for achievement. Formal education is pursued to the extent that a master's degree is often obtained.[1] He has lots of energy and is willing to drive hard to make his chosen course of action work. Moderate risks are taken but only against realistic and achievable odds. At the time of starting his first business, the typical entrepreneur is in his early thirties, has a supportive wife, and has some seed money to invest. He has developed a curiosity about technological advancements, business affairs, and people. A successful entrepreneur will also have a high awareness of himself and his environment. Although he has family responsibilities, he is nonetheless willing to make the personal sacrifices required in starting the new business.

---

[1]Studies of *non*-technical entrepreneurs, on the other hand, indicate that they have more modest educational qualifications.

1

Some people are constantly thinking about how to make a better product, provide a better service, or improve their job performance. They have a continual need for successful completion of tasks. David McClelland, in the first article, *That Urge to Achieve,* describes this drive as the person's need for achievement, and characterizes people with high *n* Ach as preferring to be personally responsible for solving problems and for setting goals to be reached by their own efforts. They are also characterized by the need for feedback on how well they are accomplishing the job and obtaining the stated goals. McClelland views entrepreneurs as having these same characteristics. He believes that a person (or an entire society) possessing a latent need for achievement can be taught achievement motivation—resulting either in the undertaking of new entrepreneurial activities or a more aggressive level of present entrepreneurial venturing.

Although entrepreneurs may be characterized by their high need for achievement, it is equally important to focus on those additional characteristics that differentiate entrepreneurs from men in general, and the successful entrepreneurs from the unsuccessful ones. It is a common observation, for example, that entrepreneurs generally work harder and longer than their subordinates. But is it sufficient to possess dynamic energy or "drive" and to work long and irregular hours? Is a high need to dominate complementary with high achievement motivation and successful business ventures? To what extent do other factors, such as talent, self-reliance, imagination, resourcefulness, leadership and competitiveness, contribute to the ultimate success of the entrepreneur?

In the second article, *Characteristics of Successful Entrepreneurs,* John A. Hornaday and John Aboud attempt to answer these questions by using data obtained from interviews and self-rating scales and from the objective personality scales of standardized tests administered to a group of 20 black and 20 white entrepreneurs. They found that entrepreneurs, compared to men in general, score significantly higher on scales measuring the importance attached to recognition, independence, and leadership, and they score lower on scales reflecting emphasis on benevolence or need for support. Except for the latter characteristics, which may reflect cultural differences and differences in socio-economic background, no significant differences between races were found.

In the third article, *The Application of Psychological Testing to Entrepreneurial Potential,* Michael Palmer cites still another characteristic that is common among successful entrepreneurs: the ability to make decisions under uncertainty. He finds the entrepreneur engaging in business venture activities that provide concrete feedback on performance (profits), some degree of risk taking, and opportunity for personal achievement.

Whether to be self-employed or to work for someone else is a major decision for many persons and warrants careful consideration. In the final section of this chapter, Joseph Mancuso cites other attributes of the successful entrepreneur and presents a self-test, *The Entrepreneur's Quiz,* to assist the reader in determining whether or not he is the type to be his own boss.

This quiz, which was developed from *Fun & Guts, the Entrepreneur's Philosophy,* is based on Mancuso's research with over 300 entrepreneurs on the East Coast. He found that entrepreneurs have common traits and characteristics, and he has devised a self-scoring system to gauge how well an individual measures up on a scale from entrepreneur to hired hand.

In summary, it can be stated that the entrepreneur is not motivated by money itself but rather by his high motivational needs, especially his need to achieve. Money is a by-product for accomplishing some nobler goal. The entrepreneur has an idea and a dream. His awareness of people and their needs, and his technical training, enable him to perceive profitable marketing opportunities that others have neglected. We know from past studies that in the more advanced countries entrepreneurial characteristics are related to certain sociological factors in the entrepreneur's childhood and to personal experiences in later adult life. Further research should reveal additional parameters that will help to explain the complex individual we call an entrepreneur.

Governments have always sought to find and develop entrepreneurs. In underdeveloped nations, these individuals often hold the key to economic growth for a whole society. So *entrepreneur* is not a dirty word or a fast-buck opportunist, but, rather, the backbone of the capitalist system.

THAT URGE TO ACHIEVE*

DAVID C. McCLELLAND

Most people in this world, psychologically, can be divided into two broad groups. There is that minority which is challenged by opportunity and willing to work hard to achieve something, and the majority which really does not care all that much.

For nearly twenty years now, psychologists have tried to penetrate the mystery of this curious dichotomy. Is the need to achieve (or the absence of it) an accident, is it hereditary, or is it the result of environment? Is it a single, isolatable human motive, or a combination of motives—the desire to accumulate wealth, power, fame? Most important of all, is there some technique that could give this will to achieve to people, even whole societies, who do not now have it?

While we do not yet have complete answers for any of these questions, years of work have given us partial answers to most of them and insights into all of them. There is a distinct human motive, distinguishable from others. It can be found, in fact tested for, in any group.

Let me give you one example. Several years ago, a careful study was made of 450 workers who had been thrown out of work by a plant shutdown in Erie, Pennsylvania. Most of the unemployed workers stayed home for a while and

*From *Think* (November-December, 1966), pp. 19-23. Reprinted by permission from THINK Magazine, published by IBM, copyright 1966 by International Business Machines Corporation.

3

then checked back with the United States Employment Service to see if their old jobs or similar ones were available. But a small minority among them behaved differently: the day they were laid off, they started job-hunting.

They checked both the United States and the Pennsylvania Employment Office; they studied the "Help Wanted" sections of the papers; they checked through their union, their church, and various fraternal organizations; they looked into training courses to learn a new skill; they even left town to look for work, while the majority when questioned said they would not under any circumstances move away from Erie to obtain a job. Obviously the members of that active minority were differently motivated. All the men were more or less in the same situation objectively: they needed work, money, food, shelter, job security. Yet only a minority showed initiative and enterprise in finding what they needed. Why? Psychologists, after years of research now believe they can answer that question. They have demonstrated that these men possessed in greater degree a specific type of human motivation. For the moment let us refer to this personality characteristic as "Motive A" and review some of the other characteristics of the men who have more of the motive than other men.

Suppose they are confronted by a work situation in which they can set their own goals as to how difficult a task they will undertake. In the psychological laboratory, such a situation is very simply created by asking them to throw rings over a peg from any distance they may choose. Most men throw more or less randomly, standing now close, now far away, but those with Motive A seem to calculate carefully where they are most likely to get a sense of mastery. They stand nearly always at moderate distances, not so close as to make the task ridiculously easy, nor so far away as to make it impossible. They set moderately difficult, but potentially achievable goals for themselves, where they objectively have only about a 1-in-3 chance of succeeding. In other words, they are always setting challenges for themselves, tasks to make them stretch themselves a little.

But they behave like this only if *they* can influence the outcome by performing the work themselves. They prefer not to gamble at all. Say they are given a choice between rolling dice with one in three chances of winning and working on a problem with a one-in-three chance of solving in the time alloted, they choose to work on the problem even though rolling the dice is obviously less work and the odds of winning are the same. They prefer to work at a problem rather than leave the outcome to chance or to others.

Obviously they are concerned with personal achievement rather than with the rewards of success *per se,* since they stand just as much chance of getting those rewards by throwing the dice. This leads to another characteristic the Motive A men show—namely, a strong preference for work situations in which they get concrete feedback on how well they are doing, as one does, say in playing golf, or in being a salesman, but as one does not in teaching, or in personnel counseling. A golfer always knows his score and can compare how well he is doing with par or with his own performance yesterday or last week. A teacher has no such concrete feedback on how well he is doing in "getting across" to his students.

THE *n* ACH MEN

But why do certain men behave like this? At one level the reply is simple: because they habitually spend their time thinking about doing things better. In fact, psychologists typically measure the strength of Motive A by taking samples of a man's spontaneous thoughts (such as making up a story about a picture they have been shown) and counting the frequency with which he mentions doing things better. The count is objective and can even be made these days with the help of a computer program for content analysis. It yields what is referred to technically as an individual's *n* Ach score (for "need for Achievement"). It is not difficult to understand why people who think constantly about "doing better" are more apt to do better at job-hunting, to set moderate, achievable goals for themselves, to dislike gambling (because they get no achievement satisfaction from success), and to prefer work situations where they can tell easily whether they are improving or not. But why some people and not others come to think this way is another question. The evidence suggests it is not because they are born that way, but because of special training they get in the home from parents who set moderately high achievement goals but who are warm, encouraging and nonauthoritarian in helping their children reach these goals.

Such detailed knowledge about one motive helps correct a lot of common sense ideas about human motivation. For example, much public policy (and much business policy) is based on the simpleminded notion that people will work harder "if they have to." As a first approximation, the idea isn't totally wrong, but it is only a half-truth. The majority of unemployed workers in Erie "had to" find work as much as those with higher *n* Ach, but they certainly didn't work as hard at it. Or again, it is frequently assumed that *any* strong motive will lead to doing things better. Wouldn't it be fair to say that most of the Erie workers were just "unmotivated"? But our detailed knowledge of various human motives shows that each one leads a person to behave in *different* ways. The contrast is not between being "motivated" or "unmotivated" but between being motivated toward A or toward B or C. etc.

A simple experiment makes the point nicely: subjects were told that they could choose as a working partner either a close friend or a stranger who was known to be an expert on the problem to be solved. Those with higher *n* Ach (more "need to achieve") chose the experts over their friends, whereas those with more *n* Aff (the "need to affiliate with others") chose friends over experts. The latter were not "unmotivated"; their desire to be with someone they liked was simply a stronger motive than their desire to excel at the task. Other such needs have been studied by psychologists. For instance, the need for Power is often confused with the need for Achievement because both may lead to "outstanding" activities. There is a distinct difference. People with a strong need for Power want to command attention, get recognition, and control others. They are more active in political life and tend to busy themselves primarily with controlling the channels of communication both up to the top and down to the people so that they are more "in charge." Those with high *n* Power are not as concerned with improving their work performance daily as those with high *n* Ach.

It follows, from what we have been able to learn, that not all "great achievers" score high in *n* Ach. Many generals, outstanding politicians, great research scientists do not, for instance, because their work requires other personality characteristics, other motives. A general or a politician must be more concerned with power relationships, a research scientist must be able to go for long periods without the immediate feedback the person with high *n* Ach requires, etc. On the other hand, business executives, particularly if they are in

5

positions of real responsibility or if they are salesmen, tend to score high in n Ach. This is true even in a Communist country like Poland: apparently there, as well as in a private enterprise economy, a manager succeeds if he is concerned about improving all the time, setting moderate goals, keeping track of his or the company's performance, etc.

MOTIVATION AND HALF-TRUTHS

Since careful study has shown that common sense notions about motivation are at best half-truths, it also follows that you cannot trust what people tell you about their motives. After all, they often get their ideas about their own motives from common sense. Thus a general may say he is interested in achievement (because he has obviously achieved), or a businessman that he is interested only in making money (because he has made money), or one of the majority of unemployed in Erie that he desperately wants a job (because he knows he needs one); but a careful check of what each one thinks about and how he spends his time may show that each is concerned about quite different things. It requires special measurement techniques to identify the presense of n Ach and other such motives. Thus what people say and believe is not very closely related to these "hidden" motives which seem to affect a person's "style of life" more than his political, religious or social attitudes. Thus n Ach produces enterprising men among labor leaders or managers, Republicans or Democrats, Catholics or Protestants, capitalists or Communists.

Wherever people begin to think often in n Ach terms, things begin to move. Men with higher n Ach get more raises and are promoted more rapidly, because they keep actively seeking ways to do a better job. Companies with many such men grow faster. In one comparison of two firms in Mexico, it was discovered that all but one of the top executives of a fast growing firm had higher n Ach scores than the highest scoring executive in an equally large but slow-growing firm. Countries with many such rapidly growing firms tend to show above-average rates of economic growth. This appears to be the reason why correlations have regularly been found between the n Ach content in popular literature (such as popular songs or stories in children's textbooks) and subsequent rates of national economic growth. A nation which is thinking about doing better all the time (as shown in its popular literature) actually does do better economically speaking. Careful quantitative studies have shown this to be true in Ancient Greece, in Spain in the Middle Ages, in England from 1400—1800, as well as among contemporary nations, whether capitalist or Communist, developed or underdeveloped.

Contrast these two stories for example. Which one contains more n Ach? Which one reflects a state of mind which ought to lead to harder striving to improve the way things are?

Excerpt from story A (4th grade reader): "Don't Ever Owe a Man—The world is an illusion. Wife, children, horses and cows are all just ties of fate. They are ephemeral. Each after fulfilling his part in life disappears. So we should not clamour after riches which are not permanent. As long as we live it is wise not to have any attachments and just think of God. We have to spend our lives without trouble, for is it not time that there is an end to grievances? So it is better to live knowing the real state of affairs. Don't get entangled in the meshes of family life."

6

Excerpt from story B (4th grade reader): "How I Do Like to Learn—I was sent to an accelerated technical high school. I was so happy I cried. Learning is not very easy. In the beginning I couldn't understand what the teacher taught us. I always got a red cross mark on my papers. The boy sitting next to me was very enthusiastic and also an outstanding student. When he found I couldn't do the problems he offered to show me how he had done them. I could not copy his work. I must learn through my own reasoning. I gave his paper back and explained I had to do it myself. Sometimes I worked on a problem until midnight. If I couldn't finish, I started early in the morning. The red cross marks on my work were getting less common. I conquered my difficulties. My marks rose. I graduated and went on to college."

Most readers would agree, without any special knowledge of the n Ach coding system, that the second story shows more concern with improvement than the first, which comes from a contemporary reader used in Indian public schools. In fact the latter has a certain Horatio Alger quality that is reminiscent of our own McGuffey readers of several generations ago. It appears today in the textbooks of Communist China. It should not, therefore, come as a surprise if a nation like Communist China, obsessed as it is with improvement, tended in the long run to outproduce a nation like India, which appears to be more fatalistic.

The n Ach level is obviously important for statesmen to watch and in many instances to try to do something about, particularly if a nation's economy is lagging. Take Britain, for example. A generation ago (around 1925) it ranked fifth among 25 countries where children's readers were scored for n Ach—and its economy was doing well. By 1950 the n Ach level had dropped to 27th out of 39 countries—well below the world average—and today, its leaders are feeling the severe economic effects of this loss in the spirit of enterprise.

ECONOMICS AND n ACH

If psychologists can detect n Ach levels in individuals or nations, particularly before their effects are widespread, can't the knowledge somehow be put to use to foster economic development? Obviously detection or diagnosis is not enough. What good is it to tell Britain (or India for that matter) that it needs more n Ach, a greater spirit of enterprise? In most such cases, informed observers of the local scene know very well that such a need exists, though they may be slower to discover it than the psychologist hovering over n Ach scores. What is needed is some method of developing n Ach in individuals or nations.

Since about 1960, psychologists in my research group at Harvard have been experimenting with techniques designed to accomplish this goal, chiefly among business executives whose work requires the action characteristics of people with high n Ach. Initially, we had real doubts as to whether we could succeed, partly because like most American psychologists we had been strongly influenced by the psychoanalytic view that basic motives are laid down in childhood and cannot really be changed later, and partly because many studies of intensive psychotherapy and counseling have shown minor if any long-term personality effects. On the other hand we were encouraged by the nonprofessionals: those enthusiasts like Dale Carnegie, the Communist ideologue or the Church missionary, who felt they could change adults and in fact seemed to be doing so. At any rate we ran some brief (7 to 10 days) "total push" training courses for businessmen, designed to increase their n Ach.

7

FOUR MAIN GOALS

In broad outline the courses had four main goals: (1) They were designed to teach the participants how to think, talk and act like a person with high n Ach, based on our knowledge of such people gained through 17 years of research. For instance, men learned how to make up stories that would code high in n Ach (i.e., how to think in n Ach terms), how to set moderate goals for themselves in the ring toss game (and in life). (2) The courses stimulated the participants to set higher but carefully planned and realistic work goals for themselves over the next two years. Then we checked back with them every six months to see how well they were doing in terms of their own objectives. (3) The courses also utilized techniques for giving the participants knowledge about themselves. For instance, in playing the ring toss game, they could observe that they behaved differently from others—perhaps in refusing to adjust a goal downward after failure. This would then become a matter for group discussion and the man would have to explain what he had in mind in setting such unrealistic goals. Discussion could then lead on to what a man's ultimate goals in life were, how much he cared about actually improving performance v. making a good impression or having many friends. In this way the participants would be freer to realize their achievement goals without being blocked by old habits and attitudes. (4) The courses also usually created a group *esprit de corps* from learning about each other's hopes and fears, successes and failures, and from going through an emotional experience together, away from everyday life, in a retreat setting. This membership in a new group helps a man achieve his goals, partly because he knows he has their sympathy and support and partly because he knows they will be watching to see how well he does. The same effect has been noted in other therapy groups like Alcoholics Anonymous. We are not sure which of these course "inputs" is really absolutely essential—that remains a research question—but we were taking no chances at the outset in view of the general pessimism about such efforts, and we wanted to include any and all techniques that were thought to change people.

The courses have been given: to executives in a large American firm, and in several Mexican firms; to underachieving high school boys; and to businessmen in India from Bombay and from a small city—Kakinada in the state of Andhra Pradesh. In every instance save one (the Mexican case), it was possible to demonstrate statistically, some two years later, that the men who took the course had done better (made more money, got promoted faster, expanded their businesses faster) than comparable men who did not take the course or who took some other management course.

Consider the Kakinada results, for example. In the two years preceding the course 9 men, 18 percent of the 52 participants, had shown "unusual" enterprise in their businesses. In the 18 months following the course 25 of the men, in other words nearly 50 percent, were unusually active. And this was not due to a general upturn of business in India. Data from a control city, some forty-five miles away, show the same base rate of "unusually active" men as in Kakinada before the course—namely, about 20 percent. Something clearly happened in Kakinada: the owner of a small radio shop started a chemical plant; a banker was so successful in making commercial loans in an enterprising way that he was promoted to a much larger branch of his bank in Calcutta; the local political leader accomplished his goal (it was set in the course) to get the federal government to deepen the harbor and make it into an all-weather port; plans are far along for establishing a steel rolling mill, etc. All this took place without any substantial capital input from the outside. In fact, the only costs were for four 10-day courses plus some brief follow-up visits every six months. The men are raising their own capital and using their own resources for getting business and industry moving in a city that had been considered stagnant and unenterprising.

The promise of such a method of developing achievement motivation seems very great. It has obvious applications in helping underdeveloped countries, or "pockets of poverty" in the United States, to move faster economically. It has great potential for businesses that need to "turn around" and take a more enterprising approach toward their growth and development. It may even be helpful in developing more *n* Ach among low-income groups. For instance, data show that lower-class Negro Americans have a very low level of *n* Ach. This is not surprising. Society has systematically discouraged and blocked their achievement striving. But as the barriers to upward mobility are broken down, it will be necessary to help stimulate the motivation that will lead them to take advantage of new opportunities opening up.

EXTREME REACTIONS

But a word of caution: Whenever I speak of this research and its great potential, audience reaction tends to go to opposite extremes. Either people remain skeptical and argue that motives can't really be changed, that all we are doing is dressing Dale Carnegie up in fancy "psychologese," or they become converts and want instant course descriptions by re-return mail to solve their local motivational problems. Either response is unjustified. What I have described here in a few pages has taken 20 years of patient research effort, and hundreds of thousands of dollars in basic research costs. What remains to be done will involve even larger sums and more time for development to turn a promising idea into something of wide practical utility.

ENCOURAGEMENT NEEDED

To take only one example, we have not yet learned how to develop *n* Ach really well among low-income groups. In our first effort—a summer course for bright underachieving 14-year-olds—we found that boys from the middle class improved steadily in grades in school over a two-year period, but boys from the lower class showed an improvement after the first year followed by a drop back to their beginning low grade average. (See Fig. 1.) Why? We speculated that it was because they moved back into an environment in which neither parents nor friends encouraged achievement or upward mobility. In other words, it isn't enough to change a man's motivation if the environment in which he lives doesn't support at least to some degree his new efforts. Negroes striving to rise out of the ghetto frequently confront this problem: they are often faced by skepticism at home and suspicion on the job, so that even if their *n* Ach is raised, it

9

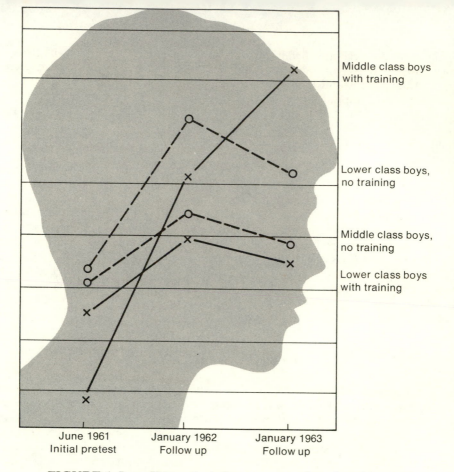

Middle class boys
with training

Lower class boys,
no training

Middle class boys,
no training

Lower class boys
with training

June 1961   January 1962   January 1963
Initial pretest   Follow up   Follow up

FIGURE 1 In a Harvard study, a group of underachieving
14-year-olds was given a six-week course designed
to help them do better in school. Some of the boys
were also given training in achievement motivation, or *n* Ach (solid lines). As graph reveals, the
only boys who continued to improve after a two-
year period were the middle-class boys with the
special *n* Ach training. Psychologists suspect the
lower-class boys dropped back, even with *n* Ach
training, because they returned to an environment
in which neither parents nor friends encouraged
achievement.

can be lowered again by the heavy odds against their success. We must learn not
only to raise *n* Ach but also to find methods of instructing people in how to
manage it, to create a favorable environment in which it can flourish.

Many of these training techniques are now only in the pilot testing stage. It
will take time and money to perfect them, but society should be willing to invest
heavily in them in view of their tremendous potential for contributing to human
betterment.

CHARACTERISTICS

OF SUCCESSFUL ENTREPRENEURS*

JOHN A. HORNADAY / JOHN ABOUD

INTRODUCTION

In an earlier article in *Personnel Psychology*, Hornaday and Bunker (1970) discuss the importance of achieving a better understanding of the psychological nature of the successful entrepreneur through a research program designed to identify and measure the personal characteristics of those persons who have successfully started a new business. Such knowledge would be of much interest to lending organizations such as banks, to enfranchising organizations such as oil companies and restaurant chains, and to federal government programs, both domestic (in loans to small businesses and in such efforts as the poverty programs) and international (as in using foreign aid more effectively to help strengthen the economy of underdeveloped countries). Further, colleges of business administration can make significant contributions in entrepreneurial education if it is possible to understand the nature of entrepreneurship and if workable programs can be developed from the results of the research.

The earlier research led to the development of a structured interview guide sheet as well as the selection of three standardized, objective tests that appeared promising in differentiating successful entrepreneurs from men in general. Although McClelland (McClelland, Atkinson, Clark and Lowell, 1953) had reported success in using both the Thematic Apperception Test (Murray, 1943) and in using his own test for this purpose, these tests are *projective* in nature and can be administered and interpreted only by a highly trained psychologist. The goal of this study was to develop *objective* tests which will be valid and will have the advantage of a simple format and ease of administration and interpretation.

Further, McClelland approaches the problem of predicting entrepreneurial success by measuring, specifically, individuals' need for achievement (*n* Ach) and he emphasizes that this characteristic is to be considered even to the exclusion of other factors. In a recent interview for *Forbes* (McClelland, 1969), he stated, "We've spent twenty years studying just this [why one businessman succeeds and another fails], twenty years in the laboratory doing very careful research, and *we've isolated the specific thing. We know the exact type of motivation that makes a better entrepreneur.* [Italics ours.] Not necessarily a better

*From *Personnel Psychology* (Summer, 1971), pp. 141-153. Reprinted by permission.

head of General Motors; I'm talking about the man who starts a business." He went on to say that the specific characteristic is the individual's need for achievement.

NEED FOR OBJECTIVE APPROACH

The earlier research by Hornaday and Bunker and the present study of entrepreneurs are predicated on two assumptions: (1) that there would be great value in a system of selection that is *objective* and *structured* so that non-psychologists could administer it, and (2) that in addition to the admittedly important *n Ach* there may be other factors which should be measured. The latter point is that our prediction of success would have higher validity if measurement were made of several factors, each of which makes some independent contribution to the ultimate success of the entrepreneur.

The need for objectivity in measuring need for achievement is emphasized by Hermans (1970). He says, "During the past twenty years, there have been a great many studies in the area of achievement motivation. These vary from psychometric investigations to theoretical discussions. One of the most difficult problems in this area is that of measurement. Projective techniques have been the principal devices used to quantify the strength of the achievement motive. . . . With regard to the projective needs for achievement measures, several critical problems arise. Klinger (1966) pointed to their lack of internal consistency, lack of test-retest reliability, their deficient validity against performance criteria, and the low intercorrelation among several projective *n Ach* measures. . . . The need for a new measure for *n Ach* still exists."

The pilot study indicated that three objective tests held promise of differentiating entrepreneurs from men-in-general. For the present study, therefore, these tests, along with the structured interview, were administered to successful entrepreneurs. As in the pilot study, the "successful entrepreneur" was defined as a man or woman who *started* a business where there was none before, who had at least eight employees and who had been established for at least five years. These criteria were selected because it was desired to eliminate the "Mom and Pop" stores and because the first five years are the most difficult. The criteria are similar to those established by Collins et al. (1964) in their entrepreneurial studies. The three tests applied to the entrepreneurs were: Kuder Occupational Interest Survey, Form DD (Kuder, 1970), Gordon's Survey of Interpersonal Values (Gordon, 1960), and a questionnaire composed of three scales drawn from the Edwards Personal Preference Scale (Edwards, 1959). Throughout this paper the abbreviations for these tests will be, respectively, OIS, SIV, and EPPS.

Forty "successful entrepreneurs," as defined above, were interviewed and tested in the summer of 1970. The sample was selected without regard for geographic location (all were located in either North Carolina, Rhode Island, or Massachusetts), but care was taken to obtain twenty black and twenty white entrepreneurs. That racial selection made possible a tentative investigation of the null hypothesis relative to racial differences.

12

In addition to these forty entrepreneurs, use was made of the twenty entrepreneurs who were interviewed and tested in the pilot study (Hornaday and Bunker, 1970) since they were given essentially the same interview and the same tests. The number of cases used for the several analyses varied because some entrepreneurs completed only a part of the forms. For all sixty, however, interview responses are available; most of the questions in the interview were the same in the two studies.

HYPOTHESES

Specifically, the hypotheses investigated in this study were:

1. A number of personal characteristics differentiate successful entrepreneurs from men in general and these characteristics can be measured by objective, standardized tests. Entrepreneurs are significantly higher on scales on the EPPS that measure need for achievement, need for autonomy, and need for aggression. On the SIV, the examinees are expected to score higher on scales measuring the importance attached to recognition, independence, and leadership.

2. Because of the nature of scoring the OIS, the scores of entrepreneurs could not be compared to men-in-general. The Form DD scores of OIS are lambdas (Clemans, 1968; Kuder, 1963), and the nature of those scores does not permit comparison of an individual to a group. The hypothesis for the OIS, therefore, must relate to the scales on which entrepreneurs are higher relative to their other scales. Entrepreneurs should score high on scales relating to business occupations and business college majors. The greatest value from the Kuder Occupational Interest Survey, however, would be gained from an entrepreneurial key for the OIS, and development of that key must await the gathering of considerably more data.

3. In answering the questions covered by the interviewers, entrepreneurs are expected to indicate that they work long hours, that the work interferes with their family relationships, that they rebel against regimentation, and it was felt that their family background might reflect, generally, a rebellion against an attitude in the father that they perceived with distaste. A number of additional areas were investigated in the interviews as a further exploration into characteristics which might be significant. On these, no specific hypothesis could be formed nor is there any control group of the general population to serve as a basis of comparison. Thus, the interview was largely exploratory.

4. On a self-rating form in which entrepreneurs subjectively compared themselves to the general population, it was hypothesized that the subjects would be above the general population in all of the significant items (a few items were "fillers"). Those are such items as: need for power over people, self-reliance, innovative tendencies, and other characteristics as listed in Table 3.

5. Relative to race, the null hypothesis is to be tested for all scales of the tests and items of the interview. Our hypotheses are that no racial differences will be found between black and white entrepreneurs. Data, therefore, are presented for the races separately and, where no difference is found, combined.

PROCEDURE

The subjects of this study consisted of a total of sixty entrepreneurs. The distribution of the sixty by race and sex is as follows:

34 white males
22 black males
2 white females
2 black females

During the early work of this study, which began in the summer of 1969, a total of twenty entrepreneurs were interviewed. It was in the process of these interviews that the Interview Schedule was developed. Development consisted primarily of devising items, reordering most of them, and, subsequently, deleting or adding a very few items. Also during this early phase of the work, the three tests used to assess the personality traits of the entrepreneurs were selected. Because some experimentation with the formats and content of these measurement devices was necessary, not all of the entrepreneurs were subjected to identical items. As will be seen later, this, plus the failure of some entrepreneurs to complete all of the forms, resulted in the sample's containing somewhat less than sixty for the various forms employed. Early experimenting with procedures of testing and interview also yielded unequal numbers of completed forms for the various questionnaires employed.

The forms which held the most promise in the pilot study and were used in this study are:

The Standardized Interview Schedule
The Kuder Occupational Interest Survey (Form DD)
The Gordon Survey of Interpersonal Values
A modified form of the Edwards Personal Preference Schedule
A five-point scale of personal self-estimates called the Self-Evaluation
Scale

RESULTS

Analyses were made separately and in combination for the white males (34) and black males (22). Because of the small number of cases for women (two white and two black), no meaningful comparative analyses could be made by sex. Inspection of the data indicated differences between the female and the male entrepreneurs, and it could not be established that the sexes could be reasonably combined; therefore, only the male entrepreneurs were used in subsequent analyses.

The structured interview was used with the full group of sixty entrepreneurs. Many of the items were administered to the total of sixty, but a few items were introduced or revised at some time during the first twenty contacts. For the last forty the interview schedule was kept constant. The sample size for interview items, thus, may vary between 40 and 56 (since the four female entrepreneurs were not included).

Table 1 presents data for black males and white males on all of the interview items that lend themselves to quantification. The items on which significant differences occurred were:

1. Length of time in business. White males averaged thirteen years and black males averaged eight years. This perhaps is a reflection of the more recent encouragement given blacks to go into business for themselves.
2. Frequency of separation and divorce from wives. In this study 6% whites and 32% blacks were divorced or separated. This may reflect a general cultural difference rather than a characteristic of entrepreneurship. (Divorce and separation is considerably higher among the blacks in the United States according to the *Statistical Abstract of the United States, 1970.*) In fact, the per cent of divorce and separation among all entrepreneurs is below that of the general population (16% among all entrepreneurs combined; approximately 33% in the general population).
3. The frequency of a special idea as the basis of the development of the enterprise was much greater for white entrepreneurs than for blacks. This may have been a reflection of the types of entrepreneurs in the two groups. A much higher percentage of the whites were in manufacturing, where a specific original idea might have been particularly important. Almost all of the blacks were in sales and services; of the three blacks who were in manufacturing, all had moved into the field because of their having an innovative idea.
4. Differences in per cent graduating from college and "seriousness" in school, as well as differences in self-support in college. Again these may reflect cultural differences and differences in socio-economic background

TABLE 1   Analysis of Quantifiable Items of the Structural Interviews

	Statistic	White Male (N $\leq$ 34)	Black Male (N $\leq$ 22)
Time required for interview	Mdn.	90	75
Number of employees	Mdn.	24	15
Years in this business	Mdn.	13	8
Hrs. work/week at start	Mdn.	68	70
Hrs. work/week now	Mdn.	60	60
Age of entrepreneur	Mdn.	46	42
Age started business	Mdn.	33	34
Previous ent. effort?	%yes	20	27
Special person import. in getting started	%yes	25	9
Special idea import. getting started	%yes	58	18
Never married	%yes	0	0
Divorced or separated?	%yes	6	32
Graduated high school?	%yes	94	82
Graduate college?	%yes	82	32
Level of school achievement	Mdn. eval.	Above Av.	Average
Serious in school	% serious	79	25
Consider dropping out	%yes	36	38
Active in extra-curricular activities in school	%yes	75	62
Financed coll. primarily through own effort	%yes (of coll. group)	45	84
Accepts regimentation?	%yes	77	68

On all other characteristics investigated in the interview, insignificant differences between races were found. It appears that each of the obtained differences resulted from socio-economic differences or from special considerations in sample selection, as in (3) above, and it does not appear that any racial differences for entrepreneurs as such were evident. The null hypothesis, therefore, cannot be rejected on the basis of interview results.

Table 2 presents the objective scales of the EPPS and the SIV for the two racial groups, separately and combined. Inspection of the raw data indicated no justification for combining the sexes in this study. In comparing black and white males, however, we find that on all scales except Benevolence there are no significant differences. The only exception was a t of 2.48 produced by the very low score of whites on the Benevolence scale. Because of the ipsative nature of the SIV, and because of the very high scores by whites on Independence and Leadership, the low Benevolence scores are interpreted as *relatively* low for the entrepreneurs, not necessarily low compared to the general population. Since the SIV is not normative, only interpretation of relative values is appropriate. The t-tests were applied for this survey only to point to direction and relative magnitude of differences. Because of the small differences between blacks and whites found in Table 2, the results of the two races are combined in the last column.

Compared to men in general, entrepreneurs are significantly higher on scales reflecting need for achievement, independence, and effectiveness of their leadership, and are low on scales reflecting emphasis on need for support. Again the low need for support score may result from the high scores of other scales of this ipsative survey.

Note that only three of the EPPS scales were investigated in this study. Only those three scales were investigated since it was assumed that they were the most likely to relate to entrepreneurship. It is recommended that, in later research, the full fifteen scales of the EPPS be included in the investigation if cooperating entrepreneurs would be agreeable to answering the full 225 items of that test.

DISCUSSION

It is surprising that the EPPS Autonomy scale yielded no significant t value ($t = 1.34$) since interest in independence *is* a characteristic of successful entrepreneurs and since the SIV Independence scale is highly significant ($t = 2.76$) and is correlated with the Autonomy scale .49 (Gordon, 1963).

On the OIS, the numbers cannot be treated as raw scores since the figures are not quantitatively comparable from one person to another. It is the relative standing that is significant. The highest 10 occupational scales and highest 10 college major scales were examined for blacks and whites separately, and striking differences were evident. Both college and occupational scales related generally to the occupations and avocations of the entrepreneurs. Since there were more manufacturers (particularly in electronics and related areas) among the whites, engineering scales were frequently high; for blacks they were infrequently in the top five scales. The interviews (Table 1) indicated that education level was significantly higher for the whites, and the kinds of occupations ranking to-

TABLE 2 Comparisons between Black Entrepreneurs, White Entrepreneurs, and the General Population on Nine Personality Scales

Scale[a]	Black		White		Combined		General Population[b]		White-Black		Black-Gen. Population		White-Gen. Population		All Entrepreneurs-Gen. Pop.	
	M	SD	M	SD	M	SD	M	SD	Diff.	t	Diff.	t	Diff.	t	Diff.	t
Achievement	15.4	2.97	18.4	5.78	17.3	3.89	14.4	4.80	3.0	1.81	1.0	.76	4.0	3.60**	2.9	3.40**
Autonomy	13.5	3.26	15.2	4.61	14.7	4.28	13.5	4.79	1.5	1.07	.2	.15	1.7	1.60	1.2	1.34
Aggression	12.6	2.65	12.4	5.12	12.5	4.48	12.5	4.74	(.2)	.14	.1	.08	(.1)	.09	.0	.00
Support	12.1	3.69	11.2	5.64	11.6	5.05	15.0	5.70	(.9)	.53	(2.9)	1.87	(3.8)	2.91**	(3.4)	2.66***
Conformity	13.4	7.12	11.1	6.04	12.0	6.53	14.8	6.50	(2.3)	1.03	(1.4)	.77	(3.7)	2.50*	(2.5)	1.86
Recognition	8.9	4.34	11.5	5.03	10.7	4.86	11.2	5.20	2.6	1.58	(2.3)	1.62	.3	.25	(.5)	.39
Independence	20.1	7.17	21.9	6.13	21.5	6.76	16.9	7.40	1.8	.80	3.2	1.57	5.0	2.99**	4.6	2.76**
Benevolence	17.5	6.18	12.9	4.46	14.7	5.76	15.8	6.80	(4.6)	2.48*	1.7	1.06	(2.9)	2.22*	(1.1)	.80
Leadership	17.9	6.63	21.1	7.09	19.9	7.08	16.1	7.70	3.2	1.34	1.8	.85	5.0	2.86**	3.7	2.15*

[a] Scores on Achievement, Autonomy, and Aggression were derived from the Edwards Personal Preference Schedule. The other scales are from the Survey of Interpersonal Values.

[b] Population is being used here to denote the norms provided in the test manuals of the Edwards Personal Preference Schedule and the Survey of Interpersonal Values.

*Significant at the five per cent level ($p \leq .05$).

**Significant at the one per cent level ($p \leq .01$).

17

TABLE 3   Analysis of Self-Ratings on The Self-Evaluation Scale for
White and Black Entrepreneurs, and Their Combined Scores,
in Per Cent Selecting Each Position

		5	4	3	2	1
1. Energy level	White	57	27	17	0	0
	Black	47	26	26	0	0
	Combined	53	27	20	0	0
2. Physical health	White	79	15	5	0	0
	Black	58	25	19	0	0
	Combined	64	21	15	0	0
3. Need achievement	White	70	18	12	0	0
	Black	56	28	14	0	0
	Combined	65	22	13	0	0
4. Willing to take risks	White	60	27	9	3	0
	Black	56	28	14	0	0
	Combined	58	27	11	4	0
5. Watch T.V.[a]	White	0	9	30	47	13
	Black	0	11	17	22	50
	Combined	0	10	24	36	29
6. Creative	White	47	37	10	7	0
	Black	43	43	14	0	0
	Combined	45	39	12	4	0
7. Need for affiliation	White	6	9	10	16	20
	Black	19	14	29	24	14
	Combined	11	13	20	24	32
8. Desire for money	White	21	35	35	9	0
	Black	55	10	25	10	0
	Combined	33	26	32	9	0
9. Tolerate uncertainty	White	30	27	20	13	10
	Black	43	29	10	14	5
	Combined	35	28	16	14	8
10. Desire for candy[a]	White	9	0	0	9	81
	Black	0	0	0	6	94
	Combined	4	0	0	7	89
11. Authoritarian in business	White	38	38	19	6	0
	Black	35	30	12	12	12
	Combined	24	35	27	6	9
12. Liking for sports[a]	White	0	27	27	18	27
	Black	6	19	6	25	44
	Combined	4	22	15	22	37
13. Get along with employees	White	54	35	8	0	4
	Black	47	35	12	0	6
	Combined	51	35	9	0	5
14. Organized	White	12	41	41	0	6
	Black	24	52	10	14	0
	Combined	31	30	19	13	7

TABLE 3   (continued)

15. Self-reliant	White	72	21	3	0	3
	Black	55	40	5	0	0
	Combined	66	28	4	0	2
16. Likes to collect things[a]	White	9	9	9	0	72
	Black	0	13	6	13	69
	Combined	4	11	7	7	70
17. Singleness of purpose	White	12	31	18	31	6
	Black	18	18	24	12	30
	Combined	15	24	21	21	18
18. Need for power	White	15	9	27	21	27
	Black	10	14	14	33	29
	Combined	13	11	22	26	28
19. Patience	White	35	18	6	24	18
	Black	30	30	18	12	12
	Combined	32	24	12	18	15
20. Competitiveness	White	33	28	22	11	6
	Black	53	24	12	12	0
	Combined	66	20	6	6	3
21. Take initiative	White	69	27	0	0	4
	Black	70	30	0	0	0
	Combined	70	28	0	0	2
22. Confidence	White	53	47	0	0	0
	Black	77	24	0	0	0
	Combined	65	35	0	0	0
23. Versatility	White	39	50	11	0	0
	Black	53	30	6	6	6
	Combined	46	40	9	3	3
24. Perseverance	White	63	31	6	0	0
	Black	77	24	0	0	0
	Combined	70	27	3	0	0
25. Resilience	White	59	29	12	0	0
	Black	65	30	6	0	0
	Combined	62	29	9	0	0
26. Innovation in business	White	45	39	12	3	0
	Black	78	16	0	0	6
	Combined	41	41	15	4	0
27. Leadership effectiveness	White	32	39	26	3	0
	Black	38	33	19	10	0
	Combined	35	37	23	6	0

[a] Indicate "filler" items which were inserted so that entrepreneurs would have the opportunity to use the entire range of the scale.

ward the top for them reflected higher educational requirements. For example, whites frequently ranked high on computer programmer, engineer, psychologist, and travel agent. Blacks frequently ranked high on television repairmen, plumbing contractor, automobile salesman, and florist. Both rank high on manager, architect, and buyer.

19

It is of interest to note that lambdas greater than .60 were attained on one or more scales by 40 percent of the white entrepreneurs but by none of the black entrepreneurs. Lambdas above .50 were attained by 80 per cent of the whites and only 30 per cent of the blacks. That difference is interpreted to mean that the interests of the black entrepreneurs are not as highly developed and are more diverse; interests of white entrepreneurs tend to be more sharply developed. This again is probably the result in a large measure of the difference in educational background.

Over-all, the OIS was not significant in selecting entrepreneurs or in differentiating blacks and whites of comparable educational level, but it still may prove to be fruitful if a scale for entrepreneurs can be developed. This aspiration is reinforced by the fact that for many blacks Business was a first or second preference as a college major. The OIS was also useful in the present study in that the V scale, a measure of accuracy of the test-taking by examinees, was checked to determine if the answers were valid. In only one case was the V scale out of the acceptable range and for that individual all of the forms were returned to the entrepreneur with the request that he take them a second time more carefully. Since they were not returned, he was not used in the test analyses.

The Self-Evaluation Scale is so highly subjective that it is of little value. To be interpreted meaningfully, it would have to be given to a standardization group for comparison. As a matter of information only, the distribution of answers for the 34 whites and 22 black entrepreneurs is presented separately and combined. Inspection of Table 3 reveals a very high similarity of self-ratings by the two races so that combination is most meaningful. Both races rate themselves significantly above average on need for achievement, self-reliance, competitiveness, initiative, confidence, versatility, perseverance, resilience, innovation, and physical health.

In addition, as part of the structured interview each entrepreneur was asked what qualities were necessary for success in business. The characteristics listed by both blacks and whites are similar, but there was some difference in emphasis.

The blacks mentioned most often the need to have "Knowledge of the Business." Also frequently mentioned was either skill in management of finances or a source of financial advice. Frequently mentioned, but not as often as Knowledge of Business, was: honesty, having a good character, possession of inner drive, willingness to work hard, and pleasing personality. This latter list corresponds very well with the characteristics most frequently mentioned by white entrepreneurs: willingness to work hard, perseverance, single-mindedness of purpose, and the ability to work with people.

CONCLUSIONS

Both the EPPS and the SIV yielded scales that significantly differentiated entrepreneurs from men in the standardization groups for those tests. These scales were achievement, support, independence and leadership (Table 2). It is recommended, therefore, that these two forms be used in further study of the entrepreneur. It is also recommended that continued use of the OIS may be fruitful in order to gather sufficient data for developing an entrepreneurial scale.

The interview items have not been analyzed for their effectiveness in differentiating entrepreneurs from men in general, but the items have been sharpened for clarity, and the authors' experience with these sixty entrepreneurs indicates that the items as given elicit meaningful responses from entrepreneurs. Compared to the laborious procedures and technical training necessary for interpreting projective tests, the administration and scoring of the objective tests is easy and accurate. Furthermore, not only does this procedure yield *n Ach* scores but also other information, obtained by structured devices and objectively evaluated, which further sharpens the differentiation of the successful entrepreneur. It is yet to be determined whether these scales will differentiate between the successful entrepreneur and the individual who has made an *unsuccessful* attempt to be an entrepreneur, but this study establishes (insofar as judgment can be made on a small number of cases) that the structured interview and tests used here are objective indicators of entrepreneurship.

REFERENCES

Clemans, William V. An analysis and empirical examination of some properties of ipsative measures. *Psychometric Monographs*, 1968, 14.

Collins, Orvis F., Moore, David G., and Unwalla, Darab B. *The Enterprising Man*. East Lansing: Michigan State University Press, 1964.

Edwards, Allen L. *Manual for the Edwards Personal Preference Schedule*. New York: The Psychological Corporation, 1959.

Gordon, Leonard V. *Manual for Survey of Interpersonal Values*. Chicago: Science Research Associates, 1960.

Gordon, Leonard V. *Research Briefs on Survey of Interpersonal Values* (*Manual Supplement*). Chicago: Science Research Associates, 1963.

Hermans, Huber, J. M. A questionnaire measure of achievement motivation. *Journal of Applied Psychology*, 1970, 54, 353-363.

Hornaday, John A. and Bunker, Charles S. The nature of the entrepreneur. *Personnel Psychology*, 1970, 23, 47-54

Klinger, E. Fantasy need achievement as a motivational construct. *Psychological Bulletin*, 1966, 66, 291-308

Kuder, Frederic. A rationale for evaluating interests. *Educational and Psychological Measurement*, 1963, 23, 3-10.

Kuder, Frederic. *Manual for the Kuder Preference Record: Form DD*. Chicago: Science Research Associates, Inc., 1970.

McClelland, David C. In *Forbes*, June 1, 1969, 53-57.

McClelland, David C., Atkinson, J. W., Clark, R. A., and Lowell, E. L. *The Achievement Motive*. New York: Appleton-Century-Crofts, 1953.

Murray, Henry A. *Manual for the Thematic Apperception Test*. Cambridge: Harvard University Press, 1943.

Statistical Abstract of the United States. United States Department of Commerce, Bureau of the Census, Washington, D. C., 1970.

THE APPLICATION

OF PSYCHOLOGICAL TESTING

TO ENTREPRENEURIAL POTENTIAL*

MICHAEL PALMER

The word *entrepreneur* carries a deluge of definitional and operational ambiguity. A review of the literature of entrepreneurship affords "strange and contradictory results." The entrepreneurial function has been identified with "uncertainty bearing . . . coordination of production resources . . .introduction of innovations . . . and . . . the provision of capital."[1] The literature also demonstrates the inadequacy of definitions to describe the entrepreneur in terms necessary for ex ante measurement. All definitions are ex post facto: a person is defined as an entrepreneur because of something he has done, in terms of a function. Although the functional definition may be constructed to indicate something he is *capable* of doing, the measurement problem is not solved. He still has to perform the function before he can be called an entrepreneur.

With these definitional and measurement problems sharply in mind we:

1. elucidate the term entrepreneur,
2. elaborate on the problems of entrepreneurial measurement,
3. propose a single definition of the entrepreneurial function for possible use in psychological testing.

Before examining various definitions of the entrepreneur, it would be beneficial to speculate why an investigation such as this is important. Arthur Cole suggests that to study the businessman is to study the main figure in economic activity.[2] However, a reason such as this does not specifically answer what important consequences might ensue from such a study. As a possible answer, I might introduce the following hypothesis (for which originality is not claimed): **a priori,** there appears to be some correlation between economic growth and business formations. **Second,** important to the formation of a business is the activity of an entrepreneur. **Third,** certain areas may possess capital and resources while suffering from a scarcity of entrepreneurs; hence, in these areas we might expect to find a lag in economic development. In other areas, where numerous entrepreneurs exist along with an adequate resource base we might expect a flourish of economic activity.

A qualification to this thesis is the reasoning that in areas void of entrepreneurial talent, if the market is right, and if opportunities are available, entrepreneurs will be forthcoming. But, this assumes perfect mobility of existing entrepreneurs.or that existing entrepreneurs have additional time to devote to the region.

Returning to our entrepreneurial depressed area for a moment, it now becomes obvious that if we understand the role of an entrepreneur it might be possible, as a short-run measure, to train or supervise people to act in an entrepreneurial manner. To develop autonomous entrepreneurs in the area, however, a longer-term remedy appears needed. For this, one must examine the sources of entrepreneurial talent, that is, the forces—psychological and environmental—which engendered the entrepreneurial personality. In summary, a functional definition might suffice for use as a short-run measure, but one must probe much deeper for an adequate long-run solution.

THE DEFINITIONAL PROBLEM

Joseph Schumpeter noted that fifteenth century economic thinkers had established ideas about the businessman and his functions. The French economist Cantillon, the first to introduce the term entrepreneur, defined him as the agent who purchased the means of production for combination into marketable products. Furthermore, at the moment of the factor purchases, the entrepreneur was unaware of the eventual price which he would receive for his products. Thus, Cantillon introjected elements of direction and speculation into his functional definition of the entrepreneur.

Another Frenchman, J.B. Say, expanded Cantillon's ideas. Say conceptualized the entrepreneur as the organizer of the business firm, central to its distributive and production functions. Beyond stressing the entrepreneur's importance to the business, Say did little with his entrepreneurial analysis.

Adam Smith, despite the detectable influence of Cantillon upon his thinking, saw the entrepreneur as cast in a minor active role in overall economic activity—he provided real capital, but did not play a leading or directing part.[3] Generally, it appears that classical economists, for the purpose of theoretical analysis, were not concerned with the entrepreneur as a human entity, but rather treated him impersonally, as the firm itself.

In the second half of the nineteenth century examining the entrepreneur's role as distinct from the capitalist's was expedited by a growing separation of corporate ownership and management. As a result of new financing methods, the distinction between entrepreneur and capitalist became salient, and in ensuing analysis, examination of the entrepreneur was accentuated.

Early twentieth century writers conceptualized the entrepreneurial function as one of promotion. One such writer, Arthur Stone Dewing, viewed the promoter as one who transformed ideas into a profitable business. In enumerating the characteristics of a successful entrepreneur, Dewing wrote of the qualities of imagination, initiative, judgment, and restraint.[4] Dewing was quite explicit in emphasizing the promoter's importance to the creation of business organizations. "No business," he stated, "ever started itself." Other writers emphasizing the promoter during this time stressed the indispensable function of the promoter to business formations.[5]

Joseph Schumpeter contributed substantially to the literature on entrepreneurs. He excluded from the term entrepreneur all heads of firms or managers who merely operated an established business. To him, carrying out new combinations covered the introduction of a new good, the introduction of a new method of production, the opening of a new market, the finding of a new source of raw materials, and the carrying out of a new organization of any industry.[6] To accomplish this, the entrepreneur must convince money holders—bankers and private capitalists—of the desirability of his innovation. After securing the funds he merely buys the necessary means of production.

According to Clarence H. Danhof, an entrepreneur "is primarily concerned with changes in the formula of production . . .over which he has full control . . . He devotes correspondingly little time to the carrying out of a specific formula."[7] Danhof divides the function of the entrepreneur into three major roles: *obtaining relevant information, evaluating the information with regard to profit,* and *setting the operation in motion.* Once the entrepreneur has determined what information should be gathered, the first two functions can be delegated. Basic to the entrepreneur function, in Danhof's analysis, is decision making, or judgment, under alternative choices.

Another concept is presented by Herberton G. Evans who views the entrepreneur as "the person or group of persons who has (or assumes) the task of determining the kind of business to be operated."[8] The decisions germane to this function involve the nature of the goods and services to be offered, the size of the enterprise, and the customers catered to. Once these decisions have been made by the entrepreneur, other decisions, that is decisions to achieve the previous goals set by the entrepreneur, become essentially management's. Evans notes that once these decisions have been made the role of the entrepreneur does not cease: instead, he must be continually alert and ready to make new decisions in light of changing market conditions and arising opportunities. In Evans' scheme we find a distinction between the entrepreneurial and managerial role. It's implicit in his article that the manager's role could be delegated, but not the entrepreneur's.

Another advocate of the entrepreneur as a decision maker is Robert K. Lamb. To him "entrepreneurship is that form of social decision making performed by economic innovators."[9] Lamb suggests that the major contribution of the entrepreneur is not the broader process of building local, national, and international communities and changing existing social and economic institutions.

All the definitions thus far examined are similar in one prominent respect—they neglect the influence of the social order on the actions of the entrepreneur. If the functions of the entrepreneur are to be thoroughly understood, all aspects contributing to his behavioral patterns must be considered social, political, economic, and psychological forces.

Joseph McGuire wrote that "Over time, and in different societies, there has evidently been a substantial change in entrepreneurial types, and presumably in the entrepreneur function."[10] In order to understand these differences, he feels one should be aware of cultural variations. Entrepreneurs in different cultures may act quite differently and these differences cannot always be attributed to economic factors, such as natural resources, money capital, and so on, for these factors may be equal. To understand the differences in business behavior, factors such as social ideology, norms and rewards for behavior, individual and national aspirations, religious doctrines, education and the like, must be examined on a comparative basis. Obviously, the need for a cultural approach is not just limited to comparative analysis, but is also indispensable for an intra-cultural examination of entrepreneurial behavior.

Some contemporary writers, like the earlier traditionalists, have held unwaveringly to the profit maximization motive (or some refinement of it) as the factor responsible for business behavior. They have continued to espouse this viewpoint despite the mounting evidence for other motivational factors being accumulated by the behavioral sciences.

Sigmund Freud, in his psychoanalytic theory, depicted the human being as driven by unconscious and innate drives. Essential to Freudian analysis was the influence of early childhood experiences on the behavior of the adult. For example, if a choice becomes fixated or frustrated during an early developmental stage, a resulting behavior pattern may carry over into adulthood. Nowhere in Freud's works is there mention of an economic motivation directed toward profits or material aggrandizement. An individual may seek out these material ends, but they will be incidental to the basic human motives. According to Freud: "The sexual are amongst the most important of the instinctive forces." They may be sublimated, however, and "their energy . . . diverted towards other ends, no longer sexual."[11]

Freud's pansexualism and neglect of cultural factors promoted the development of a school of psychology known as social psychology. Among these apostates from Freudian analysis were Eric Fromm, Karen Horney, Alfred Adler, and Harry Stack Sullivan. According to the social psychologists, man is predominantly a product of the society in which he lives. His personality is not biological, but social. The notion of unconscious drives was reduced by these psychologists. Drives were provided by the social environment in which man existed. Alfred Adler, for example, declared that the driving force in man was an innate social urge—striving to attain the goal of a perfect society.

Other psychologists, known as the self-theorists, have explained man's motivation in terms of self fulfillment, or self development. Man is viewed as a driving, seeking individual, attempting to reach the ultimate goal of self completion. Within this school are such psychologists as Carl Rogers and Abraham Maslow.

Stimulus-response theorists form still another group. Advocates, such as Dollard, Miller and B.F. Skinner, visualize the behavior of the human organism as a manifestation of stimulus-response bonds. When a certain stimulus is felt by the individual, he will react according to his learned responses. Classical stimulus-response theorists explain this bond as being automatic, while instrumental theorists, see its development according to the past reinforcements of the individual.[12]

In summary, behavior cannot be explained in simple terms, or as the classical economists would like us to believe, in terms of an economic motive. Perhaps the entrepreneur does seek profits, but that he has other motivational drives influencing his behavior patterns must be recognized. Therefore, to understand adequately the role of the entrepreneur, economic and psychological factors must be considered.

Now that various definitions have been examined, what can one say about the entrepreneur? To begin, all of the frameworks are disappointing in that they have been concerned with functional behavior, that is an entrepreneur is defined as an entrepreneur because he acts in a certain way. From Cantillon's incipient analysis to the economists of today, the functional stigma has remained. In addition, one cannot tell from these models (although a clue is offered by the cultural advocates) what factors initially contribute to the development of an entrepreneurial class, or how we may measure the existing supply curve of entrepreneurs in a given area, or how we may increase the long-run supply of entrepreneurs.

THE MEASUREMENT PROBLEM

Functional definitions, although limited, are essential. They are essential here because it is necessary to distinguish the entrepreneurs from the non-entrepreneurs. Thus, when a before-the-fact measurement is devised, we may compare its test predictions with actual behavior, hereby determining the validity of the measurement.

The most promising methods of before-the-fact measurement of the entrepreneur appear to be attitudinal and motivational tests. In general, the two types which might be employed are projective and pencil-and-paper tests.[13] The projective test is more nondirective and subjective in that the subject is instructed to write or speak candidly after having examined a picture or read a short story. The psychologist using such a test assumes that the subject projects himself—his feelings, beliefs, motivations, and so on—into the picture or the story, and although many of the subject's drives, motivations, and feelings are unknown even to him, they will become salient in his stories. A paper-and-pencil test is more directive in that the person is usually asked to rank himself with regard to an object or situation on a predetermined (like-dislike; yes-no) scale. Common among these testing techniques are the Likert scale, the Thurstone equal appearing intervals, and the Bogardus social distance scale.

Employing projective techniques, David McClelland has developed a promising method for measuring entrepreneurial potential. McClelland has hypothesized that the need for achievement is the psychological factor which engenders economic growth and decline. A society in which the level of achievement motivation is intense will produce energetic entrepreneurs. If McClelland's hypothesis is workable, entrepreneurship can be ascertained by measuring achievement motivation.

In the McClelland test, the subject is shown a picture (for example, a man sitting at an office desk looking at a picture of his family or a boy sitting at a piano looking out a window). After viewing the picture, the subject is asked to write a story about it. The psychologist assumes that the subject will project himself into the picture and his related story will actually be a narration about himself. In scoring the test, the experimenter checks for achievement in the subject's story; achievement being indicated by the subject mentioning one of the following incidents: (1) defining a problem, (2) wanting to solve it, (3) thinking of means to solve it, (4) thinking of difficulties that get in the way of solving it, (5) thinking of people who might help in solving it, and (6) anticipating what would happen if one succeeded or failed. The subject receives a +1 for each idea that shows up in his story. If none are indicated, he is given a score of −1. The best possible score would be +36 and the lowest possible score would be −6.

McClelland claims that the "coding of the stories for achievement imagery is so objective that two expert scorers working independently rarely disagree."[14]

Certain roles have been shown to delineate entrepreneurial behavior; among these roles are risk taking, innovating, and decision making. With these roles in mind, an examination of the correlations between overt behavior and achievement motivation scores may determine whether people with high achievement motivation act in ways analogous to the theorists' definitions of entrepreneurship. In a general sense, we are trying to determine the validity of the McClelland test.

A number of significant findings are available from researchers using McClelland's approach. For example, people with high achievement motivation, relative to those with low achievement motivation, are characterized by:

1. preferring tasks involving some objective risks,
2. working harder at tasks which require mental manipulation,
3. wanting to operate in a situation where he can get a sense of personal achievement,
4. not working harder under the influence of a money reward,
5. performing better under conditions where he has a positive and definite feedback,
6. tending to think ahead (long-range thinking).

No correlations have been found between organizational skill and motivation achievement, but it has been shown that people with high achievement motivation prefer working with experts over personal friends.[15]

From the results of the extensive research conducted on achievement motivation, it can be concluded that people who score high on an achievement motivation test are more likely to act in an entrepreneurial way than those who score low on the test. The remaining point is, do these people end up in business? According to McClelland, "there is a tendency to bias occupational choice toward business among boys of middle (but not upper) class status with high achievement motivation."[16] He has found that in three countries (United States, Italy, and Poland) representing different stages of economic development, executives tend to score higher on the achievement test than do other professionals or specialists of comparable education and background. McClelland hypothesizes that an individual with a high achievement motivation will be attracted to the business world because the existing situations will complement his achievement motivation in terms of risks, personal achievement, unambiguous feedback in the form of profits, and specific accomplishments.

Expanding McClelland's hypothesis, it is possible to explore the sources of high achievement as a means of stimulating the long-run supply of an entrepreneurial class. Marian R. Winterbottom suggests the seeds of high achievement motivation can be traced to early childhood. Through experiments with children she has found that early mastery training promotes high achievement motivation, provided it does not reflect generalized parental restrictiveness, authoritarianism, or rejection. Generally, those children who had been urged and expected to achieve outside their home at an early age demonstrated higher achievement motivation than those who were urged at later years. Winterbottom is quick to note that too early urging on the part of the parents can be just as detrimental to the development of high achievement motivation: it may be too early for the boy's abilities, or it may be too late for him to internalize the achievement motivation. The optimum ages for parental urging and expecting, as suggested by Winterbottom, appear to be between six and eight.[17]

B.C. Rosen and R.G. D'Andrade have also conducted studies concerned with the sources of achievement motivation. They have found three variables related to achievement motivation. These factors are parental expectations, warmth, and dominance. With regard to expectations, they found that parents of boys with high achievement motivation usually set higher standards for their children than do parents of low achievement motivation boys. Further, the parents of high achievement motivation boys showed more emotional involvement with respect to their child's activities. Finally, boys with high achievement motivation had nonauthoritarian fathers. Rosen and D'Andrade suggest that an authoritarian father transfers to the boy a dependent conception of the male figure. As a result, the boy will be less likely to set his own standards of excellence and to strive for them on his own.[18]

In summary, data suggest that the sources of achievement motivation for an individual stem from the beliefs, values, and ideologies which are inculcated into his psychological system in early childhood as they are subscribed to by the parents. Unfortunately, achievement motivation tests are still in their early stages of development. McClelland notes that the test results for groups may be valid, while those for each individual are questionable. On an individual basis, the test is also subject to faking and social desirability responses. In spite of these drawbacks, the potential for entrepreneurial measurement with McClelland's or similar tests is clearly evident. What remains is the refinement of the method.

FURTHER RESEARCH AND REFINEMENTS

There exists no universally accepted definition with respect to the meaning of entrepreneurial talent. Academicians and practitioners have suggested a plethora of skills and abilities when, for example, attempting to delineate the variables which account for a successful manager or leader (or entrepreneur). All that can be noted with certainty at the present is that the nature of entrepreneurship is indeed complex.

Skills and abilities which may be necessary for entrepreneurial success in one situation may be markedly different from those needed under changed conditions. Thus, an individual may confidently strive for entrepreneurial achievement in a particular setting, and become a passive participant in another. Furthermore, researchers have suggested the need for more than one type of leader when relating to the attainment of group goals. Robert F. Bales has found two types of leaders with a group: "task specialist" who controls the activities of the group, and the "social specialist" who manages the stresses and strains of the participants in the group.[19] Furthermore, Bales' research suggests that it would be rare for one person to perform both leadership functions.

Differences in motivations would appear to account for this. Bales suggests that task specialists are motivated by strong desires to control the activities of others while maintaining their own freedom. Social specialists appear to be motivated by desires for affiliation and affection. In addition, the task specialist, because of the nature of his position, will probably be low on likeability; while the social specialist will generally be the most popular person in the group.

One area of research would appear to involve the delineation of entrepreneurial functions. That is, *how* do we differentiate an entrepreneur from a nonentrepreneur, and *what* skills and abilities are necessary to the performance of the entrepreneurial function?

A second area in need of further research relates to the testing techniques. This appears especially relevant in the case of intercultural measuring for achievement motivation. Undoubtedly, what needs to be developed is a series of different pictures (or a series of different tests) applicable to varying cultures. Another measurement problem involves differences in interest among individuals. Psychologists should probably use a fairly large number of pictures (or tests) in an attempt to negate any personal differences in interest.

A third area open to further research involves cause and effect analysis. Investigations should attempt to answer why certain people possess higher entrepreneurial motivation than other individuals. Cross-discipline research—involving all the behavioral sciences—appears to be needed.

In summary, while present psychological testing allows us some measure of entrepreneurial potential, contemporary research would appear to be needed in the areas of defining the skills and abilities of an entrepreneur, refining the testing techniques as they relate to these defined skills, and providing answers relating to the sources of entrepreneurial motivation.

SUGGESTIONS

Decision making under varying degrees of uncertainty appears to be an underlying feature of entrepreneurship. For the most part, however, the element of uncertainty has only been implied by most writers. Cantillon, for example, introjected the element of price variability with regard to the entrepreneur's product. Schumpeter noted the innovating nature—developing new methods and enterprises—of the entrepreneur. Frank H. Knight, of course, was more explicit. In his *Risk, Uncertainty, and Profit,* in which he defines the entrepreneur as the "central figure of the system," he notes uncertainty as an integral factor in business decision making.[20]

Decision making under uncertainty appears to offer a suitable framework for the measurement of entrepreneurial potential. As suggested, previous entrepreneurial definitions appear to encompass functional activities under conditions of uncertainty, for example, uncertainty with regard to: pricing (Cantillon), innovating (Schumpeter), promoting ideas into business operations (Dewing), determining the type of business (Evans), and making decisions under alternative choices (Danhof), or changing market conditions (Evans).

In spite of McGuire's position that "over time, and in different societies, there has evidently been a substantial change in entrepreneurial types, and presumably in the entrepreneur function,"[21] the need to make decisions under conditions of uncertainty appears to be a relatively consistent part of the entrepreneurial function. For example, whether we are operating within an agricultural or an industrial society, within a small or large business organization under private or public leadership (or even within a micro versus a macro framework), the element of uncertainty cannot be eliminated.

The willingness of an individual to deal with uncertainty, therefore, would appear to be an appropriate measure of entrepreneurial potential. **Successful entrepreneurship, within this proposed framework, would involve a [1] determination of the types and degrees of uncertainty confronting the performance of a particular operation and [2] the ability to make the appropriate decision necessary for goal attainment.**

CONCLUSIONS

I would argue that the entrepreneurial function involves primarily *risk measurement* and *risk taking* within a business organization. Furthermore, the successful entrepreneur is that individual who can correctly interpret the risk situation and then determine policies which will minimize the risks involved (for example, converting uncertainty into fixed costs), given a particular goal aspiration. Both functions, I would argue, are essential for successful entrepreneurship. Thus, the individual who can correctly measure the risk situation, but is unable to minimize that risk, would not be defined as an entrepreneur. As suggested earlier, risk cannot be eliminated; the successful entrepreneur, however, can minimize the risk situation.

In addition, I would suggest that psychological testing (such as the McClelland achievement motivation) be directed most toward the measurement of an individual's perception and handling of risk. Cause and effect research should be concerned with an investigation of the motivational determinates of risk bearing versus risk aversion. Specific research in this area should be directed at a determination of the psychological and environmental sources which produce a risk functioning individual. Last, research should concern the extent to which programs can be developed for the successful training of risk measuring and risk taking.

REFERENCES

1. B. F. Hoselitz, "Entrepreneurship and Economic Growth," *American Journal of Economic Sociology* (1952), p. 97.

2. Arthur H. Cole, *Business Enterprise in Its Social Setting,* (Cambridge: Harvard University Press, 1951), p. 28.

3. Joseph A. Schumpeter, "Economic Theory and Entrepreneurial History," in *Change and the Entrepreneur* (Cambridge: Harvard University, 1948), prepared by the Research Center in Entrepreneurial History, pp. 63-66.

4. Arthur Stone Dewing, *The Financial Policy of Corporations* (New York: Ronald Press, 1919), pp. 245-254.

5. E. S. Meade, *Corporation Finance,* 1915, p. 23; R. E. Heilman, *Journal of Political Economy* (November 1915), 895.

6. Joseph A. Schumpeter, *The Theory of Economic Development* (Cambridge: Harvard University Press, 1934) in E. Okun, *Studies in Economic Development,* pp. 91-94.

7. Clarence H. Danhof, "Observations of Entrepreneurship in Agriculture," *Change and the Entrepreneur* (Cambridge: Harvard University Press, 1949), p. 21.

8. Herberton G. Evans, "A Century of Entrepreneurship in the United States With Emphasis Upon Large Manufacturing Concerns, 1850-1957," in *The Entrepreneur.* Papers presented at the annual conference of the Economic History Society at Cambridge, England, April 1957. Published by the Research Center in Entrepreneurial History, Harvard University, p. 50.

9. Robert K. Lamb, "The Entrepreneur and the Community," in *Men in Business,* William Miller (ed.) (Harvard University Press, 1952), p. 91.

10. Joseph McGuire, *Theories of Business Behavior.* (Englewood Cliffs, N.J.: Prentice-Hall, 1964), p. 238.

11. Sigmund Freud, *A General Introduction to Psychoanalysis* (New York: Washington Square Press, 1920), p. 27.

12. See Calvin S. Hall and Garner Lindzey, *Theories of Personality* (New York: Wiley 1957), esp. pp. 114-155, 324-327, 420-499.

13. For empirical observations on the two types of tests see: Irwin G. Sarason, *Contemporary Research in Personality,* pp. 1-81.

14. David McClelland, "Business Drive and National Achievement," *Harvard Business Review* (July-August, 1962), 101-102.

15. Elizabeth G. French, "Motivation as a Variable in Work Partner Selection," *Journal of Abnormal Social Psychology* (1956), 96-99.

16. McClelland, "Business Drive and National Achievement," 102-103.

17. Marian R. Winterbottom, "The Relation of Need for Achievement to Learning Experiences in Independence and Mastery," in J. W. Atkinson (ed.) *Motives in Fantasy, Action and Society* (New Jersey: Van Nostrand, 1958), pp. 468-71.

18. B. C. Rosen and R. G. D'Andrade, "The Psychological Origins of Achievement Motivation," *Sociometry* (1959), 185-218.

19. Robert F. Bales, "Task Roles and Social Roles in Problem Solving Groups," *Readings in Social Psychology,* E. Maccoby, T. Newcomb, and E. Hartley (eds.), (New York: Holt, Rinehart, and Winston, 1958), pp. 437-447.

20. Frank H. Knight, *Risk, Uncertainty, and Profit.* (New York: Houghton Mifflin, 1921), chaps. I and VII.

21. McGuire, p. 238.

THE ENTREPRENEUR'S QUIZ*

JOSEPH R. MANCUSO

My research methodology has been criticized by some academicians. They would prefer a statistical sampling technique and a hypothesis testing approach to indicate significance levels of each of the findings. Although I am sympathetic to that scientific plea, I believe it is too difficult a constraint to be operational. Not only does this approach become more an issue of standard deviation, oftentimes the hypothesis is deemed to be true when it is not. I claim there is a false sense of security in this scientific approach.

Rather, my approach of observing and probing and living among the population and drawing conclusions as I go is more suitable. When the subject matter is sensitive and the population is unknown, this research technique often produces better results. These two cases certainly exist for entrepreneurs. The subject matter is sensitive and extremely private. Mail or phone questionnaires are ineffective measuring instruments for this type of information. The population is unknown as well. Who is an entrepreneur? If you begin as other scientific studies have, the original population is drawn from a directory of small companies, or a list of existing entrepreneurial ventures, or a venture capitalists' directory. The problem here should be obvious. The unsuccessful entrepreneurs have disappeared. They are not listed anywhere. Their business is gone, and they do not maintain a phone number for the convenience of followup researchers. To give further emphasis to this point, recall that most entrepreneurs fail. Hence the majority of the breed don't exist to be discovered and interviewed. Consequently most earlier *scientific* research has been based only on successful entrepreneurs. And they, too, are a biased sample.

As an analogy, let us assume, that, given certain data, we are trying to decide whether or not a rape occurred. Now this is certainly a sensitive topic. The populations will be different but unknown. All data gathering will be suspect. In case *A*, let us say 100 witnesses were present and 80 claimed a rape was performed while 20 disagreed. Depending upon the hypothesis and significance level, one could support the position "yes, a rape occurred" on a scientific basis. In case *B*, only five witnesses were present but all five agreed a rape had taken place. None of the witnesses said it had not taken place. In which of these two cases, A or B, are the data more convincing? Which has the greatest likelihood of being right? Who was really raped?

This is a pretty classic issue and I am sure I will not answer it to everyone's satisfaction. However, the United States legal system would be more convinced in case *B*. They would agree that no evidence to the contrary exists. In turn, they are facing reality and interpreting data and drawing conclusions. While they too can be in error, their criteria are these.

In my research of a sensitive area and an unknown population, I choose a similar approach. My sample of 300 entrepreneurs in the Northeast is certainly

*Prepared especially for this volume.

biased. So my extrapolation to the whole may be wrong. However, my conclusions were based upon my interpretation. When many people provided the same answer and scattered special cases were the only contradictory evidence, I called it a conclusion. In no case are these conclusions based upon armchair observations. Each was arrived at only after the same data were generated from a number of independent sources. Although some conclusions were more overwhelming than others, that alone does not make either closer to the truth. I present these data for your own interpretation. You may disagree and you may be right. But, based upon this research, al least we have a common point of departure.

Alfred North Whitehead once said, "The greatest invention of all is the invention of inventing inventions." If that is the case, the person who introduces an invention to the world—the entrepreneur—must share that greatness. An entrepreneur is a person who creates an on-going business enterprise from nothing.

Much has been written about the entrepreneur—his desires, his motivations, and his characteristics—but most of this literature has been the result of deep scientific investigation that has neglected the human side of the issue.

Actually, it is very difficult to study the entrepreneur. Many, if not most, are absorbed into the business world and eventually cannot be separated from the whole. This is especially true of the majority of entrepreneurs whose ventures fail. Therefore, most previous studies have been made of successful entrepreneurs only.

During the past several years, I have worked directly with more than 300 entrepreneurs in a variety of businesses and industries. I have been their confidante and sounding board. I have worked with winners and losers alike.

What makes an antrepreneur run?

Why is he more at home in his swivel chair than his living room? What makes him willing to lose his wife, his wits, and even his wad—not once, but three or four times? Why can't he be happy working for someone else? Why does he always have to go it alone? What's with him anyway?

When the other kids were out playing ball, why was he busy hustling lemonade? When his friends were dating cheerleaders, why was he organizing rock concerts? Or marketing grandmother's pickle recipe? Or inventing a better fly swatter? Is he really smarter than the rest of us? Or just crazy?

What I found out was that, strangely enough, entrepreneurs do share many traits. Too many to be purely coincidental. And, when I started to dig deeper, I hit on all kinds of weird phenomena

The following questionnaire is the result of this investigation. Although it lacks hard statistical back-up, it does offer insight into the entrepreneur's philosophy. Why not try it yourself to see if you have what it takes to be an entrepreneur. You can even score it in the privacy of your home or office. No one needs to know the real truth but you.

1. An entrepreneur is most commonly the_____child in the family.
    a. oldest   c. youngest
    b. middle   d. doesn't matter

There is no doubt about this answer. All the independently conducted studies agree that entrepreneurs are high achievers. Dr. David McClelland at Harvard and Dr. Stanley Schacter at Columbia have written about achievement motivation. Along with others they conclude that the first born (or oldest) child in a family normally is the high achiever, or in my words, an entrepreneur. In my work, this single finding was almost infallible. This is especially significant when one considers that two-thirds of all people are *not* first born.

In fact, George Washington, Abraham Lincoln, Thomas Jefferson, Woodrow Wilson, and Franklin D. Roosevelt were all first children. Of the first 23 astronauts to go on United States space missions, 21 were first born. In a recent analysis of merit scholarship winners, 60 per cent were also first born children. Well over 60 per cent of the entrepreneurs I have worked with were first children.

A small point of interpretation here may be helpful. A high need achiever is normally the oldest child in the family but not always. Of late, families have had children in clusters. For instance, a family has children age 12, 10, 8 and then has a new addition to the family. This new addition can also be considered a first child. An only child is also a first child, naturally.

So, if you missed this one—watch out; you may be bucking some severe odds.

2. An entrepreneur is most commonly:
    a. married   c. widowed
    b. single   d. divorced

Here is a touchy topic. The data are fluid, and interpretations vary widely. In my research with over 300 entrepreneurs primarily based in the Northeast and on the West Coast, I concluded the vast majority were married. Most men in their thirties are married so this alone is not a significant finding. However, I did find that the successful entrepreneur had an exceptionally supportive wife. She provided love and stability to balance the insecurity and stress of the job.

Marriages without an extremely supportive wife ended in divorce. No doubt divorce among entrepreneurs is higher than competing but similar professions. In addition, unsuccessful entrepreneurs had the largest divorce rate of all.

My message is simple. A supportive (non-women's liberation type) wife significantly increases the entrepreneur's chances of success. Otherwise, a successful divorced entrepreneur is the next logical step. A strained love life is just too much to add to a strained business life.

This question was offered as an easy one to help improve your score. But it also might start you thinking.

3. An entrepreneur is most typically a:
    a. man   c. either
    b. woman

Almost everyone gets this question right. Everybody knows only a handful of women have started an on-going business enterprise from nothing. Entrepreneurship is one of the last male strongholds. Although women are making headway into business and even in sophisticated segments of business, such as management consulting, to date they have not penetrated the entrepreneurial ranks except in a few isolated but small industries (cosmetics, fashion).

So chalk up another correct answer.

4. An individual begins his first entrepreneurial company at which age?
    a. teens   c. thirties   e. fifties
    b. twenties   d. forties

The data on this topic have shifted over the past twenty years. In earlier studies Professors Collins and Moore (University of Michigan, *The Enterprising Man,* 1958) found the answer to this question to be between 38 and 42 years. Professor Edward Roberts at MIT found the average age, in the early and mid-1960s to be between 35 and 40 years. My work, conducted around the late 1960s and early 1970s indicates that the average age is between 30 and 35 years. Hence, a downward shift in age has been the trend during the past 20 years. I have noticed a number of individuals who began their first entrepreneurial venture while in their twenties.

Most people answer this question correctly, but the added knowledge of this shifting pattern may make this answer of "thirties" incorrect in the 1980s.

5. An individual's entrepreneurial tendency first appears evident at which of these stages?

    a. teens   c. thirties   e. fifties
    b. twenties   d. forties

Entrepreneurial traits show up very early in life. The enterprising boy becomes the enterprising man. I found many entrepreneurs had begun little businesses before their teens. But somewhere during high school or college these characteristics almost always blossom. This finding applies to well over three-quarters of the entrepreneurs I have surveyed. Coin and stamp collecting, rock concerts and dances, selling clothes and appliances, lawn and snow services, and a paper route are common examples.

Hence, this leads me to conclude that entrepreneurial traits are obvious early.

6. An entrepreneur has typically made the following educational progress:
    a. grammar school   c. bachelor's degree e. doctor's degree
    b. high school diploma   d. master's degree

This question is controversial. Few other writers agree with my finding. The work done in the 1950s concludes that most entrepreneurs neglected to complete high school, never mind college. Ed Land at Polaroid is a popular example of the self-made man who dropped out of MIT to begin his entrepreneurial venture.

My data conclude that the master's degree is the most common degree. It can be in either business management or a technical discipline. Contrast this finding with the obvious fact that most businessmen have at least a bachelor's degree today. Entrepreneurs are showing more respect for education (being high achievers) and obtain the master's degree. Few carry this respect to the extreme of going for the doctorate. This takes too much time and is seldom worth the extra effort, in their view.

This finding contradicts earlier research, but it appears to be accurate. Most of you probably got this question wrong, but don't worry—easier questions are coming.

7. An entrepreneur's primary motivation for starting his own business is:
    a. to make money
    b. because they cannot work for anyone else
    c. to be famous
    d. as an outlet for unused energy

The answer here is pretty well agreed upon by everyone. Entrepreneurs seldom leave a secure environment and a steady job for the primary purpose of making money. Their view, in my opinion, is that the attainment of wealth is a by-product of a more noble goal—to be famous is almost never the reason for starting a business.

An energy outlet is equally irrelevant to a would-be entrepreneur. He is usually more concerned about his use of time than to start a business simply to have something to do.

The last reason, he cannot work for anyone else, is more to the point. He is an independent, free spirit. He has great difficulty following others' directions. He seeks to do his own thing. This is central to all entrepreneurs. They have to be boss.

8. The primary motivation for the entrepreneur's high ego and need for achievement is based on his relationship with:
   a. his wife
   b. his mother
   c. his father
   d. his children

This is also an obvious question. Almost everyone guesses "father" as the answer and, from my research, they are right. The entrepreneur's children and his wife enter his life too late to do more than modestly alter his basic characteristics. The mother and father are more predominant in the entrepreneur's personality development.

The real question is the varying impact of the roles of mother and father. The mother has the greatest exposure to a growing child, but the father-son relationship is central to the entrepreneur's motivation. The entrepreneur either seeks to show his old man who's best or, in the case where the father has left the family, the oldest boy often has to assume immense responsibility early in life.

In my experience, the father provided the motivation and drive for the entrepreneur. Even when the entrepreneur is in his thirties, and his father is retired, the approval and praise of his father still provide a basis for his drive.

9. An entrepreneur takes which of these items from business to business:
   a. desk
   b. chair
   c. all office furniture
   d. none of these items

The answer is "a chair." Almost everyone guesses this answer correctly. However, this phenomenon has not been discussed by any other researcher. Others have chosen to ignore it even when they discovered it.

I discovered that entrepreneurs fall in love with a good chair—vaguely equivalent to Archie Bunker's favorite chair. It is his and no one dare sit in it for fear of offending him. It is not really as dramatic as that example, but most entrepreneurs do have a strong preference for a certain chair.

For reasons of comfort and convenience, entrepreneurs prefer a chair over any other piece of office furniture—so much so, in fact, that they strive to carry the same chair from business to business.

10. To be successful in an entrepreneurial venture you need an overabundance of:
    a. money
    b. luck
    c. hard work
    d. a good idea

Although this may cause concern for you, and most people get this question wrong, it seems to me the answer should be obvious.

We all know money alone is not enough to make an entrepreneurial venture successful. The classic story of Viatron, where about $50 million was invested before bankruptcy, indicated the ineffectiveness of money alone.

Hard work and a good idea are helpful in starting and succeeding in a small business. But mere hard work seldom can make a troublesome situation into a success. A good idea offers a greater chance of success as well, but also a good many good ideas end up in the garbage heaps.

Luck is a different matter. More and more luck significantly compensates for other weaknesses. Of the successful entrepreneurs I lived with in the past eight years, all agreed that they were damned lucky. A few key breaks early, according to them, were what made the difference. Sorry you answered this question incorrectly—you just weren't lucky.

11. Entrepreneurs and venture capitalists:
    a. get along well   c. are cordial friends
    b. are best of friends   d. are in secret conflict

The answer to this question always causes great difficulty, especially for money men. These folks universally prefer to believe they are best of friends with their entrepreneurs, and, in a few cases, it is true.

In the great success stories, entrepreneur and venture capitalist are pictured walking along hand-in-hand. My research strongly indicated this is the exception, not the rule. Most small businesses fail (some say about nine out of ten. Every business, save a handful, needs second and third rounds of financing. At these stages the entrepreneur-venture capitalist relationship shifts from cordiality to stress. Many times this causes a permanent split or, in other words, a divorce. The marriage needs more money, and this issue divides them and puts them in conflict.

For the few success stories, such as Digital Equipment Corporation and American Research and Development and Data General Corporation and Fred Adler, there are hundreds of failures. Sorry again.

12. A successful entrepreneur relies on which of these groups for critical management advice:
    a. internal management team   c. financial sources
    b. external management professionals   d. no one

The overwhelming answer to this question is "external management professionals." In fact, of the successful companies involved in my research, every single one had used a consultant of one sort or another at one time or another. Not so for the unsuccessful companies. This is a fascinating finding.

Entrepreneurs seldom rely on internal people for major policy decisions because they conclude earlier that employees have an ax to grind. Employees seldom offer serious conflicts on big decisions and, in the end, the entrepreneur is dominant in every decision. Outside financial sources are even less common sounding boards for entrepreneurs. Not only do banks and accountants lack a feeling for the real stresses of managing an entrepreneural venture—they are too conservative. They say "no" most of the time. This goes against the optimistic, fun-loving nature of entrepreneurs. They prefer outside professionals, including other entrepreneurs, consultants, college professors, or other successful businessmen.

13. Entrepreneurs are best as:
   a. managers
   b. venture capitalists
   c. planners
   d. doers

Although they are not poor managers (because they eventually succeed at accomplishing tasks through other people), entrepreneurs all have difficulty delegating responsibility. The basic reason for this is their outstanding ability as a doer. They do everything faster and always better than anyone else; hence, they are reluctant to delegate because they could do it both better and faster. They are best as doers, not planners or managers.

They are seldom effective as venture capitalists even after they accumulate wealth. They are more at home with products, markets, and technologies. The skills of a successful venture capitalist are at a much higher level of abstraction. Entrepreneurs do best not by maximizing capital but by maximizing their own *doing* talent. Managing money and making financial bets is not as much to their liking as finding market niches or exploiting new technologies.

14. Entrepreneurs are:
   a. high risk takers(big gamblers)
   b. moderate risk takers (realistic gamblers)
   c. small risk takers (take few chances)
   d. doesn't matter

Contrary to popular belief, entrepreneurs are not high risk takers. I will bet most of you answered this question incorrectly. The correct answer is "moderate risk takers." They choose moderate but reasonable risks. They set realistic and achievable goals.

They do take risks, but they are more calculated risks. They are extremely aware of the consequences of failure. They are reluctant to bite off more than they can chew.

Most previous research into entrepreneurs, especially by David McClelland of Harvard, agree with this finding. It is especially true for *successful* entrepreneurs, but it is true of unsuccessful entrepreneurs as well.

15. The first step in starting a business should be:
   a. find a product
   b. get some money
   c. select a partner
   d. consult a lawyer

Although it may be nice to have a product already, or some money or a partner, the first step should be to see a lawyer. He will set the business in motion. Once he has decided upon the appropriate legal set-up, you in fact have a business.

Neither a product, money, nor a partner alone is sufficient to classify as a business. Once the lawyer has completed his work, you are in business. He should be the first visit.

ANSWERS

1. oldest
2. married
3. man
4. thirties
5. teens
6. master's degree
7. can't work for anyone else
8. father

9. chair
10. luck
11. are in secret conflict
12. external management professionals
13. doers
14. moderate risk takers
15. consult a lawyer

SCORING

Number of Questions Answered Correctly	Score
11 or more	successful entrepreneur
10-11	entrepreneur
9-10	latent entrepreneur
8-9	potential entrepreneur
7-8	borderline entrepreneur
7 or less	hired hand

TWO

The Idea Stage

Where do ideas come from? What makes a good idea? Edwin Land (Polaroid), Ken Olson (Digital Equipment Corporation), Chester Carlson (Xerox), F.W. Woolworth, and Col. Sanders (Kentucky Fried Chicken) all had good ideas. Their ideas were sufficiently innovative to give their firms a strong and profitable market position. Usually, however, the process of starting a new company is more one of combining existing fields of technology or repackaging the old into a new product or service. The route might be depicted as follows: An individual, gaining specialized experience through working for others, senses a gap in the market that is not being filled. Getting support for his idea from one or two associates or from other entrepreneurs in the community, he forms the new business venture. The business is established amidst an aura of excitement and convictions based on the entrepreneur's perception that what is being offered is a unique innovation satisfying a growing consumer need. A market opportunity existed, a product idea was born, the manufacturing technology developed, and a marketing cycle was begun. A new company is born and a customer's problem is solved.

The new venture may find the market response to its product extremely favorable, or it may be faced with a "loser." Usually the unique ideas—those not involving merely the repackaging of other (existing) product concepts—stand a better chance of being successful.

How are unique ideas created? Arnold Cooper, in the lead-off article, *Technical Entrepreneurship: What Do We Know?*, concludes that new product ideas are most often created by placing creative people in an unconstrained environment, with organizational policy and procedural deterrents removed. It is often these restrictions, and the corresponding emphasis on short term goals, that motivate many entrepreneurs to leave their employer and start their own business. (The high technology firms from which new firms "spin-off" are commonly called "incubator organizations.") Contacts with other creative people in this entrepreneurial environment will result in the formulation of additional product innovations by the entrepreneur. And the idea from which everything began will be a new business venture.

40

One step in the profitable exploitation of a new idea is to select the right technological combination—a selection that will result in a short product development time, a high value-to-cost ratio, and economies of scale in manufacturing.

The two curves in Fig. 2-1 indicate the effect of this selection process. The products produced by each firm are assumed to be similar in function performed. Firm *A*, however, has been more innovative in that the technological approach is more optimum, giving the company a product with lower per-unit manufacturing costs than the product developed by Firm *B*. In the long run, as the market volume increases, Firm *A* will gain a relative cost advantage over Firm *B* since, for example, the spread indicated by line e-f is a larger percentage price spread than that indicated by line c-d:

$$\frac{2.8 - 1.7}{1.7} = .65; \qquad \frac{4.6 - 3.2}{3.2} = .44.$$

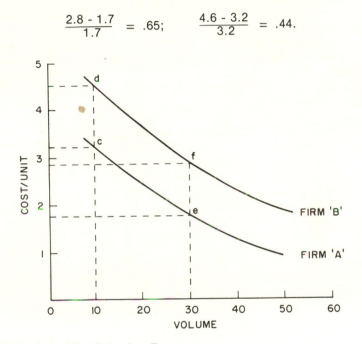

FIGURE 2-1   The Selection Process

Thus, Firm *A*, which has a competitive position that will improve as market volume increases, is likely to be the one out of ten business ventures that succeeds. A creative integration of technological disciplines is obviously an important first step.

The second article in this chapter, *Product Innovation in Small Business,* by John Doutt, identifies some of the pitfalls resulting from traditional thinking on the product innovation process and discusses some of the factors that should be considered by a small firm in approaching the competitive marketplace and planning for new products. Hiring a creative individual with sufficient curiosity and drive to successfully implement new product ideas may be a wasted effort if the firm's management is not aware of or concerned about these other factors, according to Doutt.

The need for an innovating climate is just as important in the large corporation as in the small business—although the large, generously capitalized firm can usually absorb more blunders without the same catastrophic effects that the small business would experience. But usually the scenario of the corporate-based new business venture is in many ways similar to an externally based venture activity. In the third article, *Champions for Radical New Inventions,* Donald Schon discusses the "product champion" concept. Product champions working in a stimulating and supportive environment are the key to successful product development and marketing within established companies.

Whether an internal or external venture activity, the entrepreneurial spirit must exist to provide the driving force behind the long and risky product and market development cycle. There are differences, however, in how the corporation perceives and tolerates individual mistakes, and how the organization is structured. In the final article in this series, *An Approach to New Business Ventures,* Robert Adams reviews his company's policies and procedures for internal product innovation and the process employed to tap new and profitable markets.

Recapping, we find that ideas usually result from creative people finding solutions to problems. Whether an idea is unique enough to capture a specialized and profitable share of the market must still be determined in a competitive marketplace. Sufficient analysis is required to test the idea against market needs, producibility, profitability, potential competition, market growth, and other factors related to changing consumer needs. The risks involved in exploiting the idea will generally be directly related to the potential rewards.

TECHNICAL ENTREPRENEURSHIP:

WHAT DO WE KNOW?*

ARNOLD C. COOPER

Abstract. The factors influencing the birth of new, high technology firms have been investigated in a number of separate studies. This paper summarizes and reports upon this research.

New, technologically-based firms have had, in the aggregate, substantial economic impact. The birth of these companies has been concentrated in particular places and at particular times.

From Research and Development Management, Vol. 3, February 1973, pp. 59-64. Reprinted by permission of Basil Blackwell Publications, 108 Cowley Rd., Oxford, United Kingdom.

The decision to found a new company appears to be influenced by three major factors. The characteristics of the entrepreneur, including the many aspects of his background which make him more or less inclined toward entrepreneurship, are important. The organization for which he has been working, which might be termed 'the incubator organization' also influences the entrepreneurial decision in various ways. A third factor consists of a complex of external influences, including the availability of venture capital and the collective attitudes toward entrepreneurship. Feedback processes appear to be at work such that past entrepreneurship makes future entrepreneurship more likely.

What do we know about how new, technologically-based firms are founded? What factors influence the birth of such companies? The phenomenon of technical entrepreneurship has been investigated in a number of places by a number of individuals; this paper summarizes and reports upon that research.

New, technologically-based firms contribute in a variety of ways to the growth and vitality of the economy:

1. They are important sources of innovation, sometimes achieving great success in matching developing technologies and market needs.
2. They add to the vitality of industry, serving as new sources of competition and complementing and spurring the efforts of established firms.
3. They offer alternative career possibilities for those engineers and managers who do not function most effectively in large organizations.
4. From the standpoint of regional economic development, they make pleasant neighbors, producing relatively little noise and pollution, employing highly paid technically-trained people, and broadening the regional economic base, thus lessening the reliance upon a few organizations.

Although many of these firms have enjoyed only modest success and others have failed, some have been extremely successful businesses. Companies such as Metals Research Ltd. and Nuclear Instruments Ltd. in England and Digital Equipment, Raychem, and Memorex in America have enjoyed great success. Compared to other kinds of new businesses, technically-oriented firms in America have experienced relatively low failure rates [Draheim, et al. (1966), Roberts (1972), Cooper (1971)]. The employment provided by new firms, considered in the aggregate, can be substantial. For example, spin-off firms from the major laboratories affiliated with M.I.T. provided, within a few years of founding, substantially more employment than the parent laboratories [Roberts (1969)].

The birth of these new firms seems to be concentrated in particular places and at particular times. In America, cities such as Boston, Los Angeles, San Francisco, and Minneapolis have had in recent years large numbers of new firms. There are other regions which, although they employ large numbers of technical personnel, have had relatively few new companies founded. Some of the regions in which technical entrepreneurship has been studied are indicated in Exhibit 1.

Understanding what has been learned to date about technical entrepreneurship should be of interest to a number of groups, including engineers or technical managers who envisage becoming entrepreneurs, those concerned with regional economic development, and managers of organizations interested in alternative ways of exploiting technology.

Exhibit 1   High-Technology Firms Studied*

Areas	Number of Firms Studied*
Ann Arbor, Michigan	76
Austin, Texas	31
Boston, Massachusetts	250
Buffalo, New York	42
Canada (nationwide)	47
Erie—Niagara, New York	43
Minneapolis—St. Paul, Minnesota	142
Oak Ridge, Tennessee	21
Palo Alto, California	250

*These do not represent all new firms founded in the areas indicated, only those studied.

INFLUENCES UPON ENTREPRENEURSHIP

The founding of a new firm is, in a basic sense, a decision made by one or several entrepreneurs. The influences upon this decision might be organized under three general headings:

1. *The entrepreneur* himself, including the many aspects of his background that affect his motivations, his perceptions, and his skills and knowledge.
2. *The established organization* for which the founder had previously been working, which might be termed an 'incubator organization'. Its characteristics influence the location and the nature of new firms, as well as the likelihood of spin-offs.
3. *Various external factors,* many of them regional in nature. These include the availability of capital, collective attitudes and perceptions relating to entrepreneurship, and the accessibility to suppliers, personnel, and markets.

The various influences of the entrepreneurial decision are shown in Exhibit 2.

THE INDIVIDUAL ENTREPRENEUR

What are the characteristics of these people who choose to take the unusual step of starting new companies? What prepares and propels them toward this unique activity? The longest history of research in entrepreneurship centers on the individual founder. Although the technical entrepreneur has been studied much less extensively than his non-technical counterpart, the following characteristics emerge:

1. Founders of high-technology companies often form groups to start new companies. The percentage of new firms started by groups of two or more was 48% in Austin, 61% in Palo Alto, and 59% in a study of 955 geographically diversi-

44

EXHIBIT 2   Influences Upon the Entrepreneurial Decision

Antecedent Influences
Upon Entrepreneur

1. Family and religious background
2. Educational background.
3. Psychological makeup.
4. Age at time(s) of maximum external opportunity
   and organizational 'push'.
5. Earlier career experience.
6. Opportunity to form entrepreneurial groups.

Incubator Organization

Entrepreneur's
decision

1. Geographic location.
2. Nature of skills and knowledge acquired.
3. Motivation to stay with or leave organization.
4. Experience in 'small business' setting.

External Factors

1. Examples of entrepreneurial action and
   availability of knowledge about entrepreneurship.
2. Societal attitudes toward entrepreneurship.
3. Ability to save 'seed capital'.
4. Accessibility and availability of venture capital.
5. Availability of personnel and supporting services;
   accessibility to customers; accessibility to university.
6. Opportunities for interim consulting.
7. Economic conditions.

fied firms [Susbauer (1967), Cooper (1971), Shapero (1971)]. Groups permit a
more balanced management team, one less likely to have major areas of weakness. They also provide psychological support at a time when the individual may
be wondering whether he is taking the right step.

2. Founders tend to be in their thirties when starting high-technology companies.
The average age of founders studied was 34 in Austin, 35 in Philadelphia, and
32 in Boston [Susbauer (1969), Industrial Research (1967), Roberts (1968)].
Apparently, at this time in their careers, they have sufficient experience and
financial resources, yet are still willing to incur the necessary sacrifices and
risks.

3. The typical American technical entrepreneur had at least a B.S. or first degree,
usually in engineering. In Boston and in Austin the median educational level
was an M.S. degree [Roberts (1969), Susbauer (1969)]. Since these new companies' competitive advantages are based upon the founders' knowledge, this is
not surprising.
Earlier studies of *non*-technical entrepreneurs emphasized that they tended to
have modest educational qualifications. Often, they got along poorly with their
fathers, their teachers, and their employers; they often left school at an early
age [Collins & Moore (1964)]. Available evidence on technical entrepreneurs
suggests they do *not* fit this mould, at least with respect to their tolerance for
formal education.

4. Founders appear to be more single-minded in their devotion to careers than

45

hired executives. Within the semiconductor industry, they had fewer outside civic and sports activities [Howell (1972)].

5. Studies involving psychological tests and very limited numbers of respondents showed that entrepreneurs rated higher than average in aesthetic and theoretical orientations, leadership orientation, and achievement orientation. They rated low in religious orientation, need for support, need for conformity, and practical mindedness. Interestingly, they did *not* have high scores in regard to economic values [Komives (1972)]. The high scores in need for achievement are consistent with a considerable body of research focussing upon the importance of this factor in entrepreneurial activity [McClelland (1961)].

6. A disproportionately high percentage of founders are from homes where the father was in business for himself [Roberts & Wainer (1971), Shapero (1971)].

7. In some instances, an unusually high percentage of founders are from particular segments of the population. In Canada, 50% were immigrants; in Boston, 16% were Jewish [Litvak & Maule (1972), Roberts & Wainer (1971)].

THE INCUBATOR ORGANIZATION

When a founder starts a new company, he typically leaves some organization. The characteristics of that organization, which might be termed the 'incubator', influence entrepreneurship in a number of ways.

1. The incubator organization affects the location of the new firm. Even though technical founders may have been geographically mobile at earlier stages of their careers, they rarely move at the time when they are founding new firms. The percentage of new companies started which involved at least one founder who was already working in the area was 97.5% in Palo Alto and 90% in Austin [Cooper (1971), Susbauer (1972)].

2. Established organizations also influence the nature of the new businesses established. In Palo Alto, 85.5% of the new companies served the same general market or utilized the same general technology as the parent company [Cooper (1971)]. In Ann Arbor, 83.7% of the new firms had initial products or services which drew 'directly' on the founders' previous technical employment experience and knowledge [Lamont (1971)]. The founder typically starts his new firm to exploit that which he knows best. Thus, families of related companies grow up, such as hearing-aid companies in Minneapolis or chemical firms in Buffalo [Draheim (1972)].

One study showed that spin-off firms from universities initially concentrated on providing services—R & D, testing or consulting. Spin-offs from small firms tended to provide standard products, while those from large firms tended to provide custom products [Lamont (1971)].

3. The established organization also appears to influence, to a marked degree, the motivations of the entrepreneur. In brief surveys such as questionnaires, founders tend to report the socially acceptable reasons as to why they became founders; these include the desire for independence, financial gain, etc. [Howell (1971), Roberts & Wainer (1971)]. However, depth interviews often disclose that the founder is 'pushed' from the parent organization by frustration. In one study, 30% of the founders quit their previous jobs with no specific plans for the future; 13% had to leave because of factors such as plant closings, and

46

an additional 40% said they would have left their previous positions even if they had not become entrepreneurs [Cooper (1971)].

Studies of spin-offs from individual organizations also show that internal factors influence spin-off rates. Thus, internal problems of Univac in Minneapolis and Tracor in Austin were both associated with subsequent spin-offs [Draheim (1972), Susbauer (1972)].

Spin-Off Rates

Spin-off rates appear to vary widely, even among firms in the same geographical region. Some organizations function as incubators to a much greater extent than others. In Palo Alto, the range in spin-off rates for firms with more than 3 spin-offs during the decade of the 60's was about 200 to 1. Many organizations had no spin-offs; others had as a major product—entrepreneurs [Cooper (1972)].

What kinds of firms have high spin-off rates and what kinds have low spin-off rates? In Palo Alto, small firms considered as a class (less than 500 employees) had spin-off *rates* 10 times as high as large firms considered as a group [Cooper (1971)]. Studies of four major M.I.T. laboratories also showed that spin-off rates were inversely associated with laboratory size [Forseth (1966)]. Consistent with these findings, another study showed that where a city is dependent upon one large, dominant firm, the development of new firms rarely occurs [Draheim, *et al.* (1966)].

Very limited data suggest that, within large industrial firms, spin-offs occur chiefly from the 'small businesses' within the firm and rarely from the large, dominant divisions [Cooper (1971)].

Clearly, incubator organizations influence entrepreneurship in a number of ways and some organizations make better incubators than others.

Role of Universities

Some of the major complexes of new firms have grown up around universities—such as Boston, Palo Alto, and Ann Arbor in America. Some observers have concluded that universities play a central role in the development of local entrepreneurship [Deutermann (1964), Allison (1965)].

The extent to which universities have functioned as incubators, with students or staff spinning off to start new firms, has varied widely. In Boston, Austin, and Ann Arbor, substantial percentages of the new firms studied were direct spin-offs from a university or one of its laboratories [Roberts (1969), Susbauer (1972), Lamont (1971)]. Where direct spin-offs from the universities have occurred, they have rarely involved faculty giving up full-time positions to become founders. Although faculty have been involved in a variety of roles, including sometimes being the 'driving force' and sometimes giving only advice, their commitment has usually been only part-time [Roberts (1972)]. Many spin-offs have occurred from university contract research laboratories engaged heavily in government contract research; notable examples are the Instrumentation Laboratory and Lincoln Laboratory at M.I.T.

However, a variety of other patterns also exist. In Palo Alto, only 6 of 243 firms founded in the 1960's had one or more full-time founders who came directly from a university [Cooper (1971)]. In that complex, the role of the university as an incubator appears to have been relatively more important in the earlier years. In both England and America, there are universities strong in science and engineering which have been associated with very little entrepreneurship. There are also instances of substantial entrepreneurship without the presence of a strong university. Shapero found that of 22 technical complexes studied, only 7 had major universities. Several had no colleges when the technical company formation process was getting started [Shapero (1971)].

Universities have undoubtedly played a role in attracting able young men and women to particular regions, and sometimes in giving the firms located there competitive advantages in recruiting and retaining these people. They also provide sources of consulting assistance and opportunities for continuing education for professional employees. However, the degree to which universities play a central or essential role in technical entrepreneurship appears to vary widely.

EXTERNAL FACTORS

A complex of factors external to the individual and external to the parent organization appears to influence entrepreneurship. Research to date provides us with only a limited understanding of many of these factors. Yet it is clear that they interact to create climates more or less favorable to entrepreneurship. It is also clear that climates can change over time and that, to some extent, past entrepreneurship makes future entrepreneurship more likely.

The decision to found a business is affected by the entrepreneur's perceptions of risks and rewards and his knowledge of sources of venture capital and of individuals and institutions which might provide help and advice. Past entrepreneurship creates what might be termed an 'entrepreneurial environment', in which the prospective founder is surrounded by examples and enveloped in knowledge about the process. A number of researchers report that the credibility of the act of starting a company appears to depend, in part, upon whether the founder knows of others who have taken this step [Shapero (1971), Cooper (1971)].

Societal attitudes toward business and entrepreneurship are also undoubtedly important in influencing an individual's decision. Although decisions to found technically-oriented companies have not been studied in this context, studies in a variety of countries show that some cultures are more entrepreneurially inclined than others [Hagen (1971), McClelland (1961)].

Venture Capital

Venture capital is supplied both by the founders themselves and by external individuals and institutions. In one American study, 40% of the technically-oriented firms were started primarily with founders' capital; in a Canadian study, 35% of the firms were initially financed by the founders [Cooper (1971), Litvak & Maule (1972)]. The extent to which founders can save sufficient capital depends upon salary and taxation levels. Observers believe that entrepreneurship in the United Kingdom and Canada is seriously hampered by the difficulty in saving 'seed capital' [Bolton (1972), Hodgins (1972)]. In the American electronics industry, stock options, which are often intended to bind executives to firms, sometimes make it financially feasible for them to become entrepreneurs [Cooper (1971)].

Institutions and individual investors vary substantially in the extent to which they are willing to invest in new, technologically-based firms. The prospective founder seeking capital must thus try to make contact with the 'right' sources of capital, those whose experience and attitudes make it more likely that they will assist this kind of venture. In areas of active entrepreneurship, well-developed communication channels may have developed such that it is relatively easy for the prospective founder to make contact with experienced venture capital sources [Baty (1964)].

In Palo Alto, externally supplied capital for the new firms of the 1960's often came from the successful entrepreneurs of the 1950's. Some of them had become venture capitalists after selling their businesses; others still active in their businesses, advised both entrepreneurs and venture capitalists and served as vital communication links [Cooper (1971)].

Attitudes toward investing in new, technically-based firms can change substantially over time. The success of Control Data in Minneapolis and Tracor in Austin apparently helped to change the local investment climate and made the raising of capital by subsequent waves of entrepreneurs much easier [Draheim (1972), Susbauer (1972)]. Of course, the reverse can happen also; the collapse of the American 'new issue' market in 1961 was followed by a period in which institutions and individuals were extremely sceptical of this kind of venture.

Living Conditions

To what extent are attractive living conditions essential if a complex of new firms is to develop? Clearly, established organizations consider whether they will be able to attract and keep highly trained, mobile, scientific personnel in deciding where to locate branch plants and laboratories. These organizations, in turn, can become the incubators which bring potential entrepreneurs to a region. However, available evidence suggests that, although attractive living conditions may attract technical people to an area as employees, they rarely attract men who are in the act of founding companies [Cooper (1971)]. Furthermore, one study of 22 areas of active entrepreneurship showed that only 8 had unusually attractive living conditions [Shapero (1971)]. Some men leave parent organizations and become founders, because, in part, they do not want to be transferred from a region they like [Susbauer (1972)]. However, in most instances living conditions do not appear to bear directly upon the decision to found a company.

Economics of Location

How important are the economics of location, including transportation costs and the development of complexes of related firms which buy from and sell to each other? Although more research is needed to determine the relative importance of these factors, it does appear that the growth of a complex conveys many benefits to new firms. These include pools of trained labor and the development of specialized suppliers. Although transportation costs may not be very important with many high-technology products, the ability to work closely with customers is sometimes essential. Location in a complex may be particularly important for those new firms which provide custom manufacturing services and which serve as satellite suppliers. An additional benefit is the development of specialized expertise among local accountants, bankers, and lawyers relating to the special needs of small, high-technology firms [Shapero (1971)].

Location in a complex of related firms also provides opportunities for consulting; these opportunities are particularly important for those founders who quit previous jobs with no specific plans for the future and who need to support themselves while plans are crystallizing and capital is being raised [Cooper (1971)].

Experienced Entrepreneurs and Small Firms

Past entrepreneurship creates within a particular region many new, small, technologically-based firms. As indicated earlier, these firms, as a class, tend to have high spin-off rates and to be almost ideal incubators. In addition, past foundings create experienced entrepreneurs. Later, when the founder sells out or when disputes cause the founding team to break up, what does the experienced founder do? Sometimes, he starts another firm, drawing upon his prior experience [Cooper (1971)]. In an area of active entrepreneurship, there may be hundreds of experienced founders. Their presence makes future entrepreneurs more likely.

THE DEVELOPMENT OF AN ENTREPRENEURIALLY-ACTIVE AREA

How does an entrepreneurially active area develop? There have been few studies involving systematic comparisons between regions or of environmental influences as they change over time. However, studies to date suggest that the following processes influence the regional climate for entrepreneurship.

If an area is to develop and maintain technical entrepreneurship, organizations which can serve as incubators must be present, be attracted, or be created. Since founders tend to start firms where they are already living and working, there must be organizations which will hire, bring into the area, and train the engineers, scientists and technical managers who may someday become technical entrepreneurs.

However, the nature of these organizations is critical in determining whether spin-offs actually occur. It is certainly not difficult to point to cities where thousands of engineers are employed, but where there is little entrepreneurship. Exhibit 3 indicates the characteristics of firms and the industries in which they operate which may be associated with high or low birthrates of new firms.

If the established firms serve markets that are stable or declining, there is little incentive for the prospective entrepreneur to enter the field. If the es-

Exhibit 3   Industry and Organizational Attributes Related to the Birth-Rate of New firms

Characteristics of Industry

Low Birth-Rate	*High Birth-Rate*
slow industry growth	rapid industry growth
slow technological change	rapid technological change
heavy capital investment required	low capital investment required
substantial economies of scale	minor economies of scale

Characteristics of Established Incubator Organizations

Low Birth-Rate	*High Birth-Rate*
large number of employees	small number of employees
organized by function	product-decentralized organization
recruit average technical people	recruit very capable, ambitious people
relatively well-managed	afflicted with periodic crises
located in isolated area of little entrepreneurship	located in area of high entrepreneurship

All of the attributes in a given column are not necessarily found together nor are they required to bring about a given spin-off rate. Various combinations may exist.

tablished firms are in industries which require large capital investments or substantial organizations to compete, it will be difficult to assemble the critical mass needed to get a new firm started. If the potential incubator firms hire relatively undynamic people, train them narrowly, and organize them so that engineers talk only to engineers, and so forth, it will be difficult to assemble a well-rounded founding team with the requisite knowledge and skills in marketing, engineering, and manufacturing. If the established firms are well-managed and avoid periodic crises, there may be little incentive for potential founders to leave comfortable positions.

Under such conditions, a would-be founder will find the going difficult. If he seeks to bolster his confidence or to gain advice, he will find few successful founders who have preceded him. If he seeks to support himself as a consultant while formulating his plans and raising capital, he may find this difficult if there are few small companies in the region.

Sources of venture capital experienced in investing in new, technologically-based firms are probably not available locally and making contact with possible investors may be laborious and time consuming. In such an environment, the prospective founder's personal experience is likely to have been in large, established firms. He is likely to know little about what is involved in starting and managing a new firm.

How does the first new firm become established in such a region? Sometimes it involves those rare instances in which the founder comes from another geographical location or starts a new company not related to the business of the parent firm he has left. Sometimes, it involves a technically-trained person who was working in a non-technical organization [Shapero (1971)].

The rate of entrepreneurial activity appears to be accelerated or diminished by a number of factors, although this is another subject deserving additional research. One of the most important factors is the development of the markets

51

and technologies on which the area's industry is based. If the rates of market growth and technological change decline, then technical entrepreneurship will decline, for potential founders will find fewer areas of opportunity. In America, public attitudes relating to new issues of stock from recently-formed companies are also important, for they affect substantially the availability of venture capital.

However, if these factors are favorable, a self-reinforcing process takes place. Past entrepreneurship makes future entrepreneurship more likely and, in time, a high rate of entrepreneurial activity may develop.

REFERENCES

Allison, D. (1965) 'The university and regional prosperity', International Science and Technology, April.

Baty, G. (1964) 'Initial Financing of the New Research-Based Enterprise in New England', Boston, Mass.: The Federal Reserve Bank of Boston.

Bolton, J. (1972) 'Small firms', Speech to Management Forum, University of Manchester, 26 April 1972.

Collins, D. F. & Moore, D. G. (1964) 'The Enterprising Man', East Lansing, Mich.: MSU Business Studies, Michigan State University.

Cooper, A. C. (1971) 'The Founding of Technologically-Based Firms', Milwaukee, Wis.: The Center For Venture Management.

Cooper, A. C. (1972) 'Spin-offs and technical entrepreneurship', I.E.E.E. Transactions on Engineering Management, Vol. EM-18, No. 1.

Deutermann, E. (1966) 'Seeding science-based industry', New England Business Review, December.

Draheim, K. (1972) 'Factors influencing the rate of formation of technical companies', Technical Entrepreneurship: A Symposium (eds. A. Cooper & J. Komives), Milwaukee, Wis.: The Center For Venture Management.

Draheim, K., Howell, R. P. & Shapero, A. (1966) 'The Development of a Potential Defense R & D Complex', Menlo Park, Cal.: Stanford Research Institute.

Forseth, D. A. (1965) 'The Role of government-sponsored research laboratories in the generation of new enterprises—a comparative analysis', S.M. Thesis, Cambridge, Mass.: M.I.T. Sloan School of Management.

Hagen E. E. (1971) 'How Economic Growth Begins: A Theory of Social Change', Entrepreneurship and Economic Development (ed. P. Kilby), New York, N.Y.: The Free Press.

Hodgins, J. W. (1972) 'Management challenges to the entrepreneur', The Business Quarterly, Vol. 37, No. 1.

Howell, R. P. (1972) 'Comparative profiles—entrepreneurs versus the hired executive: San Francisco Peninsula Semiconductor Industry', Technical Entrepreneurship: A Symposium, op. cit.

Komives, J. L. (1972) 'A preliminary study of the personal values of high technology entrepreneurs', Technical Entrepreneurship: A Symposium, op. cit.

Lamont, L. M. (1972) 'The role of marketing in technical entrepreneurship', Technical Entrepreneurship: A Symposium, op. cit.

Lamont, L. M. (1971) 'Technology Transfer, Innovation, and Marketing in Science-Oriented Spin-Off Firms', Ann Arbor, Mich: Industrial Development Division, Institute of Science and Technology, University of Michigan.

Litvak, I. A. & Maule, C. J. (1972) 'Managing the entrepreneurial enterprise', The Business Quarterly, Vol. 37, No. 2.

McClelland, D. C. (1961) 'The Achieving Society', Princeton, N.J.: D. Van Nostrand, Inc.

Roberts, E. B. (1969) 'Entrepreneurship and technology', Factors in the Transfer of Technology (eds. W. Gruber & D. Marquis), Cambridge, Mass.: The M.I.T. Press.

Roberts, E. B. (1972) 'Influences upon performance of new technical enterprises', Technical Entrepreneurship: A Symposium, op. cit.

Roberts, E. B. & Wainer, H. A. (1971) 'Some characteristics of technical entrepreneurs', I.E.E.E. Transactions on Engineering Management, Vol. EM-18, No. 3.

Shapero, A. (1971) 'An action Program For Entrepreneurship', Austin, Texas: Multi-Disciplinary Research Inc.

Susbauer, J. C. (1967) 'The science entrepreneur', Industrial Research, February.

Susbauer, J. C. (1969) 'The technical company formation process: a particular aspect of entrepreneurship', Ph.D. Dissertation, Austin, Texas: University of Texas.

Susbauer, J. C. (1972) 'The technical entrepreneurship process in Austin, Texas, Technical Entrepreneurship: A Symposium, op. cit.

ADDITIONAL READING

Bruce, F. R. (1972) 'Spinoff industry', Oak Ridge National Laboratory Review, Spring.

Cooper, A. C. (1970) 'The Palo Alto experience', Industrial Research, May.

Cooper, A. C. (1970) 'Entrepreneurial environment', Industrial Research, September.

Goldstein, J. (1967) 'The spin-off of new enterprises from a large government funded industrial lab.', S. M. Thesis, Cambridge, Mass.: M.I.T. Sloan School of Management.

Mahar, J. & Coddington, D. (1965) 'The scientific complex—proceed with caution', Harvard Business Review, Vol. 43, No. 1.

Mahar J. & Coddington, D. (1965) 'Academic spinoffs', Industrial Research, April.

Roberts, E. B. (1969) 'What it takes to be an entrepreneur ... and to hang on to one'. Innovation, Number Seven.

Roberts, E. B. & Wainer, H. A. (1968) 'New enterprises on Route 128', Science Journal, December.

Rogers, C. E. (1966) 'The availability of venture capital for new, technically-based enterprises', S.M. Thesis, Cambridge, Mass.: M.I.T. Sloan School of Management.

Shapero, A., Howell, R. P. & Tombough, J. R. (1965) 'The Structure and Dynamics of the Defense R & D Industry', Menlo Park, Cal.: Stanford Research Institute.

Teplitz, P. V. (1965) 'Spin-off Enterprises from a Large Government Sponsored Laboratory', S.M. Thesis, Cambridge, Mass.: M.I.T. Sloan School of Management.

Thurston, P. (1965) 'The founding and growth process of new technical enterprises', S.M. Thesis, Cambridge, Mass.: M.I.T. Sloan School of Management.

—— (1967) 'Technical Innovation: Its Environment and Management', United States Department of Commerce, Washington, D.C.: United States Government Printing Office.

PRODUCT INNOVATION

IN SMALL BUSINESS*

JOHN T. DOUTT

The charge that small businessmen are using too mush system and procedure, too much organization, too technical an approach to problem solving is a strange sound indeed. More commonly they are accused of being casual in adoption of "more business-like methods." Recent observations by the author suggest that businessmen do look on problems of product innovation and development as being technical in origin and solution. And their attempt to solve them has led them on occasion to activities that are both costly and fruitless. Findings indicate that small manufacturers tend to view the problem in terms of these concepts:

1. Research efforts should prove rewarding in proportion to the money and personnel that are given to them.
2. A useful tool for making decisions about new products is the check list. This will save time on products that "just don't fit".
3. Technically trained people can be hired who will generate new product ideas and will aid in developing them.
4. Management problems attendant to new products that are developed can be delegated to someone who is brought in to administrate the commercial aspects of the new product.

THE MECHANICAL APPROACH

Perhaps the most amusing ideas embraced are those that hold that research is something like selling life insurance in that the more money spent and the more effort made, the more certain and the more rewarding the results will be. And, much as the life insurance man is taught to believe, all one has to do is to redouble his efforts, and his redoubled reward will be forthcoming. In a rather simple simile, doubling the amount of fertilizer applied and doubling the number of gardeners does not necessarily produce a double size bloom on the flower. The climate in which new product ideas flourish cannot be purchased by simply doubling the offering price nor can new products be expected to blossom twice as large or twice as fast by doubling the number of technically trained personnel engaged in the effort.

*From *MSU Business Topics* (Autumn, 1960), pp. 58-62. Reprinted by permission of the publisher, Division of Research, Graduate School of Business Administration, Michigan State University.

One of the most generally used tools in product research is the check list. Here one can ascertain at a glance whether or not a given idea fits with some preconceived notion as to what would be a "good" product for the company to develop. While the range of items on the check lists runs from freight rates to adaptability to currently owned equipment, the common theme throughout is the belief that here is a time saver and an automatic device to screen the "good" ideas from the "bad" ones. The fact that some "good" ideas (in terms of germination potential and possible adaptability) are discarded at the very outset is accepted rather casually as inevitable. At least, management had evolved a policy, an approach, a framework for dealing with the different problem of product development.

THE FORMULA

The desirable qualities or characteristics that a new product should possess to be attractive to a small manufacturer can be summarized easily: it should serve some unique purpose in fairly wide-spread applications and should lend itself to patents or the development of a specialized market niche that will not invite or attract too much competition. The realization of this formula is almost certain to result in a product of some pulling power and with sufficiently high profit margin to make the producer happy. And the specialized market niche permits the manufacturer to schedule his manufacturing operations in a fairly serene atmosphere, the customer taking his turn at the gate and never mentioning pricing practices.

The fact that some manufacturers do find products with just these characteristics does not seem to help them in finding additional products to add to their line. Rather than regarding the experience as being unique, the finding of the proverbial needle in the haystack, the general reaction is simply to add one more criterion to the checklist—and this one well-nigh excludes any real product innovation for some time in the future It might be better for the manufacturer to regard his finding of such a product as the grandest kind of luck and rather than spend his time looking for another needle he might do better to turn his attention to the more pedestrian products that make up the product line for most manufacturers.

CURIOSITY AND CONCERN

The fact of the matter is that finding another product with the rare combination of characteristics described above is something that cannot be assured by any mechanical approach to the problem—neither amount of effort at product innovation nor the time-honored check list. The premium quality here is an intense curiosity and concern that is centered on the product by individuals within the organization—individual men who are thoroughly immersed in the notion of "doing something with our product" or some new product which they have thought about largely on their own. And, as with religion, it would sometimes appear that the best way to kill it is to organize for it, delegating, assigning, parceling out until the responsibility for the product (and the zeal for it) are pretty well dismembered.

If this quality of concerned curiosity is to be developed and implemented, top management must see their own responsibility in creating the climate so essential for its advancement. As with most characteristics of the business, this one starts at the top. If the company has been living in an atmosphere of comfortable circumstances with little or no innovation in the day-to-day tasks undertaken by the management echelon, it is unlikely that one will find any wellspring of curiosity and new ideas anywhere in the company. The zest for innovation and progress is indeed a permeating and contagious sort of thing. It cannot be purchased, pigeon-holed, channeled and controlled as one would a pound of pig iron for the store room.

THE MANAGEMENT OF IMPROVEMENT

Nor can one wait until such time as he needs a more imaginative approach to his product line and then proceed to instruct his people to think imaginatively, creatively. It is not a sort of current that lends itself to switch control. And bringing in an innovator or idea man to be superimposed on an uninspired organization is only to dramatize and accentuate the problem of the company's plodding pace. It will hardly solve it. The management of improvement is a continuing part of the management responsibility and the attitude or climate so essential for it to flourish in cannot be hired, delegated, or controlled by gimmick or device.

The company that is blessed with top management possessing this quality will be characterized by a questioning attitude throughout the organization—a ferment that soon involves all phases of the operation of the enterprise. Personnel earmarked by their intensity of curiosity will be hired for both sales and production, and they will get their greatest encouragement here not from the pay check but from top executives who are themselves responsive to this trait.

A second characteristic of the innovating company will be its concern with the finding of problems that need solutions. Involvement with solutions as such (an inevitable by-product of the research laboratory) or the purely commercial activity of new applications of the present line are not just a lesser order of the imaginative mind. They are more likely to be an actual distraction to it. If some unique purpose is to be served and some specialized market niche is to be found, it is more likely to result from the quest for problems to be solved than it is from the making of minor adjustments in the usefulness of our present product to its present customers. Herein lies the failure of much of that which is called "market research".

SURVIVAL OF THE SMALL

But the competition is keen, and it is here that the large company may find an edge over the small producer. With its reputation and larger sales force, it gains more exposure to problem situations, and when they arise, it is in a position to spend great amounts of time and money on the solving of a particular problem knowing full well that the solution could lead to a whole series of product developments. Obviously, if the small producer is to survive in such an economic arrangement, it will be by the excellent quality of what he does and not by any quantitative attempt to meet the large producer on his own playing field. His sensitivity to problem situations must be keen, his ideas unusual.

THE ACADEMIC FOUNTAINHEAD

It is becoming increasingly common for executives in the industrial world to turn to academic people for aid on this topic of product innovation. One case observed will be described by way of illustration. Believing that teachers in universities would be in the vanguard of new ideas and latest developments in scientific and technical areas, the chief executive of a small manufacturing concern contacted a number of university professors in a broad number of areas and arranged a loose organization whereby they would be called in as the need would arise. It was his hope that these people would become a fountainhead of new ideas, some of which might become the product with the unique characteristics described earlier.

Despite some lapse of time, the academic program has not turned up any ideas worth developing commercially. Apparently there is little correlation between intelligence and the sort of creative imagination required here. In fact, the more informed mind often turns out to be the more critical, not only of the efforts of others but of its own as well. The result is a barrenness in which creative ideas cannot take root.

AN ORGANIZATIONAL PROBLEM

The problem receiving the least attention from top management is the question of what they would do with a new product idea if they did get one and how they would integrate it into their present organization. In at least one case studied, the chief executive was actively seeking one or more new products to be added to the line, but confessed quite openly that he did not have the management team to handle the new product or the increased burdens that expanding production and sales would place on his present organization. In still another instance, the owner-manager of a fairly large operation (125 employees) admitted that he had surrounded himself with narrowly trained executives hired to do specific tasks, and that he had made no effort to weld them into a working team. Any new product developed, he observed, would mean that he would have to bring in some one to handle it. Just how it would relate to his present product line or how his new product manager would fit in with his going organization were problems that had been given but casual consideration.

In still another instance, the chief officer of the company claimed to be looking for new products, maintaining that his present plant and capital structure could easily support a sales volume three times its present size. While his manufacturing operations were quite systematically controlled, made possible by the fact that his chief product was free from the usual harassments of a competitive market, he relied on a constant round of visits among the executives themselves to maintain control and coordination in the higher echelons of the business. And he himself was actively engaged in reviewing inventory records of finished stock and initiating a work order for replenishment when he judged it desirable to increase quantities on hand. It is doubtful if even the slightest increase in sales volume or diversity of product line could be experienced without placing serious strains on his present administrative devices.

THE NEW PERSPECTIVE

It is apparent from these few observations that product innovation is far from the mechanical problem that it often appears to be. The priceless ingredients here are a management philosophy, an attitude, a sensitivity, a curiosity that the top executives generate and encourage and which flows from the top down through every department of the organization; it permeates every office and every function of the enterprise. In one instance this attitude was evidenced by a number of home-made machines in the shop which incorporated bicycle wheels and peculiar mechanical linkages because, as the owner explained, "nobody makes the kind of machines we need".

Until the chief executives of a company see this problem in terms of the perspectives outlined here, they will probably continue to rely on the old precepts of product development: research budget, technical personnel, and check list, complete with 5 gradations of opinion. But the race is not to the swift nor the struggle to the strong. It is to those who grasp the true nature of a problem and react with some intelligence to what it suggests.

CHAMPIONS FOR RADICAL

NEW INVENTIONS*

DONALD A. SCHON

1. Why do small companies, large corporations, military laboratory employees, and independent inventors find it so difficult to sell really new inventions to the military services?
2. What is the nature of resistance to innovation in military and business organizations?
3. What does experience show to be the requirements of successful technical innovation?

*From *Harvard Business Review* (March-April., 1963), pp. 77-86. Copyright 1963 by the President and Fellows of Harvard College; all rights are reserved.

4. What steps can management take to ensure that the necessary development work will go into promising proposals for radical new products and processes?

The military services hold up to the business community an enormous and only slightly distorted mirror in which patterns surrounding technical innovation stand out clearly. Goaded by the threat of competition and a perceived need for corporate growth, industry seeks new products. In order to "win the arms race" and "meet the Soviet threat," the military seeks new weapons systems. Both depend on technical innovation and lean on technical resources for producing change. Both are caught in the gap between the wish for deliberate and systematic methods of innovation and the uncertainty and risk inherent in this activity. In both, there is a discrepancy between formal organization for innovation and the informal organization and process by which it is sometimes accomplished (though in the military, perhaps because it is a superorganization, the informal routes are more clearly visible).

In this article I shall examine the significance of the resources for invention that are being wasted and the reasons (many of them all too human and understandable) that this waste continues to go on. Then I shall turn to the measures we can take in business and government to cope with the problem. The first and most essential step is recognizing resistance to change and accepting it rather than "driving it underground." There are a series of measures, one of the most important of which has to do with the "product champion" concept, that we can take to promote the development of promising new inventions.

Much of the information and thinking in this discussion is based on a study conducted by Arthur D. Little, Inc., under a contract administered by the National Inventors Council and supported by the military services.

SIGNIFICANT RESOURCE

In the traditional sense, "inventor" means an amateur, untrained, and independent genius of the kind supposedly typified by men like Thomas A. Edison and Samuel F. Morse. Whether or not technical heroes ever did fit this mold, it is clear that they do not fit it now. The growing technical complexity of military and industrial life has made it impossible for individuals to invent effectively without extensive technical experience. Moreover, in our culture today, the official idealization of inventors masks an unofficial contempt. "Inventor" is very nearly a dirty word. With few exceptions, industry and the military alike tend more and more to protect themselves from the apparent dangers of dealing with individuals as individuals; and as a result the individuals who might once have called themselves "inventors" are now forming small businesses or filtering into the ranks of large corporations.

For these reasons, "inventors" in the old sense are not the resource we ought to be interested in here. We should be concerned, rather, with innovative, technically trained individuals who have proved their ability to develop new products and processes and who have done so as individuals, without organizational support. We find these people operating as professional independents and in a variety of organizational settings: universities, research institutes, small and large corporations, and the military itself. What is more, our concern should be with radical innovation, such as Robert H. Goddard's early work on rockets and Sir Frank Whittle's work on the jet engine. When it comes to this kind of innovation (which is always easier to identify in retrospect than in advance), a man's residence in an organization does not guarantee him organizational support.

From this point on, when I refer to "inventors" and "inventions," I shall use the terms in the ways just described.

NUMBER OF INVENTORS

How many such men are there; how much have they contributed? This question can be answered only indirectly and by approximation. On the basis of our own estimates and interviews with technical people in military laboratories and large corporations, heads of small businesses, and professional independent inventors themselves, a good guess is that today there are several thousand independent inventors in the United States. To mention some of the pieces of evidence gathered in our study:

1. The United States Patent Office was able to give the National Inventors Council a list of 500 inventors who had accumulated many useful patents, working independently. Jacob Schmookler estimates that 40% of the patents currently granted are assigned to such individuals.[1]
2. There are about 310,000 small businesses in the United States ("small" by the Small Business Administration's standards — less than 500 employees and less than $10,000,000 in annual sales).
3. We interviewed 42 small companies which, through technically trained individuals in their employ, had developed an impressive array of new products and processes.

We have no way of estimating the number of independent innovators working without organizational support *in* military laboratories and large corporations.

VALUE OF CONTRIBUTION

How important a role have such people played in innovation? Evidence for their actual and potential contributions is, as might be expected, elusive. Nevertheless, several different kinds of evidence have been gathered:

Although patents are a doubtful sign of technical innovation, patent studies have been made which are at least indicative. Jacob Schmookler's study covering patents granted during the last decade reveals that a surprisingly high percentage were assigned to individuals working as individuals, rather than to organizations. Indeed, 40% to 60% of the patentees worked outside the organized research teams of industrial laboratories. And John Jewkes, David Sawers, and Richard Stillerman made a study which showed that between 1936 and 1955, in both the United States and Great Britian, the percentage of patents issued to individuals, as opposed to corporations, remained between 40% and 50%.[2]

[1]"Inventors Past and Present," *Review of Economics and Statistics,* August 1957, p. 321.
[2]*The Sources of Invention* (New York, St. Martin's Press, 1959), p. 105.

In a paper presented to the Joint Economic Committee on September 24, 1959, Professor Daniel Hamberg of the University of Maryland stated that 12 of the 18 inventions he had examined resulted from the work of independent individuals and relatively small companies. The authors, in their *The Sources of Invention*, show that 40 of 61 important inventions made since 1900 were the product of independent innovators, working alone, unaffiliated with any industrial laboratory. Another 6 were the product of investigation conducted in small- to medium-sized organizations. Their list cuts across technical disciplines and industrial areas, ranging from Bakelite and cellophane to safety razors and ball-point pens.[3]

In the course of our study, we assembled a list of inventions important for military uses, made within roughly the past 50 years. Individuals working without organizational support were either entirely responsible for these inventions or played a major role in their evolution:

Jet engine — Sir Frank Whittle
Gyrocompass — H. Anschütz-Kaempfe
Helicopter — Igor I. Sikorsky
Rockets — Robert H. Goddard
Many varieties of automatic guns — e.g., the Lewis gun
Suspension tanks — George Christie
Doron body armor — General Georges F. Doriot
Noiseless and flashless machine guns — Stanley Lovell
Cryotron — Dudley Buck
Atomatic submarine — Admiral Hyman G. Rickover
Sidewinder missle — William B. McLean
Project Astron — Nicholas C. Christofilos
Stainless steel — Elwood Haynes
Titanium — W. J. Kroll

Bear in mind that many of these developments, as well as a number of others which could have been included, occurred *after* the beginning of the organized research and development which has characterized the last 50 years.

It is clear, then, that in recent times individuals working without organizational support have been responsible for an extraordinarily high percentage of important, radical commercial developments. In spite of the problems in contributing to the military, they have also been responsible for a number of significant military changes. Also, these individuals have shown themselves to be particularly well equipped to do innovative exploratory work and to do it quickly in comparison to the research teams of large corporations. However, as we shall see presently, much of their potential value to business and the military has been wasted.

What are the reasons for this waste? Let us begin with a look at the military screening offices, then turn to companies and individuals who are doing (or might be doing) defense work. Later we can examine the interesting parallels with commercial innovation.

FAILURE TO GET THROUGH

Within the military, there is official recognition of the need for technical innovation. Military research and development chiefs and civilian advisers em-

---

[3] Ibid., pp. 72, 73.

phasize the need for radically new developments, for "ideas," and for more exploration. They are apt to express this need in terms of "meeting the Soviet threat," "winning the Cold War," "defending the Free World," and the like—phrases which play for the military very much the same role that "growth" plays for the industrial corporation.

The formal channel by which the ideas of individuals may enter the military is the military screening offices. The major research and development agencies of each of the three services have such offices, as do major operating groups like the Army Ordnance Corps and individual military laboratories like the Army Signal Corps Laboratories. The function of these agencies is to receive and screen the ideas of individuals, inside and outside the military, and to pass on to appropriate technical personnel those ideas which seem to have most merit.

How much innovation goes through this channel? We interviewed 14 men from 7 screening offices which receive from 40 to 2,000 ideas a month. The chief question asked of each man was whether he could identify an invention submitted through his office and later used by the military. *In not one case could he do so.*

For this reason we were led to conclude that as a means of helping the military to use resources of invention which are not now adequately used, these screening offices are virtually a hindrance. They can be best understood as a wall, rather than as a screen. They protect the main body of military R & D from the disturbance of outside inventors and inventions; they are a device for maintaining good public relations.

Many of the men we interviewed were perfectly open about this. They had long ago concluded that inventors may as well not submit inventions to the military services. They pointed to their own problems: cuts in budget, too few personnel, overlap and repetition of function within and among the services, and difficulties in getting feedback on ideas from the working laboratories. And although these men are charged officially with a constructive function, they work under conditions that permit them to perform only a secondary, defensive one.

In brief, there are significant resources of innovation for which there is expressed need, and there is a screening organization whose main function is to serve as a buffer against them. This is not the simple case of a large organization's discrimination against certain individuals. The case is much more that of a complicated social tangle in which people on all sides of the issue are caught, in spite of their best efforts.

WHY INVENTORS FAIL

The problems of contributing to the military are experienced in different ways by individuals in varying settings. Let us take a look at four groups — people in the military, large and small business, and independent inventors.

Federal Employees

Individuals in military laboratories, who are inventive and technically competent, have a unique value as a resource. They know what the technical problems are. They have access to prior art in their fields. They are subject to miminum security restrictions. And, unlike individuals in other settings, they are already organized as a resource. It is particularly significant, therefore, that where figures are available, military screening offices report that the rate of rejection of ideas submitted internally through formal channels is as great as the rate of rejection of ideas submitted from the outside.

Some of the reasons for this came out in our interviews with technical personnel in military laboratories. In spite of the fact that many of these people had records of outstanding technical contribution, there was a general sense of discouragement about the possibility of contribution apart from assigned work. The men gave several reasons for this attitude:

1. In their view self-initiated innovation was not expected of them. And where their function was not limited to testing or administration of contracts, their superiors seemed to fear that self-initiated work would distract them from assigned tasks.

2. While there was a civilian award program for self-initiated contributions, substantial awards were rarely given. (An exception was the $25,000 award given for the development of the Sidewinder missile at the Navy's China Lake Laboratory.)

3. Most important of all, discouraging delays were encountered when the men attempted to go through formal channels. This they attributed to a "reverse natural selection" among technical civil service personnel. Relatively low salaries tended to drive many good innovative technical men out of government work, and the dedicated inventors who stayed on had to cope with the remainder — many of whom come into positions of responsibility only through seniority. One laboratory experimented with an "Operation Blue Sky" in order to solicit new technical ideas. But the ideas submitted were reviewed by the same men who were believed to have blocked innovation in the past, and the experiment produced nothing but frustration.

Small Business

In the case of small business, many innovators come from universities and large corporations precisely in order to be freer and more effective in technical innovation. They tend to be men who show unusual enthusiasm for new technical developments and who, by and large, have demonstrated an unusual ability to move quickly from new technical ideas to prototype development. But they do not contribute significantly to the military for these reasons:

1. Many technically based small companies have not even attempted to gain military R & D contracts. They attribute this to the unprofitability of such contracts, inability to capitalize on later production contracts, the difficulty and cost of selling R & D to the government, and competition with large corporations.

2. Relatively few small businesses are successful when they attempt to gain technical development contracts with the military, and the successful ones tend to conform to a pattern. Thus —

    a. They gain contracts in a specialized technical area in which one or two of their staff members have considerable technical prestige.

    b. They have a man (or two) in top management experienced in dealing with the military.

c. They either bid on contracts where the technical requirement is already clearly recognized by the military, or they sponsor their own development work and apply to the military for optimization contracts.

d. In general, they do not make money on such contracts; they are lucky to break even.

All of this suggests that, in spite of efforts by the military and the Small Business Administration to increase the small business share of R & D contracts, there is still a resource of technically trained innovative individuals in small firms throughout the country whose contributions the military is not getting. This is particularly true of technical needs that the military has not yet clearly recognized and of small companies lacking the qualifications mentioned above.

Big Business

Large corporations are entirely distinct from individuals without organizational support. But the large corporation's advantages in approaching the military — its proven name, its large sales force, its capital, its ability to carry out production contracts — apply only to projects officially sanctioned by top management. Innovative, technically trained individuals within a corporation frequently have technical ideas that never get official sanction. Ideas of this kind may not look to the top management like a source of long-range profit, they may not seem to have commercial application, or they may even lie outside the corporation's pattern of technical growth. And yet they may be of great value to the military. To illustrate:

During World War II, technical staff members of a large corporation proposed water-filled protective capsules for pilots of high-speed aircraft and a new kind of aircraft thermometer. Both ideas were rejected at the time and later produced successfully elsewhere. Most technical directors of large corporations are familiar with similar cases.

Inevitably, corporate managers make some mistakes in judging the value of a proposed development for the corporation, and in many more cases they correctly judge as inappropriate for them a development which might be of great value to the military. The originator of such a development must either sell the idea "uphill" in his own organization; or he must sell it essentially as an individual to the military. The double obstacle is usually insuperable. And, what is more, the technical man usually has no incentive to overcome it. He will have signed away his patent rights, so that he cannot profit from them. He is not eligible for the civilian award program. If his project succeeds, he is likely to gain some status and prestige. But if it fails, he may very well suffer for having wasted time and money.

Independent Operators

Independent inventors constitute a special case in that their problems in relating to large organizations, both in the military and in private business, are classic.

First, there are difficulties inherent in the relation itself. Witness, for instance, the mutually frustrating, but finally successful, efforts of Alexander Zarchin to interest the Israeli government in his salt-water conversion process, and the mutual harassment that characterized the interaction of many inventors in one U.S. industry — an interaction which in the case of at least three major inventors (Rudolph Diesel, Wallace H. Carothers, and William G. Armstrong) ended tragically.

In the case of the U.S. military, this relationship has certain special features. For example, each of the services views itself as being harassed at present by one or two voluble inventors, skillful in appeal to Congressmen, who have made that service their particular target. Unfortunately for R & D administrators in each of the services, the word "inventor" is apt to conjure up an image of their particular tormentor.

What makes the situation even more delicate is that these men cannot easily be dismissed. There are the stories of Professor Robert H. Goddard who tried in the 1930's, for the most part unsuccessfully, to interest the U.S. military in rocketry; of George Christie, inventor of the suspension system for tanks — rejected by the U.S. Army, later adopted successfully by the Russians; and of Nicholas C. Christofilos, "the crazy Greek" who turned up with Project Astron.

The difficulty with these rare geniuses is that they can be recognized easily only in retrospect, never in prospect. You never know for certain that your present-day tormentor, whom you *think* is a crank, may not turn out to be another Goddard, another Christie, or another Christofilos.

Furthermore, the inventor himself may often show considerable aggressiveness, not to say eccentricity, in his dealings with the military. In many cases, his motives appear to be primarily to show up the professional military man, the professional scientist, or the professional engineer. He may present his invention so aggressively at to suggest that he is aiming not at having it accepted but at being able to complain of its unfair rejection.

At best, the preliminary judgment of new technical developments is precarious, particularly for men who do not have great technical sophistication in the field in question. Often the technical administrator must base his judgments on the soundness of the man at least as much as on the promise of the development itself. And when the man appears in sneakers and an open shirt, when he behaves queerly, or when he refuses (moved by his own perhaps legitimate and perhaps excessive fears about protection of his idea) to reveal the principle of his invention until he has been paid, he makes it extremely difficult for the military decision-maker to act favorably toward him.

While these difficulties are sharpest for the men who call themselves inventors, they extend generally to all kinds of individuals mentioned earlier. For the military, feeling that it has been burned so frequently in its dealings with individual inventors, tends to apply its defensive attitude to *all* "organizationless" individuals. Thus, we are confronted here by a vicious circle of protection and aggression, practiced by both parties.

NEED TO RESIST CHANGE

So far, the complicated social tangle responsible for the record of the military screening offices has been presented mainly from the side of the would-be contributors. But there is another side as well. And here we find striking parallels between military and commercial organizations.

"Normal" Opposition

Individuals approaching the military tend to be inattentive to the military administrator's problems. These problems make it difficult for him to invest in radically new technical developments for which there is no obvious and immediate requirement — especially when these are at the "idea" stage and are to be undertaken by individuals working without organizational support. These problems have to do, in part, with the so-called "weapons systems" approach which characterizes much of the military's technical development work:

> To ensure that no time, money, or effort will be wasted on blind alleys, almost all of the planning is done in terms of the end products that are supposed to emerge from the program — the weapon systems. Before any major project is begun, the planners painstakingly figure out what performance characteristics the weapon system is supposed to have and the technological innovations it will contain. The development program is spelled out stage by stage and then reviewed by numerous agencies within the armed services, by special committees, and by the staff of the Assistant Secretary of Defense for Research and Engineering. After the program is under way, progress is monitored at every step.[4]

Within this sort of approach, certain general technical routes to the goal are chosen. "Technical problems" are problems in implementing these routes. A military technical administrator operating within such a system cannot easily shift his attention to radical technical ideas not obviously related to his requirements, and so he finds it even more difficult to invest in risky individuals who will not be able to carry their innovations into production later on.

There is an even more general sort of resistance to radical technical change. Elting Morison describes it elegantly in his study of the introduction to the Navy of continuous-aim firing (a new combat-tested method, presenting major advantages over old ones, had been rejected by Navy officials until President Theodore Roosevelt intervened):

> The Navy is not only an armed force — it is a society. In the forty years following the Civil War, this society had been forced to accommodate itself to a series of technological changes. . . . These changes wrought extraordinary changes in ship design, and therefore in the concepts of how ships were to be used; that is, in fleet tactics and even in naval strategy. . . . To these numerous innovations, producing as they did a spreading disorder throughout a serivce with heavy commitments to formal organization, the Navy responded with grudging pain. It is wrong to assume, as civilians frequently do, that this blind reaction to technological change springs exclusively from some causeless Bourbon distemper that invades the military mind. There is a sounder and more attractive base. The opposition, where it occurs, of the soldier and the sailor to such change springs from the normal human instinct to protect oneself and more especially one's way of life. Military organizations are societies built around and upon the prevailing weapon systems. Intuitively and quite correctly the military man feels that a change in weapons portends a change in the arrangements of his society.[5]

[4] Burton Klein, "A Radical Proposal for R & D," *Fortune,* May 1958, p. 112.

[5] "A Case Study of Innovation, *Engineering and Science,* April 1950.

What Morison characterizes as the "normal human instinct" to oppose technological change is as true of the military today as it was in Theodore Roosevelt's time.

Justified Ambivalence

We come now to a most important point. Resistance to change is not only normal but in some ways even desirable. An organization totally devoid of resistance to change would fly apart at the seams. It *must* be ambivalent about radical technical innovation. It *must* both seek it out and resist it. Because of commitments to existing technology and to forms of social organization associated with it, management *must* act against the eager acceptance of new technical ideas, even good ones. Otherwise, the technical organization would be perpetually and fruitlessly shifting gears.

This is true in the military and also in almost all walks of private industry. As a matter of fact, most corporations are, if anything, *more* intensively defensive than the military. Taking the case of proposals from outside the organization first, only a few companies have maintained a tradition of receptiveness to such ideas. For in addition to sharing with the military reasons like those mentioned, many companies are afraid of being sued. Because some companies have had to pay damages to inventors, most companies have built up eleborate legal defenses. And because some companies have stolen ideas from inventor's, many would-be inventors have become gun-shy.

But the most interesting analogies refer to inside, rather than to outside, innovation. Here, too, most large corporations share the military's ambivalence over radical proposals. On the one hand, there is official enthusiasm for growth, expansion, diversification, progressiveness, getting ahead of the competition, and maintaining share of market — all backed up by the axiom that those who do not forge ahead fall behind, as well as by the *Alice in Wonderland* notion that you must run very hard even to stand still.

There is plenty of reality behind this axiom, as witnessed by the fate of many sleepy industries tied to outmoded products and processes. (I seriously wonder, however, if growth is *always* required for corporate health and whether new products are *always* the means to salvation.) The fact stands, nevertheless, that radical product innovation means radical changes in all phases of the business — new technologies, new product techniques, new channels of distribution, and perhaps even a new conception of the market.

Novelty in these areas challenges accepted ways of doing things and long-established skills. It may throw a company, including top management, into areas where it feels inept and uninformed. Also, as in Morison's example of continuous-aim firing, changes in technology tend to carry with them major changes in social organization, threatening established hierarchies, undermining the security of positions based on old products.

Moreover, the more radical the product innovation, the higher, in general, the cost of developing it. And this cost curve tends to rise sharply after the preliminary work in which the first models are built and the first market concepts are achieved. In fact, the whole process is marked by increasing risk and takes place in a context where most new product efforts fail. It is not surprising, in view of these tendencies, that a ground swell of covert resistance to change comes into conflict with official enthusiasm for it.

The pernicious part of this problem for both the military and industry is not the resistance to change, but the failure to recognize it. Here again, the rule applies to almost all types of organizations.

In the case of the military, resistance is masked by official assumptions to the effect that the services are wholeheartedly in favor of technical innovation in weapons systems and accept or reject all new ideas objectively, strictly on their merits. These assumptions conflict with reality and mislead potential innovators. For they go hand in hand with other assumptions. It is held, for example, that "civilian resources of invention are ready to be tapped" — that is, solutions to urgent technical problems are there for the taking, in the form of already worked out developments. If this is so, it is only prudent to reject solutions which have not yet been fully developed — and this, of course, includes most ideas submitted to the military.

In short, official assumptions, masking what is often legitimate resistance to change, drive that resistance underground, as in the case of the idea-screening operation itself. Once underground, this resistance to change goes out of control. Thus, the question of its legitimacy never comes up, and potential contributors to the services are bewildered by the discrepancy between words and action.

In industry, too, once resistance to change goes underground, it becomes capable of destroying most product innovation. Underground resistance paves the way for disguised defenses against change. In screening new ideas, many large corporations employ formal committees which are, in effect, buffers against new ideas. Assumptions are found to the effect that new ideas are wholeheartedly desired and are evaluated objectively, strictly on their merits — together with the further assumption that new ideas should be fully developed and ready for plucking. For instance:

> In some large companies, the "new idea forms" which must be filled out by innovators require a fullness and precision of detail impossible early in the life of a new product idea. Such screening mechanisms require that each idea be developed before support is given for its development; they have the effect either of discouraging submission of new ideas or of forcing development work underground.

PATTERN OF SUCCESS

Despite the complicated buffers and screens I have described, innovation does take place in government and industry. Radical inventions do find acceptance, and the fact that they do, and the reasons that they do, are tremendously important. Since the military is such a superb case in point, let us take its experience first.

Developments like McLean's Sidewinder missile and Rickover's atomic submarine do not fit the pattern of orderly presentation of promising technical ideas to official judges, favorable objective evaluation, and then orderly marshaling of technical resources for development. These histories look more like crusades or military campaigns, with overtones of fifth-column activity and guerrilla warfare. They present clear illustrations of four major themes.

1. At the outset, the idea encounters sharp resistance. Like Goddard's work on rockets, Whittle's work on the jet engine, and virtually every other significant military technical development, the Sidewinder and the atomic submarine at first were met with indifference and in some cases active resistance from military officials. These innovations appeared to run counter to the most sensible and established technical commitments. They looked expensive and unfeasible.

2. *Next, the idea receives active and vigorous promotion.*   In spite of the myth that valid technical ideas do not need internal sales, it is characteristic of successful technical innovation within the military that the new idea requires and receives active promotion. Often, as in Morison's description of the introduction of continuous-aim firing, there is a division of labor as to invention and promotion. In that instance, the inventor was not equally talented as a promoter, and so a second figure emerged who was able to carry the fight for its introduction and development into the highest Navy circles. In our own time, Admiral Rickover's skill in defending and promoting his ideas is legendary. Techniques for promoting new technical ideas are a matter of serious concern, even at the highest military levels, as shown by the use for this purpose of outside publication and appeal to Congress.

3. *For the introduction, promotion, and development of these ideas, their proponents make use of the informal, rather than the official, military system.*   In the early stages of development, when the idea was still in its infancy, the Sidewinder was not funded through official contracts from any of the Navy bureaus, but from the small sums detoured from official programs. Only when enough work had been done to show the strength of the idea did it fall into official contract channels. The use of such "bootlegged" research funds is only one example of the use of the informal military network. In many instances ideas now under development or test were submitted originally through personal contracts; in the matter of technical development, particularly across departmental lines, a network of good personal contacts is a cherished resource. The buffering function of the official screening offices virtually forces such a network into existence.

4. *Typically, one man emerges as champion of the idea.*   Many people do know of Goddard, Whittle, Rickover, and McLean. But in the case of less famous developments, for example, the Navy's "Ribbon in the Sky" and the introduction of frangible bullet firing as a training method in World War II, individuals also emerged as champions. There is nothing incidental or exceptional about this happening. Where radical innovation is concerned, the emergence of a champion is required. Given the underground resistance to change described earlier, the new idea either finds a champion *or dies.*

Essentially, the champion must be a man willing to put himself on the line for an idea of doubtful success. He is willing to fail. But he is capable of using any and every means of informal sales and pressure in order to succeed.

No ordinary involvement with a new idea provides the energy required to cope with the indifference and resistance that major technical change provokes. It is characteristic of champions of new developments that they identify with the idea as their own, and with its promotion as a cause, to a degree that goes far beyond the requirements of their job. In fact, many display persistence and courage of heroic quality. For a number of them the price of failure is professional suicide, and a few become martyrs to the championed idea.

All of these requirements apply to commercial organizations as well as to the military. As just one example, Arthur K. Watson has testified to the importance of the third condition at IBM:

> The disk memory unit, the heart of today's random access computer, is not the logical outcome of a decision made by IBM management. It was developed in one of our laboratories as a bootleg project — over the stern warning from management that the project had to be dropped because of budget difficulties. A handful of men ignored the warning. They broke the rules. They risked their jobs to work on a project they believed in.[6]

Product Champions

But perhaps the most challenging part of the pattern described, at least for corporate executives, is the product-champion concept. How can it be made to work (yet not work so well that the organization is in chaos)?

To begin, it is clear that the product champion must have considerable power and prestige in the organization; otherwise he will not have the freedom to play his role. He must know and know how to use the company's informal system of relationships. Also, his interests must cut across the special interests (technology, marketing, production, and finance) which are essential to the product's or the process's development.

But attention to these requirements has a curiously futile ring to it. For one thing, it is extremely difficult *in practice* for top management to admit the need for such a man, since the implication in doing so is that something is wrong with what is euphemistically called the organization's "climate for creativity." Moreover, once the need is admitted, what can be done about it? Is management to bring in individuals whose overt function is to disrupt the company order which has been so carefully built up over the years? And, if it is to do so, what evidence is there that product champions can be selected and fostered?

In fact, there is some evidence that these men can*not* be hired and "developed" the way some others can. In more than one case, companies have brought in men who were specially chosen to initiate radical product change; but since these men were chosen, in part, for their thick-skinned aggressiveness, they succeeded in alienating others on whom they depended, even to the point of ensuring failure. In still other cases, companies brought into this new product role men who were well received within the organization but who lacked the aggressive, risk-taking properties of the product champion, and failed for the opposite reasons.

Nevertheless, there have been instances in which product champions have been successfully introduced from outside, or recognized and supported within, a company. This kind of activity has occurred in at least two different ways:

1. Management resorts not to sweeping across-the-board change, but to a model for change. It sets up a pilot operation staffed by only a few men but capable of carrying ideas through preliminary development and promoting them vigorously in the informal channels of the organization. This pilot operation can be headed by a man selected because he has the characteristics of the product champion described previously, with the exception of overt aggressive-

[6]Address to the Eighth International Congress of Accountants, New York City, September 24, 1962.

ness, which often is not necessary. The function of the operation is to provide a model of product innovation, small at first, but capable of taking root and spreading.

2. The company's management makes the decision to adapt to its new technology and to the product champions who accompany that technology, rather than to force innovation into the mold of the established organization. Such a decision crucially affects the company's policy of corporate growth and diversification, since it does not require that new products mesh with existing means of production and distribution. Essentially, it gives support to certain product champions as entrepreneurs, allowing them to push their product through from beginning to end, and establishing a new division for the resulting business (that division need be only loosely related to the existing corporate structure).

More often than not, the champions are drawn from within the organization. They are given freedom to take a technical, production, marketing, and management view of their new product — in effect, to approach its development as though they were setting up a small business with corporate funding and support. They are held responsible for the success of that business, in turn, as though they were an independent corporate entity. The corporation resulting from consistent pursuit of such a policy has the aspect of a loose confederation of businesses which may or may not fall into the same product family.

Both of the foregoing patterns share recognition of the need for the product champion, a need created by the organization's own powerful underground resistance to change. The patterns are devices by which top management, shrewdly assessing obstacles to innovation, attempts to manipulate the organization. The success of the manipulation, at least on a temporary basis, is shown by the number of organizations for which one or another of the patterns described has become a standard procedure.

Needless to say, these patterns do not represent the only alternatives. Once the need for the product champion has been recognized, there are many possible social inventions for selecting and supporting him. The important point is that *some* such invention is required.

CONCLUSION

In perspective, the problem of significant innovation in business and the military raises some basic questions. For instance, it seems fair to ask if the most important aspect for top management is not formal organizational procedures but the social tangle which necessitates bringing the product champion into being in the first place. Why must legitimate resistance to change go underground? Why is it not possible to deal openly in a company with the dangers of innovation, even while proceeding with development work? Why should penalties for failure fall so heavily on one or two men, when the organization as a whole demands innovation?

The product-champion approach grows out of the sharp division between those in top management who dispose and those, lower in the organization, who propose. Product champions would be needed less if the risks of product change were more evenly distributed, that is, if top management were to give up some of its prerogatives to dispose of what others proposed. This may be seen as too steep a price to pay for innovation. But a willingness to face the price of innovation is a major part of the problem of technological progress.

AN APPROACH

TO NEW BUSINESS VENTURES*

ROBERT M. ADAMS

From time to time new terms or expressions for old situations rise to common usage in our everyday vocabulary. Such terms become so popular and so prevalent, so discussed and so disputed that we are led to presume that they describe some amazing new social, scientific, or economic phenomenon. Who has not heard about the "establishment" or the "generation gap;" the "brain drain" or the "conglomerate;" "escalation" or the "new politics." Our parents and grandparents and more ancient generations knew the phenomena described by such words, even if they didn't use these words. And so it is today with "new business ventures," an increasingly popular expression among businessmen, investors, and managers of research and development.

Our nomadic ancestors launched new ventures virtually every day of their lives. Certainly the first merchant to send goods across Europe and Asia by camel caravan was involved in a new enterprise on which he hoped to make a substantial profit. The advent of the Industrial Revolution quickened and dramatized the new business thrust of capitalism; but the Industrial Revolution is more than 200 years old so we can hardly claim that new businesses based on new technologies are recent phenomena.

If, then, new business ventures are not new, why are they the subject of so much attention and discussion these days? Why are they high on the list of suggested theme subjects for meetings of the I.R.I., an organization of people and industries committed not to what's old, but to what's new?

The answer is not simple. It's not sufficient to say that desire for growth is the answer because this merely leads to the question of why we want growth. The complete analysis of that question would yield a complex mixture of social, economic, scientific, philosophical, and psychological reasons. For some of us, the driving force is simply corporate policy, usually dictated by such factors as competition or an investment image. For others, it is the opportunity to convert the raw ore of scientific discovery into refined products for human wants.

We can accept the fact that new business ventures are regarded as

*From *Research Management* (Vol. 12, No. 4, 1969), pp. 255-260. Reprinted by permission.

necessary and presently desirable things in our business life. How, then, do we achieve such necessities and satisfy such desires?

It is my intention to discuss only one aspect of this subject: new business ventures developed within a sizable and growing industrial corporation. It will necessarily be a somewhat narrow view of the subject since my first-hand experience is largely with a single company, albeit one that has been unusually successful in this area. It is not my objective to discuss acquisitions or the formation of new businesses to exploit already established markets with known technology, although these are both well used and often suitable routes. Please note, however, that the term, "developed within", does not exclude finding new ideas, inventions, or technologies outside the company. The important point is that the development from the idea or invention stage to commercial reality comes from within the company.

Converting new technologies or new products or new business concepts to successful enterprises is not the province or property of any single organization or individual. If any company had a tried and proved answer to new business ventures that assured success for every start, that company would guard such knowledge zealously. Such a key to success would be carefully protected proprietary information. It is possible only to describe some general principles which have been found useful and to recommend them to you for our own evaluation.

A new business venture in the context of this presentation will be considered truly new only if it produces new sources of sales and profits for its sponsor from presently untapped markets. Success in such ventures hinges on many factors, not the least of which is sheer good luck. However, consistent performance cannot be achieved without three absolutely essential elements: the proper corporate climate; a good organizational approach; and people. It sounds easy, but is it?

FAVORABLE CLIMATE NECESSARY

Climate is an average condition established over long periods of time. Like the climate which prevails in our natural environment, a corporate climate is composed of several parts: attitudes, actions, and approaches. Also, like our natural environment, climatic conditions frequently start at the top. Generally, a favorable climate for new business ventures results when a company's top management demonstrates its personal interest and enthusiasm in new business activities on a daily basis; when it points with pride to a success in a new venture and is eager to try again; when it accepts a failure with constructive concern but is eager to try again. Such management must be absolutely convinced that new ventures based on new products and new technology are essential to the future of the corporation. It can be quickly recognized that a favorable climate is not easily created nor is it easily maintained. It should also be recognized that even a favorable climate is marked by the day-to-day variations which we call weather.

One other aspect of "climate" should be mentioned here: the corporate attitude toward the company's inventors, entrepreneurs, and new venture managers. More will be said about the subject of people a little later. It is sufficient here to note that those ventures promising the greatest reward are normally the ones that require the greatest risk for the company and for individuals. Mistakes are more likely to be made in probing new products, new processes, new markets, and new business concepts. Management must, therefore, learn to differentiate between mistakes made in attempts to do something new, and mistakes made as a result of inherent inability. No one expects praise for failure; neither should a man be unfairly criticized for venturing a new approach. None of this is meant to imply that inventors, entrepreneurs, and new business ventures managers should be coddled or pampered. Experience indicates just the opposite attitude works best. The key is management's willingness to move forward with a minimum of hindsight criticism and a maximum emphasis on what's next.

DEVELOPMENT ACTIVITIES BEST IN SEPARATE UNIT

The second essential ingredient in my recipe for successful new business ventures is a development concept or plan. It starts with the basic question of where the new venture work is to be done in the company. As a simple illustration, let's look at a corporation having three operating divisions, each with its own sales, production, and technical departments. These established operations are concentrating daily on producing goods, distributing them, selling them, and improving them, all within the framework of sales forecasts and profit objectives. This leads to a multitude of short-term programs and pressures which greatly limit the division's freedom to explore wholly new developments, especially in business fields not related to the existing business. New business development is a long-term proposition; if it is too closely associated with operating functions, it tends to be neglected, restricted, or even cannibalized when operating problems occur.

For such reasons as these, new venture development activities have the greatest chance for success when organized as an independent corporate function. Top management then has the opportunity to determine directly the corporation's commitment to enter brand new business fields. It can establish recognized and permissible amounts of deficit financing or investment dedicated to future long-term gains. Being closer to the new enterprises, it can be more sensitive to their progress, programs, and people.

Having found a place for our new business development activities, we must now find some ideas which promise future new businesses. Briefly, here are the usual sources of such ideas: company laboratories, observant salesmen, outside inventors, patent literature, market studies, licensing organizations, and consultants. Those charged with the responsibility for reviewing these ideas must be imbued with the power of positive thinking. If they come to a negative conclusion, it must be because they could not find a suitable answer to the positive question: "How can this idea be made into a profitable business?"

Further evaluation of promising ideas and inventions needs people competent to determine product potentialities and market possibilities. This requires technical experience and marketing experience properly blended for the selection of the best new business opportunities. My company has found that such a blend is most effective when the marketers are physically located in the same laboratory facilities used by the technical people. In fact, one scientifically trained marketing manager reduced the significance of this approach to a formula. Simply stated, the formula says that the probability of commercial success of an unrelated new venture is inversely proportional to the square of the distance between the technical point of view and the marketing point of view. Or, in other words, the chance of achieving commercial success with a new business is very low and approaches zero if the marketing view of it is a great distance from the technical view.

Following this approach, we house our technical men and marketing men side by side. We send the scientists and engineers into the market occasionally, and we involve the marketers in testing and using the products. We do all we can to get each man to appreciate the other's point of view and thereby increase our chances of commercial success.

ENTREPRENEUR SPEARHEADS VENTURE

Assuming it has been demonstrated that there is a worthwhile basis for initiating a new business venture, what's next? Continuing with my own company's concept, an entrepreneur is named to spearhead the effort to prove the business concept. He hires the people he needs from the technical and marketing staffs. He finds the facilities he needs wherever suitable space is available. He is a "venture manager," the counterpart of the president and chief executive officer of a new small company. He proves that his products have customer appeal and utility, that they can be made by feasible processes, and that they can be sold at prices which will build future profits as volume expands. He begins to establish the roots for a long-term business by creating a proprietary position with patent protection, technical know-how, and pioneering marketing methods.

Those small, new product companies which thrive and grow (many never make it) eventually assume the status of an official corporate project, though still a part of the New Business Ventures Division. Project status is a prize achieved by the small company as recognition for its achievement in proving the concept and content of the new business. This is the point at which management satisfies itself that there is a desirable new business and that the venture manager is sufficiently committed and capable to carry the business to its full potential. With management's vote of confidence, the new project manager now assumes full responsibility and authority for all aspects of the venture, including technical, manufacturing, and marketing. In every instance, his goal is to develop and establish the new business with a maximum amount of sales and profit potential, consistent with the real values that are created for the customer. He is accountable for the success or failure of the project.

This concept of new venture development has as its advantages at least the following: (1) defined individual authority and responsibility; (2) measurable results and recognition; (3) emotional involvement and commitment of people who have this project as their only job; (4) freedom from the inhibitions and pressures of an established operating group; and (5) direct top management interest and support.

Throughout this talk there have been references to people: management people, venture people, entrepreneurs, and inventors. It is impossible to talk about successful new business enterprises without talking about people.

The importance of people to business success was given a significant twist in a speech last year by 3M Company's Vice President for Research and Development, Dr. C. W. Walton, who said, "A vital ingredient in business success is excitement, primarily *people* excitement . . ." If we added dedication to that statement, we might have a nearly complete description of the new venture manager or entrepreneur. Excitement will help him to sell his ideas and concepts and products, but dedication will keep him at the task during the inevitable setbacks and downturns of new business development.

These are the kinds of qualities we look for in the people whom we select to manage our new ventures and to carry them through the process which has been described earlier. Sometimes it's the inventor who exhibits these characteristics. Often it's someone who has had to evaluate an invention in the laboratory or marketplace and has seen the outline of a promising new business. Occasionally, and we wish it were more often, it's an entrepreneur from one of our operating divisions seeking the freedom to develop his own ideas.

Of course, talent and capability are required and it takes courage and energy and a host of other virtues to be a good new business venture manager. But if there is a lack of excitement and no depth of dedication, the project is in danger. In fact, these are important signals for which to watch in judging whether to launch or to continue a new venture.

More can be said about people and their role in new business ventures, but the objective of this discussion is limited to calling attention to the need for an entrepreneur whose excitement and dedication will favorably affect all those with whom he may come in contact.

To summarize, then, internally generated new business ventures have the best chance to succeed when the corporate climate is favorable; when a development concept is adopted that gives freedom of action, individual responsibility, a chance to become wholly involved, and adequate rewards; and when the project is placed in the hands of an entrepreneur who is excited by the potential business and dedicated to making it go, go, go. . . .

THREE

The Start-Up Problem

Given that a man has what he thinks is a unique product or service to offer the marketplace, and a strong desire to be his own boss, how does he proceed to establish himself as the head of a business enterprise? What are the major factors to consider if the business venture is not to end in failure and bankruptcy—as nine out of ten do? What sources of information and outside help are available? Is there a better chance of success from acquiring an on-going business or buying into a franchise chain, rather than starting a new business from the ground up? In the first article in this chapter, *Pitfalls to Avoid in Starting Your Own Business,* Maury Delman discusses these questions, as well as the major reasons for business failures, and lists sources of help in making the initial decisions. Delman's suggestions underscore the necessity of thoroughly understanding the operational and financial considerations involved in starting one's own business. In an appendix to this book, we also list sources of help for entrepreneurs.

Complementing Delman's article is the Baumback-Lawyer *Checklist for Organizing and Operating a Small Business.* It is intended to help the prospective entrepreneur in evaluating his readiness to launch the new venture, and in sucessfully managing it after it has been gotten off the ground. What are his personal qualifications? Does he have leadership abilities, strong perseverance, an endless supply of energy, and applicable experience? Has he made an objective investigation of the probable success of his proposed ver.ture? What is the marketing plan and how will it be affected by changing technological, political, cultural, and economic conditions? As the checklist indicates, the prospective entrepreneur is faced with a wide assortment of problems and tasks during the planning and start-up stages of the business enterprise. The questions that must be answered and the decisions that must be made seem endless, but the collective responses to these questions are determinants of the success or failure of the venture.

The prospective new entrepreneur must perceive the levels of risks and rewards to expect from founding a new business. Has he really considered all the risks? Will he be able to raise sufficient start-up and operating capital?

What are the most important start-up problems to resolve first? And from whom will he seek advice and consultation if he has difficulties? Are the expected rewards sufficient to offset the risks?

Among the most important start-up problems is where to locate the firm. In the third article, *Entrepreneurial Environment,* Arnold Cooper discusses why the prospective founder of a new technologically-based firm should be particularly concerned with the region or environment in which he establishes the business. Cooper theorizes on why there are specific regions in the nation where technologically-based firms seem to concentrate. He discusses regional factors that support a differentiation between the environment in general and the more specific entrepreneurial environment, in which past entrepreneurial activities will enable the prospective founder to have an awareness of venture capital sources and individuals and institutions that provide help and advice. Thus, the region in which the business is to be located should be examined carefully for the availability of the required resources.

Having examined some of the qualifications and considerations required in starting and locating the business, the entrepreneur must next prepare his plan for making the business a success. In the final reading, *Planning for the New Enterprise,* Albert Kelley discusses the need and development of this business plan for the successful start-up of a business venture. The business plan essentially becomes a documented means for communicating the entrepreneur's strategies for producing and marketing his product. It establishes a reference framework to use in measuring the company's progress. Venture capitalists, bankers, potential professional employees, and the company's accountant and lawyer are all interested in learning what the business is all about and what the game plan is for succeeding. It should answer the question of whether the founder really has the experience, leadership qualities, and resources required for profitably expoiting his product concept. And in the end, preparing the plan provides the entrepreneur with a greater degree of awareness about himself as an entrepreneur and his firm's chances for success.

The entrepreneur will usually experience severe difficulties during his first two years in business. Delivery dates must be met, products must be reliable, and bills and employees must be paid. But mainly, the entrepreneur must convince potential customers that his gadget is better and less costly, and that his business has a long life expectancy. An obvious requirement is that the entrepreneur must have confidence in his entrepreneurial abilities and be committed to the successful exploitation of his product concept.

To repeat, both his abilities and his strategies must be documented in a business plan that is used as a tool in establishing financial support for the new venture, and as a reference framework with which to compare the future status of the business.

PITFALLS TO AVOID

IN STARTING

YOUR OWN BUSINESS*

MAURY DELMAN

U.S. Department of Commerce studies show that about half of new small businesses never make the third year. Retailing suffers the most, with only 29% surviving three-and-a-half years. Wholesaling shows best with a 48% survival after the same period.

Nevertheless, Dun & Bradstreet figures suggest that more than 400,000 firms are started annually with about an equal number being discontinued.

Survival depends upon a variety of factors. Dun & Bradstreet people have been able to pinpoint nine major reasons for failures of new businesses.

Topping the list is simply lack of managerial experience. Even those who have managed other businesses successfully have come quickly to bankruptcy when operating businesses they knew little about. For example, take the case of a young Pennsylvanian who went into the building business after nine years as an insurance agent. With his cash tied up in real estate and "receivables," suppliers were willing to sell him on a cash basis only. He couldn't buy enough to keep going. After four years, he filed a voluntary petition in bankruptcy with liabilities twice the size of his assets.

A middle-aged Texan gave up a successful career as an insurance salesman to become an air-conditioning and heating contractor. He, too, ended up in a bankruptcy court when most of his capital got tied up in slow receivables. A West Virginia doctor teamed up with a restaurant owner to build a shopping center and became a bankrupt after construction costs got out of hand.

A "receivable" is simply money somebody owes you that you can't get your hands on yet. If a builder, for instance, has given so many people long-term credit that he hasn't enough ready cash or credit of his own to pay his workmen and buy supplies to put up a new building, he has to pass up the bids on the new jobs. People who are new to business easily get themselves trapped with a shortage of enough funds on which to keep operating. In their eagerness to get their very first customers they may extend attractive credit which turns out to be suicidal for them. Experience selling insurance is hardly good training for another business that requires buy-sell judgment and heavy day-to-day expenses before the profits roll in.

But even with specific experience in some line there is no assurance of success. The importance of experience is not the time spent but what is learned. Successful businessmen underscore the need for balanced experience. This includes knowledge of your product, financial handling, buying and selling.

*From *The American Legion Magazine* (February 1971). Copyright 1971, The American Legion Magazine, pp. 24-27, 41-44, and 46. Reprinted by permission.

Insufficient starting capital ranks just under lack of experience as a cause of all business failures. The notion that a few thousand dollars and very hard work will bring success has held very little validity since the 1930's. An experienced women's-wear retailer says, "Anyone going into business now without plenty of capital in back of him should have his head examined." Even if a new business venture should survive its first year with limited capital, this disadvantage takes many years to overcome.

Borrowing the needed capital often seems an easier solution than it is. Those who don't calculate exactly how much the interest on the borrowed money will eat into their expected profits often come to grief—discovering too late that they've only been working for the bank. A man who earns 9% "clear profit" on capital that he borrowed for 9% can have a great time running his own business until he starves to death.

Yet, the attractions of being "independent" have been known to induce new "businessmen" to close their eyes to the hard fact that they won't earn a cent for themselves until they have met all operating costs *and* the interest.

Today, anyone starting a new business must first figure his normal operating expenses plus his salary. For safety, the expense figure should be adjusted upward from 25% to 50%. There are always unforeseen costs. Then, he'll have to determine the volume of business he must do to cover these expenses. The cost of supplies, merchandise, etc., to produce this volume must be figured. Finally, what fixtures are needed and what receivables will have to be carried if credit is granted to customers? In essence, what capital is needed to produce income enough for a reasonable net profit after expenses. A surprising number of people go into business without doing this hard arithmetic.

The third business pitfall is the wrong location. Inexperienced people are prone to look for inexpensive locations. Good locations are bound to cost money but the volume realized from a good location can more than offset the higher rent.

Once a business is under way it can readily fall victim to the fourth pitfall—inventory mismanagement. The common warning, "don't get too much inventory," should be modified to, "don't buy too much of the wrong merchandise."

The management of inventory is an art, if what you are doing is selling something that you keep in stock. Its ABC's are simply put, even if its XYZ's are not. The dollars you have invested in inventory must earn you money at a desirable rate. Fast turnover will earn money on goods that are priced at a small profit margin. Goods that turn over slowly only pay well if the markup is large. The great inventory tragedy is found in goods that sit on your shelves without any buyers. They represent dollars invested by you that are not earning anything—in short, precious capital that's tied up. This is all just as obvious as it can be, but, oh, the businesses that go on the rocks because of ill-judged inventory.

In the big, successful retail stores there is not love, humanity, sentiment or personal whim in the matter of inventory. The hard questions are: "What sells, at how fast a turnover, for what markup?" and buyers of stock succeed or fail on their ability to solve that equation most profitably. By contrast, I know of a successful man who quit his profession to invest his all in a store selling a "cultural" product that he thought the people "ought to" have. It bankrupted him because people buy what they want, not what you think they "ought to."

Pitfall five is too much capital going into fixed assets. Any money invested in fixtures or real estate will most likely come from your working capital or will be borrowed. Money tied up in frozen assets that aren't necessary to your business is working capital that may not be available when you need it for either a crisis or an opportunity.

The sixth pitfall is poor credit granting practices. The temptation to let customers "put it on the books" can be very strong, particularly if your competition is coming from low-margin, big-volume cash competitors. If you offer easy credit in order to get the business, some customers may be so slow to pay that they'll give *you* "the business." When you force credit on people you are in danger of attracting the poorer payers. One of the shocks lying in wait for new businessmen is that well-heeled customers are very often the slowest to pay their debts.

In granting credit two fundamental questions must be answered: Do I have enough capital? Do I know how to collect?

A general rule is that you must have additional capital on hand equal to one-and-a-half month's credit sales in order to give customers 30 days to pay. Credit granting and collecting takes skill. Many people just don't have it. One retailer with 25 years experience commented, "When I first started I also tried to sell on credit but found that I wasn't a good collector, so after several months I made all sales for cash and have since conducted a cash and carry business."

Pitfall number seven is taking too much out for yourself. It's an easy habit to fall into. Many new business starters pledge to themselves, "We're not going to take anything out of the business." And of course they can't stick to it. What's the purpose of going into business if you aren't going to take something out? The approach to what you take out for yourself should be flexible and realistic. When profits decline owners must curtail their drawing.

The eighth pitfall can come from too much success. Business is so good you decide to expand—but unplanned expansion can be ruinous. Generally businesses grow in two ways: Slow and steady from within—marked by increased sales and profits, or by rapid expansion through addition or acquisition.

Rapid expansion must be carefully planned since it requires skills to manage new people you must hire as well as additional capital. One storekeeper found out the hard way that two stores weren't twice as profitable for him as one. With one store going well he opened another across town. But the managerial help in his second store failed to grasp his successful methods. The owner had to supervise both stores with his wife helping out. When she got sick the load was too much. Eventually, physical and capital strain required that he sell the second store. Today, he operates one store profitably and without undue headaches.

Pitfall number nine—the wrong attitude—ruins many. Some businesses fail to prosper or come to grief because of wrong attitudes of their owners. Being in business is plain hard work, demanding full diligence. Some owners figure that since the business is their they'll work hours only to suit themselves. Others get involved in outside interests to an excessive extent. They may even tell themselves that social and civic interests help promote the business when all they do is take the owner away from affairs that need tending. Greed kills off still others. When products are misrepresented or shoddy, it is always found out. A well-known chain of fine restaurants had to be sold off because their owner evaded income taxes. The penalties levied by the Internal Revenue Service in addition to a jail sentence forced the sale of that restaurant chain.

But, even with all the hazards, the dream of having your own business can be realized. There are ways to overcome the obstacles and succeed. A prime source of help lies with the Federal Government through its agency, the Small Business Administration, set up in 1953 to aid small business. The S.B.A. with field offices in principal cities, as well as in Guam and Puerto Rico, is available to assist new business hopefuls as well as established small businesses.

Most people associate the S.B.A. solely with loan assistance but this is only a part of the important services the agency performs. Actually, the S.B.A. is structured to provide a wide range of advisory services to help businesses operate better. Anyone who's in trouble with his small business should at least ask the S.B.A. for advice. Maybe it can't save him—but maybe it can. And it often sets up clinics, workshops and management courses for small business owners. In addition, it guides established business owners in procuring government contracts set aside for small business.

The S.B.A.'s doors are open to anyone who seeks counseling and guidance on going into business for himself. At the S.B.A. office he is assigned to a management counselor who interviews him to determine his business objective and his qualifications for reaching it. The interview is controlled by a four-page questionnaire which probes for such information as education, work experience, knowledge of a particular business' needs, capital requirements and other pertinent data needed to evaluate fitness to start a venture.

Some people are only technically equipped, which isn't enough. For example, the young vet who served a year's apprenticeship repairing radio and TV sets before entering the military. He learned more from electronics training in the Army. Upon discharge he wanted to set up shop for himself. But while he could make a radio or TV work wonderfully, he actually knew nothing about running a business.

"Even worse, some people come through the door armed with no more than a burning desire to be free and work for themselves. They haven't got the foggiest notion of what business they'd like to get into or what knowledge is needed," confides Charles Spano, management counselor for New York's Small Business Administration regional office. "In such cases I encourage them to participate in one of our workshops for prospective business owners."

S.B.A. workshops are usually conducted on a one-day-a-month basis, teaching basic principles of financing, taxes, federal regulations and sales promotion. Workshop leaders stress additional sources of advice and assistance and encourage their students to use them. The workshops are valuable in a number of ways, Mr. Spano points out. "They teach business principles and they show up the weaknesses of many aspiring business entrants, dissuading them from going into business when they aren't truly ready."

In cases where a would-be entrant shows strong potential, the S.B.A. is prepared to act further. A counselor may help him get a loan to start the business. Once started, counselor guidance may continue until the fledgling business is on its feet.

While the S.B.A. now rarely makes direct loans, it does get involved with "participation" loans. One type, the guaranty plan, requires that a bank make the loan which the S.B.A. guarantees up to 90%.

Before the S.B.A. will involve itself in a loan it insists that an applicant first seek a direct bank loan. Only after a turn-down will the S.B.A. consider participation. Borrowers are expected to furnish such information as their experience, a financial statement reflecting all personal assets and liabilities, a detailed projection for the first year of operation and a list of all collateral at present market value.

A more modest loan is available through the S.B.A. under the Economic Opportunity program. These loans are offered to the economically "disadvantaged," particularly the minorities, who have the capability to operate a business but can't get loans through usual channels. The maximum amount of an Economic Opportunity loan is $50,000 for up to 15 years.

The S.B.A. can also put you in touch with ACE, a group of active business executives who have volunteered to help guide those in small businesses. S.B.A. has another such corps of volunteer counselors made up of retired executives. They are called SCORE. (S.B.A. also seeks more executives and retired executives who would care to volunteer for ACE or SCORE.)

Beyond personal counseling and loans, the S.B.A. produces and publishes a variety of publications of interest to the small businessman. These include lists of available books, pamphlets, technical aids, management research summaries and annuals. Many are free and are obtainable by writing your S.B.A. field office. Others sold at a nominal charge can be purchased from the Superintendent of Documents, Government Printing Office, Washington, D.C. 10402. Recommended reading includes:

Checklist for Going Into Business (Management Research Summaries No. 120). Free;

Factors in Small Business Success or Failure (Management Research Summaries No. 145). Free;

The First Two Years: Problem of Small Firm Growth and Survival (Small Business Research Summaries No. 2).

Problems of Small Business (Management Research Summaries No. 42). Free;

Starting and Managing a Small Business of Your Own (Starting and Managing Series No. 1).

An excellent source of information for anyone interested in starting a business is a trade association. Trade associations exist in every major industry and many minor ones. They are sources of surveys and studies that do economic analyses of such factors as salaries, wages, sales and labor conditions. A letter addressed to a trade association asking about the feasibility of entering an industry will often be answered with a packet of materials outlining such matters as growth trends, capital equipment, new technology, operating ratios and other pertinent data. A full listing of trade associations can be found in the *National Trade and Professional Associations of the United States.* Columbia Book Publishers, Room 300, 917 15th St., N.W., Washington, D.C. 20005.

Chambers of Commerce, both state and local, can help to get a new business started. Generally, they can assist in such matters as site location, labor information, referral work, setting up introductions and making appointments with vital sources, and they may even make loans. Thomas N. Stainback, executive vice president of New York's Chamber of Commerce and former president of the Jersey City Chamber of Commerce points out that ". . . while the services of Chambers vary widely, to overlook their facilities is a mistake since they can save people time, money and headaches along the way."

Public libraries can be gold mines of information to potential owner-managers of small businesses. Libraries offer indices to business periodicals, newspapers and selected subjects. They keep such government documents as censuses of population, business and agriculture, the *Census of Manufacturers,* the *Census of Business* and *County Business Patterns.*

Libraries hold copies of existing local, state and federal laws, as well as pending legislation. The statistics needed to make important decisions, and the precise information found in directories are all free for the asking through public library sources. Although a local library may be small and unable to furnish a particular publication, it can still be of help by borrowing the volume you want through interlibrary loan channels.

The following references are helpful in using the public library to get information on running a business:

Sources of Business Information, by Edwin T. Coman, Jr., Revised 1964. University of California Press, 2223 Fulton Street, Berkeley, Calif. 94120.

Selected Business Reference Sources. Latest edition. Harvard University, Baker Library, Boston, Mass. 02138.

How to Use the Business Library, by H.W. Johnson. 3rd edition, 1964. South-Western Publishing Company, 5101 Madison Rd., Cincinnati, Ohio 45227.

Basic Library Reference Sources for Business Use. Small Business Bibliography No. 18. Small Business Administration. September 1966. S.B.A., Washington, D.C. 20416. (Or nearest S.B.A. office.)

Starting your own business is one thing. How about obtaining a ready-made business? A franchise is a possibility. There are perhaps 1,200 franchise companies and between 400,000 and 600,000 franchise outlets that annually generate from $80 to $110 billion in sales in the United States. Franchises account for nearly 10% of the gross national product and 26% of all retail sales. Ninety percent of all existing franchises sprang up in the last ten years and franchising as a way of American business life is continuing to grow.

A prospective franchisee's choices are virtually unlimited. The variety of products and services available would cover the yellow page directory. Most prominent are the fast foods, employment agencies, financial services, tool and equipment rental, convenience grocery stores, cleaning stores and women's ready-to-wear shops.

Essentially, a franchise is a license to do business under a company's trademark. Usually the trademark covers a known or proven product or service. Along with the license goes a formal contract of continual relationship with the franchisor. The prime attraction of a franchise is the opportunity to start an independent business with limited capital and experience. Other benefits are initial training and follow-up guidance, promotional assistance and possible savings through bulk buying. Generally, franchises require an investment fee plus a continuing royalty, usually a percentage of the gross. Sometimes an advertising fee is tacked on which goes into the company's promotion fund. This is customarily a percentage of the gross, too. If products are involved, the franchising company reserves the right to sell them to the franchisee at company-fixed prices. Franchisors perform a variety of services for their franchisees, including financing, site selection, fixturing, purchasing of initial durable equipment and record keeping.

Franchise investments can be as low as $1,000 or as high as $100,000. Annual incomes from single, successful franchise operations range from

$10,000 to $250,000. Because the franchise idea appeals to the "be-your-own-boss" instinct it attracts people from every walk of life and occupation.

Leonard Morris, 46, a New Yorker, who had a radio tube distribution business, now operates a plush Management Recruiters employment agency on Wall Street. John Hannon, 42, a Mississippian, left a $135-a-week packing job in 1963 to buy a fried-chicken franchise from the original Colonel Sanders. Today, he has nine stores employing 75 people with a gross yearly volume of over $2,500,000. Jean Taylor, a secretary for the Santa Fe Railroad at Fort Worth, Tex., now runs a House of Nine dress shop on Long Island. It grosses $400,000 a year.

With the astounding number of franchisors now in the market, the question arises—are they safe? Figures compiled by the International Franchise Association based on an analysis of its members over a period of years would indicate they are. The I.F.A. claims that the average franchise operation has approximately an eight to one better chance of being in business after ten years than the average small business started by an individual operating on his own.

Despite the statistics presented by the I.F.A., franchises have proved a disaster for hundreds of innocent investors. At least five states have introduced franchise disclosure laws. The Federal Trade Commission is conducting investigations of its own. Why all the furor about a business structure which seems to be the modern day fulfillment of the American dream? Bernard Goodwin, a prominent New York attorney and franchise expert, testifying before the Texas legislature in June 1970, said: "Well, the con-boys moved in on this thing (franchising), the bunco boys, the soft-shoe operators. They said, 'Wow, we're not in the stock market anymore because we've got the SEC there watching us or the Blue Sky laws all over the country watching us, and we can't operate like we used to operate. Franchising—this is a heaven. Where did this come from? We can go around selling franchises. And who cares what happens afterwards. We collect our franchise fee, and we disappear.' "

Harold Brown, a Boston attorney and author of the book *Franchising Trap for the Trusting,* is an outspoken critic of much in franchising. He castigates such practices as kickbacks; overcharging franchisees for products, services and equipment; proliferation of outlets so as to force owners to sell back to the parent company at a fraction of their value; and arbitrary termination of contracts on flimsy grounds.

Louis J. Lefkowitz, Attorney General of the State of New York, after investigating thousands of franchises, strongly supports a full disclosure law. In particular, he finds much in franchise promotional literature which is inadequate, misleading, wholly lacking or blatantly false as to facts necessary to make a sound business decision. Take, for example, a pet-grooming service franchise seeking a $10,000 investment from a franchisee for fully equipped grooming trucks, including kits for gourmet dog food, as well as grooming supplies. It represented that potential profit of "up to $40,000 per year" was within easy reach—even without experience. The fact was that the company had only one small grooming truck, no record of performance(!) and no financial backing.

A home protective service, luring investors with the promise of earning $30,000 annually, stated to Lefkowitz's staff that it could not answer the attorney general's questionnaire. With only a few months in business they hadn't "enough of a background." Other franchise companies involved in bankruptcy reorganization continued to solicit franchisees without even a hint of their financial condition.

A random sampling of 84 different franchisors and 10,620 franchisees showed that 65.5% of the persons investing in franchises earned less than $15,000 a year in their prior occupation. It was also found that 36% of the franchisors managed to stay in business two years or less. It was further found that at least half of the franchisors went into it to make their money from the franchisees, rather than from the success of their product.

If you're considering a franchise, heed the warning of the National Better Business Bureau, Inc., which advises "investigate before buying."

The Bank of America issues a check-list of 50 questions it thinks you ought to have answers to before contracting with a franchisor. That's more than we can print here, but if you're that interested send a stamped, self-addressed return envelope to Bank of America, P.O. Box 37000, San Francisco, Cal. 94137.

Harry Kursh's big book, *The Franchise Boom—How You Can Profit in It,* is a veritable encyclopaedia of franchise information. Publishers are Prentice-Hall, Inc., Englewood Cliffs, N.J. 07632.

Franchises are listed in the "Business Opportunities" section of some newspapers and in the Wall Street Journal. Other sources of franchise information include:

> *Directory of Franchising Organizations.* Pilot Books, 347 Fifth Ave., New York, N.Y. 10016. Published annually.
> *The Monthly Report.* National Franchise Reports, 333 North Michigan Ave., Chicago, Ill. 60601.
> *Modern Franchising Magazine.* Modern Franchising Magazine, Inc., 1033 First Ave., Des Plaines, Ill. 60016.
> *Franchising Today,* by Charles L. Vaughn. 1969 edition. Farnsworth Publications Co., Inc., 381 Sunrise Highway, Lynbrook, N.Y. 11563.
> *Franchise Company Data.* Task Force for Equal Opportunity in Business. July 1969. U.S. Department of Commerce, Washington, D.C. 20230.

The Franchise Annual, National Franchise Reports, 333 North Michigan Ave., Chicago, Ill. 60601, is published [annually] by the International Franchise Association, Inc., an organization which can supply important information on member franchisors.

There is also the alternative of buying an existing non-franchise business. This approach is both advantageous and disadvantageous. On the plus side, it avoids the time and headaches involved in locating a site, negotiating a lease, fixturing, buying merchandise, installing record systems and hiring personnel. Important, too, going businesses have momentum—something a starting business lacks and must overcome. Moreover, going businesses are, for the most part, predictable as to their volume and earnings.

Hunting for a good, going business for sale can be costly and time-consuming. Acquiring a business warrants serious investigation before you lay your cash down and take title. For this, you will have to call upon the expertise of lawyers, accountants and bankers. Because a business is going it can be costly to buy—but this may still be better than starting one yourself and failing.

As a rule, service businesses can be bought for less than manufacturing or wholesaling operations. They also need less working capital to operate since large sums aren't tied up in inventory and receivables. On the other hand, service businesses have the poorest survival rate.

One road to finding a business for sale is through a business broker. They are easily found in the yellow pages of the phone book under the classification "Business Brokers." Some specialize in particular lines of business, while others handle anything that comes through the door. Telephone listings, however, are no guide to a broker's reliability. To get a reference on a good broker ask your bank.

Good brokers won't accept listings of outright lemons. They demand financial statements proving the income and net worth of a concern as well as other important details of its history. Beyond merely getting the buyer and seller together, a good broker can be instrumental in setting up the terms of the sale and sometimes steering an over-anxious buyer away from involvement in a business he couldn't handle.

Fritz Loeb, 30 years a broker with the 50-year-old David Jaret Corp. in New York, states: "A good broker makes every effort to weed out bad listings. If this is not done it is easy to ruin a reputation earned over a lifetime of service." He adds: "Many buyers are naive in that they seek to find out why the seller is selling. What really counts is the merits of the business as it stands and its future."

Another source of quick leads is the classified listings found in the "Business Opportunities" sections of newspapers. Most of them are typical small businesses such as small motels, stationery stores, cleaners, bars, restaurants and retail specialty shops. In most cases, newspaper ads give minimum information. They seldom disclose more than gross sales or weekly income, length of lease and seller's price. From that point on it will be up to you to do much investigating.

The idea that you'll come upon a real "sleeper" involves about the same odds as your breaking the bank at Monte Carlo. Generally, a business up for sale is first offered to relatives or a trusted executive, then to suppliers or even competitors. Advertising a business for sale has perils which sellers prefer to avoid. It can cause a pulling in of supplier's credit, send customers to buy elsewhere and induce key employees to begin to look for other jobs. By the time a business appears in the classified columns there can be something seriously wrong. This does not mean it should be ruled out completely. If you can recognize and cure the ills you may have a terrific bargain bought at a rock-bottom price.

Inserting your own ad to seek a business should be done with care. Your wording should be precise as to the kind of business you seek, its location and the price you're willing to pay. An imprecise ad, for example, offering to invest cash and managerial participation for a partnership will yield hundreds of replies from sour businesses, shaky start-ups and wacky inventors. Even the better replies will entail days of researching before any decision can be made. In a nutshell, it's a long and aggravating way to search.

Better sources for leads are lawyers, bankers and accountants. In the course of handling clients these professionals come into contact with businesses of all sizes and descriptions. Equally as important, they are often privy to intimate knowledge of the businesses they recommend.

Let's assume that after sifting various proposals you narrow your choice to one. This is the time to make a close scrutiny before signing. It is advisable to ask yourself such questions as: What is the growth potential? Am I buying mainly physical assets, goodwill or momentum? Could the business be duplicated more cheaply by starting my own concern? Is this a profitable investment at the price? Do I know the market? Who are the customers? Why do they buy this product or service? Is the product or service growing in popularity? Is strong foreign competition or obsolescence likely? What is the competition from larger and better capitalized firms? What is the business' reputation in trade channels? Is the business linked to the skill or reputation of the present owner? These and many more questions should be considered. In buying any business "let the buyer beware" is still the rule.

Once you've decided to buy a business, it pays to give heed to a tax plan that permits maximum cash available in the first year's operation. (Usually this is done by charging off assets as rapidly as possible, converting everything allowable into expense.) Other tax strategies are possible which will allow you a lower purchasing price yet a higher net return to the seller. A certified public accountant should be consulted to guide you with these strategies.

Upon closing title there are other details which require your attention. For example, how will accounts that are receivable when you take over be handled? Will they be assigned to the buyer or seller or to factors? Are you taking on the debts of the seller? What obligation do you assume from the seller's union contract? Here, a good attorney is well worth his fee.

If all the pitfalls and technicalities involved in modern-day business seem a bit discouraging, many people still overcome them. Beyond personal satisfaction found in operating a successful business, being in business for yourself has many tax advantages. It's about the only way an individual can accrue capital. When you consider that quality common stock may not yield 4%, a good small business returning 20%, 30% and even 40% is well worth the effort and headaches—if you know how to do it.

CHECKLIST

FOR ORGANIZING AND OPERATING

A SMALL BUSINESS*

CLIFFORD M. BAUMBACK / KENNETH LAWYER

The following checklist should be completed satisfactorily before any person is ready to enter business for himself. It follows the general plan and recommended procedures of the text, *How to Organize and Operate a Small Business,* 5th Edition. An important consideration for any prospective business owner is to plan carefully and to work out every major requirement for success

*Reprinted by permission of the publisher and authors of *How to Organize and Operate a Small Business,* Fifth Edition, Baumback, C., Lawyer, K., and Kelley, P. (Englewood Cliffs, N.J.: Prentice-Hall, Inc., 1973), pp. 583-589.

before actually starting the business. It is not enough merely to read the text and to have good intentions of applying its recommendations as each need arises. Not only is there danger that some important matters will be overlooked unless this checklist is followed seriously, but once the business is in operation the pressure of daily work greatly reduces the likelihood that the best practices will be adopted and the best decisions made on all important questions.

The plan of the checklist is simple. Each topic is presented as a question intended to stimulate analysis concerning some important point. The question should be considered carefully and answered honestly and realistically. An affirmative answer to a question means that the topic has been considered and provided for to the best of the enterpriser's ability. When further attention to a topic is needed, an attempt to answer the question should convince the prospective businessman of this need and also suggest what further action is called for. Requirements thus discovered should be recorded and checked off as completed.

I. The Decision for Self-Employment

1. Have you rated yourself and had some acquaintances rate you on the personal qualities necessary for success as your own boss, such as leadership, organizing ability, perseverance, and physical energy?

2. Have you taken steps to improve yourself in those qualities in which you are weak but which are needed for success?

3. Have you saved money, made business contacts, taken special courses, or read particular books for the purpose of preparing yourself for business ownership?

4. Have you had training or experience in your proposed line of business or in one similar to it?

5. Are you (*a*) good at managing your own time and energy? (*b*) not easily discouraged? (*c*) willing to work harder in your own business than as an employee?

6. Have you estimated the net income from sales or services you can reasonably expect in the crucial "first two years"?

7. Have you compared this income with what you could make working for someone else?

8. Are you willing to risk the uncertainty or irregularity of your self-employment income during the early years of the enterprise?

9. Would you worry less as an employee than you would as the owner of your own business?

10. Have you carefully considered and enumerated the reasons why you want to enter business on your own?

II. Buying a Going Concern

1. Have you checked the proposition against the specific warnings issued by Better Business Bureaus and other authorities?

2. Are the physical facilities in satisfactory condition?

3. Are the accounts receivable, inventory, and goodwill fairly valued?

4. Have you determined why the present owner wants to sell?

5. Have you compared what it would take to start a similar business of your own with the price asked for the business you are considering buying?

6. Has your lawyer checked to see that the title is good, that there are no liens against the business and no past due taxes or public utility bills?

7. Have you compared several independent appraisals of the business, arrived at by different methods?

8. If it is a bulk sale, has the bulk sale provisions of the Uniform Commercial Code been complied with?
9. Have you investigated possible developments, such as new shopping centers, new traffic patterns, or changes in zoning or parking regulations, that might affect the business adversely?

III. Justifying a New Business

1. Have you analyzed the recent trend of business conditions?
2. Have you analyzed conditions in the line of business you are planning to enter?
3. If your business will be based on an entirely new idea, have you attempted to secure actual contracts or commitments from potential customers instead of merely getting their polite approval of your idea?
4. Have you discussed your proposition with competent advisors who are in different occupations or who have different viewpoints?

IV. Acquiring a Franchise

1. Have you viewed the franchise offer in terms of its economic justification or business potential?
2. Have you contacted personally several of the company's franchise holders to see how they like the deal?
3. Have you asked for a business responsibility report on the franchise promoter from your local Better Business Bureau or Chamber of Commerce?
4. Have you engaged the services of a lawyer to go over all provisions of the franchise contract?

V. Selecting the Profitable Location

1. Did you compare several different locations before making your final choice?
2. Did you use one or more detailed checklists to guide your selection?
3. Have you arranged for legal counsel before signing the lease and any similar contracts?
4. Are you, and the members of your family affected, satisfied that the community in which you plan to locate will be a desirable place in which to live and rear your children?
5. If your proposed location is not wholly suitable, are there sound reasons (not merely your impatience to get started) why you should not wait and try to secure a more nearly ideal location?

VI. Building and Layout

1. Have you studied your proposed building with function, construction, and modernization in mind?
2. Have you made a personal inspection of the physical plant of other successful businesses similar to the one you plan to start, including both independents and the branches of large organizations?
3. Have you made a scaled layout drawing of your store or shop?
4. If the proposed building does not meet all of your important needs, are there any *good* reasons for deciding to use it?

VII. Financing and Organizing the Business

1. Have you written down a complete, itemized list of all capital needs for starting your kind of business, including a fair allowance for operating expenses and your own living expenses until the business is able to support itself *and* provide a substantial reserve for the "one serious error" most businessmen make during their first year of operation?
2. Have you discussed this financial prospectus with a banker and a successful businessman in your proposed field?
3. Have you used as a guide the standard operating ratios for your business in calculating your capital requirements?
4. Have you considered all the factors for and against each legal form of organization?
5. If you plan to secure much of your initial capital from friends or relatives, are you *certain* that your business will remain free of "friendly" domination?

VIII. Establishing the Business Policies

1. Have you made an objective investigation of the probable success of your proposed policies?
2. Have you written down the main provisions of your general and major policies?
3. Have you discussed your proposed policies with competent advisors to counteract the beginner's tendency to offer what *he* likes and wants instead of what his potential *customers* like and want?
4. Have you written down an adequate statement of the reputation you want your business to acquire with customers, suppliers, and competitors?
5. Have you made adequate provisions to insure that your policies will be understood and enforced and that you will receive ample warning of the need for policy adjustments?

IX. Management and Leadership

1. Have you considered the way you will organize duties and responsibilities?
2. Have you made up a tentative plan or schedule to guide the distribution of your own time and effort?
3. Have you thought about how you would go about preparing standards, budgets, schedules, and other management aids?
4. Have you provided some check on your own actions to insure that you do adequate management planning before making commitments or important decisions covering future activities of the business?
5. Have you arranged to use periodically some checklist covering detailed activities regarding customer relations, maintenance, safety, or whatever type of activity will require close attention to details in your particular business?

X. Insurance and Risk Management

1. Have you evaluated all the hazards to which your business will be exposed?
2. Have you determined the hazards for which you should provide insurance coverage?
3. Have you determined how much of each kind of insurance you should purchase, and the costs of this insurance?
4. Have you made allowances in your budget of estimated expenses for losses resulting from predictable, uninsured risks (such as shoplifting and bad debts)?
5. Have you considered the nature of the protective devices and precautionary control measures you will need to reduce the business risks you will face?

XI. Personnel and Employee Relations

1. Will you be able to hire employees, locally, who possess the requisite skills?
2. Have you prepared your wage structure, and are your wage rates in line with prevailing wage rates?
3. If you plan to employ friends and relatives, are you sure you have determined their qualifications objectively?
4. Have you planned working conditions to be as desirable and practical as possible?
5. Are you certain the employee incentives you plan to use represent the workers' viewpoint rather than what *you* think they want?
6. Have you planned your employment, induction, and training procedures?

XII. Procurement and Supplier Relations

1. Have you evaluated individual suppliers in terms of the quality and variety of goods best suited to your needs, before selecting the companies you plan to deal with?
2. Have you carefully analyzed the points for and against concentrating your purchases with one or a few vendors, taking into account your personal skill and ability as well as conditions in your line of business?
3. Have you investigated your field of business with reference to the existence of cooperative buying groups, and the advantages of affiliating with one of these groups?

XIII. Pricing for Profit

1. Have you thought through the advantages and disadvantages of acquiring the price reputation you plan for your business?
2. Have you considered the probable reaction of competitors to your pricing practices?
3. Have you compared the relative importance in your business of each major marketing instrument, including price?
4. Have you investigated possible legal limitations on your pricing plans?
5. Have you considered possible applications of price-lining to your business?
6. Have you decided on the formula or method you will use in pricing each class of goods and services?
7. Have you decided how and to what extent you will meet probable price competition?

XIV. Advertising and Sales Promotion

1. Have you analyzed your probable competition in connection with the direct and indirect sales promotional methods you plan to use?
2. Have you planned definite ways to build and maintain superior customer relations?
3. Have you defined your potential customers so precisely that you could describe them in writing?
4. Have you decided how you can measure and record the degree of success achieved with each sales promotion so that you can repeat the "hits" and avoid the "duds"?
5. Have you considered different features of your business that would be appropriate for special promotions timed to your customers' needs and interests?
6. Have you made a list of all the media suitable for advertising *your* business with some evaluation of each?
7. Have you selected the most promising reasons why people should patronize your business, and have you incorporated them in plans for your opening advertising?
8. Have you made use of all appropriate sources in the preparation of a good initial mailing list?

9. Have you given careful thought to the advertising value of the proposed names for your firm, products, and services?
10. Have you made plans for some unusual gesture of welcome and appreciation for all customers during the opening days of your business?
11. Have you planned how you can measure the effectiveness of your advertising?

XV. Credit and Collections

1. Have you carefully investigated the need for credit extension by your business?
2. Have you planned specifically the various ways you will secure and use information obtainable from your charge account customers?
3. Have you made a personal investigation of the services and costs of affiliating with the local credit bureau?
4. Have you planned the basic procedures you will *always* follow before extending credit to any applicant?
5. Have you formulated plans to *control* all credit accounts?

XVI. Inventory Control

1. Have you determined carefully what constitutes a *balanced* inventory for your business?
2. Have you recorded on paper the exact information you will need for effective inventory control?
3. Have you planned the best methods for securing this information?
4. Have you selected the most appropriate inventory control *system* to use?
5. Have you planned the best procedures to use for stock or stores keeping?
6. Have you listed the purposes and uses of the information you plan to secure from your inventory control system?

XVII. Production Control

1. Have you prepared a production control routine or "system" suitable to your manufacturing processes?
2. Have you anticipated future production requirements, and have you made plans for increasing the capacity of the plant as needed?

XVIII. Profit Planning and Expense Control

1. Do you know what your "break-even" volume is?
2. Have you made an estimate of what your volume is likely to be during the early years of your business?
3. Have you investigated the standard systems of expense classifications used in your type of business and selected the most appropriate one for your use?
4. Have you determined what are usually the largest items of expense for your type of business and made definite plans for controlling these expenses from the very beginning of the business?
5. Have you determined which, if any, expense items, though normally small for your type of business, very easily become excessively large unless carefully controlled *at all times?*
6. Have you prepared on paper a *flexible* expense budget for two or three different probable amounts of volume of business, including provisions for frequent operating expense reports to be compared with planned figures in your budget?

7. Have you determined the standard operating ratios for your field that you plan to use as guides?
8. Have you compared the expense of "farming out," or having certain activities of the business done by outside agencies, with what it would cost you to do the work yourself?

XIX. Regulations and Taxes

1. Have you ascertained from reliable sources all regulations that must be complied with in your business?
2. Have you provided for an adequate system of record keeping that will furnish essential information for all taxation purposes?
3. Have you planned your record system so that appropriate use will be made of standard operating ratios?
4. Have you provided for securing all information from employees required by law?
5. Have you obtained a Social Security number?
6. Have you complied with regulations governing the use of a firm or trade name, brand names, or trademarks?

XX. Records

1. Have you decided what records will be adequate for each division and need of your business?
2. Have you secured the necessary forms to enable you to start keeping adequate records from the first day of operation of the business?
3. Have you planned your record system so that appropriate use will be made of standard operating ratios?
4. Have you investigated the possibilities of using simplified record-keeping systems for some of your needs?
5. Have you considered applications of the "one-book" system to your business?
6. Have you decided by whom each record needed will be kept?
7. Have you investigated the record-keeping system recommended by the trade association in your field?

ENTREPRENEURIAL ENVIRONMENT*

ARNOLD C. COOPER

Most scientists and engineers probably would answer, yes, if asked whether or not they would like to start their own company. On the other hand, more than 99.9% of them never will.

Why?

Primarily because they don't live and work in the right environment. An

*From *Industrial Research* (September, 1970), pp. 74-76. Reprinted by permission.

environment, which, among other things, is populated with a variety of old and new, big and small, technologically-based firms.

From the standpoint of regional economic development, technologically-based firms often are viewed as highly desirable. They make pleasant neighbors, produce relatively little noise and pollution, and they often employ substantial percentages of highly-paid scientists and engineers.

Sometimes, they enjoy outstanding growth, with great increases in numbers of employes and with key investors and employees becoming "paper millionaires."

In their efforts to develop this kind of local industry, communities often compete to attract branch laboratories or plants of national firms. In many instances, the efforts meet with frustration and the industrial parks, developed for this pupose, are still empty. Sometimes a single large defense contractor is attracted, but subsequent heavy community dependence upon the fluctuating fortunes of a donimant firm has proved to be a mixed blessing.

In contrast to all the effort to attract firms from elsewhere, relatively little attention has been devoted to such questions as the following:

1. What factors lead to the birth and growth of *new,* technologically-based firms?
2. What accounts for the market regional differences in the birth of such firms?
3. Can anything be done to encourage the birth and growth of these new firms?

One approach to understanding how new firms come into being is to study those factors that seem influential in an area of active entrepreneurship. I was able to study (in research supported, in part, by The Center For Venture Management, Milwaukee) the birth of new firms in the San Francisco Peninsula area around Palo Alto, Cal. The findings enabled me to pinpoint certain regional factors that appear to be important to entrepreneurship.

Specifically, the research included three phases. The first involved intensive interviews with 30 entrepreneurs. In the second phase, an attempt was made to gather summary data relating to the founding of all of the new, technologically-based firms (NTBFs) started on the San Francisco Peninsula since 1960—about 250 new firms.

A third phase involved interviews with executives from established organizations about spin-offs from their firms and about internal factors that may have encouraged or discouraged entrepreneurship.

The decision to found a new firm is an intensely personal decision made by one or several entrepreneurs. Past experiences and upbringing of an individual undoubtedly affect the extent to which he may be inclined toward entrepreneurship. Whether there may be regional differences in these traits is not clear.

However, there are a number of major influences upon the entrepreneur's decision that do vary substantially from region to region. These include:

1. An *entrepreneurial environment.*
2. The existence of small, new incubator firms.
3. A pool of experienced entrepreneurs.
4. The presence of specialized sources of venture capital.

THERE'S A RIGHT TIME, BUT ALSO A RIGHT PLACE

The environment in which a prospective entrepreneur finds himself can affect significantly his perceptions of the risks and rewards involved in entrepre-

FIGURE 3   Estimated New Enterprise Formation by Year
in Palo Alto Area

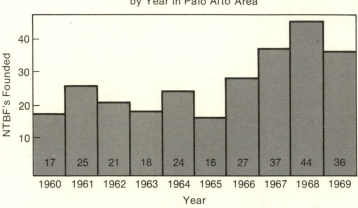

Estimated New Enterprise Formation
by Year in Palo Alto Area

1960	1961	1962	1963	1964	1965	1966	1967	1968	1969
17	25	21	18	24	16	27	37	44	36

neurship. The San Francisco Peninsula area has developed an *entrepreneurial environment,* and this has probably been an important factor in the high birth rate of new, technologically-based firms in that area.

An entrepreneurial environment might be defined as a situation in which prospective founders of new firms have a high awareness of past entrepreneurial action, of sources of venture capital, and of individuals and institutions that might provide help and advice. In such an environment, surrounded by examples of success and information about entrepreneurships, the prospective founder often may perceive the risks associated with entrepreneurship to be relatively low and the rewards to be relatively high.

Most of the founders of the 30 companies studied intensively knew of many examples of the action that they were considering. Many had observed prior spin-offs from the very firms they were leaving. At the time they made the decision, 93% of the founders knew of other founders of new firms, many being known personally. (Interestingly, they tended to know of successful new, technologically-based firms but rarely of unsuccessful ones.)

As they made the decision to start a firm, most of the entrepreneurs later described themselves as very confident—77% said they admitted almost no chance of failure. They were sure they could make the new business succeed; only 13% admitted to serious concern or saw themselves as undertaking a very risky venture.

Studying the Palo Alto area during the 1960s does not answer the question of how an entrepreneurial environment gets started. Presumably, the first instances of entrepreneurship in a region take place without this influence. Each successful new firm then provides an example for others who may follow. In time, an environment develops such that the prospective founder is exposed to many successful examples of entrepreneurship and finds it relatively easy to learn about what is involved in starting and financing a company.

A scientist or engineer who is considering the major step of founding a new firm must ask himself, "What is involved in getting a company started and do I know how to do these things?" He also must consider whether managing an established small firm will present problems similar to those he has dealt with in the past.

FAMILIARITY BREEDS SUCCESSIVE SPIN-OFFS

The fact that substantial entrepreneurship already has occurred in the Palo Alto area means that many new and small firms now are located there. In many ways these small firms are almost ideal incubators. The employes in these firms are, by definition, acquiring market and technical knowledge that can be exploited by a small firm. They are also learning what is involved in managing a NTBF.

Studying spin-off rates in the Palo Alto area indicates that firms with less than 500 employes had a spin-off rate *eight* times as high as firms with more than 500 employes. Thus, past entrepreneurship generates new, small firms that seem uniquely suited to function as incubators.

Past entrepreneurship also generates experienced entrepreneurs. Some of these men stay with their firms as they grow. However, many of the firms are acquired and many of the founding teams break up. After the merger or after the fight with the co-founder, what does the former entrepreneur do? Often, he turns to entrepreneurship again!

Eight of the 30 companies studied intensively in the Palo Alto area were founded by men who previously had been in the founding groups of other companies. One man was starting his fourth new business. Without exception, these men stated that it was easier to start a company the second time, both in regard to making the decision psychologically and in knowing what was involved in launching a firm.

In the Palo Alto area in the year 1968 alone, there were 44 new, technologically-based firms founded, involving some 118 individual entrepreneurs. There probably are now more than 1,000 experienced technical entrepreneurs in the Palo Alto area. The presence of these men makes future entrepreneurship more likely.

The birth of new firms depends upon the availability of venture capital. In the Palo Alto area, a number of sources of venture capital specialize in investing in and assisting NTBFs. The presence of some of these sources clearly is related to the high level of entrepreneurship, which has existed there in the past.

During the 1960s, a major source of venture capital was the successful entrepreneur of the 1950s. A typical situation involves the entrepreneur who has founded a successful firm and then later sold out. He usually is wealthy and still relatively young. Often, there are many investors who previously have made money through backing his judgment. He may feel the one thing, which he knows best, is how to help a NTBF get started. What does the successful entrepreneur then do?

Sometimes he starts another firm. In the Palo Alto area, he sometimes becomes a venture capitalist, investing in and advising the next generation of entrepreneurs. His influence often extends beyond his own fortune, for there are investors willing to back his judgment again.

There also are a substantial number of experienced entrepreneurs, still managing their firms, who play a key role in advising investors and prospective entrepreneurs. One company president estimated that, on the average, he judged one new company proposal per week. If the venture looked promising, he helped the prospective founder get together with what he termed his "stable of investors." This is typical of the well-developed communication net-works that permit prospective founders to make contact with sources of capital.

THE STOCK OPTION—A TWO-EDGED SWORD

The success of many of the firms in the Palo Alto area has created substantial stock values, not only for the founders but also for key employes. An important source of initial capital in 43% of the firms sutdied intensively was stock held by the founders in the firms for which they had previously worked.

Some of these men had been founders previously. Others had been able to exercise stock options. Because stock ownership is often seen as a way of tying an executive to a firm, it is interesting to note that this ownership often has made it financially possible for key men to leave and start their own firms!

Around Palo Alto, there also are a number of venture capital firms, which specialize in investing in and advising NTBFs. A continuing flow of entrepreneurs seeking capital provides the opportunity for such firms to develop there. Although there is some venture capital imported from other parts of the country, most new firms are financed locally.

Of the 30 firms studied, 18 raised outside capital, and 15 of these raised all or a substantial part of their capital in the San Francisco Bay region. Many of the founders believed it would have been much more difficult to sell stock in other parts of the country. Some had, in fact, tried to do just that, with little success.

Primary Source of Initial Capital

Founders		40%
Outside Investors		60%
Located in San Francisco area	50%	
Located outside San Francisco area	10%	
		100%

Several reasons for this belief were advanced:

1. They lacked ways of learning about and making contact with the "right" potential investors in other areas.
2. Investors in the San Francisco Bay area were more likely to understand and be sympathetic to technologically-oriented businesses.
3. Potential local investors easily could check into the background of the aspiring entrepreneur. Often, they knew him already.

4. Investors could keep in close touch with the new firm.
5. Presentations and proposals to such local investors did not have to be so elaborate.

While future entrepreneurs are by no means assured of venture capital, it is relatively easy for them to make contact with institutions experienced in helping such individuals and providing capital for their use.

A THEORY FOR ENTREPRENEURIAL ACTIVITY

In view of all this, how can we explain regional differences in technical entrepreneurship? Ideally, one would like to be able to study a region through time as the rate of entrepreneurship changes. However, based upon this intensive study of the Palo Alto area, it is possible to construct a theory about how entrepreneurially active areas get that way.

If an area is to develop technical entrepreneurship, organizations which can serve as incubators must be present, be attracted, or be created. Since founders tend to start firms where they are already living and working, there must be organizations which will hire, bring into the area, and train the engineers, scientists, and technical managers who may someday become technical entrepreneurs.

However, the nature of these organizations is critical in determining whether spin-offs actually occur. It is certainly not difficult to point to cities where thousands of engineers are employed, but where there is little entrepreneurship. If the established firms serve markets that are stable or declining, there is little incentive for the prospective entrepreneur to enter the field.

If the established firms are in industries, which require large capital investments or substantial organizations to compete, it will be difficult to assemble the critical mass needed to get a new firm started. If the potential incubator firms hire relatively undynamic people, train them narrowly, and organize them so that engineers talk only to engineers, and so forth, it will be difficult to assemble a founding team with the needed well-rounded knowledge and skills in marketing, engineering, and manufacturing. If the established firms are well-managed and avoid periodic crises, there may be little incentive for potential founders to leave comfortable positions.

Under such conditions, a would-be founder will find the going difficult. If he seeks to bolster his confidence or to gain advice, he will find a few successful founders who have preceded him. If he seeks to support himself as a consultant while formulating his plans and raising capital, he may find this difficult in a "one company" town.

Sources of venture capital experienced in investing in NTBFs probably are not available locally, and making contact with possible investors may be laborious and time-consuming. In such an environment, the prospective founder's personal experience is likely to have been in large, established firms. He is likely to know little about what is involved in starting and managing a NTBF.

If there are new firms started in such an environment, the founders are likely to come from particular "small businesses" or promising new ventures within the established firms. Possibly, they involve those rare instances in which the founder comes from another geographical location or starts a new company not related to the business of the parent firm which he has left.

If the first new companies are successful, then their success begins to change the environment. These new firms are likely to be better incubators, that is, they have higher spin-off rates than the older firms, which their founders left. Their success may begin to convince others that entrepreneurship is feasible and rewarding. Potential investors are encouraged or created by the success of the new firms. Financial consultants and venture capital firms then develop. Future founders find a more promising environment than those who went before.

The rate of entrepreneurial activity can be accelerated or diminished by a number of factors. One of the most important is the development of the markets and technologies on which the area's industry is based. If the rates of market growth and technological change decline, then technical entrepreneurship will lessen, for potential founders will find fewer areas of opportunity. Public attitudes relating to new issues of stock from recently-formed companies also are important, for they affect substantially the availability of venture capital.

However, if these factors are favorable, a self-reinforcing process takes place. Past entrepreneurship makes future entrepreneurship more likely, and, in time, a high rate of entrepreneurial activity develops. Now, what was that you said about wanting to start your own company?

PLANNING FOR THE NEW ENTERPRISE*

ALBERT J. KELLEY

Any company, regardless of size, faces two problems. First, it has only limited resources with which to work, just so much money and so many people. Second, it has certain objectives, e.g., a desire to increase total sales by 10 percent, or to introduce new products. Matching a company's objectives with its resources is, in itself, a major task; ensuring that the objectives are achieved is an even greater task. The purpose of the Business Plan is to help in accomplishing these tasks. What are the specific advantages of formulating a Business Plan?

The advantages of careful thought. So often we develop plans and ideas for the future in our heads. Yet these plans do not work out as well as we had anticipated, often because we failed to take into consideration some aspect of the problem. If the plan had been written out in a clear and precise manner, we might well have been able to identify and eliminate the flaw. [Thus], the first important advantage of developing a Business Plan is that it forces careful thought. . . .

*Excerpted from *Venture Capital: A Guidebook for New Enterprises* (Chestnut Hill, Mass.: Management Institute School of Management, Boston College, 1971), pp. 19-25. Reprinted with permission of the author and publisher.

The advantages of focusing on key issues. Even if all the important issues concerning the business and the product have been thought through, there is a danger that the planner will become involved in a mass of detail and fail to recognize that certain aspects of the company's management are critical. The Business Plan should help in deciding which are the critical factors, i.e., which factors does success depend upon?

The advantage of internal coordination and communication. Unless the enterprise is strictly a one-man organization, the need for coordinating the efforts of different people and of communicating with them will exist. With a written Business Plan in hand, most people find it much easier to coordinate their activities. Furthermore, with people who have no clear and consistent idea of the objectives of the organization, communications have a habit of being either misunderstood or ignored. An additional advantage of a Business Plan, therefore, is that it provides the members of the organization with a clear idea of what it is the organization is attempting to do.

The advantage of having a guide for day-to-day decisions, and a means of measuring progress. Throughout the year, the management will want to know exactly what was agreed upon, or just what was planned for tackling a special problem or achieving a specific goal. Obviously, the files can be searched until an appropriate piece of paper detailing that specific decision is found. However, it is far better to have all such decisions consolidated in one Business Plan to which everyone can refer on a day-to-day basis.

Furthermore, a Business Plan provides a means of measuring the company's progress toward its goals. Progress toward a goal cannot be measured if there is no clear statement of purpose. Without such a statement there is no way of determining if a company's operations are on schedule. ...

[A well-organized Business Plan can be divided into three major sections or components: 1., the General Plan, 2., the Marketing Plan, and 3., the Financial Plan].

THE GENERAL BUSINESS PLAN

The format and content of general business plans will be as varied as the entrepreneurs who create them and the venture capitalists who are expected to review them. Some venture capital firms explicitly specify not only the content but also the format required of proposals submitted to them. In the majority of instances, however, the entrepreneur must assume the responsibility for forming the business plan.

While it is not possible to specify in great detail the content of a general business plan, there are some elements or types of information common to all comprehensive plans.

Introductory material. At the outset of a business plan it is useful to include a description of the product or service to be offered by the company. At this point, it is also helpful to describe the role of this product in an industry, the particular need it will fill, or how it will relate to existing products performing a similar function. ...

Market research. The general business plan should also include both positive and negative factors about the product, industry, potential customers and competition as reported in [a market research study]. ...

101

Manufacturing. Given the market for the product, what process will be used in its manufacture? What decisions have been made with respect to facilities, plant location, space requirements, subcontracting of component parts? Have subcontractors been interviewed? What kinds of costs are involved in the manufacturing process, i.e., costs of components, plant cost, equipment cost, labor costs? At this stage, some preliminary work should have been done to identify likely costs at different levels of production over the next three years. These cost data will also become an integral part of the Financial Plan.

Timing. A plan, by definition, involves a statement of events that are expected to be accomplished during various future time periods. When will the product prototype be completed? When will the company be prepared to manufacture or assemble the product? What is the expected date for initial deliveries of the product? How will the company grow internally in response to projected sales growth? What are the expected effects of this growth on manufacturing, financial and personal requirements? When will those effects be felt? What is management's plan for dealing with them?

Organization structure. Any prospective financier will be vitally concerned about the principals of the company, their roles in the management of the firm, and their prior experience, training and educational backgrounds. A respected security analyst responded to the question, "What are the factors you consider most critical in your evaluation of a company?" by simply stating, "A strong market for the company's products **and management.**" The venture capitalist's decision will rest heavily on his evaluation of the management team and its members' ability to carry out their assigned roles within the company. ...

THE MARKETING PLAN

A marketing plan is simply a statement of **what** the company is going to do during the next six months or year, **how** it is going to do it, and **who** is going to do it. If the entrepreneur and his management team can answer each of these three questions with respect to the sale and distribution of the company's product, they have the essence of a marketing plan.

What is the company going to do? Mr. Jones of the Alpha Plastics Company had a good product, about which potential customers were enthusiastic. For a year he worked hard at developing sales contracts and encouraging potential customers to begin trial programs using his product. Yet, at the end of the year, Mr. Jones had to admit he had failed. Sales had not developed as he had hoped. Why?

The reasons for Mr. Jones' failure were numerous. Among the most important was that he had had no clear idea of what he was going to do during the year. Every day was a new day for Mr. Jones and he would rush on, in an attempt to solve whatever problems had arisen. One large customer represented more potential business than any other, and yet Mr. Jones had managed to call on him only twice during the year. On the other hand, a small customer, who represented a small potential sales volume, received more than fifty visits because he had problems and asked for assistance. *Unless management knows exactly what it wants to do, it is unlikely that it will be successful.*

How is the company going to do it? Mr. Jackson, President of Jackson's Industries, knew exactly what he wanted to do. He wanted to contact each of

2,000 potential customers in an industry not normally serviced by his sales force. Mr. Jackson decided, therefore, to advertise in the industry press. Each month he purchased a full-page advertisement in the industry journal. It provided complete information on the new product along with a coupon with which additional information could be requested. To his surprise the response was poor. He received less than twenty requests for additional information. Why? On investigation, Mr. Jackson found that very few of the potential customers regarded the industry journal as a source of product information. They all relied on industry distributors for this support. Having made this discovery, Mr. Jackson changed his approach. Now, he signed up a network of distributors to handle the product. This move also produced unsatisfactory results. Why? Mr. Jackson offered a 20 percent margin to the distributors while other products sold to the same customers carried a 35 percent margin. As a result, the distributors were relatively unenthusiastic about promoting the product. *Even if management knows what it is going to do, the appropriate steps must still be taken in order to achieve the objective.*

Who is going to do it? The three founders of the Varane Company held a meeting to establish objectives and goals for both their company as a whole and for the product which they planned to introduce, as well as to detail the means by which they would achieve these objectives. They began very well. The meeting ended and each of the founders went his own way. At a later meeting, the three gentlemen found that, although much had been achieved in the earlier meeting, many of the steps which should have been taken had not been accomplished. "But I thought you were going to do that, John." *Management must assign responsibility for executing its plan.*

These are some of the general problems that arise when a company attempts to operate without a specific marketing plan. How do we go about formulating a marketing plan?

WHAT SHOULD A MARKETING PLAN CONTAIN?

Statement of goals. A marketing plan should begin with a statement of the company's goals for the year. These goals should be quite specific. Compare:

Increase total sales by $2 million.

Increase sales on Product X in Region III by $500,000.

The second goal is specific by both product and by geographic area. It might equally well be specified by salesman or by month. The fact that it is a specific goal enables those concerned with its implementation to view it in very real terms and provide for courses of action that will aid in achieving it.

A goal, however, does not have to be expressed in quantitative terms. For example, a company may want to establish a reputation of selling a quality product. While it is difficult to measure success in achieving goals of this nature, they should nevertheless be clearly stated, if they are important to the company. Without an explicit statement of goals the organization can easily lose sight of its purpose.

Background material on each of the company's products and markets. A statement of the goal alone, for example, to increase sales on Product X by $500,000 is of little value itself. Management must decide how it is going to achieve that goal. But first it must ask the question: "Is this a realistic goal?" If the total market for Product X is $3 million and the company currently has 20 percent of the market (i.e., $600,000 in sales), an increase of $500,000 in sales would represent nearly a 100 percent increase within a year. It also represents an increase in market share from 20 percent to 37 percent. Is that expected? Or is it even wildly possible? The goal must be realistic.

Before a judgment can be made about whether the goal is realistic, the company must know a considerable amount about the marketplace. For example:

Customers
— location
— annual purchases and rate of growth
— purchasing behavior
— specialized requirements

Competitors
— market shares
— prices
— services offered
— size of salesforce or distributors

An overall picture of the marketplace must be in hand before goals can be established. The advantages of incorporating basic market data in a marketing plan is that it enables management to see later what assumptions were made about the size, nature and future of the market. The market data do not have to follow the statement of the company's goals and objectives in the Business Plan but can be placed in an appendix. In any case, they should be available to support the marketing plan.

A program designed to achieve the goals. If the goal is realistic, then decisions must be made about a program to achieve the goal. How might we achieve an increase of $500,000 in the sales of Product X? Answers might be:

Hire two additional salesmen.
Sell through distributors (in addition to the direct sales effort).
Increase the level of advertising.
Reduce the price by 5 percent.

In preparing the marketing plan, care snould be taken to consider each of the possible alternative programs. What will each of the programs cost and how likely is it to succeed?

A statement on timing. The resultant marketing plan, as with the general business plan previously discussed, should include specific statements about when the planned events are to take place. For example, when will the additional salesmen be hired?

A statement of responsibility. Unless the responsibilities for carrying out the elements of the marketing plan are clearly assigned and understood, there is the danger that the jobs will not get done or that the planned actions will not be taken.

Plans for evaluation. The marketing plan must be a "living" document. There must be a built-in reevaluation procedure for measuring the company's progress against the plan.

The plan, itself, should cover the year ahead in detail, and it might also include statements on the long-range plans of the company (i.e., 5 years). It should be reviewed and updated **quarterly.** Much can happen in a three-month period and the plan should be adjusted accordingly. There is, however, another reason to review the plan on a regular basis: to evaluate the performance of each member of the management team. If there is no reward or penalty associated with meeting or failing to meet the timetable detailed in the marketing plan, it will tend to be disregarded.

THE FINANCIAL PLAN

"At a moment in time, a company can be viewed as a pool of funds. These funds have a variety of sources: investors in the company's stock, creditors who lend the company money, and past earnings which the firm retains. Funds provided from these sources have been committed to fixed assets, to inventories, to accounts receivable and to cash or marketable securities. At a moment in time, the pool of funds of the firm is static. Over time. however, the pool changes; and these changes are known as funds flows. In an ongoing business funds flow continually throughout the enterprise. The term **financial management** connotes that these flows are **directed** according to some **plan**.... [1]

In this section we will discuss the reasons for financial planning, types of financial plans and provide some "how to" information.

The need for financial planning. Mr. Morris Chip, founder and president of Chiptek, Inc., a small profitable rapidly growing manufacturer of high density integrated circuits, was threatened with bankruptcy by his creditors. The company's rapid growth created a demand for additional working capital. A failure to provide this capital in the form of permanent new financing had caused the required increment in current assets to be financed, by default, through stretching payments to suppliers from the normal 30 days to 120 days. In spite of the fact that the company was growing and profitable, it was always short of cash. When the crisis occurred, Mr. Chip was informed by his investment banker that it would take three to six months to raise additional permanent capital.

Mr. Mason, Financial V.P. of Data-Tech Systems, Inc., approached his local banker, "Business is good, we're making money, can I borrow $100,000?" The banker was pleased to acquire a new customer and granted the loan. A month later, Mason was back at the bank, "Business is much better, can we have an additional $75,000?" The banker, worried about the first loan, responded, "Ah — will you need additional funds next month as well? When and how do you plan to repay the existing loan?"

The point is clear. It is possible to cause irreparable damage to an organization by appearing to know so little about its operational needs. It is equally disasterous to approach a venture capital firm if you are unprepared to respond to similar inquiries. In the first instance, how much better it would have been to

---

[1]James C. VanHorne, *Fundamentals of Financial Management* (Englewood Cliffs, New Jersey: Prentice-Hall, Inc., 1971), p. 3.

have projected the effect of rapid growth on capital requirements of the company and been able to make timely arrangements for raising the additional funds. In the second case, a simple cash budget made up in the beginning of the year would have permitted a visit to the bank in January with the information that the company will require $175,000 in June, July and August and will be in a position to make repayment in October.

Planning for liquidity. Financial planning falls into two broad areas, planning for liquidity and planning for profit. Planning for liquidity or solvency is planning the company's cash flow. Where will the cash come from, and when; what will it be used for? Most businesses cannot operate in a manner such that daily cash inflows match daily cash outflows. The fact that these flows vary from day to day from month to month makes it essential that the firm plan for financial solvency. The principal tool for short-term financial planning or planning for liquidity, is the cash budget. (It is not the purpose here to describe all the techniques for formulating a cash budget. This topic is treated in greater detail in many finance texts.)

Simply stated, a cash budget is a written plan detailing the amount and timing of expected cash inflows and outflows, usually prepared for one year on a monthly basis. Cash sales and the collection of accounts receivable provide the normal cash inflows while payments to vendors and employees represent typical outflows. In addition, non-recurring items such as a large insurance premium or tax payment are recorded in the months they are expected to occur. The critical elements for management purposes are (a) the extent to which cash inflows and cash outflows in any given time interval do not match and (b) the timing and magnitude of the cumulative effect of net outflows or net inflows. With this information the financial manager is equipped to approach the banker or the venture capitalist for additional short-term funds; he now knows how much financing he will need, when, for how long and how it will be repaid.

Planning for profit. The second broad area of financial planning involves a longer range projection of the company's status, its future income, the assets required to generate this income, and the sources and amount of funds that will be required to finance the assets. Here we are talking about three or five-year plans. These plans are designed to measure the impact of various policy decisions on the financial condition and performance of the firm, for example, the effect of doubling sales in two years, the effect of changing a dividend policy, or mortgaging a building. These plans also provide information about when the company may go public in order to raise additional equity capital, how much capital must be raised, etc. The principal means of accomplishing this task is to project the company's income statements and balance sheets. The former outlines the projections of sales revenues, expenses and profits, while the latter details the assets required to support the projected level of operations together with a statement of how these assets are to be financed. ...

The market research effort and the marketing plan provide significant inputs to these long-range financial plans. The single most important variable influencing future financing requirements is sales. Sales volume, of course, directly influences the level of operations and the amount and composition of plant and equipment required by the firm. In addition, a larger sales volume increases inventories and accounts receivable. A portion of this increment in assets can usually be financed through profits retained in the firm. Often, however, the level of profits generated and saved is not sufficient to support the total increase in operating assets. One prime purpose of preparing long-term financial plans is to identify the extent and timing of these additional capital needs.

An extremely useful tool now available to the financial planner is the packaged financial planning program marketed through time-sharing computer services. While insuring arithmetic accuracy, the computer allows the planner to test the sensitivity of financial plans to a wide variety of assumptions regarding growth in sales, accounts receivable collection period, alternative methods of raising capital, etc. It thereby allows management to view a wide range of possible outcomes, with little or no additional effort. This procedure also encourages continuous planning and, at times, may even suggest the most appropriate method for responding to unexpected changes in plans.

FOUR

The Venture Financing

The entrepreneur will usually require financing during three stages of the enterprise's development. During the first, or start-up, phase the entrepreneur needs seed money to purchase the materials, rent the space, hire the accountant and lawyer, and pay his employees for the time it takes to establish a productive organization. To obtain sufficient financing for this stage, the entrepreneur must invest a substantial part of his net worth in the venture to indicate his commitment to making the business a success. Even then, conventional sources of financing will generally not be interested in providing start-up funds during this highly speculative period when the reward potential is difficult to ascertain. Private placements and venture capitalists are the preferred sources. Funds from relatives and friends are acceptable if the entrepreneur has realistically considered the consequences of living with them after declaring bankruptcy.

During the second, or growth, stage the business will again require financing to cover the costs of additional new product development, building the new plant, hiring the full time salesmen and business manager, and purchasing the necessary manufacturing equipment to meet the initial demand for the company's product—which by this time has been successfully developed and marketed, giving the business and the entrepreneur a track record with a measure of success. Commercial banks and the Small Business Administration generally become interested at this stage, along with more conservative venture capitalists and SBICs (Small Business Investment Companies).

In the last stage, the enterprise has matured to the point where the above financial sources can no longer provide the magnitude of funds required for further plant and staff expansion. Investors with large sums of money must now be located—usually through the public sale of stock, from institutional investors or insurance companies, or through a merger.

If the entrepreneur has successfully maneuvered through these several stages, has managed to communicate effectively with the venture capitalists and the underwriters, and has avoided Chapter II (of the United States

108

Bankruptcy Act), he has at last established himself and his enterprise in the business community.

As noted, commercial banks and other conventional lending sources are generally reluctant to fund a business venture that is starting "from scratch," with its high risk, high appraisal cost, and low dollar investment. During the start-up or seed money stage of the venture, the aspiring entrepreneur usually turns to venture capitalists for help. In the first two readings in this chapter, *Venture Capital* and *What a Venture Capitalist Looks For,* Albert Kelley and Sam Adams concentrate on the venture capital groups and how they rank management factors against the product concept, the type of financial gains they expect, and the types and sizes of equity investments they seek. The entrepreneur usually must be willing to seat a representative from the financial group on his board of directors, to trade ownership in return for cash and possibly management assistance, and to reach other compromising agreements if he is to overcome the financial obstacles and begin the task of developing his enterprise.

Even after the financial sources are known, located, and their objectives understood, to successfully compete for these funds the entrepreneur must present a comprehensive and factual business plan. Kelley and Adams discuss the specifics that bankers and venture capitalists look for in an investment proposal. In assessing the venture risk level, they discuss various qualitative and quantitative informational requirements.

Product design, staffing plans, markets. and environmental factors must be considered, along with a measure of the entrepreneurial and leadership characteristics of the founder. Does the entrepreneur understand what is encompassed in his product development and marketing efforts? Will his entry into the market result in a meaningful market share and a strong position against traditional or potential competition? Has the entrepreneur assembled a talented and cohesive team, all striving for the same goal? Is the environment in terms of suppliers, consumers, and changing technological, legal and economic factors viewed realistically? These are all questions that the banker and other venture capital sources are trying to answer in their evaluation of the entrepreneur and his venture plans. Funds for financing an exciting new or growing business are available. However, success in obtaining such funds depends on the entrepreneur's ability to convincingly provide the kinds of information required by the venture capital sources.

A major question throughout the search for outside funds is whether the venture should be financed with loan (debt) capital or investment (equity) capital. Is it better to seek loans from private or governmental agencies, or to share the ownership and profits with those who can provide the necessary capital? Long term credit is usually obtained from commercial banks, with some loans from the federal Small Business Administration and state industrial development corporations. (Federal government capital sources are described by Anthony Chase and James Proctor in the article, *Financial Aid and Venture Capital Programs at S.B.A.*). Equity funds are principally obtained from wealthy individuals (often referred to as "angels"), family estates, and venture capital firms. Recently established SBICs combine both methods of financing by making their debentures convertible into stock of the small company; in either case, a large share of the seed money is expected to come from the entrepreneur. As the capital demands of the firm increase, public stock issues usually are floated to raise large amounts of money.

Victor Danilov, in his article *Sources of Venture Capital,* offers six major categories of capital sources. In discussing the advantages and disadvantages of each of these sources, he concludes that the successful entrepreneur carefully matches his firm's financial needs to the characteristics of the venture source. Depending upon the venture's progress, the entrepreneur will be best advised to explore a variety of options in financing his venture. This article also offers many examples of successful marriages between entrepreneur and venture capitalist.

In the concluding article by D. Bruce Thorsen, *Venture Capital: Pitfalls and Possibilities,* the author discusses strategies by which an MBA* should approach the venture capital community. Along with concrete advice on SBIC financing, Thorsen outlines several common pitfalls to be avoided. As a director of a New Hampshire SBIC, this author explains how an SBIC operates and cautions the entrepreneur not to paint himself into a corner.

The five articles within this section all offer advice on how to raise capital. Venture financing is one of the more significant milestones in an enterprise's development. Firms that excel at this facet of the business do well; those that fall short in raising funds struggle for survival. Fresh new capital is the life blood of a new or growing enterprise. A properly timed and healthy infusion of capital is a major forward step for a new enterprise.

A sound and balanced business plan is the required foundation for successful venture financing.

VENTURE CAPITAL*

ALBERT J. KELLEY

The term "venture capital" has no commonly accepted definition but conventional usage, in the United States at least, implies investment in a business enterprise where the uncertainties have yet to be reduced to risks which are subject to the rational criteria of security analysts.

The concept of venture capital is quite simple. An investor or group of investors contributes capital money to the new or small corporation in return for an equity position in that corporation. The object is that, as the business grows

*Excerpted from *Venture Capital: A Guidebook for New Enterprises* (Chestnut Hill, Mass.: Management Institute, School of Management, Boston College, 1971), pp. 27-28, 32-38. Reprinted with permission of the author and publisher.

*Holder of the Master of Business Administration degree from a college or university.

and prospers, the value of that equity position will increase. Furthermore, at some favorable time in the not too distant future (usually 3-6 years) it will be possible for the investor to convert the value of that equity position into cash or other liquid assets. Thus the appreciation of his investment will be in the form of capital gains.

What distinguishes the true venture capitalist from any other investor is the technique he employs to achieve his goals, and the degree of risk associated with this type of investment. However, even these characteristics are changing as more and more types of investors seek to become "venture capitalists." Two schools of thought are emerging on the investment of venture capital. One is the traditional concept which will be discussed shortly. The second has resulted from institutional investors becoming more adventuresome in their investing policies. These institutional investors have noticed that while their investment in a listed stock might, if they were lucky, double or triple, they were missing out on the stock's more significant gains. By the time the institutions had decided to buy, the firm's original investors had perhaps multiplied their money 50 to 100 times, and even more. However, because the institutions deal in venture capital as a secondary rather than primary interest, they are unable to devote as much time and effort to their venture investments as the traditionalists. Therefore, the new venture capitalists view the field rather differently than the traditionalists. Generally, they are unencumbered by the same philosophical and altruistic motivations, and they tend to regard a venture investment as just another investment with, of course, greater risks and potential rewards. This outlook is manifested most clearly in what might be called the "one-in-ten" idea of some of the public venture capital and letter stock funds. The theory is that nine out of every ten venture investments will probably be losers, break-evens or only mediocre gainers. But the tenth will hopefully be such a splendid winner that it will more than make up for the other nine.

While these institutions investigate and keep track of a venture investment more closely than they would a listed company, they do not see it as part of their job to assist the corporation in any but the most cursory way. Such assistance would be impractical anyway, because of the large number of companies in which these investors hold a position. They feel if a company becomes sick, that is the company's problem — a recognized hazard of entrepreneuring.

The head of the securities division of one large insurance company put it this way, "While venture capital is a lot of fun and everyone likes to spend time on it, we have a half billion dollars' worth of marketable securities, much of which is in funds that are competitive/performance oriented, and we just don't have a lot of time for a few little venture investments. Recently, we spent two man month on a single venture capital deal, and we just can't afford that sort of thing."

In contrast to the non-traditionalists, the traditional venture capitalist emphazises the creation of value and a willingness to expend the effort to create that value. This means more than just dollars. And, it means more than just monitoring investments.

One active traditional venture capitalist says: "Too many people today just let companies go adrift and down the tubes. You can't see when the yellow lights are going on unless you are intimately involved with a company. Reviewing quarterly financials of a new company is insufficient, because a small company in one quarter can go from being profitable to bankruptcy."

The traditional venture capitalists also scorn the non-traditionalists for what they term their lottery or "crap-shooting" approach. "Big institutions usually get cold feet when a company comes back for more money. They think this means the company doesn't know what it is doing, and so they figure they ought to write that one off. Hell, some good companies need four or five financings before they get into the black and start to go.". . .

THE VENTURE CAPITAL PROCESS

How does the whole process of securing venture capital work? To begin, it is appropriate to look at the background against which the new technically-oriented company must approach the capital market.

Some unique features of the new technically-oriented company are:

1. That it is generally trying to do something which no one has done before.
2. That it is frequently headed by technical people with little or no previous business experience.

The usual objectives of the technical people starting the new business include:

1. The exploitation of a new product, process or service developed in the laboratory which has not yet been utilized commercially; or
2. The expectation that new products, processes, or services will be developed by their laboratories once they are in business; or
3. Joining in the further development of a new scientific or technological field which is still in the early stages of exploitation.

To put the whole problem in perspective, what are the chances of getting a venture capitalist, either an individual or a firm, to back any given entrepreneurial endeavor? A reputable venture capital firm will, on the average, reject out of hand about 97% of the proposals submitted to it, take a first look at 3% and in-depth look at probably 1%, and will actually fund less than ½ of 1%. This may seem to be an extremely high attrition rate from the viewpoint of the entrepreneur. What is the venture capitalist looking for in a venture that causes him to reject over 99.5% of the situations that come to his attention?

The venture investor's motives include both economic and noneconomic factors. While the traditional venture capital groups are primarily motivated by the economies of the situation, the individual venture capitalist may often be motivated by additional factors as well. Such reasons as tax advantages available to the wealthy investors have already been discussed. Some additional motivating factors include the desire to build a viable business, the desire for recognition, and the desire to bring technological ideas, goods and services into the service of mankind.

Analysis of a Venture Proposal

What specifics will the venture capitalist look for in an investment proposal?

1. The people involved.   It is virtually a unanimous consensus among venture capitalists that people are the most important aspect of a venture situation. A first-rate man with a second-rate idea is preferred to a second-rate man with a first-rate idea. Most new technically based enterprises are the expressions of the personalities, technical competence, and aspirations of their founders.

The management team is the keystone of the new technically oriented business. Most venture capitalists feel that a major weakness on the part of the management team is grounds for the rejection of the proposal. Some investors say that if an idea is particularly outstanding they sometimes assist the initial group in finding additional team members with the necessary skills. The usual criterion for the management team appears to be "balance" — the presence of both technical and managerial skills in complementary proportions.

The potential investors will probe the entrepreneur's mind to find out what kind of person he is; what makes him tick; what are his goals. The best entrepreneurs are people who fundamentally like to run things, organize them and grow them — as well as to have financial rewards.

2. The technology.   In judging the venture against this criterion, the potential investor reveals his character more clearly than in any other part of the decision process. The investors' attitudes toward technology will range from considering only exciting new technological developments to anything that promises capital growth, technological or not.

A standard used by some investors is that the technology be in an area in which they already have some experience either as an investor or an operator. Still another factor might be that the technology must have some promise to civilian (vs. space and military) applications. Some investors may require that the technology have the possibility of attracting some government research and development contracts that would help support the firm in its early years.

Most researchers have reported the ultimate criterion used by investors for selecting a technology appeared to be its general excitement. A dramatic and slightly mysterious technology seemed to have a good deal of attraction even among the sophisticated investors — although not so much now as a very few years ago. For some investors an exciting technology in itself seemed to provide sufficient reason to invest.

3. The product.   It is virtually impossible today to attract backing for an entrepreneur with nothing but an idea. Even the most sanguine and patient of investors insist that a substantial amount of product and/or process be developed at the expense of the entrepreneur or someone else.

What constitutes an acceptable level of development to attract financing varies widely among investors. In the research conducted, it was found that some investors felt the existence of a working prototype was sufficient, while others felt the product should be essentially ready for manufacture and marketing. A few investors stated they would not even consider a proposal unless the first sale had already been made.

Thus, even when talking about initial equity financing, it is frequently necessary that a substantial investment have already been made by the entrepreneur, if not in money then at least in time and energy.

The product should have a natural product line or follow-on products. If the basis for the new venture is just a new and better way to make widgets, it is inevitable that a year or so later someone else will discover an even better way to make widgets.

4. The market. One area most investors in new companies carefully examine prior to investment is market growth. Naturally, this makes it more difficult to find financing for ventures which depend upon markets which do not yet exist, or are not yet developed. Some such ventures are financed, but even here almost all investors demand some substantive indication of commercial promise in the near future.

Of course, of even greater importance than the size and growth characteristics of the market, is the question of competition. If the entrepreneur proposes to sell light bulbs in competition with G.E. or Sylvania, he had better have a very unique light bulb.

In short, the investor must look at the ground rules, the competition, the pricing structure, the distribution patterns, and the industry averages for the market the company proposes to enter.

5. Size of investment. While many investors do in fact have a "minimum economic investment," the range is enormous. Several investors have put as little as one to two thousand dollars initial capital into tiny new companies. At the other end of the spectrum, one group asserted that they would not consider any investment under one million dollars. It is estimated that most initial capitalization of technology based companies (perhaps as much as 75 percent) falls between $100,000 and $300,000.

One vice-president and general partner of a well-known venture capital firm put it this way: "We aren't interested in making a $25,000 investment that may some day be worth $50,000 in a small success. We would much rather be prepared to lose all of our money. But, if we are right about the people and everything else, we will create a major success in the corporate sense and fiscally for ourselves." What the true venture capitalists aspire to, at least dream of, is to duplicate something like the Digital Equipment experience.

6. Procedures. Venture capital investors have a strong sense of risk, and usually employ methods designed to avoid unnecessary quantities of risk. Such practices normally center about the investigation of the proposal in depth, so that some set of highly individual standards may be applied to the situation.

The attempt to apply standards to a company requires some knowledge about it. The amount known about a venture by its backers ranges from 0 to 100 percent. Therefore, the investigation of a proposal by the formalized venture capital groups in particular, has evolved into a highly developed art. This process is very similar for both the publicly and privately held venture capital groups.

Typically, three levels of screening exist through which a proposal must pass before it is considered for investment. For convenience these levels will be referred to as *initial, secondary* and *final.*

Initial screening. Much of the initial screening is done on a highly informal basis. The reading of a proposal or a brief telephone conversation is usually sufficient to disqualify 80-90 percent of the possible ventures. Though some deserving projects may get rejected by this initial screening, it appears to be, on the whole, an effective and efficient process.

Secondary screening. The real scrutiny begins in the secondary screening. Some groups require the applicant to complete an extensive set of questionnaires which cover in detail such things as the technology, the product, market, fiscal and personal histories of the principals. This information is then verified and supplemented by conversations with the entrepreneur's legal counsel and auditors, suppliers, customers, dealers, competitors and the competitors' customers, present and former associates and employers of the principals, etc. In short, the secondary screening encompasses nearly any means which can produce useable information in a rather short-time span. Perhaps 25-50 percent of the projects that are subjected to the secondary screening survive it. These are then subjected to the typically longer process of the final screening.

Final screening. The usual reason given for the time delay (6-12 weeks) encountered in the final screening is to conduct a "Market Survey." Such a survey may or may not actually occur. The actual reason for the delay seems to be to provide the venture capital group an opportunity to watch the management team perform under a variety of circumstances.

While the traditional venture capital groups conduct such a vigorous and professional investigation before making a commitment, the non-traditional venture investors are not generally inclined to go to those lengths. The traditional venture capital investors rely heavily on their contacts in business and technical areas in assessing the prospects of a technology, a market, or a group of entrepreneurs. In appraising a potential market, they may also enlist the aid of a professional consulting group to do a limited study. The informal group, or individual, is more likely to simply ask his friends what they think of the prospects, or who they know that might be able to judge. This is especially true in relation to the technology since the informal investors are rarely technically trained.

In spite of all that has been said above, a great deal of irrationality runs through the investment policies of many individuals. Such things as personality conflict can cause the rejection of a very good venture. Similarly, if an investor likes the entrepreneur, he may overlook much that would ordinarily call for the rejection of a proposal.

STRUCTURE OF THE DEAL

The final structure of the venture capital financing is determined by the circumstances and situation in which the deal is made, and by the relative negotiating power of the two parties. Most venture capitalists prefer to utilize the convertible debenture as their investment vehicle. However, if the particular situation calls for some other instrument such as straight common stock so that the company can raise additional debt from commercial banks, the venture capitalist will usually adapt to the situation. Likewise, the percentage of equity sought by the venture capitalist is flexible. For example, situations are not uncommon where the financial partners take 70% of the equity at the time of the financing and then agree to turn over portions of this equity to the entrepreneur (provided he meet certain pre-established goals over the next few years) until the entrepreneur owns 70% and the financial partners 30% of the equity.

The terms of the deal are, for the most part, limited only by the imagination of the parties involved. As a result, all types of innovative arrangements can result.

Most venture capitalists seek a minority position in the companies in which they invest. Some operating corporations have venture capital subsidiaries and utilize venture capital as a technique for diversification. Such firms seek a majority position, or an agreement for future purchase of the company, but these suppliers of venture capital are relatively few.

General Georges F. Doriot of A.R.D. has stated the position of most venture capitalists when he said: "We do not want to manage companies. We do not want to control companies. The SEC deems us to be in control of a company if we have more than 10 percent of the stock. But, what is control? Suppose I finance Mr. X and I hold 99.9 percent of the stock. Then suppose that after six months Mr. X decides to leave. What do I have left? What do I have control over?"

One common thread in most deals seems to be the affinity for participation in management by investors in new companies. But, even this is not universal. The traditional venture capital groups who are more often motivated by the economics of the situation, almost always want representation in management. The individual investor usually does also, but may be much less demanding in this respect because he is somewhat like the institutional investor, in that venture capital is usually a secondary rather than primary occupation for him.

It might be said that there are two reasons for participating in management. One is defensive, that is, to protect an investment. The second is for the satisfaction of involvement, being part of something new and growing.

As for the participative techniques employed, the most customary vehicle is a directorship in the company. Occasionally, a venture capital group will even give a staff member a leave of absence from one to several months, to fill a vacant management role in the new company.

In another common arrangement, the investor wants to be considered as a consultant by management. Such a situation is often written in as a condition in the financing agreement. In a less usual, but not uncommon arrangement, the investor desires a role as a full-time officer of the firm. This situation demands a great caution. Even though the investor may be well qualified for the role, it often causes future problems such as personality conflicts in what has been a smooth running organization.

In general, the venture capital groups expect to participate to some degree in the management of nearly every venture they back. During the first year or two (often called the "hand-holding period"), the venture groups' representatives may meet with company management as often as twice a week to discuss problems of operation, finance, and planning. Even more frequent contact by telephone is not unusual in periods involving many decisions of some importance. The amount of participation by the venture capital group gradually tapers off, however, to the point where the new enterprise can stand unassisted. In describing this "hand-holding," one venture capitalist says of his portfolio companies: "We're their mother and father. We wet-nurse them, act as their crying towel, or their whipping boy or scapegoat."

The importance of the venture capitalist's participation in management has been stated by General Doriot: "Because of faster evolution of technical and commercial ideas and developments, because of keener, stronger competition, there is no time to waste. A company cannot be started slowly as it could be in the past. Shortly after it is started, a new company must obtain and avail itself of some of the good characteristics of a larger company. It must do so early in life so as to be able to survive and grow profitably. It must soon structure itself and become competitively adequate and able in all lines and in all factors of management. It must learn to foresee — to plan. It must learn how to survive accidents in spite of low momentum and lack of resources. As counselors, A.R. & D.'s staff, directors and friends try to help its portfolio companies during their growth and development period."

FINANCING THE DEAL

The techniques employed by the traditional venture capitalists for creating value vary widely from one source to another. Some firms prefer to enter the deal on an equal footing with management by taking their equity position in common stock. Others prefer to put up capital in the form of convertible debentures, or as loans with warrants for the purchase of common stock. Some venture capitalists seek a controlling interest, others do not.

In financing the new enterprise, the venture capitalist faces a part of the debt-equity dilemma. The rewards to the financier of a successful venture enterprise are dependent on participation in ownership. The supplier of debt capital, because he is granted a prior claim on income and assets, is rewarded only to the extent that he receives interest payments on the capital provided. And yet, in venture enterprises, this traditional superior claim on assets and income afforded the creditor has little real meaning, since *all capital* is exposed to the same high degree of uncertainty surrounding the fledgling enterprise's future. If the enterprise is not a success, there will be a precious few assets remaining to be liquidated for the benefit of these creditors. If it is a success, the reward to the creditor is limited to the contractual *interest rate*. To the provider of debt vis-a-vis equity financing the risk differential is small while the expected reward differential is great. There is, therefore, little incentive for the venture capitalist to provide debt capital.

On the other hand, the responsible venture capitalist must maintain some *control* over his investments. While control, in this sense, most often conjures up visions of 51 percent ownership, frequently it is not desirable or possible to attain this portion of ownership in the new enterprise. However, with debt capital the venture capitalist can often gain effective or sufficient control of key areas in the company's operations by specifying certain restrictions in a contractual agreement with the new company. For example, the venture capitalist might insist on an acceleration clause which would make the full loan due and payable within one month of default on any one of the following restrictions [among others]:

A minimum net working capital limit
A maximum limit on bank loans and long-term debt
A restriction on the creation of senior long-term debt
A restriction on dividend payments
A restriction on the acquisition of fixed assets
A restriction on major changes in the nature of the business
A restriction on merger with another company
A restriction on changes in the management of the company
A restriction on salaries and benefits paid top management

The prohibition of these actions makes them subject to the consent of the venture capitalist. The penalty for breaking any of the restrictions is the automatic acceleration of the maturity of the loan. Thus, real control can be acquired in many areas vital to the management of the new company through the use of debt.

With debt's major advantages (control) and disadvantages (risk-reward imbalance), venture capitalists frequently employ a hybrid financial instrument which combines the best of both worlds. It allows the full participation in the rewards of ownership while also permitting effective control. It even provides for a superior claim on assets and income, and returns the venture capitalist regular interest payments. The instrument is a convertible debenture, "convertible" because it can be exchanged into a specified number of shares of common stock *at the option of the holder,* and "debenture" because it is a debt instrument secured by the general credit of the company.[1]

If the venture capitalist wants to participate in potential rewards and also excercise control over his investments, there must exist *acceptable and marketable* financial instruments flexible enough to accomplish these goals. While many combinations of debt, equity, warrants and other options are used to effect these purposes, the convertible debenture is an example of an increasingly popular financial instrument employed to achieve these somewhat diverse objectives.

WHAT A VENTURE CAPITALIST LOOKS FOR*

SAM ADAMS

WHEN A COMPANY ISN'T A COMPANY

Alan Patricof's office is flooded with late spring sunlight. Its walls are covered with some of the brightly colored hard-edge paintings he began collecting before that school became faddish. His glass-topped desk is a study in translucence—clear of everything but a thick glass container of rock candy, pieces of which he crunches as he talks. Patricof reaches behind him and pulls out a small plastic cylinder with slits in its walls. "This is used instead of a toggle bolt," says Patricof. "Very strong, good product. Very interesting. But does the man who brought me this have a product or a company? We think he has a product. We don't think he has a company."

To Patricof, the distinction is crucial. Every day he and his associates listen to new business proposals, and by Patricof's count the product-company mistake is one of the commonest committed by budding entrepreneurs. In three years as the head of his own venture capital firm, Patricof has seen a lot of mistakes. He got a taste for the risk capital business in 1969 when he successfully

*Reprinted with permission from the June/July issue of *MBA* magazine. Copyright© 1973 by MBA Communications, Inc.

[1]The same goals can be achieved with a combination of debentures and warrants. For an excellent treatment of the differences between these alternatives, see Samuel Hayes and Henry B. Reiling. "Sophisticated Financing Tool: The Warrant," *Harvard Business Review* (January — February, 1969), 137—150.

lined up a wad of money to save a then tottering *New York* magazine. Then he went on to establish the Alan Patricof Organization with a pool of about $5 million. Today it owns more than half of the common stock of ASG Industries (formerly American Saint Gobain), the fourth largest glass producer in the U.S.; Childcraft Education, Inc. and RSR, Inc., a $100-million secondary smelter. It owns nearly half of publisher E.P. Dutton and has substantial investments in such companies as Wells National Serivce, a lessor of television sets to hospitals (its stock is traded on the American Stock Exchange), a consumer periodical called *Shopper's Voice,* and a bunch of high-technology companies.

But for every company in his portfolio, Patricof has turned down dozens. Many of their creators might have saved themselves some time had they gone through the obvious but often overlooked exercise of simply thinking their project through. Before an entrepreneur begins to write a business proposal, says Patricof, he should thoroughly analyze the potential market for his product and its feasibility in the current economic environment. He should submit his idea to friends and defy them to find loopholes in it. He should assure himself that there are no legal or trade secret conflicts with his present employer and that his patents are solid.

Next, the entrepreneur should take up the amount of money he needs to raise. "I am a great believer in properly capitalizing," says Patricof. "On the one hand you don't want to start an ambitious project without sufficient capital. On the other, you don't have to raise all your capital on the first day — because, if you are successful, there is no question that the initial money is the most expensive money."

Patricof's advice: Go as far as you can with close-in money — that is money of your own or money raised from friends and relatives. "I give a lot of credit to the guy who puts up his own money, persuades others to work with him evenings and weekends, and maybe lives hand to mouth until he gets to the point where his project makes sense."

"A guy from a huge diversified corporation came here with an impeccable list of credentials," says Patricof, "every one of them a national business name. I looked at his blue-ribbon list, and then I asked him: 'How is it you haven't gotten money from these guys? Why do you come to a stranger? If you could show me that a couple of these guys were investors, I would have to stand up and grab this deal. But you come in and tell me that all of these guys think you're terrific but none of them thinks you're terrific enough to back you.' "

In other words, financial support is the best reference of all. But in most cases perseverance will be more important than cash in getting a business off the ground. Patricof likes to tell the story of the entrepreneur who came to him with a new medical instrument. The instrument looked very interesting, Patricof relates. It had already been brought through design and prototype stages and a few of the units had been sold. "But he still couldn't prove to my satisfaction that the product had a sufficiently broad market. So I told him: 'Go out and develop $500,000 of backlog and I will finance that backlog.' His face dropped and he said to me, 'I was here a year ago [I didn't know this] and one of your associates told me to come back after I had my initial sales. So here I am and now you're telling me to come back after I've got my backlog.' " Patricof laughs. "Every venture capitalist wants a little more proof, and I am just as guilty of this as anyone else. But look how far he got without us."

Only after he has dealt with the concept and the financial needs should an entrepreneur proceed to a business plan. Any MBA who has taken a small business course is familiar with the contents of this document — the description of the business, cash flow, additional capital needs and so forth. But to Patricof, the most important element of the business plan is the section describing the credentials of the men who are starting the business.

Patricof looks for people with experience in the field of his new venture. "There are a lot of big problems for the guy who has been an electronics engineer and wants to start a company in the consumer product field," he says.

Next, he looks for marketing ability. "I have just about come to the point, through hard experience, that I will not back a venture unless it involves a man who is fully aware of the marketing environment — the competition, pricing, fit — and can sell the product. You can have the greatest product in the world, the greatest managerial story, the greatest financial story, but if you don't have people who know how to sell that product at a profit, I think you have a risky situation. You see a lot of production guys, engineers who design a product and assume it will fly but who really don't know what the market out there is like."

Let's say the entrepreneur has brought the company as far as it can, has determined his financial needs, and has a succinct, specific business plan. How does he deal with a venture capitlist? "You've got to appreciate the fact that these people are professionals," says Patricof. "There is going to be a lot of nitpicking. Negotiations are going to be protracted. So the worst thing you can do is to come in and say you need the money quickly."

In fact, in Patricof's opinion, the scenario should be staged as casually as possible. The ideal approach goes something like this: Make an appointment with a venture capitalist and tell him that while you are not ready to take his money yet, you've been working on something you think he might be interested in. Then keep a casual—but active—dialogue going. Let him know when you've sold an order or hired an assistant, and send him your press releases. "Very seldom is a venture capitalist going to push you because he wants your deal so badly," says Patricof. "On the other hand, you don't want to push him so hard you make him feel threatened. When the day comes that you're ready for financing, the venture capitalist will have made an investment of time, and he is going to want to see something come of it. It takes time to get a guy focused, and that venture capitalist is now focused. If on the day of the closing the deal breaks down, he'll be more disappointed than you."

Another mistake in the presentation is for the partners in a business (Patricof would much prefer to back a team rather than a single individual) to treat each other as equals. Recently three men who had been working together in a billion-dollar corporation came to Patricof with a business proposition, and he asked which of them was the president. They said that none of them was, they were equal partners. "So I said 'If you are going to run yourselves by committee, it won't work.' Later they returned and I asked again who they had appointed as president. Their answer was still wrong: 'John is the general manager.' That was a big-company answer. They were still in the corporate world." Needless to say, they went elsewhere for their financing.

Another gambit that will help the presentation is to come in with a good lawyer and a good accountant. A "Big-Eight" accountant (one of the eight largest public accountants in the U.S.) will probably be worth the 10% premium that such a firm charges because it will help identify the entrepreneur as a professional. "You reach for anything you can that will give you recognition," says Patricof.

In negotiating the financing, Patricof advises, the start-up businessman should not be afraid of performance deals; *i.e.*, contracts that link the amount of stock to be retained by the owner to the performance of the new company. "Performance deals give the investor confidence that you really believe in the proposal," says Patricof. But shouldn't the entrepreneur hang onto at least 51% of his company? No, says Patricof. "If you are really as good as you say you are, you can control your company with 1% of the stock. In the first few years, control rests with the guy who is running the company. I would be much more concerned with getting the money to do the job than getting the percentage." As the company progresses, a performance deal will make it possible for the entrepreneur to increase his ownership of his company.

One last piece of advice: Try not to live dangerously. Don't, for instance, stake everything on capturing one big account and then have to fold up shop when that account doesn't come through. "Make sure you have a survival plan," says Patricof. "Funny as it seems, sheer survival works."

PASSING A BUSINESS THROUGH THE EYE OF A BANKER

Recently an MBA now serving in the venture capital section of a large commercial bank was asked if it was difficult for MBAs to obtain seed money for new businesses. "Yes," he answered, "because other MBAs are the ones who are passing it out."

The jest is at least half true. While no one has made a strict count, there is general agreement that a disproportionate number of MBAs gravitate to the venture capital field. But contrary to the implication that MBA venture capitalists are harder on members of their own fraternity, at least one of them indicates that the MBA should have a leg up in his battle for seed money. He is University of California MBA Rick Roesch, who, as president of Citicorp Venture Capital Ltd., handles the risk money investments for First National City Corp. Citicorp Venture, a Small Business Investment Corp. with a pool of some $50 million, has investments in about 70 companies, 15 of them outside the U.S.

What would give MBAs a better than even break with Roesch? Adherence to his cardinal rule for a new business proposal: a well thought out, persuasive, *written* business plan. This, of course, is standard fare in the small business course of every business school that has one. "The most successful entrepreneurs have thought through their business plans," says Roesch. "They know their strengths and weaknesses. They know what the competition is offering." And they ought to be able to put all this on paper. Says Roesch: "The entrepreneur is doing himself a disservice to think he can go in eye-to-eye with a prospective investor and simply sell his company. It's safe to say that if it is not on paper, it is not well enough thought out for a venture capitalist to consider it."

Roesch, who with his staff looks at upwards of 2,000 business proposals a year, finds that their commonest failings are products that are not properly positioned. Frequently, they are aimed at either too well developed a market or one that is too specialized. "We're interested in the man who is determined to build a big company, one with sufficient growth potential to make it an attractive new issue." What sort of growth would be "sufficient"? "We don't have any hard and fast rules," says Roesch. "Of course, there is an industry rule of thumb that a new venture should be making $1 million after taxes within five to seven years after startup."

To Roesch, the industries that would offer the best crack at achieving that objective include some of the old favorites of the late 1960s: computer hardware, particularly peripherals, computer-related service industries and the medical electronics field. Another interesting area: industries that could receive an assist from the dollar devaluation—for example, textiles.

Finally, Roesch looks for an entrepreneur who has done his apprenticeship at a large corporation. "There is no question," he says, but what people who have had experience in big business, especially in those companies that have a rapid growth pattern, are better prepared to set up a business."

FINANCIAL AID AND VENTURE CAPITAL

PROGRAMS AT SBA*

ANTHONY G. CHASE / JAMES M. PROCTOR

Perhaps no other agency of the Federal Government is as beleaguered and at the same time as actually and potentially productive as the Small Business Administration. The Small Business Act,[1] the Small Business Investment Act (SBI Act),[2] and a number of other statutory provisions have armed SBA with an impressive array of weapons with which to stimulate and defend the small business sector of our free enterprise system.

We will discuss one SBA activity—its role in providing venture capital and other kinds of financial assistance to small businesses. SBA's full range of programs also includes its extensive activities in the areas of federal procurement, management assistance, minority enterprise and on behalf of small business before other governmental bodies.

By law, SBA is prohibited from granting financial assistance unless the assistance is unavailable from private sources on reasonable terms.[3] On the other hand, SBA is admonished by the same statute that its loans must be "of such sound value or so secured as reasonably to assure repayment."[4] Its role is not to subsidize dying businesses nor to conduct a give-away program, nor does

---

*Abridged and reprinted with permission from *The Banker's Magazine* (Autumn, 1970), pp. 11-16, 17. Loan limits and guarantees updated where necessary.

[1]Small Business Act of 1958, as amended, Pub. L. 85-699, July 18, 1958, 72 Stat. 384, 15 U.S.C. §631.

[2]Small Business Investment Act, Pub. L. 85-699, Title I, Aug. 21, 1958, 72 Stat. 689, 15 U.S.C. §§661-696 (1964 ed.), as amended, 15 U.S.C. §671 et seq. (Supp. V 1965-69).

[3]15 U.S.C. §636(a)(1).

[4]15 U.S.C. §636(a)(7).

it compete with the private banking industry. Rather, SBA's role is to make financing available to potentially profitable small concerns that cannot fit into the priority framework of the private capital markets.

SBA's guaranteed loan program is well-known; less familiar are its recent efforts to make that program more attractive to banks. Its disaster loan program is also well-known, yet it is scarcely realized that SBA aids not only victims of natural disasters but also those affected by the federal bulldozer, by product disaster, by international trade concessions, and by health, anti-pollution, and safety legislation. SBA also has a special loan program for low-income individuals, and makes unsecured long-term loans to state and local development companies and to small business investment companies. Finally, SBA can guarantee the rentals of small concerns to their landlords, thus making them more attractive tenants.

THE SBA EXPERIENCE

Despite the risks inherent in its lending policy, SBA's loss rate has not been excessive. Many would argue it should be higher. On regular business loans the rate of loss has been approximately two percent—high enough to be unacceptable to commercial bankers but low enough to demonstrate that it is a true loan program and not a system of subsidies. ...

While SBA assistance has reached significant dollar amounts, it has not gone far enough toward meeting the real needs of vast numbers of eligible concerns across the country.

Of all the independent businesses in the United States, 95 percent are considered small by SBA standards and might qualify for SBA assistance. This sector of the economy contributes roughly 37 percent of the gross national product and is responsible for over 40 percent of U.S. employment, giving SBA a potential clientele of impressive proportions. In times of high interest rates and low liquidity, the credit needs of these businesses become especially acute. Yet the aggregate level of SBA assistance has largely not been responsive to increased levels of need by small business. Clearly, there is room for SBA to expand its financial assistance role, especially at the present time. It is equally clear that no amount of government dollars alone can provide an adequate level of assistance.

No problem of SBA is more important, nor is any receiving more attention, than that of making SBA's programs and procedures more attractive to private lenders. The most extensive changes have been made in the business loan program.

THE BUSINESS LOAN PROGRAM

SBA's business loan program, under Section 7(a) of the Small Business Act, is its primary means of providing financial assistance. Under this program, SBA will guaranty up to 90 percent of a loan by a private financial institution, usually a commercial bank, to a small business concern that cannot otherwise obtain credit on reasonable terms. The private lender puts up 100 percent of the money on each such loan and stands at least 10 percent of the risk of loss. The lender also is responsible for servicing the loan. Where even guaranteed credit is otherwise unavailable, SBA may advance part or all of the loan funds itself; but the large majority of loans are now on a guaranty basis.

The maximum amount of a guaranty or direct loan to a single borrower is $350,000,[5] although lower limits have been set administratively on direct loans; the maximum term of a loan is ten years, but 15-year loans are possible for certain construction projects.

Banks are permitted to charge "legal and reasonable"[6] rates of interest on guaranteed loans. The bank pays SBA an annual guaranty fee of ¼ percent on the balance of the guaranteed portion of the loan.

Several recent innovations will make participation in the program infinitely more convenient to the banker:

Blanket Guaranty. SBA has eliminated the necessity of a separate guaranty agreement between the bank and SBA for each loan. SBA now executes one blanket agreement with the lender, under which many loans can be made, approved by SBA and thereby guaranteed. This so-called Simplified Blanket Loan Guaranty (SBLG) program has eliminated an untold amount of paper work and clerical burden. A one-page application form is used for the guaranty, separate long-form loan authorizations are eliminated, and reporting requirements are reduced. Under SBLG, SBA approves or denies each individual loan application within ten work days. . . .

Immediate Payout. In July 1970, SBA instructed its field offices that upon default of a guaranteed loan and demand by the lender for payment of the guaranty, SBA will now make prompt payment without a prior audit of the loan. The former practice was to investigate the activities of the lender in closing, disbursing and servicing the loan before paying on the guaranty — a process that often consumed months and aroused the displeasure of lenders. In eliminating the waiting period, SBA reserves the right subsequently to audit and take legal action to recover for losses arising out of misfeasance by the lender.

Elimination of Forms. The number of forms a lender must use in making guaranty loans is constantly being reduced. Banks may now use their own mortgage forms and other collateral instruments, although SBA will provide them on request for the use of small lenders. In July 1970, certain optional clauses were eliminated from SBA note forms, making it possible to arrive at a single form of note that can be used in all cases. Reporting requirements have been lightened—reports to SBA on the status of guaranteed loans are now semiannual instead of quarterly.

Revolving Credit. SBA has recently added a new tool to its business loan program, making available revolving lines of credit to small construction contractors. . . .

Within overall limitations set by a single guaranty agreement, the bank will advance funds to finance performance of multiple contracts, against pledges of contract rights by the borrower. The bank lender will be permitted to use all of its own loan closing and servicing forms, including note forms. The duration of each line of credit is normally one year, and longer terms may be authorized. Competitive interest rates are charged, and the maximum amount of guaranty is $350,000 or 90 percent of the loan, whichever is less.

---

[5]In participation and guaranty loans the individual loan can exceed $350,000 by the amount of the private lender's participation.

[6]When SBA purchases the guaranteed portion, it pays accrued interest to the date of purchase at a rate not in excess of 8% per annum. 13 C.F.R. Part 120, §120.3(b)(2)(iv), 34 F.R. 1945, 2248.

Bank Sale of SBA Paper. In recent years, low bank liquidity has inhibited the level of SBA-guaranteed financing. While SBA has primarily guaranteed loans by commercial banks, it has occasionally issued guarantees to other lenders that can exercise adequate credit judgments and perform the servicing function. Under present legislation, however, SBA has not issued guarantees directly to the bulk of the institutions, such as the insurance companies, pension funds, and foundations.

SBA has cooperated in arranging sales, to several state (public) pension funds, of the guaranteed portions of SBA-guaranteed loans. Under the normal arrangement the bank originating the loan sells the 90 percent "guaranteed portion" to the state pension fund, with SBA consent, retaining a 10 percent risk exposure and continuing to service the loan. The pension fund, since it invests in only the guaranteed portion, has a 100 percent guaranteed investment. Since the bank continues to service the loan, the fund can continue to be a passive investor.

SBA hopes to make these procedures, now used by the state pension funds, attractive to the private institutions. It is thoroughly reviewing the "packaging" of the guaranteed portions of loans into convenient investment units, that will be necessary to market them to a broad range of institutional investors and provide adequate secondary market facilities that will insure investors of a degree of liquidity. This is most difficult and may require legislation.

SPECIAL PROGRAMS

The business loan program is only one of SBA's tools. SBA's full flexibility is not generally recognized, and this lack of awareness has led to under-utilization of many of its programs.

SBA is generally known to provide disaster assistance—the ordinary disaster loan is made to a property owner or businessman to compensate for physical loss or other economic injury suffered in natural disasters.[7] It is less well known that SBA is authorized to make disaster-type loans (that is, long-term low interest rate loans) in situations other than natural disasters. For example:

Displaced Business Loans[8] can assist small businesses that have suffered economic injury by reason of being displaced by, or located in or near, a federally-assisted construction project, including urban renewal and highway projects. These loans, with no dollar limit, have up to 30-year maturity at an interest rate which is currently 5½ percent. Most of the funds for the program have come directly from SBA, but there has been a degree of bank participation (at 10½ percent interest).

Product Disaster Loans[9] are available to assist small businesses that suffer economic injury as a result of inability to process or market a product for human consumption because of disease of toxicity due to natural or undetermined causes. This authority was enacted by Congress in 1964, as a result of the botulism scare that injured scores of small firms in the Great Lakes fishing industry. . . .

Trade Adjustment Assistance Loans[10] are available to assist any business,

[7] 15 U.S.C.§636(b)(1), (2).
[8] 15 U.S.C.§636(b)(3).
[9] 15 U.S.C.§636(b)(4).
[10] 15 U.S.C.§636(e).

large or small, to adjust to increased competition from imports. This authority was enacted in 1966 and supplements the Trade Expansion Act of 1962.[11] Under the original provisions of that Act, domestic firms could apply for assistance if they could show that U.S. trade concessions were the major cause of increased imports and that increased imports were the major factor causing injury to the firm. Early applications for assistance were unsuccessful. . . .[The 1966 supplement, and more recent legislation, has made] trade adjustment assistance more readily available to industries and firms injured by import competition.

SBA has other disaster-type authority as well, such as its ability to assist small coal mine operators to meet the requirements of recently enacted *Coal Mine Health and Safety* legislation.[12] More recent bills enable SBA to extend disaster-type assistance to small businesses that must meet the requirements of local, state or federal *anti-pollution* laws.

[*Editor's note:* In 1974 at least two dozen bills were introduced in Congress to amend the Small Business Act to provide "disaster-type" loans to small business concerns affected by the energy shortage].[13]

Economic Opportunity Loans

Title IV of the Economic Opportunity Act of 1964[14] authorizes SBA to make or guarantee loans to small business concerns that are (1) located in urban or rural areas with high proportions of unemployed or low income individuals, or (2) owned by low income individuals. EO loans cannot be granted unless other financial assistance (including a regular SBA business loan) is unavailable. The maximum loan size is $50,000; SBA may lend the money directly, or may guarantee up to 100 percent of a bank loan. Despite the guarantee, only about ⅓ of the new funds going into the program are from private sources; the small size of the loans and a higher delinquency rate have discouraged bank participation. . . .

It should be noted that the Urban Affairs Committee of the American Bankers Association has been extremely active in creating a framework for increased lending to the urban poor. Among other projects, minority lending seminars have been scheduled to be held eventually in 54 cities.

Development Company Loans

Under Section 501 of the SBI Act,[15] unsecured loans are made to State Development Companies (SDCs) incorporated under specific state enabling laws. These corporations have as members (or stockholders), banking institutions, federal savings and loan associations, building associations, pension funds and insurance companies who agree to lend to the SDC certain funds for investing in small business concerns within the state. The economic growth of

[11] 19 U.S.C. § 1912.
[12] 15 U.S.C. § 636(b)(5).
[13] E.g., S. 3096, 93rd Cong., 2nd Sess.
[14] 42 U.S.C. § 2901.
[15] 15 U.S.C. § 695.

the affected area is of primary importance. Once the members or stockholders have made their capital contributions to the SDC, SBA will lend funds to the SDC in an amount not exceeding such contributions. The SBA loans are for a maximum of 20 years at the same interest rate as the SDC borrows from its members, but not more than 10½ percent per annum. Most states now permit the incorporation of SDCs. SDCs initially confined their activities to long-term collateralized loans but more recently have invested in equity securities of small business concerns.

The Local Development Company (LDC)[16] has proven to be a flexible means of promoting economic development, particularly in rural areas where money is often extremely difficult to obtain for small businesses. Local development companies are private profit-making or non-profit corporations composed of citizens and businessmen of the local area. A minimum of 25 members or stockholders, all of whom reside or do business in the area of operations, must control at least 75 percent of the voting stock of an LDC. SBA loans money or guarantees up to 90 percent of loans by other lending institutions to LDC's to assist "identifiable" small businesses in plant construction, conversion or expansion, including land acquisition. The maximum loan or guaranty is $350,000 for *each* small business to be assisted. The loans may not be used for working capital; however, an ordinary business loan or SBIC companion loan could be made to the same small business concern for working capital.

For each project assisted by an LDC, local sources must normally inject at least 20 percent of the project cost; but in some locations, including "target areas" of high unemployment or predominately low-income individuals, a 10 percent (or lower) local injection is required.[17] Loans to LDC's bear interest at 5½ percent, for as long as 25 years. Banks may charge any legal and reasonable interest rate and the loan may be 90 percent guaranteed by SBA. While LDC's have been successful in rural areas, those in urban areas have had difficulty raising the "local injection," and there is some indication that SBA may have to waive part or all of the local injection requirement in many cases.

Lease Guarantee

Another little-known vehicle of SBA assistance is the Lease Guarantee Program.[18] SBA, usually in cooperation with a participating insurance carrier, will guarantee the payment of rental by a small business tenant to its landlords, in effect making the small concern a triple-A tenant for credit purposes. This program enables him to compete with larger firms for space. The resulting strength of the lease may also help the landlord obtain financing for the construction of the leased premises. Leases may be guaranteed for terms of from five to twenty years.[19]

[16]15 U.S.C. §696.

[17]The small business concern being assisted may invest up to one-fourth of the required local injection in the LDC and this investment may be either equity or debt. (13 C.F.R. §108.502-1(e).)

[18]15 U.S.C. §692.

[19]The statute fixes no maximum on the amount of rental that may be guaranteed under a single lease; however, SBA has administratively limited this to $9 million and imposes stricter screening procedures to all guarantees above $2.5 million.

SBICs

Small Business Investment Companies (SBICs) are licensed and regulated by the SBA pursuant to the SBI Act. SBICs are privately owned and operated corporations created in order to fill the "gap" in equity capital and long-term loan funds available to small concerns, and to provide management assistance to such firms.

In order to become licensed, an SBIC must have a minimum private capitalization consisting of $150,000 of cash or eligible Government securities (though $150,000 is now rarely considered sufficient private capital by SBA). Generally speaking, SBA is authorized to furnish an SBIC with so-called "matching funds" by purchasing SBIC debentures in an amount up to twice the SBIC capitalization, but not to exceed $10 million.

The SBIC industry has a number of tax advantages. An SBIC shareholder may treat gains on sales of his stock as long-term capital gains or, if he is not so fortunate, he may take an unlimited ordinary-loss deduction on losses arising from disposition of the stock. SBICs are granted relief from the tax on excess accumulations of surplus and may qualify for relief from the tax on personal holding companies. The Internal Revenue Code allows SBICs to take full deductions against ordinary income for losses they sustain on convertible debentures, or on stock received through conversion of debentures.[20]

Over 1,000 SBIC licenses have been issued since the beginning of the program. The number of SBICs actively operating in the program has now declined to 443. Many of the early minimum size companies have defaulted on their obligations to SBA or incurred regulatory difficulties occasioning their departure from the program. In addition, a relatively small number of larger SBICs have surrendered their licenses, reportedly because of low profitability and their dissatisfaction with federal regulatory requirements. Most recently, several former SBICs have formed "two-tier" structures with an unregulated venture capital company as the parent of a subsidiary licensed SBIC.

It was not until 1966 that the SBIC industry as a whole showed a net return on invested capital (2.5 percent). Today, the industry may be approaching health and stability.

Bank Ownership

Congress attempted to remedy the early plight of the industry by enacting the SBI Act Amendments of 1967.[21] According to a study prepared by SBA in 1967, an SBIC required a minimum capitalization of $1 million in order to constitute a sound financing organization, i.e., "to assure adequate income, to employ competent management, to make the company attractive to private investors, to allow diversification of investments and to enable an SBIC to have reasonable expectations of a successful long-time operation.[22]

In support of resulting 1967 legislation to increase an SBICs minimum mandatory capitalization to $1 million, SBA took the position that bank-owned and bank-affiliated SBICs were among the best operated companies; in view of

[20]See Sections 243, 542, 1242, and 1243 of Internal Revenue Code, as amended (Title 26 of U.S. Code).

[21]Pub. L. 90-104, Oct. 11, 1967, 81 Stat. 268, effective on Jan. 9, 1968.

[22]Senate Report No. 368, 90th Cong., 1st Sess., June 27, 1967, 5-6.

the requested increase in minimum SBIC capitalization, banks should be permitted to invest up to 5 percent of their capital and surplus (as opposed to the previous 2 percent) in SBIC stock. Congress finally approved an amendment permitting a bank to purchase SBIC stock not exceeding 5 percent of the bank's capital and surplus but did not increase the required minimum capitalization of an SBIC, which remains at $150,000.

A new provision was added at the insistence of the House conferees prohibiting banks from thereafter acquiring 50 percent or more of any class of voting securities of an SBIC.[23] In support of this new restriction the House Banking and Currency Committee stated that—

> Commercial banks presently own or have an affiliation with 84 small business investment companies, 24 of which are wholly owned by banks. Your committee feels that this is an undersirable situation and one loaded with dangerous monopolistic potential.   .[24]

Matching Funds

A major concern of the SBIC industry in recent years has been the irregularity of government funding. Legislation enacted in 1969 authorized an increase of $70 million in the level of SBA "financing functions."[25] During the six months following this enactment, SBA received 104 applications for SBIC funding totaling $115.7 million and approved 99 debenture purchases for a total of $59.5 million. For Fiscal Year 1974, an SBIC program level of over $70 million has been set, but SBA's ability to use a portion of this is contingent upon its ability to guarantee loans to SBICs by private investors. A backlog of applications already exists, and pending applications for the refinancing of maturing debt add to the burden.

The SBICs will not solve their funding problems without reducing their dependence on direct government lending. Under the original Act, SBA was clearly authorized to guarantee loans by private lenders to SBICs. A quirk of the 1967 Amendments has cast a cloud over this aspect of SBA's guarantee authority and private investors have since been unwilling to place full reliance upon it, despite favorable rulings by the Comptroller General.[26]

From time to time, SBA has been able to sell blocks of SBIC debentures to the private market as an indirect source of funds for new lending. These sales, with right of recourse against SBA, give the private investors a full faith and credit government guarantee as to principal and accrued interest. Nevertheless, the procedure for selling debentures is cumbersome and the direct guarantee authority is infinitely preferable.

MESBICs

[In 1969, legislation was passed on the President's recommendations] that (1) the SBI Act be amended to allow a bank to become a 100 percent equity

---

[23]Subparagraph (2) of Section 302(b), added by Section 204 of SBI Act Amendments of 1967, fn. 5, *supra*.

[24]House Report No. 552, House Banking and Currency Committee, 90th Cong., 1st Sess., *Small Business Act Amendments of 1967*, Aug. 14, 1967, at 9-10.

[25]Pub. L. 91-151, 91st Cong., Dec. 23, 1969, 83 Stat. 371, 378.

[26]Compt. Gen. decision B-149685, Mar. 20, 1968.

owner of a Minority Enterprise SBIC, or MESBIC (subject to the "5 percent of assets" limit), (2) MESBICs be permitted to organize and operate under state nonprofit corporation statutes, and (3) ordinary income tax deductions be allowed for contributions to nonprofit MESBICs.[27] "MESBIC" is defined as a special purpose SBIC "the investment policy of which is that its investments will be made solely in small business concerns which will contribute to a well-balanced economy by facilitating ownership in such concerns by persons whose participation in the free enterprise system is hampered because of social or economic disadvantages."[28]

SBA has already amended its regulations to permit regular SBICs to own MESBIC subsidiaries and to permit MESBICs to be under common ownership with existing SBICs. An SBIC owning a MESBIC must own at least 20 percent of the MESBIC's voting securities unless it demonstrates that it will be an active participant notwithstanding a lesser percentage of stock ownership. Non-SBIC investors may also acquire a portion of the equity securities of such a MESBIC.[29]

To encourage the formation of MESBICs, SBA has issued licenses to MESBIC applicants sponsored by strong parent companies (or individuals) despite the fact that the MESBIC will have private capital of only $150,000. A MESBIC can succeed with this minimum amount of initial private capital only if its strong parent will absorb all or part of its operating expenses and stand ready to inject additional private capital as the need develops. In order to attract large firms into the MESBIC program. recognizing that returns on investment can be delayed for many years, it was considered appropriate to permit MESBIC sponsors to commit capital only to the extent necessary to cover specific investment opportunities and operating expenses.

CURRENT PROPOSALS

A variety of legislative proposals affecting small business have come before Congress. These proposals place additional emphasis on increasing private participation in financing small business.

Whereas SBA can now extend its guaranty only to lenders that qualify as "banks or other lending institutions," the new proposals would enable SBA to guarantee loans made by persons or organizations "not normally engaged in lending activity." For the first time, SBA could directly guarantee loans to small business made by trusts, foundations, pension funds, churches and community groups, as well as service the loans made by these occasional lenders.

In order to cut red tape and minimize the time required to process a guaranteed loan, the legislation would authorize SBA to delegate authority to selected lenders to approve loans for guaranty without advance SBA approval in each case. A dollar ceiling would be imposed on the total amount of a lender's non-approved loans. SBA's advance approval of each loan is now required, even under the Simplified Blanket Loan Guaranty.

---

[27]Fn. 11, *supra.*

[28]Section 201 of S.3699.

[29]SBIC Regulation, 13 C.F.R. Part 107 (Rev. as of Jan. 1, 1970), amended by addition of new §107.813, 35 F.R. 11462, July 7, 1970.

The basic economics of an SBA-guaranteed loan would be affected by the [proposed] legislation in two ways. First, small businesses would be eligible to receive an interest subsidy during the first three years of an SBA guaranteed loan, which could reduce the effective loan interest rate by as much as 3 percent. The grant would go directly to the small business concern and not to the bank lender; special care would be exercised to assure that the bank did not increase its ordinary interest rate as a result of the subsidy. Within the 3 percent limit the subsidy could not exceed one-third of the total annual interest rate and could not reduce the effective interest rate below SBA's direct loan rate of 5½ percent. From the lender's standpoint the legislation would provide for an income tax deduction (with certain limitations) of 20 percent of the gross income derived by corporate lenders from SBA guaranteed loans.

In addition, the proposal would (1) exempt MESBICs from the provision preventing more than 50 percent ownership of an SBIC by a bank, (2) permit the incorporation of non-profit MESBICs, contributions to which would be deductible for income tax purposes, and (3) permit SBA to guarantee the timely payment of 100 percent of principal and interest for the full term of debentures issued by SBICs.

Tax Aspects

The tax provisions of the proposed legislation are designed to attract trained personnel and management talent to small business. Subchapter S of the Internal Revenue Code provides that certain small businesses may elect to be taxed as partnerships. A principal advantage is that operating losses, common in the early years of a business, may be deducted directly against ordinary income of its shareholders. The new proposal would increase from 10 to 30 the permissible number of shareholders in a Subchapter S corporation (enabling a company to issue employee stock options) and would permit a MESBIC to be a shareholder without the MESBIC's shareholders being counted against the new total of 30.

The tax treatment of early losses in a business would be liberalized by extending the present tax loss carry forward period from five years to ten years. This will be of particular use to new businesses that find it necessary during the early years to spend large amounts of money on items which cannot be capitalized, such as research and development.

In order to partially offset the advantages that large businesses have in attracting management talent, the tax legislation would also revise the stock option rules for small businesses to provide that an optionee could hold his option for up to eight years prior to exercise against the present five years. Also he could hold the stock for a minimum of one year after exercise (against the present three years) and still receive long-term capital gain treatment on his profit.

A persistent problem for small construction firms—particularly affecting minority contractors in inner-city areas—is their inability to obtain adequate surety bonding. Under the proposals, SBA would be authorized to guarantee surety companies against loss resulting from the breaching by small construction firms of bid bonds, payment bonds or performance bonds, on contracts amounting to as much as $500,000. Such a guarantee could cover up to 90 percent of the amount of a surety's loss, and would constitute a strong inducement for him to provide bonding protection to small firms.

SBA will never have sufficient funds to meet the needs of qualifying small concerns, without the help of private financial institutions. Congressional and executive mandates require the participation of private lenders, and authorize SBA to guarantee their loans—sometimes fully, more often up to 90 percent of the loan amount. Private lenders can provide further help by advising small concerns on the availability of SBA financial assistance in the less well-known programs. Among these, the lease guarantee, federally displaced business, product disaster, and trade adjustment programs deserve the attention of eligible small concerns and their bankers.·

SOURCES OF VENTURE CAPITAL*

VICTOR J. DANILOV

Nearly every scientist and engineer has considered—at one time or another—the feasibility of starting his own company. He is intrigued by the responsibility of running his own business, earning a fortune, and/or developing a successful product or service.

In most instances, however, such thinking rarely goes beyond the dream stage. The individual recognizes his shortcomings.as an entrepreneur; does not want to jeopardize his security; fails to develop a marketable idea; or lacks the necessary funds to launch a new company.

The lack of sufficient capital probably is the most common obstacle to the birth and success of new science- and tachnical-based companies. Without financial resources, it is virtually impossible even for the most daring individual or the best idea to succeed.

Before World War II, there was little hope of obtaining financial assistance from the outside, unless it came from relatives, friends, or an occasional private investor.

Commercial banks were not set up to provide "venture" or "risk" capital. Restricted by banking regulations and tradition, they could make only short-term loans, and then only with ample collateral.

Investment bankers were reluctant to supply the funds or to handle the sale of securities for a new company with limited resources and little or no record of performance.

But things are different today. It is possible to obtain venture capital from a number of sources, including some commercial and investment bankers under certain circumstances.

This change was brought about by the postwar establishment of venture capital investment groups that specialize in funding high-risk enterprises, often based on scientific or technological advances.

*From *Industrial Research* (October, 1966), pp. 68-74. Reprinted with permission.

As a result, it is much easier for a scientist or engineer to start his own company—providing he is willing to share the ownership.

The venture capital groups are interested primarily in "capital gain," and therefore seek to exchange cash for "equity"—a portion of the ownership. They are not in the loan business, although they occasionally will lend urgently needed funds to companies in their "portfolio."

The amount of equity that an entrepreneur must give up will vary with the size and nature of the investment, the record and worth of the company, and the bargaining abilities of the parties involved.

Sometimes, an investment is stalled because the individual refuses to surrender a portion of the stock in return for the capital. In such cases, venture capital representatives frequently will tell the entrepreneur that he is better off with a share of a well-financed company than with 100% of a failing one. And they generally are right.

It takes more than a willingness to give up equity to obtain venture capital. The venture capital groups are besieged by men and women seeking financing at almost any cost. Perhaps that is why the odds against obtaining venture capital are so high—something like 25 or 50 to 1.

Venture capital groups usually require a detailed report that includes: a brief history of the company; a description of its facilities, products, and services; an analysis of the present and future market; financial statements; a projection of sales, cash flow, and financial needs; biographical sketches of key personnel; personal, business, and technical references; the names of principal suppliers and customers; and other such pertinent information.

It normally takes about six to eight weeks for an investment application to be proceeded. During this time, the venture capital group checks on the performance and integrity of the principals; reviews the company's products, markets, and competition; studies the firm's organizational structure, facilities, and potential; and considers the financial and other plans.

Some applications are rejected almost upon presentation because insufficient time is allowed for appraisal; the project needs further development before it can be evaluated; the company's growth opportunities appear limited; the proposed valuation of the project or stock is unrealistic; and the company's plans are inconsistent with the venture capital firm's long-range objectives.

THREE STAGES OF INVESTMENT

Venture capital groups ordinarily are interested in investing at three stages in a company's development:

1. "Start-up" or "seed" money to finance launching of an enterprise.
2. "Venture" funds to carry the company to a size where it can secure capital and loans from the public stock market, commercial banks, and other conventional sources.
3. "Growth" capital for major expansion of the company.

Of the three stages, the first appears to have the least appeal to many venture capital people. It is the riskiest type of investment. However, it also promises the greatest gain.

Most venture capital groups prefer to have what they call a "track record" on investment applicants. This means they would like to see the entrepreneur start the business on his own, and then come to them after some years of operation. In this way, they feel they are better able to evaluate the performance and potential of the man and his company.

If an applicant lacks this background, venture capital representatives sometimes will equate experience as a manager or similar position of responsibility in their evaluation.

In preparing this article, *Industrial Research* found that nearly all major venture capital groups gave as much weight—if not more—to "management" as they did to the "idea" in evaluating investment opportunities.

Most venture capital officials said good ideas are plentiful, but that good management people who can exploit ideas are rare. As a result, many promising innovations are bypassed by venture capital groups simply because the principals do not appear to possess the necessary qualities.

Venture capital groups prefer "management teams" rather than "one-man shows." They feel management depth is essential because of the diversity of talents required in a growing company built on scientific or technological know-how. They also regard the team approach as a safeguard on their investment.

The amount of capital that can be raised from venture capital sources ranges from a few thousand to several million dollars. However, most venture capital firms rarely are interested in investments below $100,000 and seldom will go above $1 million. If there is a preference, it is between $200.000 and $300,000. This is a substantial investment that gives the venture capital group a sizeable interest in the typical company—without being a drain on its resources.

If the company's progress is satisfactory and additional financing is required at a later date, the venture capital firm generally will provide the funds or arrange for credit through conventional or other capital sources.

The three most common types of equity investments made by venture capital organizations are:

1 Common stock. The exchange of cash for shares is the most frequently employed investment method.
2. Convertible debentures. In this case, the venture capital firm lends money to the company and receives a debenture (a note of indebtedness). The investment group then either can accept repayment of the loan or convert the debenture into an equivalent amount of the company's common stock at a prearranged price.
3. Loans with warrants. In return for a loan, the company issues warrants that gives the venture capital firm an option to purchase common stock—usually at a favorable price—during a specified period of time.

Venture capital groups often expect to have one or more representatives on the board of directors as a result of their investment. They also believe that serious consideration should be given to their "suggestions."

Among the typical suggestions are: a working board with regular meetings; the hiring of a competent financial officer; and preparation of periodic progress reports and financial statements.

The venture capital firm sometimes will offer so-called "management services," which may include such things as staff assistance, financial planning, and marketing guidance. A nominal fee usually is charged for such services.

In general, venture capital organizations are not interested in having controlling interest in a company. Some believe control discourages management.

On the other hand, venture capital groups tend to stay away from investments that give them less than 10% of the stock. They feel they are not able to be effective in such a minority position, and that the returns are not worth the effort. An investment of 20% to 30%, therefore, is more common.

Although goals vary, most venture capital firms hope to double their investments in three years and triple their money in five years. But it seldom works out that way. Some companies fail, while others succeed beyond the most optimistic forecasts.

The basic venture capital objective is quite simple—to make the company grow and prosper so that its stock can be traded publicly or that it can be merged with a larger company. In either case, the venture capital firm benefits by receiving a considerably higher price for its investment.

Ideally, the entrepreneur who conceived the company and led it to success also benefits in the process. In most instances, he and his associates gain even more than the venture capital group. Unfortunately, this is not always the case. Sometimes the entrepreneur loses control in his fight for survival, and occasionally he has to be replaced because of his lack of management abilities.

Today, there are at least 11 principal sources of venture capital. Of this number, five can be considered general sources and six can be classified as specialists in venture capital.

The general sources are: relatives and friends, commercial banks, investment bankers, private investors, and large companies. Each has its advantages and drawbacks.

Aside from personal savings, the most common source of new venture funding is the entrepreneur's relatives and friends. However, the financing frequently is insufficient to provide the impetus and the continuing support needed "to make it big."

Although still conservative, some commercial banks have become a source of limited venture capital. In many cases, they will make short-term loans as part of a financing package worked out with a wholly owned or affiliated small business investment company that specializes in long-term equity investments.

The investment banker can assist the entrepreneur in at least three ways— he can invest in the company himself, either personally or as a firm; he can arrange for private placement with wealthy individuals; or he can handle the public offering of the stock. Unfortunately, it usually is necessary for the company to be firmly established and to pay a premium for the service.

Private investors—who generally learn about venture capital opportunities through commercial and investment bankers—quite often are willing to invest large sums in speculative ventures. However, they sometimes are impatient about the bonanza.

A large corporation occationally will invest in a smaller company, especially if the former is interested in diversifying and the latter is a supplier. But the arrangement can be unhealthy from a business standpoint.

SIX MAJOR SOURCES

In addition to the foregoing general investment groups, there are six types that specialize in venture capital funding. It is in this area that most of the high-risk financing is taking place today.

The six major venture capital sources are:

1. The venture capital arms of family fortunes, such as the Phipps, Rosenwalds, Whitneys, and Rockefellers.
2. Publicly held venture capital corporations typified by American Research & Development Corp. of Boston.
3. Private venture capital organizations, such as Payson & Trask in New York and Davis & Rock of San Francisco.
4. Informal investment syndicates, usually made up of Wall Street financiers and arranged by investment bankers and lawyers.
5. Small business investment companies (SBICs) licensed and partially financed by the federal government to assist small businesses.
6. State-licensed business development corporations designed to further the state or regional economy. Unlike the others, the development funds usually are interested in making mortgage loans rather than equity investments.

Perhaps the best way to obtain a better insight into venture capital financing is to take a closer look at some of the organizations that are active in the field.

Although history is filled with instances where individuals—and some companies—made available venture capital "for a share of the action," it was not until after World War II that the concept was formalized with the establishment of a number of private and publicly held venture capital investment groups.

Two of the early entries in the venture capital field were Bessemer Securities Corp., established in 1924 by Henry C. Phipps, co-founder of the Carnegie steel empire, and the Starwood Corp., created in 1929 by Julius Rosenwald, then chairman of Sears, Roebuck, & Co.

Although Bessemer made an occasional venture capital investment in the 1920s and 1930s, it was not until after World War II that a "special situations" office was formed to seek out such investments.

At present, Bessemer has about $20 million in venture capital invested in some 30 companies, with approximately half in the technical field. The companies include firms in such diverse areas as magnetics, cryogenics, electronics, oceanography, testing, instruments, and mining.

The Rosenwald family investment firm was known for many years as the NWL Corp. before it became Starwood Corp. in 1960. It was named after Nathan W. Levin, who directed the investments for more than 30 years.

It was Rosenwald money that helped to establish such companies as Litton Industries Inc., Southern Nitrogen Co., and Fansteel Metallurgical Corp.

Starwood has made 14 major investments and six minor financings in recent years. Amont the current investments are Nuclear Materials & Equipment Corp., nuclear materials; Trans-Video Corp., community television antennas; and General Corp. of Ohio, insurance.

One of Starwood's most successful ventures was United Technical Publications, which publishes *Electronics Products, Electronic Engineers Master,* and other publications. Starwood and American Research & Development Corp. invested $500,000 in United Technical Publications in 1963 for a 51% interest. Early this year [1966], the stock was sold for $5.5 million.

PREWAR VENTURES PAY OFF

Some of the prewar experiences of John Hay Whitney and Laurance S. Rockefeller convinced them that they could make money while being of assistance to inventive minds.

"Jock" Whitney inherited about a third of his father's $250-million estate in 1927. Upon graduation from college, he joined the Lee, Higginson, & Co. brokerage and investment house in New York. While learning the investment business, he became acquainted with Langbourne Williams, a former Lee, Higginson man, who was fighting to gain control of a sulphur company called Freeport Texas.

Because he liked Williams and was convinced of the merits of the latter's case against the Freeport management, Whitney invested $500,000 in the company's common stock. Williams succeeded in his bid and helped elect Whitney as chairman of Freeport's reorganized board—a position held by Whitney until 1957.

Meanwhile, the company's name was changed to Freeport Sulphur and Whitney's original investment grew to more than $10 million. During this period, Whitney also dabbled in an assortment of other ventures.

He helped to finance the development and introduction of the "Technicolor" film process; backed the production of the most successful motion picture in history, "Gone with the Wind;" and put money into a number of publications, including *Newsweek* and *Scientific American*.

After returning from World War II service, Whitney formed J.H. Whitney & Co. with four partners, most of whom were lawyers or investment bankers. With $10 million in capital the partnership sought to invest in venture capital opportunities found to be "interesting, attractive, and constructive."

Among the early investments were the Spencer Chemical nitrogen chemical firm, the Minute Maid frozen orange juice idea, and San Jacinto Petroleum, an oil and gas producer. All became highly successful, with the Whitney partnership selling its stock at sizeable profits.

However, there also were failures, such as Standard Perlite wallboard from volcanic ash, Kyptar photographic film, Circuitron printed circuits, and Hodges Research & Development.

Since its founding 20 years ago, J.H. Whitney & Co. has received more than 8,000 investment proposals and made about 80 investments—or approximately 1 out of 100 solicitations. It is difficult to calculate how much of a return the company has received on its initial $10 million in capital, but a safe estimate would be that it has been multiplied at least 12 times. More than four-fifths has come from seven key investments.

Among the recent Whitney investments have been General Signal electronic and electrical appliances, Global Marine Exploration floating oil drilling vessels, Memorex computers and instrumentation, and Peninsular Chemresearch specialty flouride chemicals.

Laurance S. Rockefeller also became interested in venture capital in the 1930s. He made his first risk capital investment in 1938 when he rescued one of his boyhood heroes, Capt. Eddie Rickenbacker, who was about to lose control of the young, struggling Eastern Air Lines.

Rockefeller helped to round up $3.5 million to refinance the airline. He bought 24,400 shares of Eastern at $9. The original $219,000 investment—and subsequent purchases—now are worth millions and Rockefeller is Eastern's largest stockholder.

In 1939, the young Rockefeller helped out another pioneer in the airplane field, J.S. McDonnell, who sought funds to develop an advanced type of fighter that was still on the drawing board. Rockefeller put up $10,000 to help McDonnell Aircraft Corp. get its start. When the holdings became worth $400,000, he sold out to reinvest in another new idea.

Immediately following World War II, Rockefeller resumed his venture capital investments by putting $500,000 into a sputtering rocket company, Reaction Motors. When the firm—which helped to develop the jet engine—was merged with Thiokol Chemical Corp. in 1958, Rockefeller received Thiokol stock worth more than $4 million for his investment.

During the postwar period, Rockefeller decided to expand his venture capital operations. He added a staff to seek out promising ideas worthy of venture capital support, with the emphasis in two areas—aerospace and electronics.

In 1950, several thousands in Rockefeller money was invested in the Marquardt Aircraft Co., which was working on ramjet propulsion. A few years later, the investment was worth millions when Marquardt began making ramjets for the Bomarc missile.

When the Itek Corp. was organized in 1957 to develop optical information-handling equipment, Rockefeller was asked to provide some of the seed money. He invested $875,000, which became worth approximately $10 million in two years.

SUCCESSES—AND FAILURES

Among the Rockefeller venture capital investments in recent years have been the GCA Corp. (formerly Geophysics Corp. of America), United Nuclear Corp., Mithras Inc., Scientific-Atlanta, Electronic Specialties, Thermo Electron Engineering Corp., and Cyronetics Corp. (Magnion Inc.).

Some of the investments have been sold off, including Piasecki Helicopter (now Boeing's Vertol Div.), Airborne Instruments Laboratory (Cutler-Hammer), Aircraft Radio Corp. (Cessna), and General Applied Science Laboratories (Marquardt).

As with Whitney, a number of Rockefeller's investments fell flat. For example, the Wallace Aviation Corp. was sold at a loss when its cold-metal process for making jet engine compressors proved to be more costly than conventional methods.

Two other ventures that failed were Platt LePage & Co., in the helicopter field, and Island Packers, a canning endeavor that folded from the lack of fish.

Rockefeller's venture capital efforts differ from others in two principal respects:

1. Sometimes the idea for a new company will be conceived within the organization, and then a management team will be recruited to operate the company, as was done with GCA Corp.
2. Investments usually are made on a one-third ratio basis, with management, Rockefeller, and an investment partner sharing equally.

When GCA was founded in 1958, Milton Greenberg, director of the Air Force's Geophysics Research Directorate, was sought out and hired as the person best qualified to run the company. In return, Greenberg and other top scientists and officers in the company were given one-third of the equity.

Rockefeller is an unusual venture capitalist in several other respects. With a personal fortune estimated at around $200 million, he hardly needs high-risk investments. But he believes that the wealthy have a social responsibility to risk their riches, to assist creative minds, and to support constructive projects.

It was the early venture capital exploits of Rosenwald, Whitney, and Rockefeller that called attention to the need for—and opportunities in—high-risk investments based in science and technology.

However, it was not until after World War II that investment firms specializing in venture capital came into being. The technological explosion during and after the war constributed to this development.

The first publicly held venture capital corporation was founded in Boston in 1946. It was estabished by a group of civic-minded business leaders who recognized the need for providing financial support for new ideas that offer promise of higher production, employment, and living standards.

Today, American Research & Development Corp. is one of the largest and most successful venture capital organizations. It has investments in 44 companies and net assets of approximately $80 million.

ARD was conceived primarily by two men—Ralph E. Flanders, president of the Boston Federal Reserve Board who later represented Vermont in the Senate, and Merrill Griswold, chairman of the Massachusetts Investors Trust.

They were aided by Dr. Karl T. Compton, then president of Massachusetts Institute of Technology; Gen. Georges Doriot, a professor in industrial management at Harvard Business School who served in the Army as director of the Military Planning Div. of the Office of the Quartermaster General during World War II; and a group of financiers who helped to provide the initial capital of nearly $3.4 million.

Included in this latter group were: Paul F. Clark, president of John Hancock Life Insurance Co.; Lessing J. Rosenwald, chairman of Sears, Roebuck, & Co.; David L. Luke, president of West Virginia Pulp & Paper Co.; and Thomas Lamont, chairman of J. P. Morgan & Co.

Flanders served as the first president of ARD, but turned the job over to Doriot in the first year following his election to the Senate. The soft-spoken "General" has headed ARD ever since.

HELPS START 80 COMPANIES

During its 20 years of operation, American Research & Development Corp. has helped to father more than 80 companies—nearly all based on technological innovations.

One of ARD's first ventures was High Voltage Engineering Corp. It invested $200,000 in MIT Professor Robert J. Van de Graaff's research in supervoltages, which produced the so-called "Van de Graaff" accelerator. While ARD's holdings in the company have decreased from 55% to 6% of the voting securities, the investment has resulted in a gain of more than $16 million over the years.

There are many similar success stories among ARD's diversified investments. For instance, a $403,000 investment in Ionics Inc., which specializes in electrochemical and membrane processes for desalination, is now worth almost $3 million; a $581,339 investment in Teledyne Inc., a manufacturer of aviation and geophysical instruments, has appreciated to $5.6 million; and a $1.2 million interest in Optical Scanning Corp. (formerly Digitek Corp.), a producer of optical mark sensing equipment, grew to over $3 million within six years.

The most recent big winner is Digital Equipment Corp., which makes equipment to gather, store, and process data. ARD helped to establish the company with a $408,125 investment in 1957. Digital Equipment went public last August, and now ARD's interest in the computer upstart is worth more than $40 million.

Among the other companies in ARD's portfolio are: Adage Inc., hybrid computers; Camco Inc., petroleum tools and services; Giannini Controls Corp., electronic instruments and controls; Solid State Products Inc., specialized semiconductors; Cordis Corp., medical instrumentation; Cooper, Tinsley Laboratories Inc., pharmaceuticals, and Tridair Industries, air cargo equipment.

Under Doriot's leadership, American Research & Development Corp. has been instrumental in establishing similar venture capital investment groups in Canada and Europe in the last twelve years.

ARD has a $464,305 investment (9% of the voting securities) in Canadian Enterprise Development Corp. and a $511,642 interest (8%) in the European Enterprises Development Co.

Thus far, the two foreign groups have made only limited investments, but they show the potential of duplicating ARD's record in this country.

Doriot points out that ARD has no specific formula for financing projects. "Each investment opportunity is considered separately, and the form of participation is tailored to meet the individual requirements of the situation." However, ARD does seek an equity position or its equivalent in all ventures.

The amount of capital invested also is flexible. In general, initial investments are in the $500,000 to $1 million range. "But situations requiring capital in excess of $1 million also are of decided interest, regardless of the field," adds Doriot.

In cases where substantial capital or specialized assistance is needed, ARD sometimes will obtain the support of other groups in the investment.

Despite the care exercised in investments, ARD has had its share of losers. In fact, the very first investment—in a degreasing gun—flopped. Among its other failures have been companies involved in quick-frozen apple juice, deveined shrimp, audio devices, and tuna processing.

MARRIAGE OF MONEY AND TALENT

Another venture capital investment firm that was born following World War II was the partnership of Payson & Trask in New York. In this instance, it was a marriage of the money of Mrs. Charles S. Payson (the former Joan Whitney) and the investment skills of Frederick K. Trask, a commercial banker.

The firm was organized in 1947 by Mrs. Payson, who has used her share of the Whitney fortune to invest in industry, entertainment, and sports and to support worthy projects in medicine, education, fine arts, and charity. She is best known as owner of the New York Mets baseball team.

Mrs. Payson put up several million dollars and gave Trask a free hand in organizing and developing the firm. Since then, the firm has invested in approximately 60 companies. It currently has an interest in 25 companies, with about half being technical.

Unlike many other venture capital firms, Payson & Trask is not interested in financing the launching of new companies. It prefers to wait until the company has existed a year or two before considering investment.

Payson & Trask makes investments ranging fom $25,000 to $500,000. Although it does not seek control, the firm wants a "position of consequence" in investments, according to Marshall Rawle, managing partner. This means at least 20% to 60% of the equity and one or two representatives on the board.

'MANAGEMENT' IS KEY

The most significant factor in a company appraisal is "management," states Robert D. Stillman, one of the partners. Although the firm does not have a checklist of desirable management characteristics, it has found that successful managements usually exhibit a combination of "high character and integrity, dedication and energy, solid technical competence, humility in financial and business areas, and the flexibility to meet changing conditions," Stillman explains.

Among the investments of Payson & Trask have been: Hartford Steel Ball Co., Ohio Rubber Co., Trygon Electronics Inc., Hampshire Chemical Corp., Crystalonics Inc., United States Instrument Corp. and Maumee Chemical Co. (recently merged with Sherwin-Williams).

A number of venture capital firms have followed in the footsteps of Payson & Trask. Among the leaders are Davis & Rock of San Francisco; Draper, Gaither, & Anderson of Palo Alto; and Fox, Wells, & Rogers of Stamford, Conn.

Davis & Rock probably has had the fastest growth among all the venture capital investment firms. From a modest beginning several years ago, it has earned more than $30 million.

The man largely responsible for this success if Arthur Rock, a virtually penniless security analyst who became a millionaire through his venture capital investments.

The whole thing started in 1957 when Rock was working on underwriting deals for Hayden, Stone Inc. He learned about a group of Beckman Instruments scientists who wanted to start their own company. Within a few months, Rock helped to arrange financing for the group from Fairchild Camera & Instrument.

The new company was called Fairchild Semiconductor. It flourished so well that two years later Fairchild Camera & Instrument exercised an option and bought control for $3 million in stock.

The coup increased Rock's bankroll and threw the spotlight on a dozen glamour stocks that he had recommended in a series of market letters for Hayden, Stone Inc.

In 1961, he cautioned investors that the stocks had gone too high. Again,

Rock proved right as many of the leaders became victims of the 1961-62 crash in electronic stocks.

It was at this time that Rock left Hayden, Stone (although he remains a limited partner) and joined with Thomas J. Davis Jr., a lawyer and former vice president of Kern County Land, to form the venture capital partnership of Davis & Rock. The initial capital of $3.5 million was provided by some 30 investors.

Then came a series of investments that brought fame and fortune:

The first deal was to exchange $200,000 of D&R stock for 13,333 shares of Teledyne Inc., which was started with Rock's aid in 1961 by two Litton Industries vice presidents. Later, D&R paid $460,000 for another 15,932 shares. The investment has nearly tripled in value since then.

The second major investment was in Scientific Data Systems, formed by a spinoff group from Packard-Bell's ailing computer division. Davis & Rock invested $280,000 in SDS. In 1965, SDS netted $3 million in profits from sales of some $45 million. D&R's capital gain amounted to more than $20 million.

The third development was Astrodata Inc., a spinoff from Epsco Inc., a producer of data processing equipment. Davis & Rock bought 60,000 shares for $5 per share and earned a profit of $2 million in two years.

One of the newest partnerships in the venture capital field is Greylock & Co., a Boston-headquartered firm backed by a group of six prominent families for the purpose of equity capital investments. It was formed a year ago [1965].

The general partners are William Elfers, a former vice president of American Research & Development Corp., and Daniel S. Gregory, formerly assistant to the president of John P. Chase Inc., investment counselor and mutual fund manager.

Greylock & Co. invests principally in young growth companies having promising records and needing developmental capital, and established small- or medium-sized companies which are beginning new expansion programs or bringing in outside participants for the first time. It is interested in investments in the range of $200,000 to $600,000.

686 SBICs ESTABLISHED

The greatest number of venture capital investment firms are SBICs that were spawned by the Small Business Investment Act of 1958. At the last counting, there were 686 licensed small business investment companies. They have made available nearly $1 billion to small businesses in over 20,000 separate transactions since the act was passed sixteen years ago.

A business is considered "small" and eligible for SBIC financing if its assets do not exceed $5 million; its net assets are not more than $2.5 million; and its average net income after taxes for each of the preceding two years was under $250,000 (without benefit of tax loss carry-forward).

The SBICs come in all sizes and types. Their individual capitalization ranges from $300,000 to $29 million. Some are quite broad and others are highly specialized. Of the 686 small business investment companies, only about two-thirds are active.*

*Current (1974) SBIC statistics are provided in the updated Chase/Proctor article, pp. 128-29.

Most of the SBICs are owned by relatively small groups of local investors. However, the stock of about 50 is publicly traded; more than 80 SBICs are partially or wholly owned by commercial banks; and some are subsidiaries of other corporations.

An SBIC may borrow up to double its private investment from the federal government participation of $4.7 million. It may use this money to finance small businesses in three ways—by straight loans, equity-type investments, or a combination of the two. All financings must be for at least five years, except that a borrower may elect to have a prepayment clause included in the financing agreement.

An SBIC may invest up to 20% of its capital in a single small business. For the smallest SBIC, the maximum loan or investment is $60,000; the largest is several million dollars.

SBICs can be found in all but six states (Maine, Nevada, North Dakota, South Dakota, Vermont, and Wyoming). Nearly half (330), however, are located in only four states—California with 118, New York with 102, Texas with 56, and Massachusetts with 54.

Of the 686 small business investment companies, about 30 have scientific or technological implications in their names. To this list could be added another 20 that have extensive investments in the science- or technical-based enterprise.

Among the leading SBICs are the Boston Capital Corp. of Boston, Narragansett Capital Corp. of New York, Greater Washington Industrial Investments Inc. of Washington D.C., First Capital Corp. of Chicago, Continental Capital Corp. of San Francisco, and Electronics Capital Corp. of San Diego (which is the largest).

All have heavy investments in companies based on scientific and technological innovations. They have started or given financial assistance to such companies as Potter Instrument Co., Possis Machine Corp., C-E-I-R Inc., Defense Research Corp., Tyco Laboratories Inc., B & F Instruments Inc., Data Products Inc., Basic Systems Inc., and Alpine Geophysical Associates Inc.

The 686 licensed SBICs currently are undergoing a thorough investigation by the Small Business Administration as a result of a Congressional probe into alleged irregularities in their operations, such as impairment of capital, the making of speculative real estate loans, failure to invest government funds, and disregard for reporting procedures. However, it does not appear that any of the leading SBICs are involved

The business development corporations licensed by states are comparable—in some respects—to the small business investment companies at the federal level. The principal difference is in their primary purpose—to serve a public need rather than to make a substantial profit. Another difference is the emphasis on long-term mortgage loans.

Although most are designed only to make high-risk, long-term loans as a means of helping industry and the economy to grow, a few also are interested in minority equity investments. The Southeastern Pennsylvania Development Fund, for example, frequently will make loans in which a portion can be converted to equity at a favorable price.

There are 24 business development corporations in 22 states. Only Pennsylvania—with three groups—has more than one business development corporation.

The first state business development corporation was the Development Credit Corp. of Maine, which was formed in 1949. The newest was just established in Colorado. The stockholders in nearly all business development corporations are business and civic leaders in the state.

The venture capital concept has proved so successful in the United States that similar investment groups are being formed in other countries.

In addition to the venture organizations in Canada and Europe that were mentioned earlier, there are comparable investment groups in Great Britain, Sweden, and Japan.

There are two major groups in Great Britain—the government-sponsored National Research Development Corp. and the privately financed Industrial & Commercial Finance Corp., which recently absorbed Technical Development Capital Ltd.

Established in 1948, the NRDC is an independent corporation financed by government loans and the income from licensing. Its primary objective is to promote the adoption by industry of new products and processes invented in government, university, and private laboratories by advancing money where necessary to bring them to a commercial stage.

The privately funded ICFC offers long-term financing in return for an equity interest. It has made investments in more than 1,700 companies since it was founded more than two decades ago.

Incentive AB was organized in Sweden eleven years ago and has venture capital investments in about a dozen companies. It is patterned after American Research & Development Corp.

In Japan, three small business investment companies have been organized under a 1963 act based on the American SBIC program. The investment groups—in Tokyo, Nagoya, and Osaka—only invest in "joint-stock companies" with a capital of less than 50 million yen ($139,000) or no more than 300 employes.

There appears to be ample venture capital available in this country—and to some extent abroad—if a scientist or engineer has a good idea, possesses management talents, and wants to start his own business.

There are a variety of sources looking for high-risk investments with promising growth potential. Frequently, these sources also offer invaluable management services in addition to financial aid.

But the aspiring entrepreneur usually must pay a price—the sharing of equity and some degree of control for cash and other assistance. And if business does not develop as anticipated, he even may find his company sold against his wishes.

This may appear to be a cruel world to the person who lacks the funds to exploit his idea. However, it also can be a happy one under the right circumstances.

Venture capital meets a definite need in science, industry, and the economy. But it is not free or without risk—for either the entrepreneur or the investor.

VENTURE CAPITAL:

PITFALLS, POSSIBILITIES*

D. BRUCE THORSEN

The scenario, an all too familiar orgy of overconfidence and naivete, runs like this:

A 26-year-old MBA with a year's experience in a large corporation decides to strike out on his own. Dutifully, a PERT network is prepared: two weeks for creation of business idea, three weeks macro-market evaluation and analysis (segmentation, distribution channels, price elasticities), three weeks for market research and test marketing, two weeks for preparing a confidential investment memorandum (with, of course, five-year pro formas whose confidence intervals are based on Schlaiferian probability theory), and, finally, an unspecified period for fund-raising.

Out of all this comes a business idea—in this case, to bottle low-priced private label soft drinks in returnable bottles; retail warehouses with on-site bottling facilities, which can be observed by curious customers, will be established. Growth plan: pilot store, then expand by franchise; market segmentation: 40 million-case private label market, growing at 8% per year (low prices and ecology-oriented returnable bottles are consumer needs), which should net 3% of the market segment or 1.2 million cases per year initially, *etc., etc., etc.* The investment memorandum was finished on time . . . 30-page text, 15-page financial pro formas, and one page describing capital requirements. He needs $200,-000 cash and will give up 20% of his company (the P/E of NYSE bottlers was 30X-40X which values his company at $1 million in two years). After six weeks he closes at the investment banker's attorney's office—a successful entrepreneur with $180,000 cash (the balance going to the investment banker and his attorney), he is ready to launch his company.

INTO CHAPTER X

Nine short months later he lacks enough cash to refund deposits to his ecology-minded customers, and one month thereafter a friend directs him to law books dealing with Chapter X on bankruptcy.

At this point, the questions and self-doubts finally begin. Why did I buy new bottling equipment for $60,000—and for cash in 60 days? . . .Why did I pick that location—all the traffic was on the other side of the road? . . . Who would have known that a $3 million private label bottler sold through liquor stores in the same area—and at lower prices than mine, with non-returnable bottles? . . . How come it took so long to find a mechanic who could run the equipment—five weeks without production really cut deep? . . . Why did the

*Reprinted with permission from the December 1972 *MBA* magazine, Copyright ©1972 by MBA Communications, Inc.

cash flow stay negative when pro formas accounted for every logical detail? . . .
Why did I end up at the cash register and even have to carry cases out to cars?. .
Why did I ever leave that air-conditioned executive training program?

REAL-WORLD DOUBTS

The point of this exercise is that the real-world doubts, the real-world questions, impinged too late on what was really a textbook theory for a textbook
company.

Starting or significantly expanding a small business is a time-consuming,
iterative process requiring simulaneous commitments from customers, suppliers, employees, and financiers—all pragmatically programmed by the entrepreneur for the near-term delivery of sales for a positive cash flow (but not
necessarily for an accounting profit). It is messy and frustrating.

A good idea is important, but timing is paramount. Wait patiently to be in
the right place at the right time to start-up, buy-out, or expand a small business. Cash capital is a required catalyst for "The Business;" it is the stuff that
churns the balance sheet and attracts people, but it does not automatically generate sales, product/service, customers, suppliers, employees, and management. A business is financed exclusively by sales. All other financial arrangements are necessary but tangential to sales. Business activities which do not
generate sales are business ideas imposed upon the market place by the
ego-trips of text-book entrepreneurs—they are not businesses.

BIG BROTHER RELATIONSHIPS

Entrepreneurship involves pushing and pulling as well as enlarging on what
conservatives would define as truth. More than ideas and money are required;
relationships in, around, and for the business must be developed by the entrepreneur. It requires "big brother" customers who are willing to commit and pay
promptly because they vitally need the product/service; or it requires "big
brother" suppliers who are willing to delay trade payables (or take equity) in an-
ticipation that your sales growth will mean their future sales growth; or it requires employees who are willing to work exceptionally hard for meager pay because they have a chance to accrue wealth in proportion to the growth of the
company; or it requires a "big brother" bank which advances periodic working
capital secured by receivables or inventory because they believe the float on your
account may someday be profitable.

Combinations of these "big brother" relationships enable the prudent entrepreneur and his venture capital partner to reasonably invest their time and
money in a start-up or expansion of a small business. Absence of these relationships means you are getting involved in a business idea, not a business. You're
acting irresponsibly on an ego trip—with your time and somebody else's money.

Before jumping in, the entrepreneur should carefully consider, at an intro-
spective distance, what he is planning to do and what he has in actuality done.
He should be prepared for and welcome the inevitable skepticism and hopefully
constructive criticism offered by the venture capitalist, his potential partner. If
you can, however, put together a good business idea with the right market op-

portunity, the SBIC (Small Business Investment Company) industry can be an important source of venture capital. The Small Business Investment Act of 1958 (Public Law 85-699) establishes the basis for SBIC activity. Section 102 of the law concisely states the policy and objective of the SBIC program:

> It is declared to be the policy of the Congress and the purpose of this Act to improve and stimulate the national economy in general and the small-business segment thereof in particular by establishing a program to stimulate and supplement the flow of private equity capital and long-term loan funds which small-business concerns need for the sound financing of their business operations and for their growth, expansion, and modernization, and which are not available in adequate supply: *Provided, however,* that this policy shall be carried out in such manner as to insure the maximum participation of private financing sources.

Generally, an entrepreneur will have no problem being eligible for an investment from an SBIC. The SBA generally considers a business "small" if: (1) its assets do not exceed $5 million, (2) its net worth does not exceed $2.5 million, and (3) its average net after tax income for each of the preceding two years was not more than $250,000.

Like other "private" sources of venture capital (such as pension funds, insurance companies, large corporate "business development" departments, wealthy family partnerships), the approximately 350 active SBIC's (with over $600 million in total assets) vary significantly in size, scope, and policy definitions of venture capital. Some SBIC's only close investments which are fully collateralized by real estate (first or second mortgages), accepting a high 15% interest rate (the maximum set by the Small Business Administration regulations) and requiring no equity participation. Other SBIC's prefer "pure" venture capital investments, buying common stock at $X per share. However, most SBIC's prefer a variation on the theme of long-term debentures with interest rates from 6%—12%, some junior collateral, warrants to purchase common stock, and possibly the personal guarantee of the entrepreneur(s).

SBIC PARTICIPATION

An SBIC is generally either a group of private investors (businessmen, lawyers, accountants, bankers), a public company registered with the SEC, or a commercial bank which has chosen to be licensed by the SBA for a combination of reasons: (1) SBIC's receive special tax treatment (especially in the establishment of liberal loss reserves and carry forwards which reduce downside risk and maximize cash flow), (2) SBIC's are eligible for SBA-guaranteed long-term loans based upon a multiple of the SBIC's capital, defined as stockholders' equity less retained earnings (an SBIC with a capital base ranging from $150,000 to $1 million is eligible for SBA debentures ranging from $300,000 to $2 million, or two times its capital; and, an SBIC with capital in excess of $1 million is eligible for SBA debentures in a multiple of three times its capital), and (3) because of the SBA licensing requirements and mandatory adherence to the SBA rules and regulations, the SBIC gains a quality of respectability and professionalism which non-SBIC's must earn over time.

An SBIC cannot initially invest more than 20% of its stockholders' equity (less retained earnings) in a single small business concern. For example: an

SBIC with $500,000 in stockholders' equity, $50,000 in retained earnings, and $900,000 in SBA debentures (its maximum leverage) is restricted to a maximum investment in a single small business concern of $90,000. This SBIC may invest less than $90,000 at its own discretion, but in order to invest more than $90,000 the SBIC must demonstrate to the SBA that second-round financing is required to protect its initial investment. Also, an SBIC cannot take control (*i.e.,* own more than 50%) of a small business unless it demonstrates to the SBA that its control position is required to protect its initial investment. Generally, the entrepreneur and the SBIC manager make the decision, and then the SBIC manager prepares the paperwork for SBA discussion and authorization.

SPREADING THE RISK

Because an SBIC is limited by the "20%-capital" rule, it is common for SBIC's to participate jointly in an investment. There are numerous cliques of SBIC's which regularly participate together in the same "deals," and in many instances they prefer to participate below their 20% maximum in order to spread the risk and to establish a wider scope of accessibility to good deals. Usually, the SBIC initially contacted by the entrepreneur will act as sponsor, and its managers will sell participations to other friendly SBIC's. This practice of sharing deals is not a disadvantage of an SBIC because, generally, any type of venture capital firm will attempt to involve others in order both to spread the financial risk and to confirm their own judgments as to the desirability of making the investment.

Contacting an SBIC should be done carefully and intelligently. An SBIC in your own geographical area is a reasonable place to start because, typically, venture capital participants (both SBIC and non-SBIC) like to know that the sponsor is able to regularly review and monitor the performance of the portfolio company. However, geography is only a preference, not a mandatory requirement of most SBIC's. Generally, small SBIC's have no full time person investigating potential investments; the stockholders moonlight as required. SBIC's with full-time professionals usually have one person per $1 to $2 million in total assets. Therefore, the staffing of most SBIC's is limited to from one to 20 professionals. They are pitched many deals, so they spend considerable time only with people by whom they are intuitively impressed during the initial encounter.

SBIC INFORMATION

There are several directories which include descriptions of SBIC's: (1) the SBA publishes on a quarterly basis a complete directory of SBIC's, listing name, address and size category. Generally, an individual SBIC's maximum investment per small business concern can be estimated by taking 20% of one-third of the "private capital size" detailed on the first page of the SBA directory. (Write: SBA, Investment Division, 1441 L Street N.W., Washington, D.C. 20416.) (2) Stanley M. Rubel publishes a *Guide to Venture Capital Sources* containing some interesting text and listing SBIC and non-SBIC venture capital firms (a rather detailed code system aids in understanding the unique features of each firm listed—write: Capital Publishing Corporation, 10

South LaSalle Street, Chicago, Ill. 60603). (3) The Management Institute, School of Management at Boston College prepared a study entitled *Venture Capital—A Guidebook for New Enterprise* for the New England and Regional Commission which was published on March 22, 1972 by the U.S. Government Printing Office. The 134-page study is a guide for the new entrepreneur and unique in its detailed sketches of many leading venture capital firms in the East and Mid-west. (Write: U.S. Government Printing Office, Re: Committee Print No. 75-292, Washington, D.C.)

A limited number of SBIC's are authorized by the SBA to invest predominately in a specified industry (primarily in real estate oriented industries); however, most SBIC's will review "any deal that makes sense"—which is not an especially meaningful or helpful policy. Yet, it is a realistic policy because the content of the business (*i.e.*, its industry) is only one factor considered within the total framework of criteria important to decision making.

Many SBIC's and non-SBIC's listen to entrepreneurs pitching start-ups—few, however, commit to such projects. A venture capitalist generally does not want to buy paper clips, rent typewriters, pay incorporation fees, advance deposits for office leases, or supply eating money for the entrepreneur. He wants to invest cash capital in activities and materials which produce "now" sales. Therefore, a going concern with a basic positive cash flow on which a significant expansion effort can be built (in the same or other product/service areas) is more desirable from the viewpoint of the venture capitalist.

SBIC's are a reasonably effective attempt by government and private financiers to solve the "chicken-or-the-egg" problem on which Darwin only hedged be recognizing that the fittest survive and the surviving are related to each other. Venture capital can be either the egg or it can be the chicken. It can help the fit survive, or it can inadvertently help the weak survive longer—the key is in the mind and hands of the lucky entrepreneur.

FIVE

The Growth Crisis

The man and his idea have made it through the start-up stage. The entrepreneur can now concentrate on the application of business fundamentals to take the firm through the growth stage. The unusual talents that were required to start the business will not necessarily ensure its survival during the growth stage. Sources of additional new capital must be located for major expansion; the owner-manager must learn to delegate some of his responsibilities and reduce his work load; personnel administration procedures must be developed; product life cycles must be monitored, and new products added; long-range planning must be implemented; and the consumer markets must be reexamined to determine the characteristics of the heavy users. As the business grows, the methods and procedures used to manage the business must change. New practices must be integrated into the changing business environment. A complete understanding of basic business fundamentals is vital during a rapid growth if these changes are to be effectively managed. It is now time for the venture to be placed in perspective as an on-going enterprise.

The entrepreneur also has a life cycle, as does the company. It is during the growth stage in the company's development that the entrepreneur typically begins to be ineffective in managing the business. He discovers that organizational and long-range planning, personnel supervision, and staff meetings and consultations are not satisfying his motivational needs. The characteristics that made him a successful entrepreneur, able to create a product to capture an unfilled market need, are not the same characteristics that will enable him to become an effective executive. If the entrepreneur is concerned about the future growth of the business, he will gather together a professional management team to manage the firm's operations, while he either sells out or heads up new product ventures within the firm.

The entrepreneur who is successful will have brought his business through three critical stages of growth. In the first article, *Critical Stages of Small Business Growth,* Lawrence Steinmetz presents his business growth model and reviews the three crisis phases. Using the conventional "S" curve,

150

Steinmetz takes the reader through the slow start-up stage, involving direct involvement of the entrepreneur in every facet of the business, to the high growth stage, involving the transformation of the entrepreneur into a manager; and to the final maturity stage, where the entrepreneur-manager has divested himself of direct operating control. Each of these stages ends in a crisis involving personnel expansion, competition, and operating and profitability problems.

The first stage ends with the entrepreneur faced with an overburdening work load. Success in the business has resulted in excessive amounts of record keeping and personnel administration. The second stage crisis results from an excessive business overhead growth, power plays in the organization, and production problems. At the last critical stage, significant competitive forces exist, the rate of return on invested capital decreases, unprofitable products exist, and large amounts of capital resources are needed for expansion into national markets. If the owner-founder is to remain in control of his company, his actions must be managerially effective, especially during these three critical stages, otherwise the venture will end in failure.

It is during the second or high-growth stage of the business that plans must be made for its long-run continued success. Informal planning by the entrepreneur may overlook some of the factors affecting the growth of the business—factors that in some cases may result in a business failure. A more formalized and comprehensive examination of the company and its environment is required. The need for new product development and organizational, marketing, and financial changes in the company is not as likely to be obscured if sufficient forethought is being given to the firm's operations. The second article in this chapter, *Approaches to Long Range Planning in Small Business,* by George Steiner, discusses a variety of approaches that the small firm can use in formulating its objectives, strategies, and policies.

How other than through a systematic planning process will the entrepreneur be able to take advantage of all profitable opportunities that may occur in the future while avoiding major crises in the business? He must plan strategically if he is to effectively achieve future company goals and objectives. What resources and alternatives are available to the firm to handle these growth crises? How will future changes in the environment influence the firm? What steps are required to meet future product promotion and distribution goals that will maximize the market opportunities? Steiner presents a conceptual model depicting the types of business plans and outlines the necessary steps in their development, implementation, and monitoring. Various planning procedures and techniques are examined, including check-off lists, master planning guides, return-on-investment calculations, break-even analysis, cash flow forecasts, and pro forma financial statements. To ensure that the value from the planning process exceeds the planning costs, Steiner urges that the planning tasks be minimized to satisfy only the entrepreneur's situational needs.

During the high growth stage many entrepreneurs are limited in their effectiveness in managing their companies by an underlying emotional need to control every aspect of the firm's operations. In the fourth article, *Lengthening Your Shadow — The Key to Small Business Growth,* O. G. Dalaba contends that one of the most important factors in the firm's continued growth is the entrepreneur's ability to recruit and motivate the types of managerial and professional talent necessary to achieve the objectives formulated in the long-range planning process.

Equally important, according to Frank Friedlander and Hal Pickle, is the satisfaction experienced in their work by the personnel at the operating level of the organization. In their article, *Components of Effectiveness in Small Organizations,* they also stress the importance of the firm's societal relationships, that is, the degree to which it contributes to community progress, meets its responsibilities to governmental regulatory and taxing bodies, and satisfies the needs or fulfills the expectations of its customers, suppliers, and creditors. These considerations, too, should be reflected in the firm's long-range growth plans.

To recapitulate, during the high growth stage the firm may be in danger from the entrepreneur who, having started the firm with an idea and a dream, continues his romance with his product. Maximizing profits may no longer be the chief concern of the entrepreneur. It is during this stage that the firm's management must become more deeply involved with human relations or behavioral problems, with the application of basic business planning procedures, and with the variety of demands made upon the firm in its external environment. To continue a successful business development, management must be able to reflect back on itself and determine where changes in its plans and products are required. It becomes an organizational crisis when the entrepreneur cannot recognize that he may no longer possess the proper blend of talents for running his company.

CRITICAL STAGES

OF SMALL BUSINESS GROWTH*

LAWRENCE L. STEINMETZ

Are you working longer hours and enjoying it less? Has it seemed that your business expands but your profits do not? Are the "little guys" taking all the gravy business? Do you feel you have to do something, but you don't know what? Maybe an explanation is in order.

Most men who have been successful in operating their own businesses seem to have been able, intuitively or instinctively, to figure out what causes waning profits, organizational headaches, and acute personnel problems. They have

*From *Business Horizons* (February, 1969), pp. 29-36. Reprinted with permission.

managed to revitalize their businesses when—if not before—such problems occur. Unfortunately, many small businessmen have not had such insight. For these, this article will describe the three critical phases of small business growth. These phases are critical because failure to live through them will result in the death of the business, either because the business must be liquidated or sold to another company because continued operations would be unprofitable.

THE TYPICAL GROWTH CURVE

It has been known for some time that the growth pattern of the typical small business is S-shaped. This growth curve shows the stages of a firm's growth and their critical phases (see accompanying figure). The three critical areas are Stage 1, which occurs in the direct supervision stage of growth; Stage 2, which occurs in the supervised supervision stage; and Stage 3, which occurs in the indirect control stage.

Stage I problems occur about the time the organization has 25 or 30 employees and $500,000-$750,000 in invested capital. If the organization lives through its problems and difficulties at this stage, it develops into a Stage II business. At this point, the organization experiences very rapid growth, increases in sales volume, additions of personnel, and improved profitability. Most organizations having between 30 and 300 employees, and with assets of perhaps $5-$10 million dollars, are in Stage II. It is far away the most profitable stage of growth for the small business, the time at which the *rate of return* on in-

FIGURE 4   Stages of Organizational Growth and
Their Critical Phases

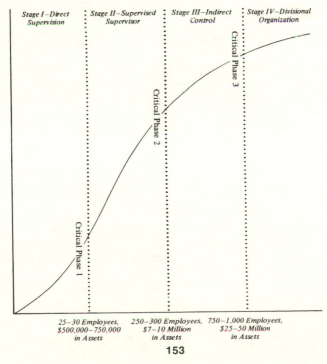

vested funds will far exceed the returns in Stages I and III. Unfortunately, a critical point is reached in Stage II (when the firm has 250-300 employees, $7-$10 million in assets)—a point where the rapid rate of growth begins to hit its peak and, again, death of the firm may occur. Death here usually does not mean liquidation, but it does mean failure (usually via merger) and loss of identity of the original small business.

If the small businessman has enough foresight or luck, he will guide his business through this second critical phase and will arrive at Stage III. Stage III is delightful for the small businessman, because the odds of death of the business are now considerably reduced; the firm has "arrived" by most people's standards. It is characterized by total indirect control on the part of the small businessman.

Now for the real question at hand: what are the tip-offs that should alert the small businessman that his business is approaching the critical phases in its growth, and what can be done to obviate the accompanying problems?

STAGE I—LIVE OR DIE

The prognosis for the small businessman just starting out—even if he is successful—is a fairly limited rate of return on his investment. At this stage the small businessman is a rather pathetic individual. As Collins and Moore have said:

> The image of the entrepreneur as a great inventor and great promoter or the great and daring risk-taker simply doesn't square with the facts. Reality is far less spectacular than this. In fact, the beginning entrepreneurship turns out to be a mundane affair and not at all heroic. There is the entrepreneur without capital resource, without apparent social skills, and without even a good idea. No respectable element in the community is even aware of him, let alone ready to help him.[1]

In short, the stereotype of the small businessman in the early stage of organizational growth is an unimaginative man who feels he has a good idea; whose role as a leader of his business is largely a result of his ownership rights rather than leadership talents; and who may or may not be able to develop a few loyal employees. Fundamentally, he is relying on personal skills or a unique product (or method or market) of which he can take advantage. He is usually not concerned about the rate of return, being more concerned with keeping the sheriff away from the door. However, assuming that he is successful—that he is not among the 50 percent of the people who will lose their business and 44 percent of their savings[2]—he will experience a slow but sure increase in sales and profitability. Unfortunately, this is where his problems come in; he is at the threshold of the first critical stage in his organization's growth.

A critical stage in growth is reached at this point because prior to this time the business has been a one-man operation, experiencing no real management problems other than "buying low and selling high." However, as the level of business increases a myriad of problems develop: paperwork multiplies,

[1]Orvis F. Collins and David G. Moore with Darab B. Unwalla, *The Enterprising Man* (East Lansing, Mich.: Michigan State University Press, 1964), pp. 242-43.

[2]Lawrence L. Steinmetz, John B. Kline, and Donald P. Stegall, *Managing the Small Business* (Homewood, Ill.: Richard D. Irwin, Inc., 1966), p. 29.

personnel must be added to the payroll, promised dates are not met, facilities get crowded, and so on. At first, of course, a few extra working hours are sufficient to cope with these problems. However, if business is good these minor problems rapidly assume major proportions. Paperwork is not only time-consuming, but more and more is required: the Internal Revenue Service begins to demand more elaborate tax information; bills begin trickling in at all times of the month; and accounts receivable begin to lag merely because statements are not mailed.

Furthermore, the increasing number of personnel begins to complicate matters. First, of course, the manager must spend more and more time in recruiting, selecting, developing, and training new employees. Then there is the problem of maintaining an acceptable relationship with employees already on the payroll. Once enough employees are added, the small businessman must begin to comply with unemployment compensation, minimum wage laws, and so on. The problems confronted by the small businessman, once he achieves a modicum of success, may be enumerated briefly:

1. His organization becomes too large to permit him to supervise the efforts of all his people directly.
2. With inadequate supervision, some of his employees become disloyal and begin to resent the hard-driving attitude of the owner, thus creating motivational problems.
3. Competition sets in and gets keener because others see a "good thing" going and sense the possibility of quick or easy profit.
4. The owner-manager (who heretofore has not had to be a real manager but just an owner-worker) is under increasing pressure to delegate work. He usually delegates ineffectively because he is not comfortable in this role.
5. Some of the growth pains of the success image begin to set in—the garage-factory gets too small, the rented facilities somehow seem cluttered, and new quarters seem to be urgently (and expensively) in order.
6. The market for the unique skill (or product or service) of the small businessman begins to dry up, shift toward some other skill, product or service, or, worst of all, is stolen by a (giant) competitor.
7. The manager is continuously pressed for "time to do what needs doing."
8. The manager experiences an overload of worry.
9. All difficulties become problems of crisis proportions.

These problems normally beset the small businessman when he is hiring between ten and thirty employees, and indicate the point on his growth curve where he faces the first serious threat to the continued existence of his business. And the facts are that if he does not begin to think in terms of overcoming these problems, he can expect to go out of business. His competition will become increasingly strong, he will have more personnel problems, his accounting and record-keeping problems will become a "stone around his neck," and he may find that he is being outstripped by other small businesses or by a giant that "doesn't like him."

At this stage, unfortunately, either the small businessman will succeed or he will fail. Statistics show that he cannot stagnate and stay small, nor can he even entertain the notion of hoping that his business will stabilize. He must press on or his business will die. Of course if he is a man who is aware of what it means to manage—to plan, organize, direct, and control—he will pass through this critical phase, will move into Stage II, and become a capable supervisor of supervisors. If not, his business is doomed. But how does he move successfully into Stage II?

STAGE II—BEING A MANAGER

The activities of those small businessmen who successfully enter Stage II in the normal growth pattern of their firms are entirely different from those actions taken by the owner-worker of the Stage I business. The stage II small businessman truly becomes a manager rather than a mere owner of his operation. He assumes a certain entrepreneurial aura, partly because of success (he has, after all, become successful) and partly because of charisma. Further, both of these images feed on each other and combine with the fact that normally he will be making more money than ever before in his life—probably more than 95 percent of the working population in his community.

Being a successful, charismatic individual is not the only characteristic of the owner of the small business during growth in Stage II. Typically, he devotes a great deal of attention to being a manager. Suddenly, perhaps accidentally, he learns how to delegate. Furthermore, he learns how to delegate through one or two levels of command and develops good "lieutenants." Another characteristic of the manager in this stage is that he usually develops a new method or gimmick to enhance or capitalize on the unique skill, product, or service which he found so useful in Stage I. He may diversify his line or service, capitalize on the use of waste material, or perhaps even integrate horizontally or vertically.

In addition, he now becomes a far more adept financial manager and managerial expert. He becomes aware (by observing competition, talking to other successful small businessmen, reading, or other education) that there are accepted norms or standards of performance which he should be obtaining in his business. He may discover, for example, that in his particular industry it is an accepted fact that a 12 percent return on investment is the minimum acceptable. Thus, he will begin to develop ways to measure his business performance, because at this point he will have left the stage of survival and can turn his attention to growth and expansion. Furthermore, his attention to the financial aspects of his business—like rate of return, profit margins, and so on—will take on a different meaning to him. Growth and expansion, for example, begin to concern him because at this point his income will have gone up enough in absolute dollars to allow him funds to plow back into the business; in addition, he recognizes that he must make a more formalized investment decision. Thus, at this stage, his actions become far more typical of those of the true entrepreneur, being more concerned with taking calculated risks than simply keeping his doors open for business.

Fortunately, although the Stage II business manager is far more willing to take risks, he still tends to be a bit conservative because he can remember the wolf at his door. Therefore, even though he is willing to engage in diversification of activities, he looks primarily for lucrative opportunities and is concerned with target rates of return. This thought pattern, in turn, causes him to engage in the practice of management by objectives, a technique he finds useful in managing men, materials, and machines, as well as money. Furthermore, the results he obtains from this technique generally are most satisfying both financially and emotionally.

Thus all would appear rosy in Stage II of the economic growth cycle of the normal firm. However, just as the firm in Stage I begins to sow the seeds of its own destruction, so does the small business in Stage II. The demon of success again emerges, and the resulting problems are serious enough in their own way to merit separate attention.

Rigidity of Thinking. One of the first problems that crops up in Stage II is in the thought processes of the owner-manager. Whereas the very reason for his success is that he was able to change from the thinking of an owner to a manager in going from Stage I to Stage II, many managers at the same time become very rigid in their thinking or too speculative as a result of their previous triumphs. Any hang-ups in thinking at this point can ring the death knell for the manager because he will not continue to adapt with the times or will commit "speculative" errors.

Surreptitious Actions by Subordinates. A second problem that crops up in the supervised supervisor stage of small business growth is that the subordinates—particularly the lieutenants developed by the small business manager—often behave in ways not beneficial to the small business. This behavior manifests itself in several actions: fouling up projects and denying responsibility for it; becoming greedy and resenting the small businessman's financial success; fighting among themselves in an effort to enhance or establish individual positions; or the development of blind resentment of the boss's son (or wife, father, brother, and so on).

Business Overhead Growth. A heavy increase in business overhead is another tip-off to entry into the second critical phase of growth. This usually happens as a result of real financial success in the business and manifests itself in increased travel by the owner, grandiose ideas about building new plants, moving to a new location, and particularly, the construction of a lush office with all the accessories, like a refrigerated bar, good-looking secretary, and two telephones. Unfortunately, most of these fixtures are deemed essential only when they are purchased, not being recognized as superfluous until it is too late.

The Union Moves. An additional problem that tends to complicate the life of the small business man approaching critical Stage II is that of unionization. Ironically, the prospects of unionization tend particularly to unnerve the hard-charging, successful, charismatic small businessman. He feels insulted because his employees no longer look to him as the "great white father" and because the union's philosophy of the strong helping the weak is the very antithesis of his personal philosophy. Unionism per se runs against his grain, and he feels his employees have deserted him.

The Informal Organization Gains Power. The informal organization becomes more and more of a burden to the successful small businessman in Stage II. The small businessman, who was successful in reaching the rapid growth phase of Stage II by learning how to be a manager, still has not learned how to be an administrator. That is, success through Stage I does not require human relations and employee behavior savvy by the small businessman, but success in Stage II does. He can no longer get by just by barking orders; he must truly learn to administrate.

Diseconomies of Scale. Diseconomies of scale form the sixth problem that normally acccompanies movement into the second critical phase of economic growth. For example, H.O. Stekler has found that small businessmen in Stage II begin to encounter certain difficulties that theoretically should not even develop, but do.[3] For example, theoretically it is expected that the bigger the small business gets the more able it is to take advantage of such principles as buying in bulk quantities, selling at lower prices because of higher volume, and so on, and still make increased profits. However, the practicalities of life teach otherwise. Stekler argues that there is relatively no advantage with respect to economies of scale realized by firms the size of those in their second stage of growth. In fact, the opposite seems to be true: diversification of products and markets causes some losses, which tend to force a *reduced* rate of return over what had been previously experienced by the small business manager in the rapid growth phase of Stage II.

Production Problems. The glow begins to wear off the rapid growth phase of the small business as production problems arise. This does not occur because the manager fails to supervise his subordinates effectively, but because his organization has become big enough, with so many intermediate levels of managers, that some of them simply are no good. The manager may not know how to find out about any unsatisfactory performance on their part.

Family Problems. The final difficulty that arises for the small business-man at critical Stage II is that of family problems. The difficulty here can be capsulized: either the man, his wife, or his children have not managed to grow up with his income. It is not uncommon for the small businessman at the peak of his growth years to discover that he is making ten times what he had ever dreamed of, but that he is spending eleven times that amount, his wife thinks he is stingy, and he resents his "social obligations."

MAKING IT TO STAGE III

The foregoing may lead the reader to believe that it is almost impossible for the small business manager to pass successfully through Stage II of his organi-zation's growth. In reality, many small businessmen easily cope with the pro-blems enumerated and manage to enjoy the good life of the relatively stabilized small business. However, all that glitters is not gold, and, as in the other two stages of small business growth, the critical point arrives at Stage III when the small businessman must successfully overcome his problems or be absorbed by the giant organizations. Fortunately, however, the small businessman at this stage is no longer small, and he is far better equipped to fight giant industry than is the tiniest of the small businessmen. Ironically, however, it is not really the giants that cause him the trouble at this phase; rather, his main problems are created by other small businesses. Let's briefly evaluate these problems so that the aspiring small businessman may duly be forewarned as to what awaits him at the end of the road.

The Greediness of Others. One problem that the small businessman must effetively cope with upon entry into the third stage in his organization's growth is the disloyalty of some of his divisional managers. If the businessman is suc-cessful in training his divisional managers to manage his small business, they will have learned to manage their own small business and may be induced to strike out on their own, leaving the small businessman holding the bag.[4]

---

[3]H. O. Stekler, *Profitability and Size of Firm* (Berkeley: Institute of Business and Economic Research, University of California, 1963).

[4]*Managing the Small Business,* pp. 33-38.

New Small Businesses Take Markets. This problem is partially an outgrowth of the first problem, but is nevertheless a singular problem in itself. If and when his divisional and departmental managers abandon ship, they usually end up in industries competitive with the business they have abandoned. When they do decide to take on the "old pro," they will do so in his most profitable lines because they know which ones are the most profitable.

The Institutional Toll. Increasing overhead costs are a third nemesis of the larger business. These costs usually begin to mount when the small businessman feels the need for institutional advertising, "national" distribution outlets, and so on. In fact, these costs are why real economies of scale never seem to be realized by the larger small-businesses, which one would theoretically expect.

The Diminishing Absolute Rate of Return. The fourth problem of the small business in its plateau stage is that the rate of return on invested capital decreases. Innumerable studies attest to this fact, all of which add up to an "iron law" of small business ownership: once the small businessman has reached full bloom, a disproportionate and diminishing return on invested capital must be expected by the owner(s).[5]

Organization Top-heavy with Staff Personnel. Overstaffing, particularly at the middle-management levels, is a serious problem with most businesses in the United States, including larger small-businesses.[6] Furthermore, it appears that all businessmen at this stage of development seem to arrive at some point where they feel they must surround themselves with staff men who can "keep them informed." Obviously, such hired help are an expensive luxury and take a heavy toll on the newly-arrived small business' overhead.

The Staff Starts Infighting. As the business becomes top-heavy with staff personnel, most large small-businesses also experience a certain amount of infighting among personnel, which not only results in serious morale problems but sometimes causes vital breaks in their performance capabilities.

A Full Line Causes Some Products to Become Unprofitable. Growing businesses in the maturity stage must diversify in the products, or markets, or services they offer. This diversification, unfortunately, carries with it the inherent probability that some of these diversified lines will fail, and, as Stekler[7] says, this creates a high probability that any given *marginal* project will actually yield a return which is lower than the previous *average* rate of return for the firm's other projects. This, of course, reduces the new rate of return realized by the business.

There is no question that small businesses experience growing pains. The ability of the small businessman to cope with these pains will determine whether or not he will be successful. Unfortunately, however, he will never outgrow such pains and still be a small businessman. Therefore, those who undertake a venture thinking that all would be nice if he could stabilize his business at $2

---

[5]See, for example, *Profitability and Size of Firm;* Ralph C. Epstein, *Industrial Profits in the United States* (New York: National Bureau of Economic Research, 1934); William L. Crum, *Corporate Size and Earning Power* (Cambridge, Mass.: Harvard University Press, 1939); and Joseph Steindl, *Small and Big Business* (Oxford: Oxford University, Institute of Statistics, Monograph No. 1, 1945).

[6]Charles Lupton, "Watch Your Management Weight," *Management of Personnel Quarterly,* I (Winter, 1962), pp. 11-17.

[7]*Profitability and Size of Firm,* p. 82.

million or $10 million or $20 million may as well forget it. There will always be critical stages of growth for the small business.

Fortunately, these stages of growth arise only from success. Anyone who commits himself to managing a small business must recognize one irrefutable fact: the minute he commits himself, he is on the treadmill of forced growth, growth that requires his ability to change from an autocratic to a professional manager. Furthermore, there is no escape from this escalator unless he is willing to accept the demise of his small business and the probable loss of nearly 50 percent of his assets. On the other hand, the rewards for success are phenomenal and few successful small businessmen will fail to agree that it is the climbing of the stairs that is important, not the arrival at a plateau.

APPROACHES TO

LONG-RANGE PLANNING

FOR SMALL BUSINESS*

GEORGE A. STEINER

There is little doubt that the great majority of small businesses do little, if any, long-range planning. While the virtues of long-range planning have been rather well "sold" to most of the large corporations, the job still remains to be done among the small business community.

Expansion of long-range planning among smaller enterprises can best proceed upon two platforms.

1. The small businessman must be convinced that long-range planning is worthwhile, and he must develop a genuine desire for it.
2. He must adopt methods and principles suitable to his situation.

The essence of long-range planning is thinking systematically about the future and making current decisions on that basis. Implicit in this concept is the idea of examining future consequences of present decisions, as well as choosing bases for making current decisions from among future alternative courses of action. Long-range planning, therefore, is not without current impact.[1]

Every businessman thinks ahead. But what is new in long-range planning today is looking ahead in a methodical, organized, and conscious fashion. Man-

*©1967 by the Regents of the University of California, Reprinted from *California Management Review*, Vol. 10, No. 1, pp. 3-16, by permission of the Regents.

agers have found that the formalization of the long-range planning process produces better results.

This new concept of long-range planning does not imply an exhaustive inquiry into the future. The process actually used in a company should merely be adapted to the particular circumstances existing in the company.

The typical small businessman is likely to give one or more of the following responses when asked why he does so little (or no) long-range planning:

That's for big companies, not me.

Why should I? I'm doing O.K.

You can't forecast the future, so how can you do long-range planning?

I am in a cash squeeze, and that's all I can think about now.

It's too complicated.

My business is simple, and I know what the problems are.

I can do all the planning I need in my head. Anyway, I don't want to discuss my plans with anyone. Why give someone a chance to find out and lose my competitive advantage?

The average small businessman is faced with many barriers to long-range planning. He is pressed for time. He has most of the problems of an executive in a medium-size company, but must solve them without helpers. He is constantly fighting "brush fires," and, as anyone who has followed business planning knows, these pressures drive out long-range planning. He is a man of action and has a habit of doing things by himself. Typically, the small businessman keeps his ideas, plans, and intentions secret. He is reluctant to discuss plans which may not materialize because he does not want to be thought foolish or inept.[2]

Finally, although the literature on long-range planning is increasing, most of it is not very helpful to the small businessman. He needs detailed guides to tell him how to go about long-range planning, which are not easy to find.

Yet none of these obstacles can justify a businessman's avoiding systematic long-range planning.

The matter of forecasting the future seems to bother many businessmen. Of course, no one can foresee the future. Forecasting, however, is making a judgment about the future on the basis of present knowledge. The more accurate the forecast, the better a plan will be, but planning can be effective even if a forecast is not too accurate at first. Whether they realize it or not, all businessmen forecast. The only difference is in how well they do it. If a manager, for example, decides not to purchase a new machine, he is in effect forecasting that his profits will not be increased in the future by the purchase.

The meanings of forecasting and planning are confused in the minds of some businessmen. Forecasting is not planning, but only a part of it. Planning is determining what a manager wants in the future and developing methods to achieve it. Forecasting may tell which type of environment can be expected; planning will determine how to take advantage of it or, if it is inhospitable, how to prevent it from taking advantage of the firm.

Answers to some of the other reasons given for failure to plan ahead are obvious. If long-range planning is important, a businessman simply must and can find the time to do it. Actually, long-range planning is simpler than many businessmen imagine. The businessman who rejects planning for the future because he is doing so well today could not be more misguided. Products as well as production methods are growing obsolete faster, and customers are becoming more fickle. Prosperity today is no assurance of tomorrow's profits.

Long-range planning is essential for a small as well as a large business for no other reason than that it permits them to take better advantage of the opportunities which lie in the future and to forestall the threats which it contains. This is the essence of entrepreneurship. Long-range planning should stimulate this function. Only a few small businesses have the financial reserves to cover the unexpected loss that occurs when they must shift from dependence on a single obsolete product or a few major customers. Yet this sort of crisis may be avoided by recognizing that it can happen and taking early action to avoid it. And there are other advantages to long-range planning for a small businessman. For example, he will find banks and other sources of cash much more willing to finance his needs if he has a well-designed long-range plan. He may be able to "go public" much more easily and without fear of losing his business. And he can be sure of perpetuating his business beyond his retirement.

Before discussing a variety of possible approaches to long-range planning, it is useful to set forth a simple conceptual frame of reference for types of business plans and steps in their development. Figure 5 is a simplified sketch of different types of plans needed in a business. It also shows the general flow of action in the process of planning.

Two important facts should be mentioned before discussing Figure 5:

1. A very large number of companies doing long-range planning have systems that fit this model.
2. The structure is exceedingly flexible and can be adapted to just about any size of business, style of management, type of business, or stage in the development of organized planning.

So long as a manager is really interested in long-range planning, this conceptual model can be used with any magnitude of resources, and it can be applied equally well to a very small and a very large enterprise.

To the left of the chart are the fundamental premises that go into any planning effort. First are the basic purposes of the firm, usually expressed in broad terms. Many companies have only recently written out their basic purposes, but it is not necessary to put them on paper so long as businessmen think about them, for they are the starting point in long-range planning. Of major significance, too, are the values, ideas, and philosophies which a businessman holds. These, of course, permeate all he does and are major determinants of all the decisions he makes. For example, a businessman who is working to enlarge a small business will go about his long-range planning in a far different manner from one who wishes to work alone to invent new products in his own small laboratory.

Planning also must be based on an assessment of the future environment, both within and outside the firm. The possible number of elements to be examined is very great, and the art of long-range planning involves an ability to choose those which are of major importance to the firm.

Upon these bases the over-all objectives, strategies, and policies of the firm can be set forth. They can be few in number or many. They can concern any element of the business. The more concrete they are, however, the better the plans are likely to be. The time dimensions of objectives, strategies, and policies

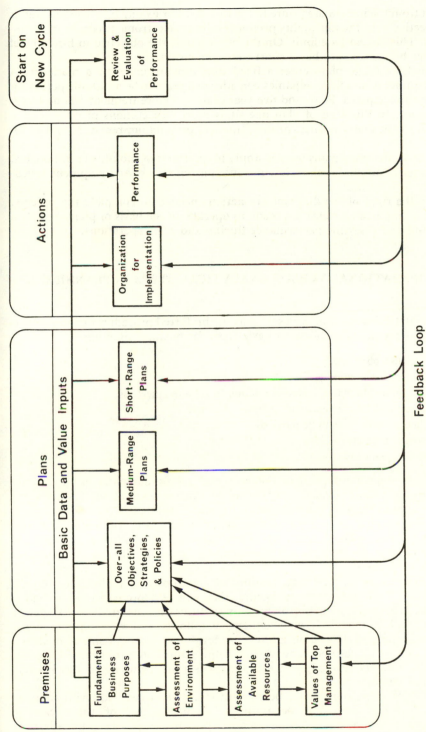

Feedback Loop

FIGURE 5 The Structure and Process of Planning for a Business

extend from the immediate future to the infinite. For example, a firm may set as its objective to be the top quality producer of microelectronic products in the industry. This has no time limit. On the other hand, the objective to hire a chief engineer by next month has a short time dimension.

Medium-range plans cover a fixed time dimension set by a manager. A large number of smaller companies consider two years to be a suitable period for medium-range plans. Four- and five-year plans are more frequent among larger companies. In this kind of plan one finds more expectations placed on such parts of the business as sales, profits, finance, production, research, and facilities.

The short-range plans usually apply to quarterly or monthly cash budgets, raw material purchase schedules, production schedules, and shipment schedules.

To the right of the diagram are actions needed to complete the process, assuring that arrangements are made to operate on the basis of plans and then reviewing and assessing performance during and after operations.

OPERATIONAL VERSUS ANALYTICAL STEPS IN PLANNING

Analytical steps have been set up as the preferred procedures in all problem solving. They take the following basic form for business planning:

1. Establish objectives
2. Prepare basic premises.
3. Determine alternative courses of action to achieve objectives.
4. Examine different alternative courses of action.
5. Choose alternatives to be followed.
6. Put the plan into action.
7. Review plans periodically.

These steps are implicit in Figure 5 and are fundamental in all effective planning. But a businessman may not follow this sequence at all. The sequence of operational steps in planning may be much different from the analytical steps. For example, it is rare to find a planning program proceeding from one step to the next without retracing or overlapping. A tentative goal found too high or too low may be changed after examining various alternative courses of action to achieve it.

In the following sections a number of operational steps for planning are presented. While they differ markedly, they will be more easily performed if both the conceptual model of planning structures and the analytical steps are kept in mind. But precisely what sequence is followed and what depth of analysis is employed will depend on many considerations: type and size of business, nature of top management, available help, nature of problems facing the business, and whether long-range planning is just beginning or has been in operation for some time.

The following suggestions begin with simple and conclude with complex methods—which need not be mutually exclusive. All of them can be incorporated into advanced, sophisticated systems, and all have actually been used with success by small businessmen.

Asking Questions. Columella is as correct today as he was centuries ago when he said, "The important part of every business is to know what ought to be done." But this is not as easy as it sounds. Consider the case of the small businessman whose sales grew rapidly but whose receivables did not turn over quickly enough to finance his current needs. He had to borrow, but, because he was not well established he had to pay high interest rates for his loan, and this wiped out his profit. This man was not asking the right questions.

A survey of over one hundred small manufacturers concluded that "the hardest part of planning seems to be getting started."[3] A simple way to get started in long-range planning is by asking some basic questions. A good place to begin is with objectives. It is most naive to say, "Our objective is to make a profit—period." Of course it is, but maximizing profits involves answering questions such as:

What business am I in?

What is my place in the industry?

What customers am I serving? Where is my market?

What is my company image to my major customers?

What business do I want to be in five years from now?

What are my specific goals for profit improvement?

Need I have plans for product improvement? If so, what?

What is my greatest strength? Am I using it well?

What is my greatest problem? How am I to solve it?

What share of the market do I want? Next month? Next Year?

Are my personnel policies acceptable to employees?

How can I finance growth?

For those small businessmen who are preparing such lists and are answering the questions, this is one excellent way to get started down the path of systematic and useful long-range planning.

It is readily apparent how a decision about any one of these questions can have an important impact on most of the others. What is most useful is to get at the major issues, think about them continuously, and set up specific plans of action.

Key To Success

Every business, both large and small, will succeed or fail depending on a limited and variable number of strategic factors. The best way to get started in long-range planning is to try to discover those few strategic factors which will be responsible for future success. Since finance is such a critical factor to most small businessmen, this area is traditionally the prime subject of analysis for them as well as for scholars who are interested in small business problems.

But other factors may be just as important strategically. Imagination may be the strategic factor responsible for the success of a toy company or an advertising firm. Quality may be the strategic factor responsible for the success of a company making components for a complicated aerospace product. Cost control and cost reduction may be the strategic factors responsible for success of a company producing standard metal stampings for an automobile manufacturer.

165

TABLE I   A New Product Check-Off List

Relationship to Present Operations
1. Does the product fall within the manufacturing and processing know-how of the company?
2. Will the product benefit by the present research and engineering activities of the company?
3. Does the product fit into the lines now handled by our sales organization? Will it permit more efficient utilization of our present sales organization?

Character of the Product
1. Will the product capitalize on the engineering strength of the company?
2. Is there a reasonable volume potential?
3. Can the product maintain a high degree of distinctiveness in comparison with competing products?
4. Will the product contribute to the company's reputation?

Commercial Considerations
1. Is the product necessary or desirable in maintaining completeness of line?
2. Does the inclusion of this product in the line have any effect on the other lines?
3. Will it strengthen our position with distributors?
4. Will the company name be of aid in marketing the product?

Strategic factors like these should come to light in a comprehensive long-range planning program. But if no such program exists, a small businessman may start his long-range planning simply by drawing up a list of possible strategic factors which may be responsible for his future success. Once the pertinent ones are identified, they should, of course, be the subject of deep thought and appropriate action.

Check-Off Lists

Some firms use so-called check-off lists to guide their planning. These lists cover important elements of planning such as sales and marketing, research and development, products, land and property, personnel, organization, finance, and competition. The list of questions in Table I concerning the addition of new products illustrates this approach. For many of the questions absolute measurement is difficult, if not impossible; simple ratings, therefore, are usually given for each question, such as: "excellent," "good," "average," "poor," "unsatisfactory."

Simplified Master Planning

Questions like those in Table I are helpful, but more systematization is desirable. Roger A. Golde, a small business consultant, has devised a form to help the small businessman organize his planning (Tables II and III).[4]

A manager-owner can work with Golde's form at odd moments, informally with or without help. This form has the great virtue of getting at the major elements of success or failure of a firm. Working with it will raise questions and encourage decisions. For many small businessmen, starting with comparatively abstract goals and strategies is difficult. The practical approach of Golde, however, should eventually lead them to a better understanding of objectives and strategies.

TABLE II   Master Planning Form

Item	Change		Comment
	Next Year	Year After Next	
Research & Development			
Products			
Product Mix			
Service			
Supplies			
Suppliers			
Inventory			
Subcontracts			
Storage & Handling			
Quality Control			
Space			
Leasehold Improvements			
Equipment			
Employees			
Fringe Benefits			
Customers			
Sales Outlets			
Terms of Sale			
Pricing			
Transportation			
Advertising			
Promotion			
Packaging			
Market Research			
Financing			
Insurance			
Investments			
Management Reports			
Management Procedures			
Management Organization			
Governmental Environment			
Economic Environment			
Industrial Environment			
Competition			
Community Environment			

INSTRUCTIONS: All changes are estimated in relation to the preceding year.

If a quantitative change is anticipated—i.e., change in size or amount—use the following symbols: L=large, M=medium, and S=small. Quantitative changes are assumed to be increases unless preceded by a minus sign.

If a qualitative change is anticipated, use the following symbols: l=large, m=medium, s=small.

Note that the notions of small, medium, and large changes are obviously subjective and will vary with the person using the form.

In general, a small change denotes some sort of minimum level of change which is thought important enough to make note of. Most of the expected changes will probably fall in the medium category, indicating significant change of some magnitude. The large category will usually be reserved for unusual changes of striking impact.

The notion of qualitative changes may need some clarification. This category of change would cover such items as a change in customer mix (which might or might not result in an increased number of customers). Using a new source of supply for raw materials and changing the media allocation of the advertising budget would also be examples of qualitative changes.

SOURCE: Roger A. Golde, *Harvard Business Review,* XXIV: 5 (Sept.-Oct. 1964), 151 f.

TABLE III   Hypothetical Completed Master Planning Form

Item	Change		Comment
	Next Year	Year After Next	
Research & Development	Mm	—S	Start development of new altimeter for executive planes.
Products		Ss	First sales of new altimeter.
Product Mix			
Service		s	Slightly different for private planes.
Supplies		s	Needed for new altimeter.
Suppliers			
Inventory			
Subcontracts		S	Most of subassemblies will be subcontracted.
Storage & Handling			
Quality Control			
Space		S	Little bit of production space for new altimeter.
Leasehold Improvements	M		Need for dust-free area.
Equipment	S		New test equipment.
Employees	S		Couple of technicians for development work.
Fringe Benefits			
Customers		sS	Plan to hit owners of executive planes.
Sales Outlets		Mm	Will need more sales representatives rather than own sales force.
Terms of Sale			
Pricing			
Transportation			
Advertising		—M	Not so effective to private owners.
Promotion		m	Will switch to more demonstrations and trade shows.
Packaging			
Market Research	S		Informal poll of private owners known by company.
Financing	S		Additional working capital for production.
Insurance			
Investments			
Management Reports		1	Need for simple product costing system.
Etc.			Etc.

Source: Roger A. Golde, *Harvard Business Review*, XXIV: 5 (Sept.-Oct. 1964), 151 f.

Selecting Concrete Key Objectives

Not all objective setting need be abstract. An approach developed by Dr. Gunther Klaus, a small business management consultant, is concrete, pragmatic, and leads directly into systematic planning. He begins with a framework for decision which is illustrated in Table IV. This particular exhibit concerns sales objectives, but it could also be used for profit. The assumption here is that, if sales are considered first, the profit objectives will follow in logical fashion.

TABLE IV   Sales Objectives

Area	First Year	Second Year	Third Year	Fourth Year	Fifth Year
Product modification					
New products					
Joint ventures					
New markets					
Acquisition					
Totals	►————————►			BEGIN HERE	

Klaus begins with an objective for sales as far in the future as it is practicable for the small businessman to contemplate, in this case five years. The question is, What dollar volume of sales do I want five years from now? When that question is answered, it naturally raises a great many more. One immediate question is whether the present product line will permit the achievement of that objective. If not, a number of questions arise: Can the target be met by product modifications? If so, which ones? If not, what new products can be produced? If this will not permit target achievement, should a joint venture be considered? Penetration of new markets? Acquisitions? Dealing with these questions opens up a "decision-tree" with many other branches. What manpower will be needed? What financing will be required? What will my costs be? Must some employees be sent to an executive training program to get prepared to assume larger responsibilities?

This approach, like the preceding ones, is quite adaptable to different conditions and sizes of businesses.

The Planning Gap

A modification of this approach is to identify the so-called planning gap.[5] This calls for the establishment of tentative sales goals and the forecasting of current momentum, or what present and anticipated lines of business will produce in the future. The difference, as shown in Figure 6, is the planning gap. The issue is, how will the gap be filled? (Similar charts can be drawn for profits, costs, personnel, floor space, etc.) Asking and answering this question leads to the same sort of analysis as that discussed above.

169

FIGURE 6   The Planning Gap

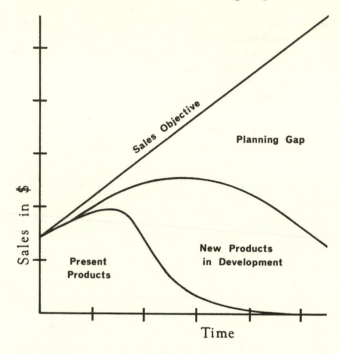

Return On Investment

Another approach is to concentrate on the return on investment calculation for a firm. The elements of this calculation are shown in Figure 7. As in the previous approach, a return on investment objective can be tentatively established for selected time periods. The analysis then begins by probing (in a fashion similar to that described above) what is necessary to achieve the objective. This approach is flexible in dealing with both short- and long-range factors in business life.

For many years, this has been the approach of the planning and control program of E. I. du Pont de Nemours & Company. It is, of course, usable by a small company as well. But a small company would find (as does du Pont) the approach more useful when accompanied by other elements of planning noted in Figure 5.

Break-Even Analysis

The break-even point for a business is that point in production at which sales volume equals costs. At that point there is neither a profit nor a loss. Figure 8 shows a break-even analysis. A simple formula will also yield the break-even point:

$$\text{Break-even} = \frac{\text{Fixed costs}}{100\% - (\text{Variable costs} / \text{Sales})}$$

FIGURE 7 Return on Investment

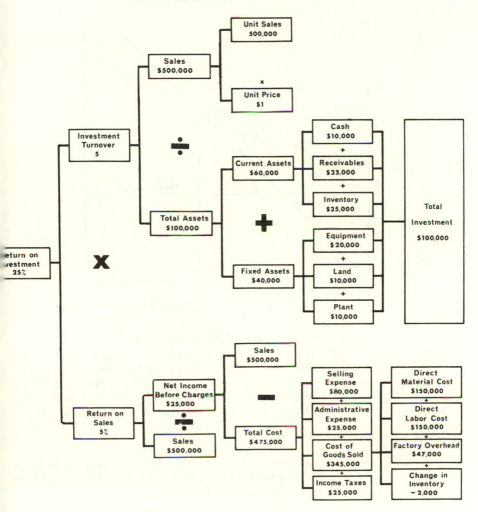

The break-even analysis is a powerful tool to answer puzzling questions such as: What is the impact on profit if fixed costs rise 10 per cent and sales decline by 10 per cent? Or if variable costs increase by 15 per cent and volume drops by 14 per cent?

This is a simple method to get at some major issues important in company planning. If break-even analysis is used to ask a widening range of questions, as illustrated above, it can be the starting point for a long-range planning program.

Economists have criticized this tool because they rightly claim that cost curves are curves and not linear as drawn on the chart. Furthermore, the technique assumes many things that may not be true; for instance, that productivity remains the same over time, or that fixed and variable costs can be separated. This is not the place to argue the merits of such criticisms. It is in point here to

171

FIGURE 8   A Break-Even Analysis

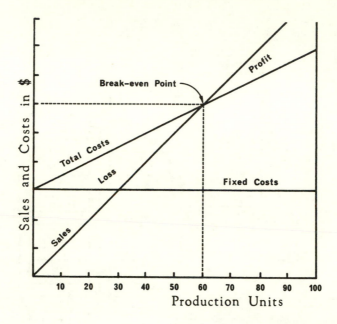

observe, however, that within a "range of relevance," the functions of a break-even chart are rather linear. For many companies within a range of ten to fifteen per cent on either side of the break-even line, an assumed linear relationship can be approximated closely enough to form a solid basis for planning. Hence this is a useful short- and long-range planning tool. Its value does, however, decrease the longer the time span covered and the wider the ranges of output.

Standard Accounting Statements

Standard accounting statements are excellent bases for developing long-range planning. They can be very simple for a very small enterprise or developed in complex detail in a comprehensive planning program.

In a simple approach, and one which is indispensable to proper management in small as well as large enterprises, cash forecasts are prepared. What is involved is the identification and forecast of all important future sources and uses of cash available to the enterprise. Table V gives an elementary arrangement of items to be forecast to determine net cash flows. A number of different formats are contained in Schabacker's *Cash Planning in Small Manufacturing Companies.*[6] Most commercial banks have developed cash flow forms which are available to businessmen. These forms can be used to forecast cash flows for any period of time chosen—daily, weekly, monthly, quarterly, or over a number of years.

The revenue-expense forecast can also be used as a beginning point for long-range planning. Table VI shows a simple revenue-expense forecast format. Here the task is to identify and forecast all important elements of cost and revenues. The difference will show profit or loss, and this in turn will provide the basis upon which simple or sophisticated rates of return on investment may be

TABLE V Five-Year Forecast of Cash Sources and Needs for a Small Business

Item	First Year	Second Year	Third Year	Fourth Year	Fifth Year
Cash sources:					
Opening balance					
Revenue from sales					
Depreciation					
Borrowing on facilities					
Borrowing on inventory and receivables					
Total cash sources					
Cash expenditures:					
Direct labor costs					
Materials purchase					
Payments to subcontractors					
New machinery and tools					
Increases in inventory					
Increases in receivables					
Increases in operating cash					
Payments on loans					
Factory burden					
Officers' salaries					
Selling costs					
Taxes:					
Employer's share of Social Security					
Local property					
Income					
Total cash disbursements					
Net cash change					

calculated. Revenue-expense forecasts can and should be prepared for each important product of an enterprise as well as for the enterprise as a whole. Revenue-expense forecasts for individual products should at least extend over the major part of the life span of the product.

An important feature of the revenue-expense forecast is that when depreciation is added to net profit the result is cash gain from operations. As noted in Table VI, this does not, however, represent net cash flow. So, when simple revenue-expense forecasts are used in planning they should be accompanied by cash flow analyses.

Complete balance sheets and profit and loss statements constitute a more complicated basis for developing long-range planning. When a company gets to the point where it can develop such documents for the length of time for which organized future planning is done, it has demonstrated high capability for planning. Consequently, the company might just as well develop a more comprehensive formal long-range planning program in which these documents are included as parts.

TABLE VI   Five-Year Revenue-Expense Projection for a Small Business

Item	First Year	Second Year	Third Year	Fourth Year	Fifth Year
Sales revenues:					
Product A					
Product B					
Operating expenses:					
Direct labor					
Overhead					
Materials					
Selling expenses					
Depreciation					
Total					
Non-recurring expenses					
Total operating expenses					
Interest and loan amortization					
Net profit before taxes					
Taxes					
Net profit after taxes					
Cash gain from operations (net profit after taxes plus depreciation reserve)					

As companies grow in size and experience with organized long-range planning, it becomes possible and desirable to have a more complete planning program than those discussed up to this point. The shape of the planning program follows more closely the conceptual model presented in Figure 5 and results in a comprehensive set of objectives and plans covering all major parts of the business.

[Following] is a brief description of an actual comprehensive planning program. This five year plan was prepared by the president [of Magnetic Design, Inc.] and his four major department heads, who worked evenings and weekends to complete it. The firm had less than $200,000 annual sales and about one hundred employees at the time the plan was prepared.

I. Corporate Purposes: the fundamental purposes of MDI. Two basic purposes are given, which is about standard. The four modifiers, however, are a little unusual.

A. Two prime objectives of MDI are:
    1. To improve earnings through productive effort primarily applied (but not limited) to the manufacture of magnetic devices and power supply equipment.

2. To conduct the business in a manner that is constructive, honorable, and mutually profitable for stockholders, employees, customers, suppliers, and the general community.
B. These objectives are amplified further:
   1. To earn a reasonable return on investment with due regard to the interests of customers, employees, vendors.
   2. To expand sales while increasing profits.
   3. To support the military effort of the United states by producing top quality products.
   4. To grow at a steady rate.
C. Departmental purposes: Administration, marketing, production and engineering, and finance. It is a little unusual for departmental purposes to be specified at this point in a plan; they are usually blended into specific goals set for their operations. Following are the objectives of the production and engineering department:
   1. Manufacture and design quality products with cost and delivery schedules which will be attractive to prospective customers.
   2. Stay alert to developments that promise new and improved company products.

II. Basic Corporate Five- and Ten-Year Sales and Profit Objectives:
A. The five-year annual sales and profit objectives are:

	Sales	Pretax Profits	Pretax (%) Profit	Federal Tax	Posttax (%) Profit
First year					
Second year			[Specified in dollars and percentages.]		
Third year					
Fourth year					
Fifth year					

B. The ten-year sales and profit objectives are:
   1. After taxes, sales will be $5,000,000 and earnings will be $750,000.

III. Basic Premises: forecasts of future markets, technology, competition, and evaluations of internal strengths and weaknesses. A framework of premises, with illustrations from the MDI plan, follows:
A. External projections and forecasts:
   1. Survey of general business conditions, including Gross National Product forecast.
   2. Survey of the market for company products, based upon general economic conditions for industrial products and estimates of government spending for company products.
   3. Forecast of company sales based on the above two forecasts. (MDI made forecasts for each of the next five years. Since the company is in the Midwest, government spending for its products in the Midwest was estimated. Included were the Department of Defense, the National Aeronautics and Space Administration, and the Federal Aviation Agency.)
B. Competition: Because competition is keen for most companies, objective

estimates of its strength are important. After looking at what its major competition was likely to do, the firm looked at itself.

1. Several advantages have placed MDI several years in advance of competition in the magnetic devices equipment field. These are cryogenic magnets for commercial applications and high reliability power supplies for long-endurance military application.
2. However, in order to realize fully the growth commensurate with the above advantages, several weaknesses must be overcome by developing an ability to construct crystals as well as developing more sophisticated test procedures.

C. Internal examination of the past and projections: Analyses of various parts of the enterprise, e.g.

1. Product line analysis:
   a. Product(s) performance (i.e., sales volume, profit margin, etc.).
   b. Customer class served.
   c. Comparison with major competitors' product(s).
   d. Comparison with substitutes and complementary performance.
   e. Possibilities for product improvement.
   f. Suggestions with regards to new products.
2. Market analysis:
   a. Important factors in projected sales changes: product success; marketing organization; advertising; and competitive pressures.
   b. New markets to be penetrated (i.e., geographical areas and customer classes).
3. Financial analysis:
   a. Profit position.
   b. Working capital.
   c. Cash position.
   d. Impact of financial policy on market price per share.
   e. Prospects for future financing.
4. Production analysis:
   a. Plant and equipment (maintenance and depreciation).
   b. Productive capacity and productivity.
   c. Per cent of capacity utilized.
   d. Suggestions for: productivity improvements; cost reduction; utilizing excess capacity; and planning expansion.
5. Technical analysis:
   a. Research and development performance.
   b. Suggestions for improving research and development effectiveness.
6. Employees:
   a. Employment and future needs.
   b. Technical manpower deficiencies.
   c. Appraisal of employee attitudes.
7. Facilties:
   a. Evaluation of current facilities to meet new business.
   b. Machine replacement policy and needs.

IV. Basic Objectives, Policies, and Strategies: This covers every important area of the business, but most companies concentrate on A through F of the following:

A. Profits.
B. Sales.

C. Finance.
D. Marketing.
E. Capital additions.
F. Production.
G. Research.
H. Engineering.
I. Personnel.
J. Acquisitions.
K. Organization.
L. Long-range planning.

This list can be expanded. As noted elsewhere, the more concrete the specification here can be, the easier it usually is to implement the plans. It is especially important for a small businessman to know precisely what he is seeking and the method to be employed to get there. For example, MDI marketing objectives were set forth as follows:

1. Increase sales of magnetic devices 100 per cent in the next five years. Increase sales of power supply equipment 200 per cent during the next five years.
2. Increase total volume of industrial sales from today's 25 per cent to 50 per cent of total sales at the end of five years.
3. Penetrate the western market to the point where the company will control 10 percent of it at the end of five years.
4. Enter the foreign market within five years by a licensing agreement, a joint venture, or manufacturing facility.

For each of these objectives, the company prepared a detailed series of strategies ranging from a strategy to "sell custom designs directly to prime contractors in geographic regions where their main plants are located" to details such as special services to selected specified customers, training programs for employees, and top management meetings with customers.

Further strategies which might be included in this section of the plan, with special regard to marketing, are organization, use of dealers, possibility of distributing products manufactured by others, salesmen's compensation plans, and pricing policy.

Drawing a proper line of demarcation between the strategic plans and the detailed operational plans is difficult. Ideally, the two blend together in a continuous line. This was the case with MDI, where those making the strategic plan also were the ones to implement it.

V. Detailed Medium-Range Plans: more detailed plans growing out of the above. For MDI these plans were developed for each of the succeeding five years:

A. *Pro forma* balance sheet, yearly.
B. Income statement, yearly.
C. Capital expenditure schedule, yearly.
D. Unit production schedule for major products, yearly.
E. Employment schedule, yearly.
F. Detailed schedule to acquire within three years a company with design capability in solid state magnetic devices.

VI. One-Year Plans: the year's budgets. The first year's budgets for items A through N were, in the aggregate, the same for the first year of the five-year plan, but broken into quarterly time periods. In addition, MDI had other budgets, principally purchasing schedules for major components and raw materials and typical detailed administrative budgets covering such things as travel and telephone.

Comprehensive Planning In Decentralized Companies

When divisions are established as profit centers, a new dimension is added to the planning process. At first, long-range planning is usually done for the entire company by the central office. But once the process is established the central office usually concentrates on over-all company objectives, strategies, and policies and leaves the detailed medium- and short-range planning to the individual divisions, reserving only the right of review and approval. Sometimes the divisional plans are aggregated into one composite company plan. The structure and substance of the plans parallel that given for MDI.

Help For The Chief Executive

One of the major problems of the chief executive in doing long-range planning is getting adequate help. It is important for the manager-owner of a very small enterprise, as well as the president of a medium-sized business and the chief executive of a large one, to recognize that help is available. Each needs only to understand what is available and learn how to use it.

His own staff is a prime resource. A manager always can do the planning himself—almost obligatory for a very small firm. As firms grow larger, however, it becomes impossible. Growth leads to staff help. Methods which have been employed in using staff successfully are:

1. The chief executive can conduct a freewheeling "think" session to get long-range planning started. Many companies take their top executives away from daily routine to some spa to engage in thinking and planning about the future and conduct these sessions as part of a well-entrenched planning program. These sessions are useful to get the process started.
2. The chief executive can first prepare objectives for the firm and then ask each functional manager to prepare plans for his own area of responsibility.
3. The chief executive can ask each functional manager to tell him what his plans are for the future and then develop over-all objectives and strategies on the basis of them. Or, to initiate the process, he can ask each functional officer what he thinks ought to be done by the firm to get long-range planning under way.
4. The chief executive can assign to one functional officer the job of starting planning. This man can monitor the process in progress.
5. The chief executive can get together with his functional officers to form a committee to prepare strategic over-all as well as working plans for his company. This is what MDI did. As the number of employees increases, there may be great advantage to this method. A committee can offset some traits of chief executives, such as the desire for one-man authoritative control, making snap judgments, preoccupation with short- at the expense of long-run planning, and secretiveness which hurts the firm more than it helps it. Committees of this sort bring to the front different points of view, which is usually healthy. Better communications are promoted, and individuals are likely to feel more intimately associated with the prospects and problems of the firm.
6. When a firm gets larger it may be able to afford one person or a small staff to

devote full time to planning. Such a staff is especially useful in decentralized, divisionalized companies. The staff coordinates work of the central headquarters' functional officers in the development of over-all firm objectives and strategies, aids the divisions in improving their planning capabilities, and helps the central headquarters management review plans. Sometimes the director of such a staff serves as the secretary to a corporate planning committee.

Outside sources of help are available, including consultants for all the major problems of the firm. These are well known and need no further analysis here. One of the most neglected sources of help, particularly for the small businessman, is his board of directors. Small businessmen should think seriously about the advantages of placing on their board one or more individuals with talents that can be used in actually performing long-range planning or advising the president about the use of outside consultants.

Summary

Many small businessmen do not engage in effective long-range planning because they are puzzled about how to begin the process and execute it so that its value exceeds its costs. Many of these approaches have been tested by small, as well as large firms, and they have been found operational and valuable in doing effective long-range planning.

REFERENCES

This article is based on a chapter from a book edited by Professor Irving Pfeffer, entitled *Financial Aspects of Profit Planning for Small Business,* to be published later this year [1967].

1. For a fuller definition of long-range planning, see my "The Critical Role of Top Management in Long-Range Planning," *Arizona Review,* XV:4 (April 1966); and my "Long-Range Planning: Concept and Implementation," *Financial Executive,* XXXIV:7 (July 1966), 54-61.
2. For a profile of the successful small businessman, see Orvis F. Collins, David G. Moore, and Darab B. Unwalla, *The Enterprising Man* (East Lansing, Mich.: Bureau of Business and Economic Research, Graduate School of Business Administration, Michigan State University, 1964).
3. Delbert C. Hastings, *The Place of Forecasting in Basic Planning for Small Business* (Minneapolis: University of Minnesota Press, 1961), p. 23.
4. Roger A. Golde, "Practical Planning for Small Business," *Harvard Business Review,* XXIV:5 (September-October 1964), 151 f.
5. See my "Making Long-Range Company Planning Pay Off," *California Management Review,* IV:2 (Winter 1963), 28-41.
6. Joseph C. Schabacker, *Cash Planning in Small Manufacturing Companies, Small Business Administration* (Washington, D.C.: U.S. Government Printing Office, 1960).

LENGTHENING YOUR SHADOW—

THE KEY TO SMALL BUSINESS GROWTH*

O. G. DALABA

It was the philosopher Emerson who said: "An institution is but the lengthened shadow of one individual." Like most homilies, this one, no doubt, has many exceptions. However, nowhere is its truth more evident than in the history of many or our major industrial organizations. Names like Ford, du Pont, Morgan, Chrysler, Penney and many others are now intricately woven into our social awareness. Any of us can also immediately associate such individual names as Rockefeller, Carnegie, Watson, and others with the major enterprises which exist today as living monuments to one man's early enterprise.

Conversely, we are also familiar with the extremely high mortality rate of the small business. What is the difference? Why is it that only a few develop into large and successful enterprises while the majority, after an initial spurt of growth, either stagnate at very modest levels or, even worse, just wither away into oblivion? Is it just plain luck? Is it fickle and unpredictable consumer tastes and desires? Or, if you prefer, is it the frequently used explanation of being undercapitalized or of being at an unfair competitive advantage with "the big boys?"

Undoubtedly, the answers to these questions are complex and may involve any or all of the factors listed above. However, new and successful companies are being launched and built, sometimes with minimum starting capital and often in competition with large industrial giants. The dinosaur undoubtedly had the strength and size to crush the hare, but which was able to adapt and react faster and, consequently, to survive?

It is the contention of this writer that if there is any one most important key to small business survival and growth, it lies in the ability of the entrepreneur or chief executive officer to lengthen his own shadow through the recruiting, selecting, and motivating of the types of managerial and executive talent necessary to achieve this objective.

In theory, this all sounds reasonably simple. But the application is much more difficult. A great many entrepreneurs and small business executives as individuals are aggressive, resourceful, hard-working, and highly competent. Far too often, however, their competence is limited by an underlying emotional need to control every minor decision point. Consequently, far too many of these same individuals are quite insecure about letting their own shadow grow beyond the point where they can see and control its every little movement.

Case illustrations from my personal consulting experience could fill this article. Instead, I shall just briefly illustrate:

The president of a small medical instruments company was brilliant. He could do every job in the company better than any employee there, and wasn't at

*From *Journal of Small Business Management* (July, 1973), pp. 17-21. Reprinted with permission.

all reluctant to let the individuals concerned know it. These included not only his chief engineer. marketing manager. and controller, but also the workers on the line blowing glass pipettes and the machinists and welders. As might be expected, his turnover was horrendous, and he eventually had to sell the company to a major corporation.

The president and chief stockholder of a successful heavy equipment company which bears his name requested my help in selecting a highly competent controller. I did so only to have the controller come and tell me six months later that he was quitting. The reason for this was that what the president wanted primarily was a 50-page financial summary each month which would show such details as every quart of oil and gallon of gasoline consumed by each vehicle in the fleet. This company is still successful and profitable, but it has not shown any significant growth in the last ten years.

The suburban highways outside the electronics centers built around Stanford University and Massachusetts Institute of Technology are decorated with many industrial "for rent" signs placed on empty monuments to men of technical creativity and innovation who were unsuccessful in "lengthening their own shadows."

A PRESCRIPTION FOR GROWTH

If you, as an enterpriser, really want to extend your shadow, here are some questions which you need to answer to your own satisfaction; it is not enough to have someone else answer them for you.

1. *Do You Really Want Your Company to Grow?* Before you answer that too hastily, give it some careful and reflective thought. To say "no" is about as socially acceptable in our culture as to hate football, motherhood, or hot apple pie. However, there is nothing wrong with running a small, but successful, business as long as it serves a legitimate purpose and this limited objective is acceptable to you and to your fellow shareholders or investors. If your primary objective or psychological need is to stay small, it is certainly better to recognize that and be honest about it with yourself and others than to create false hopes and expectations which you are either unable or unwilling to fulfill.

If, on the other hand, after careful introspection and soul searching, your answer to the preceding question is a definite "yes,"then you need to answer the three additional questions discussed below.

2. *Can You Attract Effective Management Talent to Work with You?* A clue to the answer is likely to be found in your present reputation as a leader—in the community, among your peers, among your customers, and among your employees. As an additional clue, how often have you had individuals of excellent reputation and proven track record approach you and say, "If you ever have an appropriate opening, I'd like an opportunity to explore it with you?" Still another clue lies in what happens when you interview someone for a key position. Do you spend the major portion of your time telling the applicant about all the great things you have accomplished and how fabulous you are? Or, instead, do you show a sincere interest in letting the applicant tell his or her story; what they have accomplished, what they are proud of, and what their aspirations and objectives are. Everyone is more attracted to a sincere, interested listener than to someone who has to impress and dominate. There is a time and place, of course, to present realistically the challenge and opportunity

which you have in mind, but that should follow rather than precede your giving the applicant a chance to express himself.

3. Can You Select Effective Management Talent? Here is one of the most critical tasks facing the small business enterprise which wants to grow. Paradoxical though if may seem, the small business enterprise can require people of broader imagination, drive, and competence in its officer and key management positions than many major corporations. General Motors, ATT, U.S. Steel, or many other such corporate giants might well be able to lose a dozen vice presidents or have as many positions poorly filled without even seeing a wrinkle in the year-end results or long-term growth pattern. However, in the small enterprise, one such loss or significant misfit might well be seriously damaging, if not fatal.

As a helpful clue for answering this question, do you recognize your own strengths and weaknesses and look to compensate for your weaknesses in your selection of others? Or instead, do you tend to hire "in your own image?" Do you try to balance your own temperament; for example, if you tend to be overly optimistic or overly pessimistic, do you select an individual for your management team who tends to be just the opposite? Or instead, do you tend to select only people who think the way you do? Like a happy marriage, an effective management team requires a certain degree of mutually respectful differences and conflict.

Even more importantly, do you select people primarily on the basis of personal bias, prejudice, first impressions, and superficial characteristics, or are you just as thorough in gathering and evaluating all the objective facts about an individual's background and accomplishments as you would be in considering a major capital investment in plant, equipment, or raw materials?

One client I knew claimed he had a "sure fire" screening test for evaluating executive talent. He would take the prospective applicant to lunch and offer to buy him a drink. If the applicant accepted, he was immediately disqualified. Another small company president used exactly the same test—only he interpreted it completely differently. His explanation was, "I'd never trust a man who doesn't drink." In another situation, a highly qualified controller was turned down only on the basis that he wore a mustache.

The point is, all of us have our preconceptions, biases and past experiences which can easily lead to our developing stereotypes about people. Evaluating management and executive talent is not easy, but it should be based on a logical and thorough consideration of verified past accomplishments and facts, not emotional predispositions. If your record of success is poor in this area, you may find it worthwhile to seek competent professional assistance.

4. Can You Motivate Capable Management Talent? First, I would like to make one point quite clear. The unequivocal answer to this question is "no." In spite of the plethora of articles, books, seminars and management training programs devoted to the subject of "how to motivate your employees," you or I can't motivate anyone. Motivation is internal. It is not something we do to people or put in them. In very simple terms, motivation is nothing more than the difference between what a person has, what he wants, and his perception of what behavior on his part will reduce that difference. If you can accept this, you will realize that while you cannot motivate, you can determine whether or not you will provide a motivating or demotivating climate or environment for the kinds of people you want and need in order to "lengthen your own shadow."

In determining the answer to this question, there are two critical steps to be taken. First, it requires an analysis of the kinds of motives that are likely to be of primary importance to the people you seek. Again, here are some helpful clues:

Is it security?

Not likely. In view of the high risk factor associated with small business survival, you are not likely to appeal to or want the individual to whom security is of primary importance. This type of person is more likely to gravitate to a civil service job, a bank, or a major utility—organizations that seldom have major lay-offs or cut-backs because of minor economic fluctuations. And yet, over and over again I've seen small businesses recruit people from that type of background. This seems to happen because the small businessman goes after the people he can "afford" rather than the people he really needs. You may be lucky, but the probabilities are against you if you go after the individual who has always been with one employer and at age 40 or so is coming to you because he is still well behind his peer group in both salary and level of genuine responsibility and authority. For the small business, at least, I would also be wary of the individual whose first interest is in how long an employment contract you are willing to give.

Is it the potential for significant financial reward?

Probably. That tends to be highly correlated with risk behavior. Professor Herzberg is correct in saying that money doesn't motivate, and therefore you don't pay an individual a lot of money in advance just to buy him. However, the desire and hope for money is a powerful drive for some people and leads to a lot of high risk behavior, such as working for small businesses.

The managers and executives you are likely to want and need are not likely to demand an exorbitant guaranteed base salary. But they are likely to expect an appreciable share of the additional profits which result if they are able to achieve significant but realistic objectives. This should not come as a surprise; after all, what took you into this business in the first place?

Is it the opportunity to exercise individual imagination, responsibility and authority?

Yes, indeed. This, more than anything else, is probably what drives a lot of managerial talent to seek opportunities with small businesses. Quite often, after a few years in the big organization with all of its restraints, regulations, policies, manuals to follow, and complete inaccessibility to the decision-making process, such individuals "have had it." If you can catch them early enough, before they have completely surrendered, you may have something to offer that will motivate more effective performance than they have ever been able to demonstrate before.

However, analyzing the individual's primary motivations and determining whether or not they are appropriate to your organization's needs is just the first step. The second step is analyzing your own ability and willingness to gratify these motivations.

Are you willing to pay for the kinds of talent you need, rather than only for what you can "afford?"

Some men are willing to invest a million or more in equipment and product development before expecting a nickel of profit, but reluctant to pay even $20,000 a year to bring in a competent controller, chief engineer, manufacturing manager, or marketing manager. Such economizing can be fatal.

A frequent barrier to sound business judgment appears to be an underlying, perhaps even unconscious, resentment of someone who wants that kind of salary when the entrepreneur or small business manager remembers so painfully his own days of struggle and personal financial sacrifice and uncertainty just to hold the business together and to get it off the ground. Consequently, a frequent reaction is, "What right does this upstart have, who has never been through what I have, to come in here and expect this kind of income?" However, the more logical question should be, "On the basis of his past proven accomplishments and abilities, what might I expect from this amount of investment?" If you want to hold your talent, then an ancillary question should be, "How willing am I to share the rewards of accomplishment, even though I feel I am the one who is taking the bigger risk?"

Can you satisfy a competent individual's motivation for exercising imagination, decisiveness, authority and responsibility?

No matter how motivated an individual may be when he or she joins your organization, you can quickly kill this valuable trait if you continue to run it the way you did when you first started, or if, by temperament, you find it impossible to delegate any significant authority or decision-making. You certainly have the right and the need to set up reasonable controls and guidelines, but once those are established and agreed upon, can you make yourself live with them?

Can you tolerate mistakes—not only your own but also those of your subordinates?

For example, if your vice president of marketing, after being on the job a reasonable period of time, feels that he has to replace the sales manager who has given your firm ten years of loyal service, how do you react? Do you immediately say, "Absolutely no," or do you simply say, "That's completely your responsibility—do what you want." Either response could be wrong. As a manager, you should be willing to explore the reasons why such a conclusion has been arrived at—delegation is not abdication. However, once you have explored these reasons, considered with your vice president of marketing any feasible alternatives, and brought to his attention any factors or implications of which he may not have been aware, then indeed he should have your support and backing as long as his value to the organization is greater than his liability. And this does not mean you ignore your human responsibility to the individual leaving in terms of fairness, reasonable separation pay, short-term continuation of benefits such as life and health insurance, and any assistance which you and/or your associates might provide in terms of helping him find a more suitable new placement.

SUMMARY

Small business is vitally important to the future of the American free enterprise system. It is not, as some people think, merely a vehicle through which millions of Americans find an avenue of individual expression and autonomy frequently lacking in the large stratified bureaucratic structure. This sector of our economy has traditionally been and will continue to be an important incubator and cradle of innovation, creativity, and human resourcefulness.

If the small businesses of today are going to realize their potential for tomorrow, then some, at least, are going to have to grow and step into the leadership roles that are reserved largely for major corporations. This can be done. There are many names listed on the New York Stock Exchange today that were unheard of ten years ago. But to achieve growth of this magnitude requires continually "lengthened shadows." While business success is the product of many ingredients, one of the most important is the ability of the firm's chief executive officer to attract, select, and motivate people who can complement his own imagination and decision-making abilities.

COMPONENTS OF EFFECTIVENESS

IN SMALL ORGANIZATIONS*

FRANK FRIEDLANDER / HAL PICKLE

A primary focus for those interested in understanding or changing organizations has been upon the internal dynamics of the organization. This focus has led to emphasis on methods of enhancing the worth of the employee (to himself or to the organization) through selection, training, group participation, job restructuring, etc.; and consequently to criteria of effectiveness that are limited to the internal dynamics of the organization. The criteris have typically been of two kinds: those dealing with individual human resources such as motivation, mental health, cohesiveness, satisfaction, etc.; and those concerned with individual performance, such as amount produced, quality of output, error rate, etc. The generally low relationship between these two sets of criteria has been disturbing for the researcher and has resulted in numerous dilemmas for the practitioner.[1] Since these two criteria have for the most part been uncorrelated, it appears useless to attempt to maximize them both. On the other hand, favoring one over the other produces either inefficiency for the organization or dissatisfaction for the individual. This dilemma has spurred some researchers to expand the scope of their analyses to encompass situational determinants of the satisfaction-performance relationship.[2] Others have, in one way or another, explicitly recognized the inescapable tension between the individual and the organizational goals[3] and have concentrated upon the reduction of these tensions.

For the most part, theories and research concerned with individual performance, employee satisfaction, and reduction of tension between individual and organizational goals are dealing only with internal aspects of the events, relationships, and structures that make up the total organizational system. If the organization is viewed as an open-energy system, however, it is apparent that it is dependent for survival and growth upon a variety of energy transfers not only within the organization, but also between the organization and its external environment.[4] It is obvious, then, that the internal and external dynamics

*From *Administrative Science Quarterly* (September, 1968), pp. 289-304. Reprinted with permission.

[1] S. Seashore, *Assessing Organization Performance with Behavioral Measurements* (Ann Arbor, Michigan: The Foundation for Research on Human Behavior, 1964).

[2] R. Katzell, R. S. Barrett, and T. C. Parker, Job Satisfaction, Job Performance, and Situational Characteristics, *Journal of Applied Psychology*, 45 (1961), 65-72.

[3] H. Levinson, Role, Personality, and Social Structure in the Organizational Setting, *Journal of Abnormal and Social Psychology*, 58 (1959), 170-180; C. Argyris, *Interpersonal Competence and Organizational Effectiveness* (Homewood, Illinois: Dorsey Press, 1962); H. A. Shepard, "Changing Interpersonal and Intergroup Relationships in Organizations," in James G. March (ed.) *Handbook of Organizations* (New York: Rand McNally, 1964), pp. 1115-1143.

[4] Daniel Katz and Robert L. Kahn, *The Social Psychology of Organizations* (New York: Wiley, 1966).

of the organization are complementary and interdependent. Modifications in one of these structures have an impact upon the other. This perspective of the organization is similar to the model proposed by Parsons,[5] in which four fundamental processes are specified for every social system: adaptation, goal achievement, integration, and latency. These functions provide a structural framework within which internal and external relationships may be explored.

A perspective that includes the organization's societal relationships can account for the full cycle of energy, since it incorporates both the importation of energy from this societal environment and the output of energy into that environment. The relationship between organization and environment is recognized by several research workers. For example, Bennis[6] claims that bureaucracy is least likely to cope and survive if unable to adapt to a rapidly changing, turbulent environment. Emery and Trist[7] stress that the primary task of managing an enterprise as a whole is to relate the total organizational system to its environment, and not just internal regulation. If the organization is to survive and grow, it must control its boundary conditions—the forms of exchange between the enterprise and the environment. Strother[8] reverses the direction of this influence process by claiming that one must allow for control of the organization by an outside and changing enrivonment. Pepinsky, Weick, and Riner[9] observe that the organization must adapt to regulatory control by the environment. Typical models of organization behavior, however, treat the organization as a closed system and concentrate upon principles of internal functioning as if these problems were independent of the external environments.[10]

SYSTEM EFFECTIVENESS

Parallel to the need to understand the total organization system as interdependent with its environment is the establishment of criteria of organizational effectiveness that reflect these interdependencies. Such criteria include those with some element of the organization's contribution *to society,* and those that describe effectiveness in terms of maximization of return *from society* to the organization. Bass,[11] for example, suggests that an organization be evaluated in terms of its worth to the individual worker and the value of the worker and the

---

[5]Talcott Parsons, Edward Shils, Kaspar Naegle, and Jesse Pitts, *Theories of Society* (New York: The Free Press, 1961), pp. 38-41.

[6]Warren G. Bennis, Organizational Developments and the Fate of Bureaucracy, address presented at the meetings of the American Psychological Associations, Los Angeles, Calif., September, 1964.

[7]F. E. Emery and Eric L. Trist, Socio-Technical Systems, paper presented at Sixth Annual International Meeting of the Institute of Management Sciences, Paris, France, September, 1959.

[8]G. B. Strother, "Problems in the Development of Social Science of Organization," in H. J. Leavitt (ed.) *The Social Science of Organizations* (Englewood Cliffs, New Jersey: Prentice-Hall, 1963), pp. 3-37.

[9]H. B. Pepinsky, K. E. Weick, and J. W. Riner, *Primer for Productivity* (Columbus, Ohio: Ohio State University Research Foundation, 1965).

[10]Katz and Kahn, *op. cit.*

[11]Bernard M. Bass, Ultimate Criteria of Organizational Worth, *Personnel Psychology,* 5 (1952), 157-173.

organization to society. Similar criteria suggested by Davis[12] include broad social values, economic values and the personal values. The emphasis is in a reversed direction for Katz and Kahn,[13] who describe organizational effectiveness as referring to the maximization of return to the organization by all means—technological, political, market control, personnel policies, federal subsidies, etc.

Most behavioral scientists have come to realize that organizational effectiveness is not a unitary concept. Guion, for example, points out that "the fallacy of the single criterion lies in its assumption that everything that is to be predicted is related to everything else to be predicted—that there is a general factor in all criteria accounting for virtually all of the important variance in behavior at work and its various consequences of value."[14] The assumption of unitary criteria of organizational effectiveness has its counterpart in the concept of utility maximization, in which utility is defined as the value to an individual of all things he can possible enjoy or possess. All of the nonmonetary components are assumed to be translatable into a single utility scale, which allows trade-offs between the nonmonetary and monetary components. The behavioral theory of the firm, by contrast, is rooted in the "satisficing" concept of individuals searching until a satisfactory (not an optimal) solution is found.[15] Individuals are not likely to combine their various sources of satisfaction into a single function, and certainly are not likely to maximize such a function. They are likely to seek satisfactory solutions in the several areas of their activities, with a few trade-offs.

These differences in assumptions parallel those of organizational behavior, not only in terms of the criteria of organization, but also in terms of the criteria of organizational effectiveness. In the behavioral theory of organizations, it is assumed that goals are formulated for organizational activity in several areas. The rational-man assumptions of economics for the individual become profit maximization for the organization. If organizational goals are extended beyond profit maximization, the organizational utility function must incorporate effectiveness in these other areas.[16] If satisficing in these several activities rather than profit maximization is an organization goal, relative independence in their attainment might be expected.

Although the degree-of-fulfillment terminology is used in this article, fulfillment is probably more accurately represented in terms of the degree to which the organizational or environmental component is satisficed. Furthermore, it is probable that the expectations which a component holds of the organization in general, and the specific organization with which it transacts, affect the degree to which that component it satisficed with the organization.

Clearly, effectiveness criteria must take into account the profitability of the organization, the degree to which it satisfices its members, and the degree to

[12]R. C. Davis, Industrial Organization and Management (New York: Harper, 1940).

[13]Katz and Kahn, op. cit.

[14]Robert M. Guion, Criterion Measurement and Personnel Judgments, Personnel Psychology, 14 (1961), 141-149, esp. p. 145.

[15]Herbert A. Simon, Models of Man (New York: John Wiley, 1957).

[16]A. Charnes and A. C. Stedry, Quasi-Rational Models of Behavior in Organization Research (Management Sciences Research Report No. 31; Pittsburg: Graduate School of Industrial Administration, 1965).

which it is of value to the larger society of which it is a part. These three perspectives include system maintenance and growth, subsystem fulfillment, and environmental fulfillment. Each is obviously composed of several related components, and each component is hypothetically related to the other. The degree to which these several components of organizational effectiveness are interrelated is a primary focus of this paper.

The purpose of this study, then, was to explore the concept of total organizational effectiveness by studying the relationships between internal and external system effectiveness. Internal system components were those within the formal boundaries of the organization. Societal components with which the organization transacts by exporting and importing energy were considered part of the larger environment in which the organization is located. Effectiveness was viewed as the degree to which the needs of components were fulfilled (or satisficed) in their transactions with the organization. The specific interest was in the degree of interdependence in the satisfaction of components.

The particular subsystem components chosen for study do not exhaust the variety of components, but were selected to include seven of primary importance for the maintenance and growth of the organization in its society: the owner, the employees, and five societal components—the customers, the suppliers, the creditors, the community, and the government.[17]

DATA

Sample

Small organizations were preferred as sample units in the study because it was felt that whatever relationships exist among components might be explored more adequately, since the links among these components are presumably shorter and less numerous. The sample included 97 small businesses, each with only one level of management, and each employing from four to about forty employees.

A random stratified technique was used. The distribution of types of small businesses in the United States was determined from various census data and this distribution was approximated in a random selection of small businesses within the state of Texas. Since responses from two of the initial 97 business organizations were suspect, two additional organizations were substituted for these. The final sample of 97 small businesses was composed of 54 retail establishments, 26 service establishments, 8 wholesale establishments, 6 manufacturers, and 3 mineral extraction firms.

Societal Components

The data for measuring the degree of fulfillment for each of the five societal components for each of the 97 organizations were gathered by questionnaires

[17]While customers, suppliers, creditors, communities and governments were grouped in the general category of the organization's societal environment, other models are obvious. In accord with Parson's AGIL model (adaptation, goal attainment, integration, latency), for example, owners and customers are crucial to goal attainment of product exchange; creditors, communities, governments, and suppliers provide necessary resources and support for the organization and are thus instrumental in the organization's adaptation to its environment; and employees perform integrative functions within the organizational system. Talcott Parsons, Edward Shils, Kaspar Naegle, and Jesse Pitts, *Theories of Society* (New York: The Free Press, 1961), pp. 38-41.

and interviews. All data were collected in quantified form, either in a Likert-type, multiple-choice format, or in specific dollar amounts or frequency information.

Initially, satisfaction for each of the five societal components was measured by from five to thirty-seven items. Correlation co-efficients were then computed among all items within each of the five components. Items within each of the five components which correlated highly with each other were then selected to represent that component, so as to maximize its internal consistency or cohesion. The items so selected were then given equal weight and averaged to form mean scores for each of the components. As a final check on this process and on the internal consistency of each component scale, reliability coefficients for internal consistency[18] were computed for each scale with the following results: customers, .96; suppliers, .77; owners, .92; communities, .65; and governments, .60. This method of scale construction, based upon maximizing the internal consistency of items within each scale, yielded improved results over some of our earlier procedures which did not utilize this method.

The data gathered and the methods used follow:

1. Community. Community fulfillment was measured in the general areas of membership and leadership in local and nonlocal organizations, the number of committees and drives that managers participated in during the past two years, and their attendance at community affairs such as fund-raising dinners, bazaars, etc. These data were obtained through a questionnaire survey administered to the managers in directed interviews.

2. Government. Relations with the federal, state, and local government were measured through the administration of a questionnaire to managers. Items concerned questioning by officials of the Internal Revenue Service on income tax returns, penalties paid on local, state or federal taxes, or reprimands or censures by tax officials. In general, these items reflected the degree to which the organization carried out its explicit and implicit responsibilities with governmental agencies.

3. Customers. Customers were surveyed by the use of a questionnaire administered in an interview. The sample size for each organization was proportional to its total number of customers within a framework of a minimum of 15 and a maximum of 25 customers per organization. Customers rated the respective business on a five-point scale on each of the following features: quality of goods or services; quantity of goods or services available; neatness, cleanliness, and uniformity of appearance of product; management's knowledge of product or service; speed of service; dependability of business; rank of this business in relation to others in its field; helpfulness, friendliness, and appearance of employees.

4. Suppliers. Supplier fulfillment was measured in the following areas: promptness of payment of accounts, fairness in transactions, receptiveness to suggestions, and overall evaluation as a customer. Of 403 survey questionnaires

---

[18]The internal consistency of each total societal component scale was computed using Kuder-Richardson's formula 20:

$$\gamma_{TT} = [\frac{\eta}{\eta-1}][\frac{\sigma_I{}^2 - \Sigma \rho q}{\sigma_I{}^2}].$$

Essentially, this formula measures the proportion of the total scale variance $[\sigma \gamma^2]$, which is composed of the sum of the inter-item covariances $[\gamma_{12}, \sigma_1 \sigma_2]$. This formula was not applied to the creditor scale, since data were gathered from different types of statistical and financial records and were, therefore, not comparable.

mailed, 208 were completed and returned, representing a return of approximately 52 percent.

5. Creditors. Levels of creditor fulfillment with each organization were obtained from statistical data gathered during interviews with banks, retail merchant associations, and Dun and Bradstreet.

Owner Components

The degree of satisfaction for the owner of each organization was primarily financial. The score was composed of equal weights of the average yearly profit for the owner for the last ten years and the average yearly profit as a function of the hours per week that the owner worked for the organization. Since the correlation between these two measures was .95, the component was essentially a measure of owner financial profit.

Employee Component

The SRA Employee Inventory, a measure of employee satisfaction was administered to all employees of each organization having ten or fewer employees. For organizations having more than ten employees, ten were randomly selected to represent the organization. A total of 513 inventories were completed, representing an average of 5.29 employees per organization.

Five types of employee fulfillment were measured within each organization. These types of fulfillment had been previously derived from a factor analysis of the SRA Employee Inventory.[19] Types of fulfillment included the following:

1. Satisfaction with Working Conditions: nine items related to adequacy of working conditions, effects of these conditions on work efficiency, adequacy of equipment, reasonable hours of work, and absence of physical and mental pressures.

2. Satisfaction with Financial Reward: seven items related to adequacy of pay, effectiveness of personnel policies with respect to pay, and benefit programs and pay in comparison with other companies.

3. Confidence in Management: nineteen items related to management's organizing ability, its handling of employee benefit policies, its adequacy in two-way communication, and its interest in employees.

4. Opinion about Immediate Supervisor: twelve items related to how well the supervisor organized his work, knowledge of the job, ability to get things done on time, supplying adequate equipment, letting employees know what was expected, emphasizing proper training, making employees work together, treating employees fairly, keeping his promises, giving encouragement, and interest in employee welfare.

5. Satisfaction with Self-development: five items related to employee's feeling of belongingness, of participation, of pride in the company, of doing something worthwhile, and of growth on the job.

[19]Zile S. Dabas, The Dimensions of Morale: An Item Factorization of the SRA Employee Inventory. *Personnel Psychology.* 11 (1958), 217-234.

TABLE 1   Relationships Among Societal Fulfillment, Owner Fulfillment, Organizational Size, and Employee Fulfillment.

Components fulfilled	Employee fulfillment				
	Working conditions	Financial rewards	Confidence in management	Immediate Supervisor	Self-development
Societal components					
Community	.33*	.06	.28*	.23†	.24†
Government	—.09	.00	—.06	—.03	—.12
Customer	.11	.20†	.21†	.23†	.32*
Supplier	.11	.12	.16	.05	.10
Creditor	.09	—.03	.09	.15	.16
Owner					
Financial profit	.12	.07	.20†	.22†	.23†
Organizational size					
(size of work force)	—.03	—.21	—.10	—.03	.01

* p<.01.
† p<.05.
N = 97.

RESULTS

Correlation coefficients were computed in order to explore the relationships among the components.[20] The relationships between external and internal criteria of organizational effectiveness were considered first. External criteria were those related to fulfillment of the needs of the five components of the societal system; internal criteria were those related to the five needs of the employees.

In a moderate number of instances, organizations were able to satisfice both societal needs and employee needs simultaneously, as indicated in Table 1. In almost all cases where significant relationships do exist, however, these are of a relatively low magnitude. Thus, while some mutual satisficing of employees and societal components does occur, the degree of this concurrent satisficing is rather low. Of the five societal components, only community and customer satisfaction seem to vary consistently (and positively) with the several types of employee satisfaction. In the case of community fulfillment, this finding is understandable. Organizations that recognize community needs and fulfill them are likely to be effective in providing similarly for their employees. Furthermore, in smaller communities, the membership of community and employee groups may overlap to a considerable degree. The reasons for the

[20]To check for curvilinear relationships between variables, scatter plot outputs from computer runs were examined visually. In those cases where some curvilinearity was suggested, tests of curvilinearity were made. In no case was the appropriate coefficient (η) significant.

employee-customer satisfaction relationship are perhaps similar to those of the finding on the employee-community satisfaction relationship. Furthermore, in retail and service organizations, close contact between customers and employees may serve as a mechanism of contagion of satisfaction. Customer satisfaction may fulfill employee service needs, thereby causing employee satisfaction which, in turn, is sensed by customers. Finally, both the community and customer components represent more personal and less organized entities within the society. A management which takes action to increase employee fulfillment might thus tend also to focus upon increased customer and community satisfaction.

In the association between employee satisfaction and owner fulfillment, several significant relationships were found. Financially successful organizations were also those in which employees had confidence in management, held higher opinions of the supervisor, and sensed opportunities for self-development. Although these correlations were not of a high magnitude, they do point to the tempting conclusion that satisfied employees contribute toward (or are a product of) an organization profitable for the owner. The relationship is highest between owner fulfillment and employee self-development, a finding that seems understandable since the self-development measure reflects the employee's feelings of belongingness, participation, and pride in the company—a sense of "psychological ownership" in the organization. Previous findings in this area are ambiguous, however. Bass, McGhee, and Vaughan[21] found that satisfaction with one's particular job in the company did not seem particularly related to financial performance of the company. Katzell, Barrett, and Parker,[22] however, reported about three-fourths of their attitude items correlated positively with organizational performance and no items correlated negatively with performance. They also reported consistently negative relationships between job satisfaction and size of work force, a finding validated to some extent in this study. Table 1 reveals consistent (but generally not significant) negative relationships between organizational size (as measured by size of work force) and employee fulfillment. The single significant relationship indicates that employees are less satisfied with pay policies in organizations composed of larger work forces.

Since the relationships between internal and external criteria of organizational effectiveness were relatively weak, the relationships among the several external criteria were of interest, as well as those between external criteria and owner fulfillment and organizational size.

The relationships among the external components of the organizational system show no definite pattern, as indicated in Table 2. Only five of the 15 relationships are significant. Customer satisfaction is correlated positively with supplier and owner fulfillment, which is understandable, since both are societal units with which the organization exchanges services directly for financial remuneration. This is also the case for exchanges with the employee components of the organization.

There was a negative relation between government and customer fulfillment, which was unexpected. It appears that organizations that focus upon goal

[21] Bernard M. Bass, Walter P. McGhee, and James A. Vaughan, Three Levels of Analysis of Cost-Effectiveness Associated with Personnel Attitudes and Attributes, prepared for the *Proceedings of the Logistics Research Conference*, Warrenton, Virginia: Department of Defense, May, 1965.

[22] R. Katzell, R. S. Barrett, and T. C. Parker, *op. cit.*

TABLE 2   Relationships Among Societal Fulfillment, Owner Fulfillment, and Organizational Size.

Components fulfilled	Fulfillment of needs of					
	Government	Customer	Supplier	Creditor	Owner	Org. size
Societal components						
Community	.00	—.04	.03	.03	.32*	.29*
Government		—.25†	—.11	.20†	—.11	—.07
Customer			.20†	.10	.21†	.20†
Supplier				.09	.08	.13
Creditor					—.02	.10
Owner						.28*

* $p < .01$.
† $p < .05$.
$N = 97$.

achievement through customer interactions are less concerned with the adaptive functions of fulfilling governmental obligations. However, the adaptive function of fulfilling community needs does appear to be related to the goal of achieving organizational profitability; organizations whose managers are actively involved in community affairs are also those that are most profitable for the owner.

Perhaps one of the most direct exchanges leading to goal attainment is that between the owner and the customer of the organization. Table 2 indicates that organizations in which owner needs are fulfilled are also those in which customer fulfillment is high. The tempting conclusion is that the successful organization (for the owner) is one which satisfices customer needs also.

As might be predicted, government and creditor fulfillment were moderately correlated. The needs of both of these components can be viewed more as financial obligations of the organization. These needs are fulfilled as they are continually reduced to a minimum.

Organization size is also related to the ability of the organization to fulfill the needs of the societal component. The larger the organization (in number of employees), the more likely it is to fulfill the needs of its community, its owner, and its customers. Organizations with larger human and financial resources can be expected to provide greater support for the community in which they exist; they are able to offer a wider variety of products and services to customers, and thus greater psychological and financial satisfaction for the owner. Two notes of caution should be mentioned in connection with these inferences. First, one cannot be sure as to the causal direction of these relationships. It it possible that because an organization provides fulfillment for its community, owner, and customers, it has grown larger. It is more probable that causality changes its direction over time: at one time the organization grows because it fulfills societal needs; subsequently, society's needs are fulfilled to a greater extent because the organization is larger and offers greater resources. Second, organizational size in this study was limited to organizations of forty employees. In organizations with many more than forty employees, it is probable that the size-fulfillment relationship becomes asymptotic; similar increments in size may produce decreasing gains in societal fulfillment.

DISCUSSION

In this study we have attempted to avoid the dichotomy of satisfaction versus productivity, by which organizational effectiveness is traditionally gauged. This dichotomy has left both organizational researchers and practitioners with discomforting dilemmas, and resulted in a focus on internal criteria to the exclusion of the demands of the organization's environment. Instead, the organization has been conceived as interdependent components or subsystems through which energy is transferred; and energy exchange occurs both within the organization and also between it and its environment. In this light, organizational effectiveness is the extent to which all forms of energic return to the organization are maximized.

The five societal components upon which the organization is dependent for its survival and growth include the community, government, customers, suppliers, and creditors. The organization is also dependent upon maximizing energy transformation within the firm, a process in which its employees play a major role. A third component important in the survival and growth of the organization is its owner. The focus of the study was on the degree to which fulfillment of the needs of the organization's environmental components was related to fulfillment of the needs of the organization's internal subsystem components, and whether organizational size was related to these.

Findings of this study indicate that there are only a moderate number of relationships between the degree to which the organization concurrently fulfills the needs of its internal subsystem components (its employees), its owner, and the components of its larger society. Concurrent fulfillment of the needs of the five societal components is also of a rather low magnitude.

Evidently, organizations find it difficult to fulfill simultaneously the variety of demands made upon them. Whether the organization *can* concurrently fulfill all or even a major share of the divergent demands made upon it is a provocative and hypothetical question. It is probable that organizations do not strive to maximize fulfillment of any one system component, but operate in accordance with a policy of satisficing several system components. A no-layoff policy, for example, may partially fulfill employee needs, but might do so at the cost of diminishing fulfillment of other societal components. Fulfillment of needs of the various organizational components must, therefore, be treated separately and, apparently, independently. Components in the organization's system are linked together more by the flow of energic activities than by common goal attainment.

From a broader vantage, then, the manager's task is not only to coordinate functions within the organization, but to relate these internal functions to the organization's societal environment. Lack of concurrent maximization of the organization's components calls for greater focus upon the role of the manager as a systems balancer as well as a mediator of the boundaries of the organization.[23]

The inability of the organization to fulfill concurrently the needs of its societal components, its owners, and its employees presents dilemmas for theorists in organizational behavior as well as for practitioners in industrial organizations. If prophesies and predictions[24] are correct, the tasks and goals of

---

[23]K. Davis and R. L. Blomstrom, *Business and Its Environment* (New York: McGraw-Hill, 1966), and B. M. Bass, *Organizational Psychology,* (Boston: Allyn and Bacon, 1965).

[24]W. Bennis, *op. cit.*

organizations will become far more complex in the future and will require greater adaptive and innovative capabilities. These increasing organizational complexities will demand the articulation and development of meta-goals that shape and provide the foundation for the goal structure. For example, one meta-goal might be the creation of a system for detecting new and changing goals of the organization or methods for deciding priorities among goals.

Finally, as Bennis [25] predicts, there will be an increase in goal conflict, more and more divergency and contradictoriness between and among effectiveness criteria. While at this date, the different effectiveness criteria among the variety of organizational functions appear unrelated and divergent, lethargy by management may allow these relationships to become negatively related to each other. Management's awareness of these relationships and of how they may change with differing goal structures seems a first step toward maximizing future organizational effectiveness.

[25]*Ibid.*

SIX

The Maturity Crisis

The business has now reached a level of maturity that presents new challenges to the management team. Since the initial start-up, the firm has changed from having an almost exclusive concern for the product and its production and marketing to a more people-oriented, regimented and more risk-averse organization. If the entrepreneur-founder is still with the business, then he also will have changed—most noticeably from an autonomous leader to a delegating manager. He must now learn to work from reports and meetings, rather than from direct day-to-day interaction with marketing, production, and accounting personnel.

It is during this stage that business firms will often outgrow their ability to generate sufficient cash from internal operations to finance expansion in plant and equipment, the development of new products, or the addition of new markets—some or all of which may be required to meet major competitive forces or increased consumer demand. Several alternatives exist for securing this financing, each having its advantages and disadvantages. There can be the outright sale of the firm, resulting in the entrepreneur becoming either an employee of the purchasing firm or unemployed. Alternatively, a merger may enable the entrepreneur to retain some control over the combined business while obtaining the resources required to meet the company's expanded business objectives. But the merger transaction may be difficult to consummate, especially if the company's stock is closely held and not readily marketable. A public offering has many advantages but only if the placement is successful. One advantage is that the market value of the firm will be established, allowing a realizable value to be placed on the stockholder's investment. Establishing the liquidity of the stock will usually also make any future acquisitions or mergers more attainable and profitable, especially for the high-growth company in a period of rising stock market prices. A successful stock placement will bring an influx of capital, but the entrepreneur must relinquish some control over the business.

The first article by F.W.Copeland, *When Companies Reach the Awkward Age,* portrays an entrepreneur-founder during a period of changing long-term needs for his business. He has successfully developed his idea for a unique and better product into a profitable venture that over time has grown modestly in number of employees and dollar sales. But now the entrepreneur is faced with his first major expansion. The autonomous owner must now become the managing owner who delegates major responsibilities to the newly hired managers in his expanded organization. Copeland's story about the composite Mr. X is very real in the events that take place: the consultant who proposes the gold-plated plan without establishing an adequate means for implementation; the hiring of managerial types to assume major departmental positions but restricting their effectiveness by imposing unrealistically low salaries; and then, after choosing the best men from those available, assuming that the business is in the responsible and reassuring hands of managing experts. The lack of inter-department communications and feed-back monitoring almost brings Mr. X's firm to a state of collapse.

There are several significant points in Copeland's article. If additional capital resources are required beyond what it is presently available to the firm, outside capital must be raised to cope with the maturity crisis. The availability of these funds in the amounts required must be ensured before major expenditures for expansion can be made. But no amount of capital resources will result in a successful expansion unless the new organization is staffed with competent men, and the operations are continually monitored to sense marketing, personnel, product and finance problems. The only factor that measures the worth of a small business's struggle for survival is its profitability. An overzealous owner can endanger his company by too many frills, resulting in too high an overhead and insufficient capital resources to support this overhead. The next two readings provide insight into the means of obtaining financial resources to support expansion and reorganization during the maturity crisis.

In addition to reorganizational problems, involving the adding of more personnel to meet a more intense competitive demand for the company's product, the small business that has effectively exploited its product idea will also find that success has resulted in greater competitive pressures. Maintaining or expanding the rate of company growth under this threat may require the addition of distribution channels and more warehousing, or horizontal integration in the form of additional manufacturing capacity. Sufficient capital and management resources may not be available for implementation of these necessary changes.

Edward Fillion, in A Way Out for Small Business, proposes mergers as a viable alternative in meeting and overcoming these competitive threats. It may also be a way for the founders to liquidate their investment profitably. Fillion reviews the need for careful consideration of the operational and management needs of the business and the legal and tax requirements imposed by government. One of Fillion's main points is that mergers should be considered in a positive sense as a strategic technique to use in achieving planned business objectives. Merging should not be viewed as a stop-gap measure for saving the business after errors of management have been made—although it may very well provide the only means for survival.

As stated above, the small business affected by changing technological and competitive environments must implement compensatory changes if it is to retain its growth rate, market share, and position. The required strategy for overcoming difficulties may overburden the small company's capital resources, both from internal operations and external credit arrangements. Instead of merging to acquire the supplementary capital that it needs, as the article by Fillion suggested, the company could raise the funds through a public offering of stock. Gerald Sears, in *Public Offerings for Smaller Companies,* considers the advantages of going public and offers some suggestions on selecting the underwriter and preparing the offer or prospectus.

If the marketing of the stock is successfully managed, the firm can expect future financing to be easier, more timely, and less costly. Borrowing capacity will be increased as a result of the firm's improved financial ratios and the increased confidence of its management. The firm's fair market value will be established for use in any future acquisition, merger, or selling negotiation. As Sears emphasizes, many of the potential advantages of going public will depend on the selection of a competent underwriter, experienced and familiar with the issuer's industry, to develop and implement an effective stock-offering strategy.

A successful public offering, however, will depend on the complementary occurrence of several factors. First, the firm should have a growth rate attractively higher that the average for the industry; the stock will reflect this intrinsic growth value and will be priced by the investors accordingly, resulting in a rapid placement and a high P/E ratio. Secondly, the entrepreneur-owner in his new role as an officer in a public company must be able to communicate effectively with the financial community and stockholders. A third requirement for a successful public offering is that the competitive position of the firm not be impaired by the disclosure of profit margins, market-share estimates, and similar data contained in the prospectus.

In the final article, by G. H. B. Gould and Dean C. Coddington, *How Do You Know What Your Business is Worth?,* the authors offer three methods of valuing an ongoing business. They conclude the capitalized earnings approach is the most valid because this technique of valuation is all-encompassing. Without a doubt, placing a value on a small privately held concern is a subjective process. How to do it fairly and accurately is the subject of this article offered as a management aid by the Small Business Administration.

To survive during this critical maturity period, special consideration needs to be given to evaluating the products' life cycles, intruding market competition, and changing or increasing consumer needs. Strategies must be developed for meeting the changing environment, for exploiting new business opportunities, and generally for preparing the company for future growth. Capital resources must be obtained for supporting this growth, usually through a merger or a public stock issue.

WHEN COMPANIES REACH

THE AWKWARD AGE*

F. W. COPELAND

Five years ago, Mr. X was earning $20,000 a year as an engineer with a big defense manufacturer. Then he quit to launch the XYZ Company. It grew from a staff of three, working in his garage, to a force of 50 people turning out billings of $40,000 a month in a 10,000-foot leased shop. Getting orders was the easiest part of the operation. Mr. X could quote fixed prices on jobs that were headaches for a prime contractor because of mysterious "bugs," or because the quantities were so small. Purchasing agents were tickled pink to get the order off their desks, and a "fixed price" instead of "cost-plus" in their over-all cost estimates. Mr. X figured material cost at $50 per unit and quoted $500 apiece for a lot of ten. Nobody batted an eye. Then he devoted the brains and skill of a $20,000-a-year man to the task of designing and making a successful prototype. He worked, ate and slept with the problem until he either licked it or decided it was hopeless. In the first case, he had a good chance of getting the pre-production order of 100 units at $200 apiece. If he failed, he lost nothing but his own time and a little material. When he had a $20,000 backlog, he leased more space and hired a few people. In due course, Mr. X's special training plus the cut-and-dry experience at customers' expense made him known as an expert in his specialty field. Inquiries and orders began to come automatically.

In flexibility and speed of quotation and delivery he could run circles around larger competitors, because he personally initiated, specified and implemented every phase of design, procurement, and production. He could quote a lower price yet make a wider margin of profit because he had no overhead except rent, utilities, and the salary of a part-time bookkeeper. Another advantage was in income taxes. If he considered it good business to charge off a 100 per cent tax reserve against work-in-process inventory and all drawings, special tooling, jigs, fixtures, and so on, and this happened to wipe out all or most of his operating income, nobody could challenge him, for there were no cost or turnover records to contradict his pessimism. (But if somebody asked him to put a value on his company for sale or merger, how fast those values soared!)

Mr. X enjoyed another extraordinary advantage—the microscopic amount of capital required. Since his operation consisted largely of assembling small, light pieces, his fixed assets were few and inexpensive. The principal outlay was for testing and inspection equipment, some of which could be borrowed, some bought second-hand and some included in the cost estimate of the first jobs and charged off accordingly. The only inventory required was for specific orders, self-liquidating on completion. Accounts receivable were low because the large

*Reprinted by special permission from *Dun's,* February 1961. Copyright, 1961, Dun & Bradstreet Publications Corporation.

customers were sympathetic, paid promptly or prepaid. Suppliers and even bankers gave very liberal terms of credit hoping to win the gratitude of the little company if and when it orbited. Although it was impossible to figure the net worth of the XYZ Company, it appeared to be turning its capital ten to twenty times a year.

THE GREAT DIVIDE

When the company hit the 50-employee mark, Mr. X was unaware that he had reached a milestone—the limit of his capacity to do everything and boss everything himself and the loss of some of the important advantages of smallness. He did, however, realize that although he was enormously proud of his accomplishment, and rated locally as an industrialist, he was running breathlessly on a treadmill. Mrs. X was complaining that for five years she had had no husband. His children hardly knew their father, and his doctor had hinted of ulcers.

Mr. X pondered three alternatives: to disregard the doctor and leave it to chance whether the business would expand or shrink, to cut back to a comfortable volume based on his personalized efforts, or to take the plunge—to think big, act big, grow big. Of course, he picked No. 3.

As a starter, Mr. X hired a "management consultant" with a degree from a famous business school, two years as a junior employee of a nationally known management firm, and three months on his own—admittedly young, but eager and cheap. Mr. X told him to study the picture carefully and bring in a complete set of recommendations for an expanded operation, based on an annual gross income of $1 million. "If we can do $500,000 a year with me doing all the selling, it's a cinch to do twice that with a real sales organization."

MAN WITH A PLAN

The expert returned a month later with a 50-page report and a wall-size organization chart elaborately diagramming an impressive array of management functions. The book of procedures outlined in detail the exact duties and responsibilities of each department head and tactfully quoted from various reports that stressed the need for the president to delegate authority and refrain from breathing down anyone's neck.

The organization chart fascinated Mr. X, and it pleased his ego that it should take all these people to accomplish what he had been doing all by himself, but he was appalled at the prospect of spending so much money unproductively. Still, the expert showed him figures proving that billings of $80,000 a month, with a normal margin of gross profit, would absorb all costs and expenses and leave a net of 15 per cent before taxes. Groggy but game, Mr. X said he would buy the package—but would select the personnel himself.

The employment agencies were excited when he said he wanted five department heads immediately, though when he limited salaries to $500 a month, and said he expected "damned good men," the applicants seemed to fall into two categories: elderly men with long lists of jobs and lukewarm references, and young men with excellent references but in positions well below department head level.

When the smoke cleared, the XYZ Company had engaged five men at $500, two girls at $300, and one trainee at $200. Some 1,000 feet of additional floor space had been leased and two toilets added. There was a great deal of new office equipment, a switchboard, and an intercom system.

Although he suffered nightmares of apprehension, Mr. X kept his hands off the reins. Theoretically he was supposed to keep in touch through reports from the controller, but the latter was honest enough to admit that his monthly P & L reports and balance sheets were unreliable until his newly established systems of job-costing, perpetual inventory, depreciation, etc., could build up a historical record.

One evening Mr. X was surprised to receive, at his home, a phone call from the loan officer at the bank. The officer asked him to drop in for a chat, without bringing the controller.

When Mr. X appeared the next day, the banker said: "Please understand, Mr. X, we have great confidence in you and only want your assurance that this tight-money situation is due to a temporary surge of business and is self-liquidating." Mr. X was deeply hurt and indignant. He explained in detail his expansion program and showed the forecasts of income and profit. The banker spent the next hour patiently explaining the difference between credit and capital. What the XYZ Company needed was a base of permanent capital, and since the amount would be in excess of collateral and beyond expectancy of early repayment, it should be considered "risk capital." If the company contemplated marketing proprietary items in addition to its custom business, this would mean substantial amounts tied up in finished inventory. And if the largest manufacturers in the country could not turn their capital more than three or four times a year, the XYZ Company had to figure on at least $200,000 net worth if they anticipated doing $1 million a year.

WAKING UP TO REALITIES

Mr. X staggered back to his office in a daze, called a staff meeting that included the management expert, and told them what the banker said. "What the hell have you done to my company?" he shouted. "It looks as if we were broke."

The management expert asked quietly, "Where is that income of $80,000 a month?"

The sales manager said, "How can I get sales when it takes a month to get a price and delivery to quote?"

The chief engineer said, "How can I design, or even write up specs when the sales department keeps me swamped with cockeyed inquiries? Why doesn't somebody sell something standard now and then?"

The production manager said, "How can I turn out production when the engineering department won't release specifications, the purchasing department won't bring in enough material, the inspection and quality control departments are always feuding, and the financial department keeps me so busy with paper work that I can't get into the shop?"

Each department head had been so fearful of deviating from the system that he dodged taking any responsibility. Although the backlog of orders was building up to record figures, little was being shipped and all the cash was frozen in inventory.

Did Mr. X fire the lot and go back to one-man supervision? Did he keep on doggedly and go broke—or get an angel to finance him for a while? Or did he compromise by keeping one or two of the department heads, taking back from them the authority he had delegated?

In any case, Mr. X had to look for new capital unless he wanted to sell out or merge. It is a safe bet that he went to the Small Business Administration and asked for a long-term capital loan—and was quite properly turned down for lack of either collateral or an earning record. He probably went to one or more of the small business investment companies for a debenture loan and was told that his operation did not have enough glamor to assure a resale market. The investment bankers shied away when they saw his figures. He flirted with a small-issue specialty house, but backed down when he learned the cost. Private investors offered him the capital he needed but demanded a straight equity position and control (Mr. X said he would "burn down the plant first"). If he did solve his problem it was probably via a facesaving compromise: For a substantialsweetener in free common stock, an outsider loaned him the money on a term basis, retaining control until repaid. Under this arrangement, Mr. X kidded himself that surrender of control was only temporary.

THE ROOT OF THE TROUBLE

Mr. X was not a stupid man. His mistakes were due to wishful thinking, oversimplification, and possessiveness. What could have appeared more coldly logical than the assumption that if he was turning away as much business as he was accepting he could double his volume by doubling his production force? The expense scared him but the cleancut figures of the expert would be impressive to any layman, particularly when they confirmed his aspirations. Nor should be be blamed for ignoring the need for an expanded capital base under expanded volume: He had been besieged by "deal men" hinting they could raise $299,000 for a third interest, and by mystery men representing undisclosed principals with unlimited funds to invest. Even his bank had phoned him periodically to ask if he couldn't use more credit.

It is doubtful that any one had risked Mr. X's displeasure by preaching two simple facts of business: 1) It takes money to make money, and if the owner's ambitions carry him beyond his own personal resources, he must attract outside money by offering inducements comparable to the risk. 2) Good management is as important as capital, and when an operation gets too large for one-man dominance it must be strenghthened from the top down, not from the bottom up. The $500-a-month department worker is as essential to a manufacturer as the non-com is to the army, but in today's market, one cannot get a proven, competent executive for that figure.

But if Mr. X ruined his company by too much salaried overhead, how can he be criticized for not employing bigger men? The answer to this apparent riddle is that if, instead of Mr. X and five subordinates, the XYZ Company had had two topnotch men of Mr. X's caliber dividing the functions of engineering, sales, production, and finance according to their respective aptitudes, they could have kept up the skills, flexibility, and speed of the company. They could have continued doing this until the force had reached 100 or even 150. And there is a strong probability that Mr. X could have found his counterpart in a junior executive in a large company—who, for a chance to bet on himself, would have been willing to accept a 50 per cent cut in salary.

For a small manufacturer the problems of acquiring growth capital and executive help are not insurmountable if the owner is willing to share with both investor and executive the possible fruits of success. But the possessive owner who insists on retaining all the glory, all the profits, and all the ownership can only succeed if the glory, profits and ownership are kept small.

A WAY OUT FOR SMALL BUSINESS*

EDWARD P. FILLION, JR.

Talk to almost any economist, corporate planner, or corporate president, and a generally pessimistic outlook as to the future of small business is forecast. While varied substantiations are put forth, most could be paraphrased as the dominance of size.

Many manufacturing companies are scurrying to grow faster than their competitors; others, already gigantic, are continuing to grow at a rate that is somewhat embarrassing to their management. While in most cases a portion of this growth results from expanding markets, no small amount is coming from increasing market share—to the detriment of small business. U.S. Department of Commerce figures state that the average monthly rate of business formation in 1964 was 16,477. Business failures during the same period were almost 10% of this figure.

Most of the business failures occur early in corporate life for a number of well publicized reasons, but what is not pointed out is the growing number of businesses failing after a ten year life. In 1953, of all business failures, 14.8% occurred after 10 years. By 1963, the percentage had jumped to 22.9%. How many of these faltered because they could no longer compete? While the figure is sizeable to begin with, not included are the small businesses which do not die, but which hang on indefinitely to only a marginal existence. For every one failing, we suggest there might be 50 going nowhere.

Undoubtedly there is ample opportunity for the formation and growth of certain types of small business. The July 31, 1965 issue of *Business Week* pointed out opportunities in service businesses. However, their statistics and outlook for the future of small manufacturing companies were far from enthusiastic.

MARKETING PROBLEMS

Probably the major deterrent to growth is inadequate or incomplete distribution. Most small companies sell only regionally, or in cases where there is

*From *Advanced Management Journal* (January, 1966), pp. 27-33. Reprinted with permission.

national distribution, it is spotty and at a high sales cost. While this can be corrected by adequate financing, the dollar figure required to bring the sales message to the total market is staggering.

A case in point is the experience of a West Coast specialty soap manufacturer. After running through six figure investments on two occasions, the company, although considered to be successful, had made no market penetration east of the Rockies. It required sale to a large eastern company, well-known in the consumer goods field, to achieve its real potential. The parent was willing to commit substantial sums to television and other consumer promotion programs because the high profit margin of the product would return the advertising budget quickly. Other selling costs would decrease because the buyer had an existing national sales force and warehouse system which could move the product rapidly. In five years, sales volume went up about 100 percent. Alone, the West Coast company could not hope to approximate these results.

Another marketing problem is created by too short a product line. This is particularly true in the industrial market, where increasingly complex assemblies require consideration of entire systems.

A Midwest metal products company developed a very high pressure hydraulic pump which was reputed to be excellent. The pump did not sell. Being small, the company had to rely on "reps." The reps did not have the background to provide the application engineering required. Potential customers stated they would rather buy a lesser pump from a company offering additional components and able to take responsibility for the entire system.

These and other examples in our files point out that today it is not enough to have a good product to achieve success. Of course, if limitless funds were available, distribution, product development, and management could be purchased, but what small company has access to funds of that magnitude? Slow growth of a product financed totally from within, may only invite Chinese copies.

While any given company may prove to be the exception, Department of Commerce statistics show that in the 15 year period 1947-1962, the two hundred largest manufacturing companies increased their percentage from 30% to 40% of total value added through manufacture. In 1958, four companies in each field controlled these percentages of total output:

Vacuum cleaners	70%
Transformers	71%
Primary batteries	84%
Domestic laundry equipment	71%
Surgical supplies	54%
Abrasive products	58%

Faced with the growing pressures of bigness, what can the small business do? No one answer is without objection, but the following are suggested:

1. Pick a small localized market area. Stay put and be content to remain small. The large company, with its greater overhead and administrative costs will not find it economically feasible to attempt to invade your area. In certain cases this may not work, as the dominant companies in the industry may enter your market for non-financial reasons.

2. Seek a big brother. If a portion of your production capacity is unused or

is returning an insufficient profit, the solution may be to find a captive customer. The very nature of contract manufacturing removes merchandising and distribution burdens from the manufacturer. Many companies have achieved substantial growth by being pulled along as their customer grows. There also are many cases where the opposite is true. The customer fails or at some point decides it makes more sense to perform the manufacturing function in-house. The small company may not be able to recover from the loss of business on which it is dependent.

3. Completely forego current enjoyment and plough all funds back into the company. Most small businesses are under-capitalized to begin with. The creation of capital is compounded as each succeeding profit is reinvested, and internal growth should accelerate. When all available funds are devoted to increased research and development, advertising, or in support of new salesmen, little is left for management compensation. It may be extremely difficult to attract the much needed competent middle management talent on only the promise of added compensation at some unspecified future date.

Stock options may be an answer, but of course the owner's equity is diluted. In practice, many businesses find it hard to adhere to such a Spartan plan. The hard working owner of a business may not resist the temptation to show off his success. In addition, as the equity grows, the risk of actual loss increases even though the degree of risk remains unchanged. Events outside the control of the business, such as the merger of a competitor with a big power, may show the prior frugality to have been in vain.

4. Join a big company through merger. The problems of remaining small are side-stepped by becoming big. The steadily increasing number of mergers between manufacturing companies attests to the logic of such a move. The question of small size versus bigness is relative and depends on the particular industry.

Not long ago, the chief executive of an auto parts manufacturer said that there was no place in his industry for a company of its size. At the time, annual sales were in excess of $60 million. The company subsequently merged and is now a division of one of the country's fifty largest corporations. While a transaction can be geared to answer practically every other requirement, the chief objection to a sale or merger is loss of independence.

MERGER CONSIDERATIONS

What constitutes independence is as relative as size. One company president who championed his independence had to clear every decision with his bank and a factoring company. At the same time a substantial customer and the local union dictated many operations. The "independence" was wholly in the owner's mind and was a fallacy. In another company, which had gone public, the stockholders found themselves locked in, although the public issue had been made to get more flexibility.

If viewed objectively, there are many positive reasons to consider merger with a larger company. Excluding an incentive type transaction, the doubts of the future are resolved at the time of the closing. The liquidity or marketability of the seller's investment is improved. In one motion he has capitalized his past successes and realized the fruits of his labor. Dependent on his willingness to accept new risk, his funds can be reinvested in anything from government bonds to speculative real estate.

In a high percentage of cases, the owner who merges his company, receiving stock of the acquirer, will lighten up by selling some of these new shares to get diversity of investment. The recent success of exchange type mutual funds attests to the desire to spread the risk. Prime targets for exchange fund salesmen are stockholders of recently merged companies who would rather have a dozen blue chip stocks than one.

After the business owner has fully explored the personal benefits of a merger, he may then consider the benefits to his company. Can he develop a proposal for his business which will better enable his company to grow? The merged operation may result in marketing, production, or clerical economies for both parties, but in all too many cases the cost of coordination of activities outweighs the savings. It is important to pick the right partner and evaluate each operational phase of the combined business.

Since the major part of any negotiation involves the "coming to terms" between the owners, operational considerations often are skipped over lightly. When buyer and seller sense a deal in the making each is hesitant to rock the boat by bringing up points of possible dispute. Obviously the buyer takes the responsibility for making the merger work, but if the seller is going to continue in any capacity, he also should be very certain that the business combination is on sound footing. With or without outside advice, the seller should satisfy himself that he has picked the right prospect before entering into serious talks.

Management of a company interested in making an upstream merger must first determine its requirements. Specifically, what do they hope to accomplish operationally? In the area of marketing, they may seek a national system of warehouses, direct selling or jobber contacts among a new class of customers, or additional promotion or advertising funds. In production they may be interested in vertical help—by associating themselves with a company processing at a more basic level, such as the spring company that merged with a wire drawing business. It may be wise to merge with a company nearer the ultimate consumer. This generally would involve merger with an existing customer. A horizontal combination is indicated where additional manufacturing capacity is required.

Other requirements which may dictate consideration of merger are insufficient research and development facilities or talent, lack of depth in management, or need for additional working funds to support growth. All of these requirements are positive ones indicating growth problems of the smaller company. The time to merge is when the company is healthy and growing but could grow faster with help.

An entirely different set of requirements exists for the company that waits too long and has started to experience the problems of shrinking market, product obsolescence, burdensome financing charges, and flight of competent middle management. Regardless of the circumstances, the situation must be faced squarely and the requirements objectively drawn.

In addition to operational requirements, there are those of management. Should the company continue to operate with its personnel intact, do some wish to leave the business, or should some be replaced? Must the company look for a prospective parent able to supply some talent, or should the company seek a buyer able to utilize its rising stars who will go elsewhere if greater challenges cannot be found?

GOVERNMENTAL REQUIREMENTS

A third requirement area of growing importance is observance of government policies. Anti-trust and taxation requirements are a substantial concern today, and may in the future override operational and management considerations. Governmental requirements are negative, requiring a broad knowledge of limitations. A good deal of confusion exists as to the inner workings of accounting, legal, and taxation aspects. The term, "pooling of interests," is often used to describe a tax exempt deal, but a pooling of interests really only has to do with a method of accounting.

Owners seeking a "tax free" deal generally think the exchange must be purely stock for stock or stock for assets. If, however, a statutory merger (legal basis) is accomplished, a pooling of interests can still be used (accounting basis), and tax exempt treatment will result on any stock exchanged (taxation basis), yet a substantial portion of the price can be in cash. Coordination of effort of the corporate attorney, accountant, and tax counsel are essential in any merger negotiation. This coordination must stem from top management or its merger specialist advisor.

Management also must clearly understand the impact of Sections 1245 and 1250 of the IRS code of 1962, dealing with taxation on depreciation. In the past, only legal considerations dictated whether stock or assets of a company should be sold. Today the tax implications of the two procedures are great, and may have a substantial impact on the selling price.

Another problem which will greatly affect merger strategy in the future is the handling of goodwill from the SEC standpoint. The effect of the new requirement is to benefit the buyer's earnings when the seller is merged below book value. If goodwill is involved, the results are opposite and may have a terrifically depressing effect on reported earnings per share. In most mergers today, the price paid is in excess of book value, adding to the complexity of making a deal.

THE PROPER APPROACH TO MERGERS

Once all the requirements are known, the prospective seller is in a far better position to pick the right potential buyer. Conducting acquisition explorations with "anyone showing an interest" or with "only those people who approach us" is both detrimental to the business and largely a waste of time. It can only be meaningful when the owner plans to completely walk away from his business and admits that what he wants is an auction-sale at the highest price, regardless of who the buyer is or what the consequences to the business or employees may be. In all other cases, pre-screening of the prospective buyer is essential.

Once armed with a set of requirements, and a list of prospects fitting the requirements, the next step is the proper preparation of underlying data. When a company goes public, it issues a prospectus. When interested in merger, a document should be prepared which makes the prospectus look like a first grade primer. A full description of the business, the requirements, and the way in which it is felt the requirements can be met is necessary. This does not mean that you have to wear your heart on your sleeve. Properly prepared, such a report can tell what is necessary without becoming intimate to the point of destroying the romance.

A proper approach to the prospective buyer is equally important. Big companies don't have time to play cat and mouse.. At the same time the smaller company does not wish to appear too eager. If all the proper groundwork has been laid, the company approached will be impressed with the businesslike manner, thoroughness, and logic of the exploration.

As talks are being held, it becomes equally important for the seller to analyze and evaluate the buyer. If the seller takes the buyer's stock, he has not sold out, he has traded. What is he getting? If a cash transaction, the seller still must evaluate the position his company will continue to hold unless he is one of those owners who doesn't care what happens as long as he gets his share. In many cases the buyer may think it presumptuous of the seller to pry into the buyer's motives and philosophies, but not if the preparation and approach have been properly handled.

Once buyer and seller are at the hand holding stage, someone has to ask the big question—what price! In a business marriage virtually every transaction hangs on the ability of the two parties to reach a fair and equitable price. Stated simply, it means compromise. Generally it is reported to the press that a merger is in the wind, "subject to working out the details." That little phrase is comparable to the part of the iceberg above water. There are many technical problems which must be worked out, but these are small in relation to the problem of reaching agreement as to price.

The price a company *should* sell for depends on the nature of the transaction, the compatibility of buyer and seller, the existing conditions in the industry, and the state of the economy. The price a company *does* sell for depends on the personalities involved. Recently several "how to" books on merger have been published. Each attempts to supply answers to the question, at what price should. . . . No one gives more than passing treatment to the question, at what price does. . . . This is understandable because the culmination of any negotiation represents a total of all the tangible and intangible relationships that have developed in the exploration. The accountant, attorney, production or marketing analyst is the catalyst in arriving at the tangible answer. A catalyst for the intangibles may be a great deal more important. Gererally this function is filled by an intermediary.

THE ROLE OF THE INTERMEDIARY

The intermediary may not be a third party, but few companies have successfully developed one internally who can retain third party objectivity. Merging companies may ask a banker, investment banker, business broker, finder, or other outside party to act as intermediary. In many cases the intermediary is ineffective, because he has not been involved from the inception of the idea. Someone called in at the last minute has not experienced the total intangible relationship.

The proper intermediary is one who is willing to provide, and is capable of providing, a full range of services. These include advice as to the requirements of a company, the screening of prospects, development of background information, making the approaches. analyzing the buyer, being knowledgeable in tax and accounting matters, and to no small extent having the experience of many past transactions. With this background, the intermediary is then in the best possible position to act as a sounding board, keeping the exploration and negotiation alive—avoiding the problem of face to face confrontation from which one party must retreat. Without a sounding board, many mergers have not taken place because of injured pride; or worse, they have taken place with one or both parties later discovering that "the deal was not what it seemed."

A great deal of criticism has been leveled at the broker or finder. Much of this may be warranted, but in a large number of cases the buyer or seller thought he was retaining an intermediary when such was not the case. The finder has no capability to evaluate or analyze. The accountant or attorney is not versed in marketing or production problems. The management consultant generally prefers not to become involved in the negotiation. The banker is not equipped to find or analyze. The proper intermediary is a merger specialist, knowledgeable in all these areas. In many cases, the principal, himself, may be to blame, for being less than completely candid with his representative.

Most intermediaries work, at least in part, on a commission basis. Compensation is predicated on success. We find no fault in the statement that the intermediary's prime concern is to see the deal, any deal, go through. This is precisely why he was hired. Fees vary widely and are a source of irritation to the principals and intermediary as well. In every case, the fee schedule should be agreed to in advance, at the same time the range of services to be performed is determined. The fee should be considered as part of the investment or sale price as the case may be. Certainly a deal looks better the lower the fee is, but it is a mistake to tie up the intermediary in compromising a fee at the very time the intermediary should be working for his client to compromise the price. Select the right intermediary to begin with and then devote all effort to the acquisition.

For a small businessman, consideration of merger often is not given serious attention. While merger may not be the answer, it should be viewed as objectively as a make-or-buy decision. In a great many cases merger is not considered until it is too late—when there is no other way to go.

Viewed objectively, a merger should be neither more nor less than a tool for achieving primary corporate goals, i.e. a means for expanding production, developing existing markets or pioneering new ones, increasing productivity of fixed assets, or better utilizing key personnel. Its degree of effectiveness in any small business situation often is determined by counseling talents available to the seller, as well as by the nature and timing of exploration made in his behalf.

The decision to merge, if approached only on an "if all else fails" basis rarely represents a decision at all. Being the last "independent," next door to a division of a major competitor, can be awfully lonely.

PUBLIC OFFERINGS

FOR SMALLER COMPANIES*

GERALD A. SEARS

In recent years, stockholders of small, closely held companies have increasingly chosen to sell their interests to larger, publicly held companies in order to get a more liquid holding. This has resulted in a fast-paced merger and acquisition momentum that is unparalleled in the history of the United States.

A public offering of part of the stock can often be a better solution, because it permits the owners to retain control of their company and reap the benefits of an increasingly more valuable equity position if the company continues to grow. Moreover, "going public" can sometimes result in getting a higher long-term price than selling out to a single buyer.

In this article I shall discuss the pros and cons of going public and offer some suggestions on establishing a public market and selecting an underwriter for the consideration of stockholders of privately owned companies who wish to create more liquidity for their investment.

NOT EVERY FIRM A GOOD BET

There are three main reasons why owners of companies sell their interests to a publicly held corporation or make an offering of a portion of their stock to the public:

1. They desire to diversity and take some of their eggs out of one basket.
2. High federal estate and income taxes force the owners to alter the foundation of their estate so that they can leave their heirs with maximum assets.
3. Because of expanding markets and new technology, many small companies suffer acute growing pains and need infusions of capital beyond their own resources and the credit available from financial institutions.

The need for working capital was by far the most important motive for a public offering given by 209 presidents of small companies in one survey.[1] The results are shown in *Exhibit I.* A need for operating cash was the impetus behind one third of the stock issues of these companies.

Half the presidents gave corporate financial needs, including working capital, as the primary reasons for their public issues. This is not surprising; we are a technology-oriented society, and as long as one or a very few men can to-

*From *Harvard Business Review* (September-October, 1968), pp. 112-120. © 1968 by the President and Fellows of Harvard College; all rights reserved.

[1]Cited in Solomon J. Flink, *Equity Financing for Small Business* (New York, Simmons-Boardman Publishing Corporation, 1962), p. 87.

gether push the state of the art in any technology, small companies will be formed to capitalize on this ability. Their growth can be rapid, creating acute cash needs.

EXHIBIT I   Reasons for Going Public Given by 209
             Small-Company Presidents

	Percent of total
To meet company objectives	
Financial needs	
Working capital	36.0%
Fixed capital	9.5
Research and development funds	5.7
Investment activity	
Establish market for later offering by shareholders	9.5
Probable purchase of another firm	3.8
Contemplated merger	2.4
To meet owners' personal considerations	
Minimize estate taxes	13.4
Resolve personal conflicts	2.4
Provide "nest egg"	4.8
Diversify investments	4.8
Take advantage of a bull market	3.8
Other reasons	3.8

But whatever the motives for making a public offering, success in doing it is limited to companies that meet certain criteria. I shall list these criteria and describe what happens after the offering to a company that fails to meet each one:

The Company Should Have a Growth Rate Higher Than its Industry if it is to Attract Investors. Consider the small company that staggers on from year to year showing below-average growth. Since the stock market is mainly a vehicle for capital gains—few investors nowadays buy equities for dividends—the slow-growth or no-growth company soon falls into that vast wasteland of "lost" public issues.

Financing becomes difficult to obtain. Because the company's price/earnings ratio is very low, a great amount of stock would be needed in a subsequent offering to raise even a moderate amount of cash. And when the market price of the stock falls near or below book value, debt financing can be impaired as well. The result is that the company has few of the advantages of the public market.

Owner-managers, Accustomed to Answering to No One in Running Their Businesses, Must be Able to Adjust to Operating in the Sometimes Uncomfortable Spotlight of Attention. The creation of a public market brings with it the "financial crowd" of brokers, analysts, auditors, and stockholders. They feel they have a right to be given certain information about the company, and some of them place no reasonable limit on this right. Management can find itself in the annoying position of fielding myriad requests for explanations about actions that previously have gone unquestioned.

When the company's performance is good, management can bask in the applause. But it may not be easy for onetime entrepreneurs to handle critical questions on operations, on executive salaries, or on stock option plans, not to mention explaining a downturn in the business. Often they react to such questions as if they were personal reflections on them. If management is uncomfortable in the spotlight, the result can be strained relationships with the financial community which can cause more harm than the public market does good.

The Effect of Public Disclosure Must Not be to Compromise the Company's Business. In a case where concealment of profit margins, share of market, and so on, is essential for competitive survival, the required disclosure of these facts by a company issuing a prospectus can spell disaster. This is particularly true for a one-product business. Even with a multiproduct company, however, disclosure of sales by product or product group—increasingly demanded by government agencies and investors—can affect the company's competitive position.

A public offering is not appropriate for a small company with slow growth, a company whose owner-manager is a prima donna, or a company dependent on a single major, nonproprietary product with a high profit margin and large share of the market.

The proceeds from a public issue of stock can flow to either the company or the selling shareholders, or both. With some investors there remains a lingering suspicion of an initial offering that mainly benefits the selling shareholders. This stems largely from the "bail out" theory—the idea that management has information on a future downturn for the business. Though this occurrence is rare indeed, the suspicion lingers. A wise management will think twice about proceeding with an offering if it will benefit only the principal shareholders' personal interests.

ADVANTAGES OF GOING PUBLIC

The advantages of a public offering are not always clear. Small-company owner-managers who are considering selling their interests, or a part of them, generally hold certain beliefs about selling to another company which in my view are erroneous. Let us use the case of "Mr. Jones," who sells his company to "Big, Inc.," a publicly held corporation, to illustrate these largely unfounded beliefs:

1. Jones believes he should get a price based on as high an earnings multiple as he would have obtained if his company had gone public. But Big, Inc. recognizes that if comparable publicly held companies are selling at 10 times earnings, Jone's lack of a public market should knock down the price a few multiples to 8 or 9 times earnings. In short, Big, Inc. will avoid "giving away" the many expenses it incurs as a publicly owned company, maintaining a market liquid enough to attract Jones. As a rule, the more liquid the buyer's stock, the greater the discount the seller must accept from the buyer's price/earnings multiple.

2. Jones's contemplated position with Big, Inc., as either an executive or a consultant, gives him a security that often turns out to be false. Big, Inc. has control after the sale, and Jones's position continues only at the company's pleasure.

3. Jones's only certain stream of income is from the investments he makes with the cash proceeds of the sale. But if Jones takes Big, Inc. stock in exchange for his with the idea that he will have a "management-free" investment in a marketable stock, he will have traded the uncertainties of running a small business for the vagaries of the market.

4. Jones may have elected for a private sale because it is supposed to be quicker than a public offering. While the preparation for a new public issue can take as long as a year, a private sale seldom takes less time and can take longer. The initial contact, the evaluation, research, investigation, and negotiation precede the sale. A small company seeking the best deal often goes through this procedure from two to six times before it concludes a satisfactory sale. The duration of the courtship with each prospect is seldom less than three months and often is five or six months, meanwhile draining enormous amounts of top-management time.

Rising Market Values

On the other hand, entrepreneurs like Jones can find in a public offering a potentially profitable alternative to outright sale of the company. The success of the offering depends on creation of a liquid public market, which takes time and good management of the new issue and the all-important after-market. The time factor poses a greater risk for the company than is present in an outright sale, but the rewards can outweigh the risk.

In the last few years the demand for equities has made the public market increasingly attractive to smaller companies. Institutions are putting more of their portfolio resources into seasoned equities, creating a market shortage of them that spurs investing in less-tested issues; mutual funds, feeling an urgency to show "performance," are looking harder for stocks with high growth potential; the sales forces of brokerage firms have grown substantially in size, resulting in pressure to build greater retail volume; and the long economic boom, coupled with inflation, has stirred investor interest in common stocks (which, in bull markets, has caused rampant speculative fever).

That small companies have taken advantage of these conditions is evident from a look at the over-the-counter market. Some 10,050 issues were quoted in the National Quotations Bureau's daily listed services as of early this year [1968]. This figure compares with 7,930 as of early 1959. That is an average annual growth rate of 3%. But a 1966 study for the National Association of Securities Dealers showed that unlisted stocks have declined rapidly in both volume of trading and dollar value compared with volume and total values on the stock exchange.[2] This indicates that the OTC market has become one of the smaller publicly owned companies.

A sample of OTC companies by market value and assets, taken from the Securities and Exchange Commission's study of the securities markets in 1963, supports that conclusion.[3] The results are shown in *Exhibit II*. The companies whose assets totaled less than $1 million, for instance, comprised 23% of the

[2]Booz, Allen & Hamilton Inc., *Over the Counter Market Study* (August, 1966).

[3]*Report of the Special Study of the Securities Markets*, 88th Congress, First Session, House Document 95.

total, while those concerns whose stock had a market value of less than $1 million made up 38% of the total.

EXHIBIT II Sample of Issuers of Over-the-Counter Stocks, Classified by Market Value of Outstanding Stock and Amount of Assets

| Market value and total assets (in thousands of dollars) | Number and percent of issuers | | | | | |
| | Market value | | | Amount of assets | | |
	Number	Percent	Cumulative percent	Number	Percent	Cumulative percent
$1-$249	238	14.6%	14.6%	105	6.5%	6.5%
$250-$499	153	9.4	24.0	111	6.9	13.4
$500-$999	229	14.2	38.2	161	10.0	23.4
$1,000-$4,999	449	27.8	66.0	483	29.9	53.3
$5,000-$9,999	166	10.3	76.3	245	15.1	68.4
$10,000 and over	308	19.1	95.4	504	31.1	99.5
Not reported	75	4.6	100.0	9	0.5	100.0
	1,618	100.0%		1,618	100.0%	

By-Products of a Public Market

Once a small company's stock is in the public domain, and if the company's growth continues at the same rate, the company derives some benefits other than the rising market value of the stock:

1. Since the advent of stock option plans and high personal income taxes, privately held companies have been at a competitive disadvantage in compensating management, as all executives know. Beyond a certain level, higher cash compensation enriches the tax collector more than the recipient. Because of this, managerial talent has tended to migrate toward companies that offer less heavily taxed compensation through stock option plans. To net an executive the same after-tax income as the option-compensated officer of the publicly held company, the privately held firm must pay him almost twice the amount of cash.

Cash salaries come out of company earnings, while stock option gains are "paid for" by the rising market value. The exercise of options may have a slight effect on earnings per share, but none on aggregate earnings. Moreover, one of the better ways to encourage good performance is to make the rewards to an extent depend on how valuable management makes the stock.

2. Obviously, a company can sell additional stock more easily in an already established market. Another source of financing growth is the increased borrowing capacity which is a result of the public market.

The company has increased its borrowing ability to the extent that lenders use a debt/equity ratio as a guideline. The sale of stock increases paid-in capital and therefore net worth, or book value. Thus borrowing capacity has been enhanced, if lenders use book value as a yardstick. If the company's stock enjoys a high price/earnings multiple, lenders using market equity value as a guideline will be even more receptive to meeting the company's capital needs.

Moreover, the strict reporting requirements for publicly owned companies give lenders more confidence in their financial statements, resulting in a better reception for their managements. Finally, in addition to having a greater borrowing capacity, management can be more flexible in its borrowing, using the public debt market for both straight and convertible debt. Convertibles, in particular, can help to free management from the shackles of tight money.

3. Because of the tax laws, sellers are more interested in a tax-free exchange of stock than in a taxable cash transaction. The acquisition business is intensely competitive—a seller's market. So the ability to compete is enhanced by having a marketable stock.

Smaller public companies may even have a certain advantage over large ones in this competition, since they are generally interested in acquisition of even smaller companies ignored by many large corporations. I am not making the suggestion that every small private company should go public and then set out to build another Litton empire. But frustration at seeing their suppliers, competitors, and customers acquired has led many small company owners to "sell out" themselves. Creating a public market and using the stock for growth through acquisition can combat this trend.

4. Even if a small company plans an eventual sale of the assets after it has gone public, the market value of the stock can provide a base for negotiations by establishing a minimum price that the buyer must pay. In that event, assuming that the initial offering and after-market have been handled competently, the final net price to the selling shareholders can be considerably higher than if the stock had been disposed of another way.

5. The first time a company goes to the equity market, great interest is created in it. Customers, suppliers, and competitors treat the company, its products, and services with a new respect. The reputation of being substantial, which most publicly held companies enjoy, also may enhance consumer acceptance of their products. While it is difficult to tie increased sales to the publicity arising from the market, it seems to do the recipients of this attention no harm.

BROKER AND UNDERWRITER

In considering whether to go public, and in order to understand better the mechanics of the market, the owner of a small company should be familiar with how the over-the-counter market functions and with the role of the underwriter.

The Float

The buyer of a security wants the market for that security to have sufficient depth and liquidity. He must feel assured that he can buy the desired amount of stock at a price he is willing to pay; and when and if he decides to sell his shares, he will want assurance that he can find a buyer with little delay and sell to him at a fair price. Brokers, of course, make markets in OTC stocks to facilitate these transactions, adding markup to the price in lieu of a commission.

The market must be capable of handling a volume large enough to cause little or no change in price in each transaction. This is ideal liquidity. Between the ideal and the inability to trade at all are an infinite number of shades of

215

liquidity. In its Special Study of the securities markets, the SEC reported on a sampling of the National Quotation Bureau's daily price quotations of OTC stocks (known as "the sheets"), from which it tried to determine what proportion had a liquid market. Over a 10-day period, two or more dealers entered quotations on 161 of the 300 stocks sampled, or less than 54%. By this measure, only about one half of the OTC securities have a reasonably liquid market, since one measure of liquidity is both a bid and an offer on a firm basis from two or more dealers in the sheets. (Since the sheets quote stocks with a degree of national investor interest, there is no telling the extent of liquidity of the thousands of issues traded only locally over the counter, nearly all of which are small companies' securities.)

The liquidity of a small OTC issue depends directly on the amount of stock changing hands—"the float." This is the stock held by short-term investors or speculators that comes into the market regularly (obviously, the stock held by long-term investors seldom comes into the market). The ratio of the float to the total shares outstanding depends on such factors as the type of company the issuer is, whether or not it has few controlling interests, its growth potential, and so on.

To understand better the nature of competition in the OTC market, it is helpful to look at the market from the dealer's standpoint. He advertises his willingness to buy or sell for his own account by placing a bid or an offer in the sheets. In doing this, he is in direct competition with other dealers who are in the sheets in the same stock and in potential competition with all dealers who may decide to make a market in that stock.

If the dealer has no competition, he will make the spread between his bid and offer wider, in order to compensate for possible losses from inventory and make his profit equal to what he is gaining from more liquid stocks. He will probably also keep his inventory very low, which, with the wide spread, can result in poor liquidity. If the float should increase, more dealers would be attracted to make a market in the stock.

To enable two or more dealers to make a competitive market, the float should be a minimum of 50,000 shares. This is not an absolute figure, but it is difficult to maintain a market if the amount of float declines below that figure. It is a general rule of small OTC markets that the annual trading volume is about three times the float. So, assuming that two dealers are equally sharing a 50,000-share float market, each will trade about 75,000 shares a year and will probably have an average spread of about ¼ to ½ of 1% (25 to 50 cents per share). This would be a trading gross profit of $18,750 to $37,500, before expenses and inventory losses, for each.

Selecting an Underwriter

Until about 50 years ago, the underwriting function was the principal source of income for the securities industry. Since that time, firms for which underwriting is a principal source of income have declined to only 1.7% of the total broker-dealer community, according to the 1966 OTC market study for the NASD. The principal activity of 80% of the 2,483 firms reporting was selling existing securities; firms retailing listed and OTC stocks accounted for 45.6%, while 34.4% dealt primarily in mutual funds.

Substantially all the underwriters in this 1.7% are large organizations; it is difficult to name more than a handful of small underwriting firms. So there are very few bases of performance comparison between large and small. *Exhibit III* shows the percentage of new issues that were at or below the offering price one month after the offering, broken down by size of the underwriting firm. It indicates some tendency for a more favorable after-market performance as the size of the underwriting firm increases, but not enough to make a direct correlation between market performance and size.

EXHIBIT III Percentage of New Issues at or Below Offering Price One Month Later, by Size of Underwriters

Adjusted net capital of underwriters (in thousands of dollars)	Percentage
$0-$9.9	33.8%
$10-$24.9	40.9
$25-$49.9	35.3
$50-$99.9	22.7
$100-$499.9	31.2
$500 or more	30.5

Source: Securities and Exchange Commission, *Report of the Special Study of the Securities Markets*, 88th Congress, First Session, House Document 95.

The typical national underwriting house requires a company to have had at least $750,000-$1,000,000 in net earnings before it will consider a public offering of the company's stock. A regional house with underwriting capability will generally scale the minimum down to $500,000 or $400,000. This income may be either for the fiscal year completed just prior to the contemplated offering or for the year ending immediately thereafter. In the latter case, it is assumed that there has been a record of earnings growth in previous years.

Many large underwriting firms have a continuing financial advisory relationship with their large clients, but this is not as common in the case of smaller firms. The NASD study attempted to classify these relationships by size of firm. Large firms indicated that they have been the underwriters, if not managing underwriters, of about one third of the issues in which they maintained active trading markets. The firms were asked about other traditional relationships—a directorship, a financial advisor, and past underwriters for the same issuer. Less than 8% of the small firm market makers had had any one of these three relationships, compared with 14% of the medium-sized firms and 43% of the large firms.

Selecting an underwriter is not an easy job. Not only must the issuer make a decision as to the underwriter's technical ability, but he should also try to find an underwriter who is familiar with and understands the issuer's industry. In addition, the underwriter should have he ability, either alone or through correspondent relationships, to distribute the stock in a geographic pattern that closely follows the geography of interest in the stock.

There are very few other business relationships which reflect as much deep mutual understanding as that of the issuer and the underwriter. The Special Study included a statement by one underwriter that expresses well the nature of this relationship:

"We are frequently asked to help new issuers with general problems of a company going public for a first time, such as advising them on the basis of our experience on handling stockholder relations, meetings with the investment community. . . . Related to this, we are a sounding board as to how the financial community and the public generally might react to proposed corporate actions. . . . We advise the company on a broad range of their financial problems, including such matters as the need for new financing, the methods of obtaining new financing, either publicly or privately, dividend policy, the desirability of mergers, acquisitions. . . . We feel a responsibility for seeing to it that an orderly after-market in the security is maintained so that persons who have purchased the issue will be able to liquidate or increase their investments if they desire."

Underwriting remains a very personal business. The "personality" of a firm is directly attributable to the one or two key people in the organization who decide underwriting policy. So a firm's policy on the size, industry, and other criteria of companies which it is willing to underwrite can change as fast as the makeup of the top echelon changes.

Often there are not enough comparable publicly held companies to arrive at a clear-cut determination of the public's interest, the issuer's industry, and an estimate of its potential for growth. Nevertheless, the underwriter must make a judgment. The judgment about public reception is an area where reasonable men can differ. This is particularly the case with small new issues, where public receptivity to the issuer's industry is crucial.

An underwriter may have managed one or more public offerings in the issuer's industry, so he would be a likely prospect. But the underwriter might be precluded from managing another offering in that industry because of conflict of interest. Because of the constantly shifting underwriting marketplace, the best course of action for a small company is to rely on the advice of its auditor, banker, and lawyer in suggesting two or three underwriters. After interviewing them, the company will select one as the managing underwriter.

Preparing the Offering

Making an initial public offering of stock is a complex process. *Exhibit IV* lists the major functions of an underwriter in preparing for the offering. Some of them are entirely the underwriter's responsibility; in others, he works with lawyers or auditors; and, in this example, the firm is managing the offering in association with other underwriters. If the offering is more involved than the relatively simple one illustrated in *Exhibit IV*—presenting tax considerations, for instance—the 40 steps could easily be increased to 100.[4] It has often been said that the underwriter must know his business and understand the issuer's. From this list, some appreciation can be gained of the technical complexity of the underwriting business.

---

[4]For a discussion of the complex subject of taxes, see James R. Wimmer, "Tax Effect of the Privately Held Corporation 'Going Public,'" *TAXES—The Tax Magazine,* December 1967, p. 932.

EXHIBIT IV Managing Underwriter's Selected Steps in Preparing a New Issue.

1. Review with company SEC rules regarding public statments.

2. Decide on financial data to be included.

3. Prepare underwriters' memorandum.

4. If offering to employees or other special persons, determine price, liability for unsubscribed stock, time schedule, subscription and confirmation mechanics.

5. Prepare S-1 registration statement.

6. Decide on form of stock certificate.

7. Obtain indemnity insurance policy, if appropriate.

8. Prepare prospectus.

9. Prepare agreement among underwriters (AAU).

10. Prepare underwriting agreement (UA).

11. Prepare underwriters' questionnaire to make sure they have not recommended the stock.

12. Prepare blue-sky memorandum (preliminary).

13. File registration statement with SEC.

14. Clear proposed underwriters' comfort letter with company's auditors.

15. Advise as to the number of copies of preliminary prospectus ("red herring") necessary.

16. Clear with NASD.

17. Issue invitational letters to prospective underwriters.

18. Determine makeup of underwriting group.

19. Coordinate with syndicate department for any directed sales to officers, other employees, stockholders, or creditors.

20. Compile summary report of the distribution of the red herring and amendments thereto.

21. Furnish own accounting department (for closing) with tentative time schedule, copies of propsectus, AAU, UA, and other pertinent documents.

22. Arrange "due diligence" meetings with company and underwriters.

23. Arrange (with underwriters, company, auditors, sellers, and counsel for underwriters) inspection of company's facilities, time of signings of underwriting agreement, and requested effective date of SEC registration.

24. Prepare memorandum to salesmen.

25. Prepare copy of published announcements and schedule of publications and tentative dates.

26. Determine where offering will be advertised.

27. Clear deficiencies with SEC and revise documents.

28. Send red herring distribution list to SEC.

29. Request SEC acceleration.

30. Establish final terms.

31. Prepare sets of AAU and UA and sign with underwriters and with company (and with selling stockholders, if any).

32. Recheck final prospectus.

33. Release offering for sale on telegraphed receipt of SEC clearance and after confirmation of good standing from state of incorporation of company.

34. Send copies of prospectus to underwriters, selected dealers, financial services, publications, and others.

35. Send copies of agreements to underwriters who gave power of attorney.

36. Decide on closing date with counsel, auditors, transfer agent, and registrars.

37. Advise underwriters and own accounting department as to stabilization of stock in after-market and closing arrangements.

38. Send legal opinions, comfort letter, and other closing papers to underwriters.

39. Take steps to get new issues quoted in newspapers and listed in stock guides.

40. Advise company of its responsibilities after offering.

Many questions about the offering naturally will occur to the company's management. For instance, if the underwriting is done by a syndicate, how should the stock be distributed to its members for sale? What is a reasonable gross spread or underwriting commission? How much information should be included in the prospectus? Should the managing underwriter be represented on the board of directors? What part should the company play in determining if the underwriter and other market makers are inventorying enough stock?

Any one of these questions requires far too much detailed analysis to be addressed within the scope of this article. Company management, however, should bear these points in mind:

1. The underwriter takes the same civil and criminal risks as the company for the representations made in the prospectus. So he will be careful to make adequate and truthful disclosure. (And in an important recent federal court case, lawyers, outside auditors, and company directors have also been held liable for false information in the prospectus.[5])

2. The prospectus is by law the underwriter's only permitted selling document. Therefore he will make sure it is well done.

3. While the terms of an underwriting will vary widely according to the size and industry of the issuer, any aspect of an offering has enough published prior practice so that the underwriter should be able to show why he is making a particular recommendation. Whenever company executives are uneasy on a point, the underwriter should be able and willing to show them sufficient evidence of prior practice for companies of comparable size in the same industry. Enough information is available in any situation so that reasonable men should not differ.

Perhaps the most severe test of the underwriter-issuer relationship comes at the time of pricing the new issue. Although it is not always immediately obvious, the goals of the underwriter and the issuer are the same. Both are concerned that the offering price be sustained in the intermediate and long-term market. But since the long-term market is very difficult to forecast, the responsible underwriter is usually most concerned with pricing for the foreseeable future.

The pricing decision is largely based on comparability. The underwriter is strongly influenced by the price/earnings ratios at which comparable companies are selling in the public market. An issuer can obtain a range of his probable P/E ratio by doing this analysis himself. It should encompass at least 6, but preferably as many as 12, comparable companies, and it should include information on their growth rates, balance sheets, cash flow to earnings ratios, proprietary products, and depth of management. A comparison of this type will show why companies sell at significantly different P/E multiples. It will also show the issuer's management where the company stands relative to its industry.

This comparative "spread" is one of the major tools any underwriter uses for pricing. Since no two companies are alike and no company is exactly like an average, however, the final decision on the P/E ratio must depend on the underwriter's judgment.

CONCLUDING NOTE

The public market gives the smaller company an opportunity to expand with its own resources.

[5]*Escott v. Barchris Corp.*, 283 F. Supp. 643.

Not every such company, however, meets the growth, management, and product requirements for success in that market. For the company that does not, a public offering can have a devastating boomerang effect. For those that do, it can bring substantial long-term capital gains. When a small company meets the criteria for a public offering, an outright sale of the stock to another company can be equivalent to selling the horse for the money to buy its feed.

The underwriting fraternity is increasingly recognizing that its customary reluctance to take on small-company public offerings needs reevaluation. Smaller companies will always be more vulnerable than large ones. But the demand for equities, as well as a lack of other suitable vehicles to enable investors to participate in the exploitation of new technology, is lowering the size minimums.

HOW DO YOU KNOW

WHAT YOUR BUSINESS IS WORTH?*

G. H. B. GOULD / DEAN C. CODDINGTON

Corporations whose stocks are actively traded on the major exchanges are valued continuously by the investing public. But how do owner-managers of small closely held companies determine how much their business is worth when they, for instance, seek outside financing?

Or how do you value a business for situations such as those involving estate and gift taxes? And what about the value of a company which you may purchase in order to strengthen your own business?

NO SET FORMULAR FOR VALUATION

Various methods can be used for computing a company's worth, but no set formula exists. Keep in mind that the buyer, or investor, wants an answer to one question: What percent of return can I get on my investment? Or said another way: What is the value of the future earning power of this company?

The best way to answer that question is by using the capitalized earnings method for evaluating the worth of a company. But first, look at two other commonly used methods: (1) asset valuation, and (2) market valuation.

*Management Aids No. 166 (August, 1964). Reprinted by permission of the Small Business Administration, Washington, D.C.

Asset Valuation

Companies are often evaluated by their assets as reflected in book value, reproduction value, and liquidation value. However, assets are significant only as they enable a company to manufacture and sell products, or services, that will generate profits.

Book Value. Sometimes a company's book value does not hold up in the marketplace. One company, for example, sold for $300,000 even though its net worth or book value was $600,000. The reason: a large part of the assets was tied up in specialized equipment and slow-moving inventory, sales volume was down, and the company's net income after taxes was only $30,000. The purchasers decided that the company to them was worth only 10 times earnings, or $300,000.

Another disadvantage of valuing a company on its net worth is that book value can be high because of retained earnings over a long period of time. The company can still be a poor investment because its current earnings are down and prospects for increased future earnings are dim.

Reproduction Value. Many small businessmen value their companies in terms of reproduction value—the current cost of reproducing the assets of the business. They reason like this: The cost of duplicating my business will be higher than what is shown on my balance sheet because many items have been depreciated. Also inflation has increased the prices of certain pieces of machinery.

A disadvantage of reproduction value is that it tends to set a high asking price on a business. Often a man can start a new one with less capital than it takes to buy a company on its reproduction value.

Liquidation value is the amount that would be available to the common stockholders in the event that a small business is liquidated. In liquidation, time is often a factor; outside pressures demand action; and the business is sold at a sacrifice. However, this method has some use in placing a floor under the value of a company—determining the minimum asking price.

Market Value

Quoted prices on stock exchanges constitute market value of common stock. Usually such prices in a broad and active market can be considered the current value of a company. But even so a company is sometimes merged or sold at quite a different value from the current value of its marketable common stocks.

Market value can be subjected, for example, to short-term swings caused by rumors, opinions, and other factors. The fickleness of over-the-counter stock prices tends to be even greater than that of the major stock exchanges. For example, the announcement of potential contracts often raises the over-the-counter value of the stock of an electronics company out of proportion to its real value.

Where thin, limited markets exist, differences between the current value and market price of a company's stock are apt to be great. For example, a company with 300,000 shares outstanding might sell at 5 to 10 times earnings and under book value per share because demand for that stock is slight. The industry is highly competitive, the company's sales are down, and profits have been declining. At the same time, another company with 300,000 shares out-standing—but with strong earnings and growth prospects—might sell at 30 to 50 times earnings and many times book value.

CAPITALIZED EARNINGS VALUE

Whether you buy or sell a small company you need to know about the company's ability to earn profits—especially future profits. The capitalized earnings approach considers a business as a living, changing organism which uses its assets to produce the greatest possible returns on investment.

Two steps are used in capitalizing earnings. First, you find a company's true earning power, based on both its past experience and future probabilities. Second, you capitalize these earnings at a rate which is realistic for the risks involved.

Finding a Company's Earnings

A company's *past earnings* record gives a buyer, or investor, an indication of what he might reasonably expect in the future. He learns about this record from past income statements. Looking at them for a 5-year period helps him to see trends.

The buyer should make adjustments to the income statement for: (1) non-recurring items that a buyer should not expect to encounter in the future, (2) unusually large bad debts, (3) inventory write-offs, (4) excessive salaries, (5) low salaries that might have to be raised in order to get qualified assistants, and (6) nonbusiness ventures.

The kind of accounting procedure used can also have a direct effect on reported earnings. For example, one company may charge the cost of tools and dies as expense items in the year in which they were bought. Another may amortize the cost of such equipment over a period of years and thereby increase earnings.

When a potential buyer adjusts for nonrecurring items and for varying accounting practices, he is trying to judge what future earnings might be under his ownership. His return on investment has to come from possible *future earnings*.

Therefore, the buyer needs income statement projections based on what he thinks he can do with the company. Often an independent study of the company's prospects for sales helps to give a sound basis for earnings projections.

Even though selling may be your last thought at this point, it is a good idea to look ahead. Make sure that your accounting system records the information necessary for making realistic earnings projections. Thus you can base your negotiations on facts should you ever decide to sell. Also, don't buy, or sell, without having an independent audit of the company's books.

Finally, from the 5-year period, you have to pick one annual earnings figure as the true *earning power* of the business. If the company has a proven record, current earnings can often be used. In well-established companies, *proven past profits* and *projected income* for the current year usually go together to make the true earnings figure. However, when a company is fairly new but with good potential, future earnings estimates are weighed heavily.

What Capitalization Rate Should Be Used?

The rate at which you capitalize a company's average earning power depends on the risks involved. The higher the risk of generating projected earnings—and thus creating a return on the buyer's investment—the lower the capitalization rate.

Suppose, for example, that the earning power of two companies is the same—$100,000. Suppose further that Company A has a proven record of profits and a very substantial annual earnings growth rate. With highly favorable prospects for the future, Company A might be capitalized at 20 times earnings for a value of $2 million. At the start, the investor would get 5 percent return on investment, and the proven growth of earnings would increase his possibility for a greater return in the future.

However, keep in mind that valuation is also subjective—what the buyer thinks the business is worth to him. Some may be willing to pay a much lower multiple of earnings for a closely held company even though the present owners have built an outstanding record for growth and prospects appear favorable.

On the other hand, Company B is relatively small and in a highly competitive industry. The company is growing but has not established itself. A buyer would need a high percentage return—20 percent or more—on investment. If he needed 20 percent, earnings could be capitalized at 5 times for a value of $500,000.

External Influences

When determining the proper capitalization rate, or price-earnings multiple, external influences have to be weighed. Some of them are:

1. *Economy.* What effect will the state of business and the regional and national economic outlook have on the company?
2. *Industry.* Do industry factors—such as competitive structure, cyclical, seasonal and Governmental influences, and industry glamour—make the company attractive to investors? Unattractive?
3. *Company position.* How does the company compare with its competitors in size, growth, margins, order backlog, suppliers, patents, and freight advantages?
4. *Financial strength.* How do the company's balance-sheet and income statement ratios compare with competitors, and with credit statistics for the industry as a whole? A debt-free company, of course, can borrow capital for expansion and diversification.
5. *Management.* Is the company's management strong? Does its past performance indicate that it can maintain and increase profits in the future?
6. *Character of investment.* In a closely held company—one person or a small group owning more than half the stock—the price-earnings multiple will be lower because of the nonmarketability of the investment.

Factors Which The Buyer Injects

In additions to these external influences, the price earnings-earnings multiple is often determined by factors which the buyer, or investor, may throw into the situation. Some examples are:

1. *Buyer's price-earnings multiple.* If an investing company can buy a company at a price-earnings multiple below its own, its stockholder's position is not diluted. For example, if a buying company's stock is selling at 15 times earnings, it can afford to issue stock with a value up to—but not more than—15 times earnings for an acquisition. However, if the buying company pays more than 15 times earnings, its stockholders will earn less per share on the combined earnings.

2. *Competitive investments.* When buying for investment, the return on the purchase price of a company must compare favorably with other things—such as stocks, bonds, real estate, or savings deposits—for which the buyer could spend his money.

3. *Job money.* Companies are often sold to buyers who want to take over active management, and such a buyer may be willing to pay a little more.

4. *Buyer's needs.* Another company might pay a higher price than an individual buyer in order to fill needs such as management, products, brands, patents, franchises, or licensing agreements.

5. *Method of payment.* Tax factors have to be considered. Acquisitions effected through merger, sale of stock, or sale of assets for either cash or stock depend on tax factors involved with the corporation's assets and net worth as well as each stockholder's personal position.

6. *Minority stockholders.* The value of a minority ownership position in a closely held company is not as great as a majority stockholder because of the additional risks associated with lack of control.

7. *Cash flow.* Cash flow—net profits after taxes plus non-cash charges, such as depreciation, depletion, and amortization, has become an important factor in valuation. The cash generated from operations can be used for capital expenditures, reduction of debt, payment of dividends, and expansion. So a company may be sold at a very high multiple of earnings yet at a reasonable ratio to cash flow. This cash "payout" often determines the ultimate value of a business and is becoming increasingly important.

APPLICATION OF METHODS

When determining how much your company is worth, keep in mind that its marketable value may vary according to what you are planning to do.

If you set a value in order to get *public financing*, bear in mind that a public underwriting of securities should be priced so that the investment will be attractive in comparison with stocks of other companies in your industry. Such pricing should also give the stock room to rise after the issue has been floated.

The situation is somewhat different if you seek *private financing*. When buying non-marketable securities, an investor needs a higher return. Usually private venture capital sources seek investments which will double in value and be marketable within 3 years.

In a *private sale* to one individual, he buys on what he thinks he can earn from the company. If he plans to operate the company himself, he may pay more for the intangible benefits of having managerial responsibilities.

Above all, in buying or selling, keep in mind that value varies with individuals. The worth of a going company is largely a subjective matter—what a person thinks the business is worth to him. But even so, the capitalized earnings approach embodies facts which can be used to arrive at a realistic value.

The capitalized earnings method helps you to: (1) find the true earning power of a business and (2) then find the investment necessary to earn a rate of return that is in line with the risks involved. This method also considers all of the external influences—such as the economy and industry conditions—which bear on a company's prospects.

SEVEN

The Impossible Transition

Having succeeded in his "impossible dream" of starting his own business and nurturing it through the critical stages of its growth, the entrepreneur is now faced with problems and challenges of a different sort. His business venture has long passed from being a one-man show. It is now a successful and probably large enterprise, having needs totally unlike the needs of a new venture.

If the entrepreneur is nearing the end of his active career, he should now be planning a successor to assume his position. For the family-owned company, this may present special problems. In a non-family business, the transition of the executive function will usually be uneventful if the successor is at least as competent as his predecessor, and if the organization has had some turnover in this position. Donald Trow's main focus in the first reading in this chapter, *Executive Succession in Small Companies*, concerns the factors that influence the firm's preparedness for this transition.

If the entrepreneur is still relatively young, then he is faced either with making a reassessment of his abilities as an effective manager (if this has not already been done by stockholders or creditors), or selling his interest in the business and reinvesting his talents and funds in starting a totally new venture. Similar periods of personal reassessment occur at different times in everyone's life. In the first case, the entrepreneur may find that he no longer has the qualities and attitudes conducive to profitably managing a mature enterprise. His skills may not be optimum in terms of the company's needs. His choice is either to attempt the learning and application of the required managerial skills, or to leave the business.

The second case is somewhat different, in that the entrepreneur perceives his position in a constrained environment rather than as an ineffective manager, and he makes the choice to be free from the bureaucracy of the business. He seeks to regain his autonomy and his freedom to participate more actively in the innovation process by establishing a new business venture.

In any business succession is important in ensuring a continuation of managerial control and involvement in organizational, business, and financial matters. In a family business, an important factor in the succession planning process is the availibility of a son as a potential successor. Where there is no son, or if the son's ability is suspect, a succession is complicated by friction arising from rivalries involving a father and his son, brothers, or other family members who have positions in the business. In the second article, *Conflicts that Plague Family Businesses,* Harry Levinson discusses management development, executive succession, and other kinds of problems that can disrupt an otherwise productive organization in a family owned and perpetuated business.

A common error in a family business is to start the heir apparent too high in the organization, without his having acquired ground-up business experience. This often leads to a lack of acceptance by subordinates, the eventual collapse of the organizational heirarchy, and the loss of the productive work environment. To be successful, the succession. strategy must be developed early and implemented carefully. The plan should contain a specific timetable for advancing the prospective successor through the various management development stages and assignments, and it should be well understood by both the successor and the head of the business. An aggressive son with a recently acquired MBA, who is expecting to assume control of the business, is bound to be impatient and disappointed at being told that he must wait five years to allow him time to learn the business before the father retires from active participation.

If a family is not available, leadership must be obtained from outside the firm. The problem of succession then becomes complicated by the conflicts between the traditional family goals and objectives and the newly hired professional manager's views. The new head must be willing to learn and respect the sensitive family relationships. The family relationships are as vital as the business relationships.

After the entrepreneur has managed to bring his idea successfully to the marketplace, has labored with the business through its growing pains, and finally is secure in knowing that a stable foundation has at last been built, what does he do next? The alternatives, of course, are to plan for more expansion through acquisition or internal growth or to sell or merge the business, giving up controlling interest in the process.

Based on the third article in this chapter, *The Incurables,* an entrepreneur is usually not content to be in a position where he must manage and where he cannot react immediately and with complete authority to develop a challenging idea. Men like Fairchild and Lear have continued to start new ventures after starting and selling past businesses. Managing a mature organization typically does not satisfy the need for the entrepreneur to achieve. He prefers the challenge of beginning with a vision of a new product and building a profitable business from scratch—willing to take the high risks involved. His rewards from innovating are more meaningful (and often more profitable) than simply filling a slot in a large corporation. It is during the transition stage of the entrepreneur's life cycle, after his venture has become a success, that he is likely to choose the alternative of reaping the reward, bailing out, and attacking the business environment fom the angle of a new venture formation.

When another business is formed, it is likely to be more successful than the old one, according to Lawrence Lamont, the author of the concluding article in this chapter, *What Entrepreneurs Learn From Experience.* This is because the entrepreneur has an opportunity to apply his previous small business experience—experience that is reflected in the second-generation firm's having (1) a product orientation, (2) adequate initial financing, and (3) a better balance of business skills. The entrepreneur will have learned that contract-oriented businesses are highly unstable, that most new firms are undercapitalized, and that technical talents must be combined with marketing and management skills if the business is to be successful.

To summarize: The entrepreneur faces many difficult personal choices during the maturity phase of the business. If a successor to the business must be found, then he must prepare a plan for the effective and non-interruptive transfer of his duties. If he is either not competent as an executive or finds his motivational needs are not being fulfilled, then he is likely to sell his interest in the business and start a new venture.

EXECUTIVE SUCCESSION

IN SMALL COMPANIES*

DONALD B. TROW

Chester Barnard once speculated on the consequences if, except for himself, the entire management team of his company, New Jersey Bell Telephone Company, were replaced overnight by executives from other companies in the Bell system.[1] He predicted chaos within twelve hours, in spite of the fact that the companies in the Bell system were essentially alike and the executives' knowledge and skills immediately transferable. He was emphasizing the importance of established interpersonal relationships even in supposedly impersonal organizations.

Results of a recent study of rapid succession in much smaller and contrived laboratory organizations suggest, however, that if his speculation were put to the test, the consequences might not be as disastrous as he foresaw.[2] Two conditions in the laboratory organizations' transition of the executive function without chaos (in addition to the successors having had experience in a similar organization) were: (1) that the successors be at least as able as their predecessors, and (2) that the organizations have previous experience with a high rate of turnover in these positions. The influence of another potentially important condition, namely, conscious organizational planning for the succession process, was

*From *Administrative Science Quarterly* (September, 1961), pp. 228-237. Reprinted with permission.

[1]Chester I. Barnard, Education for Executives, *Journal of Business*, 18 (1945), 175-182.

[2]Donald B. Trow, Membership Succession and Team Performance, *Human Relations*, 13 (1960), 259-269.

difficult to assess in the experimental data. The benefits of such planning, however, as well as the conditions for its occurrence, have been investigated in a sample of over one hundred small manufacturing companies by C. R. Christensen and reported in his book, *Management Succession in Small and Growing Enterprises.*[3]

The purpose of this paper is to present the results of a reanalysis of Christensen's data, which was undertaken with three objectives: (1) estimation of the average rate of succession in top management positions in these organizations, (2) assessment of the effect of the rate of succession and of the ability of the successor (the two factors found important in the laboratory organizations) in these nonlaboratory organizations, and (3) quantitative assessment of factors conducive to planning for succession.

The data consist of short case descriptions of small companies in which succession had recently taken place or appeared imminent. The general pattern of presentation in the original study was for two to five case accounts to be used to illustrate each of several types of succession plans and each of several factors that appear to account for lack of planning for succession, as well as to illustrate the main thesis that lack of such planning tends to lead to lowered profitability. The fact that almost every case contains information about several characteristics of the process of planning for succession permits reanalysis of the data using cross tabulations and simple tests of significance of relationships.

Altogether, data are presented on 108 small manufacturing companies, all but three approaching or just past a succession. A few involved more than one succession, and in these cases only the most recent succession is used for the present analysis. The selection of companies was made on the basis of accessibility and cooperativeness rather than any planned statistical sample of a defined universe of small companies; alumni of the Harvard Business School, where the cases were compiled, were *not* used as sources of contacts with companies.[4]

The typical company in the sample is a family-owned manufacturing firm with a management group numbering five or six and fewer than one hundred employees. While large firms are excluded from the study by definition, extremely small firms are probably also underrepresented. The *Census of Manufactures, 1954,* shows the median number of employees of manufacturing establishments to be less than ten and firms of this size appear to make up only a small part of the sample.[5] (The number of multi-establishment companies that might account for some of the discrepancy is negligible.) Manufacturers of metal products and machinery are considerably overrepresented: two-thirds of the 84 sample companies for which the product is named are in these industries as against one-fourth of all manufacturing establishments. Finally, there is undoubtedly an underrepresentation of companies that had neither recently experienced succession nor were expecting it in the near future. This last bias is of course entirely appropriate in view of the subject of the study.

---

[3]Boston, 1953.

[4]C. R. Christensen (personal communication).

[5]U.S. Bureau of the Census, *Census of Manufactures, 1954, Preliminary Report* (Washington, 1956).

RATE OF SUCCESSION

The annual rate of succession of managers in this sample of companies can be estimated from the average tenure of the predecessors in those companies in which succession had recently occurred and the tenure of the then current managers (on the assumption that they were not far from retirement) in the remaining companies. This figure is given or can be surmised in 29 out of the 51 cases of completed succession and in 22 out of the 57 others. Determination of the exact number of years is not possible in all cases, but the median of each distribution appears to be between 20 and 25 years. Assuming an approximately symmetrical distribution and no bias in the cases for which the figure cannot be ascertained, this gives an annual succession rate of 4 or 5 per cent.[6]

As might be expected in a sample of relatively small companies, a number of the retiring presidents had been the founders of their companies, and their average term was longer than that of nonfounders. About one-third of the cases specify that the president had been the founder or co-founder, and the true proportion may be nearer one-half, since only in about one-third of the cases is it specified that the president was *not* the founder. The median number of years in office is over 30 for the 18 founders for whom this datum is given or can be estimated, and between 15 and 20 for the 15 nonfounders. The rate of succession in these companies when founders are excluded is thus probably between 5 and 7 per cent. The rate is slightly greater for managers who are neither founders nor principal owners. These total 14, and their median term in office was 14 years. Managers who are not owners are presumably older, on the average, when they assume the presidency, and they may also retire earlier.

Even the rate of 7 per cent, however, is low. Nelson found a rate of 12 per cent for presidents of a random sample of small companies in the shoe, brewing, and automotive industries over a ten-year period, and the rate was 15 per cent for presidents of the larger organizations in these industries.[7] Even this is low in comparison with turnover of managers in the Russian industrial bureaucracy. Granick reports that in Russian firms in heavy industry only 3 to 8 per cent of the company directors (that is, managers) studied had held their posts for more than five years, the median being between one and three years.[8]

There is no evidence in Christensen's companies that a higher rate of succession reduces its detrimental effects, as was the case in the laboratory organizations. Only two or three companies had, however, what could be called rapid turnover of presidents (say, more than two successions in a ten- or fifteen-year period), and very little turnover in other management positions was recorded, so the succession rate for the management group as a whole, which was the rate used in the laboratory study, could not be computed nor could its effect, if any, be determined.

---

[6]Here and in subsequent tabulations the proportion of "not ascertained" cases is relatively large. The assumption that they are distributed in roughly the same way as the others does not appear unwarranted for any of the data presented.

[7]Joel Nelson, "Executive Turnover" (unpublished paper).

[8]David Granick, *Management of the Industrial Firm in the USSR* (New York, 1954), pp. 47-48.

SUCCESSION PLANNING AND SUBSEQUENT PROFITABILITY

Christensen's analysis begins with the thesis that lack of planning for succession tends to be followed by a post-succession period of lowered organizational performance. Before examining the quantitative support for this, it is necessary to specify more precisely what is meant by planning for succession. Implicitly in Christensen's presentation and explicitly here a plan for succession is considered to consist of three elements, all of which must antedate the actual succession by an interval of months: (1) the designation of the successor by the predecessor or by appropriate higher authority, which in a small company may involve bringing in a "crown prince" from outside; (2) a period of apparently effective training of the successor-designate in the top management tasks of the particular organization; and (3) acceptance of the planned succession by the successor-designate himself and by other major power figures (for example, major stockholders, senior but nonsuccessor vice-presidents) who could later successfully dispute the succession. The first part of this definition, designation of the successor, must be construed loosely enough to include cases in which the successor is an interim management council of some kind and cases in which an individual successor is to be chosen at the time of succession from a designated and trained group of two or three vice-presidents.

Under this broad definition 54 of the companies can be said to have had a plan, judging from the case presentation, and 45 no plan, with nine unclassifiable (and omitted from further analysis). The coding reliability of this classification is estimated at .90, based on this percentage agreement on a 20 per cent sample coding by a second coder. Of the 54 with a plan, two designated group managements and 20 deferred final choice from among a designated group of candidates.

In making the point that lack of planning tends to be followed by a post-succession period of lowered organizational performance, Christensen exhibits seven cases in which this proved true and two cases in which it seemed likely to prove true although succession had not yet taken place. When all 51 cases of completed succession are considered, the results, shown in Table 1, give strong *quantitative* support to the suggested relationship. Lack of planning does appear to be followed by lowered profitability. It may be presumed that lack of planning operates as a contributing *cause* of lowered performance, although it is possible that in some cases the absence of a plan may itself have been caused by reluctance on everyone's part to volunteer for command of an already failing organization.

TABLE 1   Association Between Profitability after Succession and Prior Planning for Succession in 51 Companies (Christensen Data)

	Planned succession	Plan absent or incomplete	Not ascertained
Profitability undiminished	12	3	(1)
Diminished profitability	7	14	—
Unreported profitability	(12)	(2)	—

$p = .007$ (Fisher's exact test for 2 x 2 tables).

Examination of the exceptional cases gives some confirmation of the importance of the ability of a successor. The three companies that were successful in spite of having had no plan for succession were two that brought in experienced presidents from outside and one in which the treasurer became president, solved the company's financial difficulties, and instituted an advantageous merger. The seven companies that were not financially successful in spite of having had planned succession were two in which deteriorating conditions prior to succession merely continued; three in which the successors were the sons of the predecessors and apparently not competent enough; one in which the successor "did not have a strong organization to support him"; and one in which the planned successor died soon after taking office. While the validity of assessment of the reasons for success or failure in these cases is necessarily uncertain, the ability of the successor appears to play a part in the majority of them. And among the 14 companies that experienced decline after an unplanned succession, the decline is explicitly attributed to lack of ability in five and is definitely ruled out in none. These, of course, are judgments of ability after the fact; nevertheless, the cases may be taken as giving some support to the conclusion drawn from the laboratory study (where ability was measured *before* succession) that even within a restricted range of variability the level of ability of the successor is an important determinant of organizational performance in the period immediately following succession.

REASONS FOR LACK OF PLANNING FOR SUCCESSION

Although there is strong support for the proposition that lack of planning is followed by decreased performance, the support for factors proposed as inhibitors of planning is more uncertain. Christensen proposes the following principal reasons for lack of planning in small companies:[9]

1. Size of management group: The smaller the firm, the more difficult it is to support a successor-designate.
2. Growth: Growth is conducive to planning for succession; where it is absent, planning is less likely.
3. Ownership: Smaller firms are more likely to be family owned and managed; this makes planning for succession difficult if there is no available successor within the family.
4. Predominance of short-term management problems: The manager of a small firm is likely to be concerned largely with the problems of day-to-day operation, very often in a specialized area (sales, design, and so on) on which company success has been built, and may not have the time or ability to train a successor.
5. Outside counsel: Small firms are less likely than large firms to have access to outside advice that might encourage planning for succession.
6. Retirement: Managers of small firms are frequently in a position to refuse to retire, in which case planning for succession is likely to be postponed, or a successor-designate may become impatient and leave.
7. Procrastination: Managers of small firms often have the attitude that "time will produce a successor," an attitude that excuses lack of planning and may also serve to postpone it further.

[9]The wording of these propositions is mine, not Professor Christensen's.

Only the first three of these—size, growth, and ownership—can be coded directly from the data. As shown in Table 2, each is associated with planning for succession within the group of companies in which succession had not yet occurred at the time of case collection, but not within the group of companies in which succession had already occurred. (The former effects are substantially independent, as evidenced by significant partial relationships not shown.) There appear to be at least two plausible explanations for significant relationships in one group and not in the other. The first is that smaller, nongrowing, family companies tend to delay making succession plans until quite close to the retirement date of the president (or delay retirement until plans can be made and sufficient training given to the successor), but they do not fail to plan any more than do larger firms. This incidentally would tend to confirm the attitude of managers who felt that "time till provide a successor." Another possible explanation for the finding is that prior to succession some of the larger firms claim to have plans for succession when in fact they do not, or when their plans

TABLE 2   Association Between Planning for Succession and Selected Organizational Variables in 99 Companies (Christensen Data)

	Following succession		Prior to succession	
	Planned	Unplanned	Planned	Unplanned
Size:				
Management group under 6	6	7	7	13
Management group 6 or more	7	9	14	3
Not ascertained	(16)	(4)	(3)	(9)
	not significant		$p = .005$	
Growth:				
Reported present	2	2	10	5
Absent or not reported	28	18	14	20
	not significant		$p = .09$	
Ownership:				
Family or partnership	21	13	12	17
Nonfamily corporation	5	5	8	2
Not ascertained	(4)	(2)	(4)	(6)
	not significant		$p = .04$	
Son as potential successor				
Reported present	16	6	4	10
Absent or not reported	14	14	20	15
	$p = .09$		$p = .07$	

Fisher's exact test used throughout.

are only provisional; this they can do more easily than smaller firms since they are more likely to have second-level executives who could conceivably succeed to the top position even though they are not slated to. Doubt is cast on the second explanation, however, by the fact that if companies whose plan involves a deferred final choice are defined as having *no plan* (that is, tightening the definition of "plan" to require actual designation of the successor), the relationship between size and planning is still significant at the .07 level.

An additional factor in the succession-planning process is the availability of a son as a potential successor. This relationship is shown at the bottom of Table 2. In companies in which succession had taken place, the availability of a son is associated with prior planning; but in companies in which succession had not yet occurred the presence of a son is associated with *lack* of planning. The variable that appears to make the difference is the son's ability: when it is low, a succession plan of any kind is less likely, and presumably succession itself tends to be postponed. Of the 16 companies with a son as potential successor but without a plan, the son is explicitly stated to lack competence in 11 cases, and in two additional cases lack of competence appears probable. A son with insufficient competence was also reported in four of the six companies in which succession occurred without a prior plan.

SUMMARY AND DISCUSSION

This secondary analysis of data collected by Christensen about management succession in a sample of over one hundred small- to medium-sized manufacturing companies has indicated the following:

1. The median length of service of the company presidents is about 20 years. It is somewhat higher than this for founders of companies and lower for nonfounders, and it is still lower (about 14 years) for managers who were not principal owners.
2. There is a strong association between planning for succession and subsequent profitability: companies in which a successor had been chosen and trained appear much less likely to have suffered a period of financial difficulty while the new president learned to manage.
3. The size and growth of the management group and the pattern of company ownership are associated with planning for succession. In the cases studied prior to succession the smaller, stable, family-owned companies tended not to have chosen and trained successors; when succession had actually occurred, however, there was no difference in planning between these companies and larger, growing, publicly owned ones. The difference is attributable to later planning in the smaller companies.
4. Management ability appeared to have two different effects on the succession process. In companies in which the manager's son was the potential successor, a low level of competence on his part seems to have delayed both planning for succession and the succession itself. Secondly, among all companies in which an unplanned succession occurred, subsequent company profitability appears to be associated positively with the successor's ability.[10]

[10]This relationship is suggested by Christensen, *op. cit.*, p. 29, but is not documented.

These results largely support the conclusions of the original study. In addition, however, they suggest a change of emphasis in the conclusions concerning the effects of company size, growth, and ownership upon succession planning: these factors appear to affect the *timing* of planning rather than its likelihood. In addition, the analysis indicated that management ability plays a larger part than was suggested in the original study. While it is hardly surprising that managerial ability is found to be related to company performance, the analysis goes beyond this in revealing the particular ways in which ability interacts with the succession process to produce its effect.

The general pattern of the succession-planning that appears to underlie the results is that of a decision problem extending over time. During the latter part of the manager's career, succession begins to loom as a problem requiring action. If there is a son (or a son-in-law or nephew) of the principal owner, then he is the first possible successor considered. If he appears to be interested and competent, then action is taken to assure his succession and to see that he gets adequate training; that is, a plan (in the sense used in this study) is formulated.

If there is a son, but he is too young, is not interested, or appears to be of borderline ability, then a decision is postponed to see whether he will become interested and/or whether further experience in lower management positions will increase his competence sufficiently for him to be the successor. In the meantime, however, the company is without a plan, and if the death or forced retirement of the manager brings about succession anyway, then the son is likely to be the successor. If there has been no change in his level of interest or competence, then he is not likely to have the full support of other organization members. Because of this problem or because he makes poor decisions the profitability of the company is likely to decline.

If there is no son, then present members of management are considered as possible successors. Here, the likelihood that there will be someone of sufficient ability to be considered as a successor is greater in larger, growing companies where there is a level of management between the president and the shop foreman; therefore a plan can readily be formulated.

Finally, if there is no one within the company who can be considered for succession, then an outsider is sought, and the same factors—size, growth, and ownership—influence the attractiveness of the position and hence the amount of delay in getting a plan for succession formulated. Smaller family-owned companies find greater difficulty in attracting managers from outside and because of the high cost of a successor-designate may tend to delay even seeking one.

Although this general pattern of the succession-planning process serves to link together the factors and relationships that this analysis has shown are involved, the pattern does not of course convey a picture of the variety of ways in which the succession problem is handled by individual companies. For this the reader is referred to the original case material.

CONFLICTS THAT PLAGUE

FAMILY BUSINESSES*

HARRY LEVINSON

In U.S. business, the most successful executives are often men who have built their own companies. Ironically, their very success frequently brings to them and members of their families personal problems of an intensity rarely encountered by professional managers. And these problems make family businesses possibly the most difficult to operate.[1]

It is obvious common sense that when managerial decisions are influenced by feelings about and responsibilities toward relatives in the business, when nepotism exerts a negative influence, and when a company is run more to honor a family tradition than for its own needs and purposes, there is likely to be trouble.

However, the problems of family businesses go considerably deeper than these issues. In this article I shall examine some of the more difficult underlying psychological elements in operating these businesses and suggest some ways of coping with them.

THEY START WITH THE FOUNDER

The difficulties of the family business begin with the founder. Usually he is an entrepreneur for whom the business has at least three important meanings:

1. The entrepreneur characteristically has unresolved conflicts with his father, research evidence indicates. He is therefore uncomfortable when being supervised, and starts his own business both to outdo his father and to escape the authority and rivalry of more powerful figures.[2]

2. An entrepreneur's business is simultaneously his "baby" and his "mistress." Those who work with him and for him are characteristically his instruments in the process of shaping the organization.

If any among them aspires to be other than a device for the founder—that is, if he wants to acquire power himself—he is soon likely to find himself on the outside looking in. This is the reason why so many organizations decline when their founders age or die.

[1]For two thoughtful views of the subject, see Robert G. Donnelley, "The Family Business," HBR July-August 1964, p. 93; and Seymour Tilles, "Survival Strategies for Family Firms," *European Business*, April 1970, p. 9.

[2]See Orvis F. Collins, David G. Moore, and Darab B. Unwalla, *The Enterprising Man* (East Lansing, Michigan State University Bureau of Business Research, 1964).

3. For the entrepreneur, the business is essentially an extension of himself, a medium for his personal gratification and achievement above all. And if he is concerned about what happens to his business after he passes on, the concern usually takes the form of thinking of the kind of monument he will leave behind.

The fundamental psychological conflict in family businesses is rivalry, compounded by feelings of guilt, when more than one family member is involved. The rivalry may be felt by the founder—even though no relatives are in the business—when he unconsciously senses (justifiably or not) that subordinates are threatening to remove him from his center of power. Consider this actual case:

> An entrepreneur, whose organization makes scientific equipment and bears his name, has built a sizable enterprise in international markets. He has said that he wants his company to be noted all over the world for contributing to society.
>
> He has attracted many young men with the promise of rapid promotions, but he guarantees their failure by giving them assignments and then turning them loose without adequate organizational support. He intrudes into the young men's decision making, but he counterbalances this behavior with paternalistic devices. (His company has more benefits than any other I have known.)
>
> This technique makes his subordinates angry at him for what he has done, then angry at themselves for being hostile to such a kind man. Ultimately, it makes them feel utterly inadequate. He can get people to take responsibility and move up into executive positions, but his behavior has made certain that he will never have a rival.

The conflicts created by rivalries among family members—between fathers and sons, among brothers, and between executives and other relatives—have a chronically abrasive effect on the principals. Those family members in the business must face up to the impact that these relationships exert and must learn to deal with them, not only for their own emotional health but for the welfare of the business.

I shall consider in turn the father-son rivalry, the brother-brother rivalry, and other family relationships.

FATHER-SON RIVALRY

As I have indicated, for the founder the business is an instrument, an extension of himself. So he has great difficulty giving up his baby, his mistress, his instrument, his source of social power, or whatever else the business may mean to him. Characteristically, he has great difficulty delegating authority and he also refuses to retire despite repeated promises to do so.

This behavior has certain implications for father-son relationships. While he consciously wishes to pass his business on to his son and also wants him to attain his place in the sun, unconsciously the father feels that to yield the business would be to lose his masculinity.

At the same time, and also unconsciously, he needs to continue to demonstrate his own competence. That is, he must constantly reassure himself that he alone is competent to make "his" organization succeed. Unconsciously the father does not want his son to win, take away his combination baby and mistress, and displace him from his summit position.

These conflicting emotions cause the father to behave inexplicably in a contradictory manner, leading those close to him to think that while on the one hand he wants the business to succeed, on the other hand he is determined to make it fail.

The son's feelings of rivalry are a reflection of his father's. The son naturally seeks increasing responsibility commensurate with his growing maturity, and the freedom to act responsibly on his own. But he is frustrated by his father's intrusions, his broken promises of retirement, and his self-aggrandizement.

The son resents being kept in an infantile role—always the little boy in his father's eyes—with the accompanying contempt, condescension, and lack of confidence that in such a situation frequently characterize the father's attitude. He resents, too, remaining dependent on his father for his income level and, as often, for title, office, promotion, and the other usual perquisites of an executive. The father's erratic and unpredictable behavior in these matters makes this dependency more unpalatable.

I have observed a number of such men who, even as company presidents, are still being victimized by their fathers who remain chairmen of the board and chief executive officers.

Why Don't You Let Me Grow Up?

Characteristically, fathers and sons, particularly the latter, are terribly torn by these conflicts; the father looks on the son as ungrateful and unappreciative, and the son feels both hostile to his father and guilty for his hostility.

The father bears the feeling that the son never will be man enough to run the business, but he tries to hide that feeling from his son. The son yearns for his chance to run it and waits impatiently but still loyally in the wings—often for years beyond the age when others in nonfamily organizations normally take executive responsibility—for his place on the stage.

If the pressures become so severe for him that he thinks of leaving, he feels disloyal but at the same time fears losing the opportunity that would be his if he could only wait a little longer. He defers his anticipated gratification and pleasure, but, with each postponement, his anger, disappointment, frustration, and tension mount.

Here is a typical situation I know of:

Matthew Anderson, a man who founded a reclaimed-metals business, has two sons. John, the elder, is his logical successor, but Anderson has given him little freedom to act independently, pointing out that, despite limited education, he (the father) has built the business and intuitively knows more about how to make it successful.

Though he has told John that he wants him to be a partner, he treats John more like a flunky than an executive, let alone a successor. He pays the elder son a small salary, always with the excuse that he should not expect more because someday he will inherit the business. He grants minimal raises sporadically, never recognizing John's need to support his family in a style fitting his position in the company.

When John once protested and demanded both more responsibility and more income, his father gave Henry, the second son, a vice presidential title and a higher income. When Henry asked for greater freedom and responsibility,

Anderson turned back to John and made him president (in name only). The father, as chairman of the board and chief executive officer, continued to second-guess John, excluded Henry from conferences (which of course increased John's feelings of guilt), and told John that Henry was "no good" and could not run the business.

Later, when John sought to develop new aspects of the business to avoid the fluctuations of the metals market, his father vetoed these ideas, saying, "This is what we know, and this is what we are going to do." He failed to see the possible destructive effects of market cycles on fixed overhead costs and the potential inroads of plastics and other cheaper materials on the reclaimed-metals business.

The upshot was that profits declined and the business became more vulnerable to both domestic and foreign (particularly Japanese) competition. When John argued with his father about this, he got the response: "What do you know? You're still green. I went through the Depression." Once again Anderson turned to Henry—making the black sheep white, and vice versa.

Angered, John decided to quit the business, but his mother said, "you can't leave your father; he needs you." Anderson accused him of being ungrateful, but he also offered to retire, as he had promised to do several times before.

Despite his pain, John could not free himself from his father. (Only an ingrate would desert his father, he told himself.) Also John knew that if he departed, he could not go into competition with his father, because that would destroy him. But John shrank from entering an unfamiliar business.

Nevertheless, from time to time John has explored other opportunities while remaining in the business. But each time his father has undercut him. For instance, John once wanted to borrow money for a venture, but Anderson told the bankers that his son was not responsible.

Now, when John is middle-aged, he and his father are still battling. In effect John is asking, "Why don't you let me grow up?" and his father is answering, "I'm the only man around here. You must stay here and be my boy."

'He's Destroying the Business'

The son also has intense rivalry feelings, of course. These, too, can result in fierce competition with his father and hostile rejection of him, or abject dependence on him. Sometimes the competition can lead to a manipulative alignment with the mother against him. Consider this actual case:

Bill Margate, a recent business school graduate, knew that he would go into his father's electronic components business. But he decided that first he should get experience elsewhere, so he spent four years with a large manufacturing company. From his education and experience, he became aware of how unsophisticated his father was about running the business and set about showing the senior Margate how a business should be professionally managed.

Margate can do no right in Bill's eyes, at least not according to the books which he has read but which his father has never heard of. Bill frequently criticizes his father, showing him how ignorant he is. When Margate calls his son "green," Bill retorts, "I've forgotten more about managing a business than you'll ever know."

Bill's mother is also involved in the business; she has been at her husband's side for many years, though their relationship is less than the best. Mrs.

Margate dotes on her son and complains to him about her husband, and she encourages Bill in his attacks on his father. When Bill undertook several ventures that floundered, she excused the failures as being caused by his father's interference.

But whenever the father-son battle reaches a peak, Mrs. Margate shifts allegiance and stands behind her husband. So the senior Margate has an ally when the chips are down, at the price of a constant beating until he gets to that point.

The struggle for the business has remained a stand-off. But as the elder Margate has grown older, his son's attacks have begun to tell on him. Bill has urged him to take long Florida vacations, but Margate refuses because he fears what would happen when his back is turned. For the same reason, he does not permit Bill to sign checks for the company.

Now Margate has become senile, and Bill's criticism of him continues, even in public. "He's destroying the business," Bill will say.

However, Bill cannot act appropriately to remove his father (even though he is now incompetent) because of his guilt feelings about his incessant attacks. That would destroy his father, literally, and he cannot bring himself to do it.

'The Old Man Really Built It'

The problem for the son becomes especially acute when and if he does take over. Often the father has become obsolete in his managerial conceptions. The organization may have grown beyond one man's capacity to control it effectively. That man may have been a star whose imagination, creativity, or drive are almost impossible to duplicate. He may also have been a charismatic figure with whom employees and even the public identified.

Whatever the combination of factors, the son is likely to have to take over an organization with many weaknesses hidden behind the powerful facade of the departed leader. For these reasons many businesses, at the end of their founders' tenure, fall apart, are pirated, or are merged into another organization.

The Ford Motor Company, at the demise of Henry Ford, was a case in point; a completely new management had to be brought in. Henry Ford II was faced with the uncomfortable task of having to regenerate a company that appeared to have the potential for continued success, but which, according to some, could easily have gone bankrupt.

While the son is acting to repair the organizational weaknesses left by his father, he is subject to the criticism of those persons who, envious of his position, are waiting for him to stumble. They "know" that he is not as good as his father. If he does less well than his father, regardless of whether there are unfavorable economic conditions or other causes, he is subject to the charge of having thrown away an opportunity that others could have capitalized on.

The scion cannot win. If he takes over a successful enterprise, and even if he makes it much more successful than anyone could have imagined, nevertheless the onlookers stimulate his feelings of inadequacy. They say, "What did you expect? After all, look what he started with." To illustrate:

Tom Schlesinger, the president of a restaurant chain, inherited the business after his father had built a profitable regional network of outlets with a widely known name—a model for the industry.

Tom has expanded it into nearly a national operation. He has done this with astute methods of finance that allow great flexibility, and with effective control methods that maintain meal quality and at the same time minimize waste. By any standards he has made an important contribution to the business.

But those who remember his father cannot see what Tom has done because the aura of his father still remains. They tend to minimize Tom's contribution with such observations as, "Well, you know, the old man really built that business."

Tom cannot change the attitude of those who knew his father, and he feels it is important to keep lauding his father's accomplishments in order to present a solid family image to employees, customers, and the community. But he is frustrated because he has no way of getting the world to see how well he has done.

BROTHER-BROTHER RIVALRY

The father-son rivalry is matched in intensity by the brother-brother rivalry. Their competition may be exacerbated by the father if he tries to play the sons off against each other or has decided that one should wear his mantle, as I showed previously. (In my experience, the greatest difficulties of this kind occur when there are only two brothers in the organization.)

The problem is further complicated if their mother and their wives are also directly or indirectly involved in the business. Mothers have their favorites—regardless of what they say—and each wife, of course, has a stake in her husband's position. He can become a foil for his wife's fantasies and ambition.

The rivalry between brothers for their father's approval, which began in childhood, continues into adult life. It can reach such an intensity that it colors every management decision and magnifies the jockeying for power that goes on in all organizations. Consider this situation:

Arthur, five years older than his sibling, is president, and Warren is an operating vice president, of the medium-sized retailing organization which they inherited. To anyone who cares to listen, each maintains that he can get along very well without the other.

Arthur insists that Warren is not smart, not as good a businessman as he; that his judgment is bad; and that even if given the chance, he would be unable to manage the business.

Warren asserts that when the two were growing up, Arthur considered him to be a competitor, but for his part, he (Warren) did not care to compete because he was younger and smaller. Warren says that he cannot understand why his older brother has always acted as if they were rivals, and adds, "I just want a chance to do my thing. If he'd only let me alone with responsibility! But he acts as if the world would fall apart if I had that chance."

Every staff meeting and meeting of the board (which includes nonfamily members) becomes a battle between the brothers. Associates, employees, and friends back off because they decline to take sides. The operation of the organization has been turned into a continuous family conflict.

The Elder. . .

Ordinarily, the elder brother succeeds his father. But the custom reaffirms the belief of the younger brother (or brothers) that the oldest is indeed the

242

favorite. In any event, the older brother often has a condescending attitude toward the younger. In their earliest years the older is larger, physically stronger, more competent, and more knowledgeable than the younger merely because of the difference in age, as in the case I just cited.

Only in rare instances does the younger brother have the opportunity to match the skills, competence, and experience of the elder until they reach adulthood. By that time the nature of this relationship is so well established that the older brother has difficulty regarding the younger one as adequate and competent.

Moreover, the eldest child is earlier and longer in contact with the parents, and their control efforts fall more heavily on him. Consequently, older children tend to develop stronger consciences, drive themselves harder, expect more of themselves, and control themselves more rigidly than younger ones. Being already, therefore, a harsh judge of himself, the eldest is likely to be an even harsher judge of his younger siblings.

. . . And the Younger

The younger brother attempts to compensate for the effects of this childhood relationship and his older brother's efforts to control him by trying to carve out a place in the business that is his own. This he guards with great zeal, keeping the older brother out so he can demonstrate to himself, his brother, and others that he is indeed competent and has his own piece of the action for which he is independently responsible.

If the brothers own equal shares in the organization and both are members of the board, as is frequently the case, the problems are compounded. On the board they can argue policy from equally strong positions. However, when they return to operations in which one is subordinate to the other, the subordinate one, usually the junior brother, finds it extremely difficult to think of himself in a subservient role.

The younger one usually is unable to surmount this problem in their mutual relationship. He tends to be less confident than his brother and considers himself to be at a permanent disadvantage, always overcontrolled, always unheeded. Since the older brother views the younder one as being less able, he becomes involved in self-fulfilling prophecies. Distrusting his younger brother, he is likely to over-control him, give him less opportunity for freedom and responsibility—which in turn make for maturity and growth—and likely to reject all signs of the younger brother's increasing competence.

If for some reason the younger brother displaces the older one, and particularly if the latter becomes subordinate to him, the younger brother is faced with feelings of guilt for having attacked the elder and usurped what so often is accepted as the senior brother's rightful role.

INTRAFAMILY FRICTION

The problems of the father and brothers extend to other relatives when they, too, become involved in the business. In some families it is expected that all who wish to join the company will have places there. This can have devastating effects, particularly if the jobs are sinecures.

The chief executive of a family business naturally feels a heavy responsibility for the family fortunes. If he does not produce a profit, the effect on what he considers to be his image in the financial markets may mean less to him than the income reduction which members of his family will suffer. So he is vulnerable to backbiting from persons whom he knows only too well and whom he cannot dismiss as faceless. Consider this case:

Three brothers started a knitting business. Only one of the brothers had sons, and only one of those sons stayed in the business; he eventually became president. The stock is held by the family. Two widowed aunts, his mother, his female cousins (one of whom was already widowed), and his brother, a practicing architect, depend on the business for significant income.

When business is off, the women complain. If the president wants to buy more equipment, they resist. If they hear complaints from employees or merchant friends, they make these complaints known at family gatherings. The president is never free from the vixens who are constantly criticizing and second-guessing him.

Perhaps more critical for the health of the business are the factional divisions that spring up in the organization as associates and subordinates choose the family members with whom they want to be identified. (Often, however, those who take sides discover that in a crisis the family unites against "outsiders," including their partisans, who are then viewed as trying to divide the family.)

If the nonfamily employees or board members decide not to become involved in a family fight and withdraw from relations with its members until the conflict is resolved, the work of the organization may be paralyzed. Worse yet, the dispute may eventually embroil the entire organization, resulting in conflicts at the lowest levels, as employees try to cope with the quarrels thrust on them.

Now the business has become a battleground that produces casualties but no peace. Such internecine warfare constitutes a tremendous barrier to communication and frustrates adequate planning and rational decision making.

A business in which numerous members of the family of varying ages and relationships are involved often becomes painfully disrupted around issues of empires and succession. Its units tend to become family-member territories and therefore poorly integrated organizationally, if at all.

As for succession, the dominant or patriarchal leader may fully expect to pass on the mantle of leadership to other, elder relatives in their turn. He may even promise them leadership roles, particularly if he has had to develop a coalition to support his position.

But for both realistic and irrational reasons he may well come to feel that none of the family members is capable of filling the role. He cannot very well disclose his decision, however, without stirring conflict, and he cannot bring in outside managers without betraying his relatives or reneging on his promises. On the other hand, he fears what would happen if he died without having designated a successor.

He may decide that the only way out is to sell the business (at least each relative will then get his fair share). But that solution is costly—it signifies not only the loss of the business as a means of employment, but also the betrayal of a tradition and, inevitably, the dissolution of close family ties that have been maintained through the medium of the business.

FACING UP TO IT

What can be done about these problems?

Most entrepreneurial fathers seem unable to resolve their dilemma themselves. They tend to be rigid and righteous, finding it difficult to understand that there is another, equally valid point of view which they can accept without becoming weaklings. Well-meaning outsiders who try to help the father see the effects of his behavior and think seriously about succession usually find themselves rejected. Then they lose whatever beneficial influence they may have had on him.

Several approaches have worked well. In some instances, sons have told their fathers that they recognize how important it is to the father to run his own business, but it is just as important for them to have the opportunity to "do their own thing." They then establish small new ventures either under the corporate umbrella or outside it, without deserting their father.

In a variant of this approach, a father who heads a retail operation opened a store in a different community for each of his sons. They do their buying together, with appropriate variations for each community, and maintain a common name and format, but each son runs his own operation while the father continues to run his.

In still another situation, the father merged his company into a larger one. Each of his two sons then became president of a subsidiary, and the father started a new venture while serving as a policy guide to his sons.

The Son's Role

Whether such alternatives can work depends in part on how the son conducts himself. He must be honest with himself and consider his paternal relationship candidly. He must take steps like these:

1. He must ask himself why he chose to go into the family business. Most sons will say it is because of the opportunity and the feelings of guilt if they had not done so. Often, however, the basic reason is that a powerful father has helped make his son dependent on him, and so his son is reluctant to strike out on his own.

He rationalizes his reluctance on the basis of opportunity and guilt. Struggling with his own dependency, he is more likely to continue to fight his father in the business because he is still trying to escape his father's control.

2. Having examined this issue, and recognizing whatever validity it may have for him, the son must realize how often his own feelings of rivalry and anger get in his way. The more intense the rivalry, the more determinedly he seeks to push his father from his throne and the more aggressively the latter must defend himself. The son must therefore refrain from attack.

3. He must quietly and with dignity, as a mature man, apprise his father of the realities—that he needs an area of freedom and an independent medium to develop skills and responsibilities. He can do so within the company framework or, if that is not feasible, outside it. In his own self-interest, as well as the company's, he must be certain that he gets the opportunity.

4. He must not allow himself to be played off against his brother, and he must

not allow his guilt to be manipulated. By the same token, he himself must not become involved with others in manipulation.

5. He must honestly recognize and request his father's achievement and competence. To build a business is no mean task, and usually the father still has useful skills and knowledge. Furthermore, the son should recognize the powerful psychological meaning of the business to his father and not expect him to be rational about his relationship to it.

If the son is still unable to make choices about what he wants to do, then, despite his pain and his father's reluctance to seek help, he himself must do so. Only he can take the initiative to relieve his anguish. Here is an example of how a group of sons has taken the initiative:

In Boston, a group calling itself SOBs (Sons of the Boss) has been formed to encourage men in that position to talk over common problems and share solutions. After educating themselves about the psychological dimensions of their situation, the group will make it a practice from time to time to invite their fathers as a group to discuss their problems openly. Then fathers and sons will get together separately.

This procedure may enable fathers and sons to realize that their particular problems are not unique to themselves, and to obtain support from those in a similar predicament.

Another approach for a son would be to ask his father to read this article and then discuss it privately with a neutral third party of their choice, to develop a perspective on their feelings and behavior. Having done so, a father is then in a better position to talk with his son, in the presence of the third party.

The third person must use his good offices to subdue recrimination. At the same time he must foster the father's expression of his fears over losing control, being unneeded, and suffering rejection, as well as the son's concerns about being overcontrolled, infantilized, and exploited.

If meeting with the third party fails to help, the next step is consultation with a psychologist or psychiatrist. There are rare instances, usually when conflict becomes severe, in which father and son are willing to go to a professional together or separately. In such cases it is often possible for the father to begin to make compromises, learn to understand his and his son's motivations, and work out with him newly defined, more compatible roles. Usually, however, such an effort requires continued supportive work by the professional and strong desire on the part of both men to resolve their differences.

If all these measures fail, those who work with patriarchs must learn to tolerate their situation until the opportunity arises for a change.

Fraternal Spirit

With respect to the brother-brother conflict, it is important for brothers to see that in their relationship they recapitulate ancient rivalries, and to perceive clearly the psychological posture each assumes toward the other. Once they understand these two issues, they must talk together about them. They should try to discuss freely the fears, worries, anger, and disappointments caused by each other. They should also be able to talk about their affection for each other.

Since there is love and hate in all relationships, theirs cannot, by definition, be pure. They should not feel guilty about their anger with each other, but they do need to talk it out. Having done that, they then must consider how they can divide the tasks in the organization so that each will have a chance to acquire and demonstrate competence and work in a complementary relationship with the other.

A brother cannot easily be subordinate at one level and equal on another. If a brother is an operating executive subordinate to the other, he gets into difficulty when he tries to be an equal on the board of directors. If more than one brother is on the board, then only one, as a rule, should be an operating executive. Of course, such rules are unnecessary if the brothers work well together.

If the brothers still cannot resolve their conflicts, then it becomes necessary to seek professional aid. If that does not help, they should consider being in separate organizations. In such a case, the big problem is the guilt feelings which the departing brother is likely to have for deserting the other and the family business.

Toward Professional Management

Where there are multiple and complex family relationships and obligations in a company, and particularly problems about succession, the best solution is a transcendent one. The family members should form a trust, taking all the relatives out of business operations while enabling them to continue to act in concert as a family.

The trust could allot financial support to every member who desires it to develop new business ventures on behalf of the family, thus providing a business interest that replaces the previous operating activity. This also helps maintain family cohesion and preserve the family's leadership role in the community.

In general, the wisest course for any business, family or nonfamily, is to move to professional management as quickly as possible. Every business must define its overriding purpose for being, from which it derives its objectives. Within this planning framework, the business must have a system for appraising the degree to which it and its components are achieving the goals that have been set.

All organizations need to rear subordinates in a systematic manner, thus creating the basic condition for their own regeneration. I know of no family business capable of sustaining regeneration over the long term solely through the medium of its own family members.

Where there is conflict, or inadequately rationalized territories, members of the family should move up and out of operations as quickly as possible into policy positions. Such movement recognizes the reality of ownership but does not confuse ownership with management.

It also opens the opportunity for professionally trained managers to succeed to major operating roles, instead of having to go to other organizations as soon as they are ready for major responsibility. The more competitive the business situation, the more imperative such a succession pattern is.

More than others, the family members need to have their own outside activities from which they can derive gratification equal to what they can obtain in the company. Otherwise they will be unable to let go and will continue to be barriers to others. Moreover, they will make it difficult to recruit and develop young persons with leadership potential who, as they mature, will see the inevitable barriers.

A number of family businesses have handled these issues wisely and have become highly professional in their management. The Dayton-Hudson Corporation and E.I. du Pont de Nemours are examples. Family members in both organizations must compete for advancement on the same terms as non-family managers. This practice is reinforced, at least at Dayton-Hudson, by a thorough performance appraisal system which includes appraisal of the chairman and president by a committee of the board.

CONCLUDING NOTE

It is very difficult to cope with the problems of the family business. That does not mean, however, that one should merely endure them. There is no point in stewing in anger and guilt, since chronic irritation is only self-flagellation. It solves no problems; it only increases anger and hostility and paves the way for explosion, recrimination, and impaired relations.

The family member can do something about such problems, as he can with any other. If reasonable steps to solve the problems do not work and he continues to feel bound to the organization, his problem is largely psychological. To free himself to make choices about what he wants to do, he must talk his feelings out with his rival in the organization, which is best done in the presence of a neutral third person. Somtimes professional help is necessary.

This will reduce sufficiently the intensity of the emotions generated by the problem, so that he can see possible alternatives more clearly and make choices more freely. That is better than the years of agitation that usually accompany such problems, unless of course the rival needs to expiate his guilt by continuing to punish himself. In that case, it is his problem and not necessarily that of the family business.

THE INCURABLES*

FORBES MAGAZINE

A good many Americans dream about starting their own companies, but most of them never get beyond dreaming. They're simply not entrepreneurs. There are others, however, a handful, so thoroughly entrepreneurial they're not satisfied with starting one company and spending the rest of their lives running it. They start company after company. For these people, entrepreneur-ing is a way of life.

Neison and Irving Harris of Chicago built the Toni Company from scratch, then sold it to Gillette for $20 million. That was in 1948, when $20 million was

*From *Forbes* (July, 1969), pp. 21-23, 60. Reprinted by permission.

as good as $30 million is today. And what did the Harris brothers do? Retire? No, they bought an old corporate shell and turned it into a $64-million-a-year industrial products maker called Pittway Corp. At that point, more money was the last thing they needed, yet they kept going. "Retire?" snorts Neison Harris. "I just don't know what the hell I'd do in the morning if I couldn't go to work."

The Harris brothers are not unique. In recent weeks, *Forbes* reporter Alex Block has talked with others like them, outstanding examples of the entrepreneurial breed, individuals who have started not one but two or more successful enterprises. He found them a diverse lot. Some were born to wealth; others rose from poverty. Some were salesmen, some technicians, some plain businessmen. They operated in widely diverse fields, from pet foods to jet aircraft, from publishing to transistors. But they had, he found, certain things in common:

They were not interested primarily in money but in creating and building companies. In several cases, when they sold a company they had started, they received so much stock for it they could have taken over control of the company to which they sold it. They didn't, because that wouldn't have been any fun; they would be running something that somebody else created. They would be managers, not entrepreneurs.

The companies they created and built were substantial and profitable but hardly in the billion-dollar class. They did have the base on which to build a billion-dollar conglomerate, but, again, that would have meant taking over businesses established by others. That's not for them. They have an ill-disguised disdain for the men who put together conglomerates. Such men are not creators.

Ask them why they refused to retire, and the usual answer given is, "How would I spend my time?" That obviously is not the real answer, because there are dozens of ways in which a retired man can spend his time—in public service, in politics, by going into Wall Street, by going fishing. To the born entrepreneur, building a business from scratch is a way of life. It's not only his occupation; it is also his vocation and his relaxation.

The classic example of the entrepreneurial breed probably is Sherman Fairchild. His father was a founder and the largest shareholder of International Business Machines. Obviously, every door at IBM was open to Sherman. He turned his back on the company. It was not that he scorned his father's money, but IBM was his father's baby, already grown to manhood. He wanted to build something he could proudly call his own. He founded Fairchild Camera & Instrument, the Fairchild Hiller Corp., then Fairchild Recording Equipment. Money? What did he need money for, especially after his father's death, when he became IBM's biggest stockholder? He had an urge to create that has grown stronger with the years. He says: "The truth is that the man who just thinks of making money usually doesn't make much money. You've got to have your eye not on the money but on the job. I've never met a real entrepreneur for whom getting wealthy was the sole object."

Superficially, no one could seem more different from Fairchild than Jeno Paulucci. Yet, basically, they are alike. Jeno Paulucci, son of an imigrant iron miner is, by his own estimate worth about $100 million at the age of 51. In 1966 he sold Chun King to Reynolds Tobacco for $63 million and began building a corporate shell he had held for several years into a brand-new food business, Jeno's, Inc. He gets to his Duluth, Minn. office at 6 a.m. and often works seven days a week. Paulucci says an entrepreneur is a man "who sacrifices everything to his work," not just for money, but for a burning desire to meet a challenge. The money's just a way to measure how successful you are.

William Lear comes from a very different background. A school dropout in the eighth grade, Lear started out as an airplane mechanic for the U.S. Airmail base at Grant Park in Chicago. But he agrees with Paulucci that the entrepreneur can do things no big company can.

"I want to be in a position where I can put an idea into effect," Lear says. "I don't want to have to sell it to four or five different levels of people. If my idea loses *I* lose. If it wins I win. You can't do that in many big corporations."

Says Jeno Paulucci, echoing Lear's dislike of depending on others: "I can't wait even a few days to convince people that what I'm doing is right. I'm in a hurry even when I may be wrong."

William Lear founded Lear, Inc., a manufacturer of aviation electronics; sold the company to Siegler and founded Lear Jet; sold that to Gates Rubber and now runs Lear Motors. His background is just as different from Paulucci's as Paulucci's is from Fairchild's. But he agrees with Paulucci that money is secondary. "I think I'd work even harder if I had a *trillion dollars,*" says Bill Lear. "When I see a good thing that needs doing I want to do it. Like the thing I'm working on now, steam power plants for automobiles."

For a while Lear headed a good-sized public company, Lear, Inc. But he quit in frustration when his board of directors refused to let him build his now-famed Lear jet. "Why I might as well have been the janitor there," he says. "At least the janitor could decide on his own where he wanted to sweep."

Jack Kent Cooke, a Canadian, sold his interests in radio and publishing in 1959 when he was 47 and came to Los Angeles to retire. "I found I missed the fun and hurly burly of business," he says, "and in 1965 I went back to work." Cooke is president and owner of the L.A. Lakers basketball team, the L.A. Kings pro hockey team and the Forum, a new $16-million sports arena.

With a personal wealth estimated at nearly $40 million, Cooke could easily have bought control of a large business and tried to make it bigger. But that wans't what he was after. "I need the feeling that I'm in effective control of the business. That's what makes me different from the professional managers. I guess it isn't fair to call them mercenaries, but their attitude is different from the entrepreneur's."

"THEY ARE STOOGES"

German-born Max Ries, 68, has started successful companies on both sides of the Atlantic. In 1940 he fled from Hitler. "I had to make a living here," he says, "and so I started peddling cheese from store to store from my car." Before he was finished, Ries had built his company, Reese Foods, into a $7.5-million-a-year seller of specialty food items. He sold it to Pet Inc. in 1964. Two years later he was back in business, partly because he was bored and partly because he disapproved of what the new owners were doing with his old company. "These big companies," he says in his German accent, "they are very funny. They are stooges. They're more interested in showing what *can't* be done than in what can be done." Ries is now in the snuff business. He says: "All the kids in England are using it, soon they will be here also."

250

Richard Rich, 38, got a degree in business administration from NYU before entering advertising. After bouncing around several agencies he helped found the now-famous Wells, Rich, Greene advertising agency which he left this past April. Rich, who still holds several hundred thousand shares of Wells, Rich, Greene stock valued at over $3 million, is now starting his own advertising consulting service. Work for someone else or be part of a big agency? "Would you ask Howard Hughes that? I've been at the very top of the most glamorous agency ever to hit Madison Avenue. I couldn't see myself working for someone else." Says Jeno Paulucci: "As soon as Reynolds acquired my company and put me on salary I felt inhibited. So I left."

Eduard Baruch sold his Heli-Coil to Topps Industries in 1956 and bought it back 13 months later. Since then he has built its sales from $2 million to $20 million. "These big company people," he says, "are good to move into an organization that already has been created. But they haven't had the exposure to run on their own. They learn about business in graduate school but they haven't actually been out on their own. They should get out and work on the factory floor and get out in the field and sell and find out how people think—what motivates them."

Max Geffen . . . has started two successful magazines and several companies and sold them to bigger companies, including McGraw-Hill where he is one of biggest shareowners. He [recently launched] a new magazine, *Family Health*. Geffen is worth maybe $50 million and, at 73, needs another business like a hole in the head. But he says, "Working is so much more fun than sitting around."

Geffen, too, scorns the idea that money is the main motive for the successful entrepreneur. "I always start a publication when I think it can perform a public service. That's the only kind that makes money. If you're doing a good job, then somebody wants it. Otherwise you're just forcing it on the public, and that's no damned good.

"I never started anything to make money. I've been wealthier than I want to be for 20 years. I don't want to be Charlie Allen or Howard Hughes. I know some of these really rich men and they haven't got anything I can't have. I play golf with a man who is worth about $1 billion and I walk down the fairway with him and he hasn't got a thing I haven't got. In fact, I have to give him strokes."

DREAMER vs. DOER

What are the qualities that an entrepreneur needs? Perhaps these people aren't the most objective observers but we asked them all the same.

"They have to have vision," says Sherman Fairchild. "As contrasted with just having a dream. We have lots of dreamers. Not so many entrepreneurs. The dreamer figures, 'Wouldn't it be nice to have so-and-so.' But he doesn't have any idea how he is going to accomplish this. Real talent has organized vision. The fellow who says, 'Wouldn't it be nice to have an automobile that ran on half the amount of gas? Think of all the money it could make' is a dreamer. I say to him, 'Come up with an idea how you are going to accomplish this.' "

Bill Lear says: "I'm not a good manager. I have an enormous distaste for management. Every minute I spend on it makes me just much less useful at what I am good at.

"What I'm good at is interphasing. That's not the same as being an inventor. An inventor thinks of things that have never been done before. An interphaser is a guy who puts things together that already exist and makes new and better combinations." Lear regards his Lear jet as an example of interphasing. "I wanted to make it so bad I could taste it," he says, explaining why he quit the chairmanship of Lear, Inc. when the board of directors refused to let him go ahead with the project.

Jeno Paulucci says much the same thing in different words. "It's not just a question of long hours and hard work. It's guts. You have to go at it with sheer determination. Otherwise the pitfalls will put you off.

"This is why big companies have to go out and acquire smaller ones. There is a quality in starting a business that only an entrepreneur can provide. My accolades to Reynolds for what they've done since they took over Chun King. But no big company can do as good a job as the individual entrepreneur."

EXPENSIVE IS CHEAP

Another trait these brilliantly successful entrepreneurs share is a belief in the importance of supplementing their own talents with those of others. They know their limitations. Self-confident though they are, they don't regard themselves as gods. "The most important thing in business," says Neison Harris, "is having people work with you, not for you." Even Lear, who has a reputation for being a lone wolf, emphasizes people. "The greatest mistake I ever made was hiring the second-best man for the job. You pay a terrible penalty for that. No matter what it costs, it's cheaper than hiring the second-best man."

"The most important thing in any business," says Max Geffen, "is attaching the right people to you. The people below you. The people next to you. And the people above you."

Sherman Fairchild waxes eloquent on the subject of getting the best people. Fairchild says that as an entrepreneur he gets as much kick out of devising new organizational tools as out of inventing such things as the aerial camera. New ways to get and keep top-notch people, for example.

"One thing I try to do is regard my executives as partners. My father used to tell me, 'Son, don't worry about how much money you're going to make. Get the right guy in and make *him* a lot of money and that's all you'll need.' I've always followed that advice."

In getting Dr. C. Lester Hogan to leave Motorola and come to Fairchild . . . , Fairchild found a new way to follow his father's advice. He lent Hogan $5 million, interest free, to buy Fairchild stock. "This was a very new thing," Fairchild says, "but a very logical thing. I didn't get him on the basis of 'Look, I'm going to pay you more money.' I talked with him, found out what he wanted in life. I put myself in his place. I asked what would attract him. That's when I came up with the restricted options and interest-free loan."

Fairchild has thought a good deal about the characteristics he wants in his executives. "I look for the ability to study a situation and not be blinded by a lot of past statistics that say it can't be done. Sure it's going to be tough. If it wasn't some dope would have done it already. The man I want thinks the thing through. He thinks what are the factors that have to be put together. You can't decide this on an accountant's report. There are too many factors that just don't show up in the figures.

"What I want is to surround myself with entrepreneurs. A foreman in a shop can be an entrepreneur if he takes existing things and puts them together in a new way. That guy usually ends up being head of the company."

"BAH!"

Perhaps it's the generation gap, but many of the entrepreneurs *Forbes* interviewed professed scorn for today's younger conglomerators. Eduard Baruch says: "I wouldn't give you a dime for some of these hotshot boys who are forming conglomerates. They're financial manipulators, pure and simple." Sherman Fairchild criticizes a good deal of today's acquisition-mindedness. "Too many of these people are just not entrepreneurial. They pay through the nose for acquisitions instead of trying to put small things together into bigger, better things." Max Ries says: "They give people watered stock. It's a swindle. Bah!"

However, at least two of these men singled out Dan Lufkin, chairman of Wall Street's Donaldson, Lufkin & Jenrette, as being a true entrepreneur of the younger school. They admire his refusal to allow New York Stock Exchange rules to prevent his firm from going public. Max Geffen calls him "the most brilliant young man I know today." Eduard Baruch also singled out Lufkin, saying: "He sees opportunities and he moves ahead."

Sherman Fairchild, perhaps because he runs bigger companies than the others, disagrees with the general idea that big companies always smother the entrepreneurial spirit. "They don't at IBM," he says. "They don't buy things outside. They start them themselves. They're their own entrepreneurs. They avoid the costly business of having to buy a going organization and product acceptance."

Max Ries has some advice for executives who work for big companies and want to preserve their entrepreneurial spirit: "Be true to yourself. Do not crawl to the president or kiss the chairman's shoes. Do whatever you think you should do and if they won't let you, then leave. That's the only way."

WHAT ENTREPRENEURS LEARN

FROM EXPERIENCE*

LAWRENCE M. LAMONT

There is an old saying that practice makes perfect. Applied to business, it means that a task can always be performed more effectively the second time it is attempted. Surprisingly, the same principle applies to technical entrepreneurship. Entrepreneurs with previous experience in founding and developing a company exhibit substantial learning when they start another business. More often than not, their experience is reflected in superior corporate performance.

The importance of prior experience becomes meaningful when one examines the self-generating nature of the entrepreneurship process.[1] The creation of a technology-based enterprise (called a "spin-off") occurs when an entrepreneur starts a business to commercialize technology transferred from his previous source of employment. As the new firm develops, it in turn becomes a source of technology and entrepreneurs for a second generation spin-off, and so on. Entrepreneurial learning becomes apparent when the principal of a first generation spin-off leaves to start another technology-based firm. Arnold Cooper's recent research on technical enterprise formation in the Palo Alto area summarizes the pattern:

> Past entrepreneurship also generates experienced entrepreneurs. Some of these men stay with their firms as they grow. However, many of the firms are acquired and many of the founding teams break up. After the merger or after the fight with the co-founder, what does the former entrepreneur do? Often he turns to entrepreneurship again.
>
> Eight of the 30 companies studied intensively in the Palo Alto area were founded by men who previously had been in the founding groups of other companies. One man was starting his fourth new business. Without exception these men stated that it was easier to start a company the second time, both in regard to making the decision psychologically and in knowing what was involved in launching a firm.[2]

What does the technical entrepreneur do differently when he participates in the formation of a second generation spin-off? Why does his technology-based firm typically perform in a superior manner? These questions are examined in the present article. The answers are of interest to existing and potential entrepreneurs because they can shorten the learning process and improve their

*From *Journal of Small Business Management* (July, 1972), pp. 36-41. Reprinted by permission.

[1]Dean C. Coddington and James F. Mahar, "The Scientific Complex—Proceed with Caution," *Harvard Business Review,* XLIII (January-February, 1965), pp. 141-44.

[2]Arnold C. Cooper, "Entrepreneurial Environment," *Industrial Research,* XII (September, 1970), p. 75.

chances for success. Venture capital firms, private investors, and businesses interested in acquiring technology-based companies will also find this article useful because it provides insight into the decision to invest in a small business.

My comments are based on an empirical study of a matched sample of 24 technology-based enterprises located in a major scientific complex. Twelve of the firms are first generation spin-offs founded by individuals without previous entrepreneurial experience. The balance of the sample consists of 12 second generation spin-offs founded by technical entrepreneurs who had been previously involved in the formation and management of a technology-based enterprise.

Aside from differences in the business experience of the entrepreneurs, the firms were similar in many respects. New businesses having less than $100,000 of sales were included as well as firms with annual sales of several million dollars. Both groups ranged in age between 1 and 11 years and averaged 3.5 years of business operations. The firms were also involved in similar technologies, primarily electronics and optics.

COMPARATIVE PERFORMANCE

Part of the entrepreneur's ability to perform more effectively the second time is reflected in the various measures of corporate performance. Several were examined, including sales growth, profitability, and financial strength. Comparative sales performance shows that the second generation firm experiences a greater rate of sales growth. This is reflected in Table 1 where first year sales are shown for each group of firms.

TABLE 1   First Year Sales Performance

Sales	First Generation Spin-off Firms		Second Generation Spin-off Firms	
$0-100,000	11	91.7	3	25.0
Over $100,000	1	8.3	9	75.0
Total Firms	12	100.0%	12	100.0%

Over 91 percent of the first generation firms reported sales in the range of $0-100,000 during the first complete year of operations. By comparison, 75 percent of the second generation enterprises reported sales over $100,000 during a similar period. The differences in sales performance were not a short-run phenomenon. After each group of firms had completed an average of 3.5 years of business, 83 percent of the second generation firms reported sales over $100,000 compared to 58 percent of the first generation spin-offs.

Profitability data confirms the superior performance of the second generation firms during their latest year of business. Over 60 percent of these firms reported profitable operations, while only 25 percent of the first generation spin-offs earned profits. The second generation firms also achieved profitability earlier in their life cycle, were financially stronger and had better credit ratings as reported by a leading business information service.

255

WHAT DO ENTREPRENEURS LEARN?

During the formation of a second enterprise, the entrepreneur has an opportunity to apply his previous small business experience. Typically it is reflected in a firm having a product orientation, a higher level of capitalization and a better balance of essential business skills.

A Product Orientation. Technology-based firms can engage in a variety of different business activities. They include consulting, research and development, engineering, and manufacturing [both] on a contract bases and the provision of proprietary products. Table 2 indicates that first generation firms were performing contract activities during their first year of business, while the second generation spin-offs were usually involved in the development and marketing of proprietary products.

TABLE 2   First Year Business Activities*

Type of Business Activity	First Generation Spin-off Firms		Second Generation Spin-off Firms	
Contract	11	91.7	5	41.7
Product	1	8.3	7	58.3
Total Firms	12	100.0%	12	100.0%

*Firms are classified as product or contract oriented on the basis of sales data and the major focus of their business.

What accounts for the significant variation in business orientation? Most of the difference can be attributed to the entrepreneur's previous small business experience. He has learned that contract-oriented businesses are highly unstable and that products are needed to maintain a profitable level of operations. The point is illustrated by the comments of a first generation entrepreneur. After several years of business his contract engineering firm decided to develop and market an industrial control instrument. He remarked:

> The development of products is a natural extension of our contract capability. These developments give us an opportunity to share on a continuing basis the things we have been doing for other companies on an hourly basis.

The comment illustrates another important characteristic of the technology-based enterprise. As the firms mature, their development is marked by dramatic changes in the nature of their business. Several development patterns are possible, but generally contract-oriented firms move toward a product orientation. A first generation spin-off included in the study illustrates this common pattern.

> The firm began business in contract research and development performing environmental studies for the government space program. Two years after formation, two electronic measuring instruments were developed using technology transferred from the government research. In a short period, the first generation spin-off's business had changed from a research and development orientation to a product orientation.

This type of change was quite evident in the sample of firms studied. In the latest year of business operations reported, 33 percent of the first generation spin-offs had achieved a product orientation and 75 percent of the secondary spin-offs had completed the transition. Obviously, the second generation firm has a head-start on the product development.

How does the experienced entrepreneur assure a product orientation for his new firm? To form the technical base for the business he transfers technology from his previous source of employment. Usually this technology includes information related to the development and manufacture of specific products. The entrepreneur takes advantage of the product knowledge the first firm may have taken years to develop.[3] A case in point: One second generation entrepreneur interviewed developed nine products during the first year of business. Prior to starting operations he had completed the design and engineering for these products so that most of the first year of operations was devoted to developing a manufacturing capability and organizing a distribution network. All of the products were improved versions of those marketed in the first business he was associated with. To a large degree, the product orientation of the entrepreneur's second firm accounts for the superior sales performance.

Adequate Initial Financing. The significance of financing to new technical firms is confirmed by the research of Dr. Edward B. Roberts, Massachusetts Institute of Technology. He notes that one of the essential characteristics of successful spin-off firms is "large initial capitalization, preferably $25,000 to $50,000."[4] However, obtaining the capital to initially finance the technology-based company is a difficult problem according to Kenneth G. Germeshausen, a first generation entrepreneur and board chairman of EG&G.

> The principal problem is the convincing of financial sources that the idea really is a good one and in obtaining the required financial support without losing control or too much of the equity.[5]

Many of the technology-based firms in the study were undercapitalized at the time of formation and throughout the early stages of development. Again, the second generation entrepreneurs' experience was worthwhile. Their firms had an average initial capitalization of $33,700 compared to the first generation spin-off's average of $19,600. Part of this difference reflects the business orientation of the second generation firms. Product oriented firms simply require higher levels of initial capitalization to finance the product development and the requirements for plant and equipment, inventory, and labor. Much of the difference, however, is the result of the experienced entrepreneur's knowledge of sources of venture capital, his ability to make a convincing presentation to potential investors and the lower level of risk involved in a business having a tangible product.

[3]Victor J. Danilov, "The Spin-Off," *Industrial Research,* XI (May, 1969), p. 58.

[4]Edward B. Roberts, "Influences Upon Performance of New Technical Enterprises," A paper presented at the Symposium on Technical Entrepreneurship, Co-sponsored by the Krannert School of Industrial Administration, Purdue University, and the Center for Venture Management, Milwaukee, Wisconsin, October 7-8, 1970, at Purdue University.

[5]Danilov, *op. cit., p. 58.*

A Balance of Business Skills. The majority of first generation spin-offs are founded by scientists and engineers having only a casual interest in the business activities required to successfully operate a business. In many firms the situation is perpetuated by hiring only technical personnel whose interests are compatible with those of the original entrepreneurs. The entrepreneur of the second generation firm usually realizes the need for help in management, production, and the other functional areas of business. When it is financially possible, he carefully selects his employees to complement the existing technical and business skills present in the firm.

As shown in Table 3, all firms reported that either a principal founder or employee had research and development or engineering experience at the time of founding. This was expected because the technical experience of the personnel is the primary basis for the firm's creation. However, when the presence of various business skills is considered, the second generation firms clearly have an advantage. They are more inclined to have production, general management, and marketing skills initially present in their organization.

TABLE 3 Business Experience Present at the Time of Founding* (Percent of Firms Reporting Each Type of Experience)

Type of Experience	First Generation Spin-off Firms		Second Generation Spin-off Firms	
Research, Development and Engineering	12	100.0%	12	100.0%
Production	1	8.3	10	83.3
General Management	1	8.3	9	75.0
Accounting or Finance	6	50.0	4	33.0
Marketing or Sales	3	25.0	7	58.3
Total Firms	12		12	

*Percentage total exceeds 100.00% because of multiple response.

The difference is due not only to the learning that occurs during the process of entrepreneurship, but it is also the result of a need for a broader range of business skills to successfully operate a product-oriented business. This explains the higher percentage of second generation firms reporting production experience in their business. The contrast in the percentage of firms having marketing and general management experience is a reflection of the fact that first generation spin-offs are frequently weak in marketing and less concerned about the personnel and project management aspects of the business. Experienced entrepreneurs recognize the significance of marketing and management skills and are more willing to hire specialists to handle the business functions.

TAKING ADVANTAGE OF EXPERIENCE

The fact that learning occurs in technical entrepreneurship implies that existing and potential entrepreneurs can improve their business skills by taking advantage of the experiences of successful entrepreneurs. However, understanding what entrepreneurs learn and do differently does not automatically lead to concepts that can be applied in a small business setting. In the following sections are discussed some specific ways in which a new enterprise may benefit from the previous entrepreneural experience of its founder.

Market Planning. Entrepreneurs with previous small business experience are able to transfer important market knowledge to their new firms. They are usually aware of specific business opportunities and know in advance where their sales are going to come from. Without the benefit of experience, extensive market planning must be performed to focus the company's product and marketing strategy. More specifically, the plan must define market opportunities, product requirements, potential customers and competition. It also specifies the sales techniques needed to penetrate potential markets, sales goals by product and market, and a detailed marketing budget.

Most experienced entrepreneurs have completed the market planning phase when they begin operations. Even though the approach may have been informal, it helps to direct the operations and maximize the efficient use of the firm's financial and technical resources. By comparison, first time entrepreneurs usually begin business without clear corporate goals and fail to define the scope of their technical and marketing effort. Only after several unsuccessful projects does the entrepreneur begin to realize the necessity for market planning.

Financial Planning. A well prepared marketing plan specifies the financial requirements of the business. Experienced entrepreneurs recognize this and carefully project working capital needs to finance the marketing program, product development, inventory, and work in process. These financing needs are then matched with sources of funds, including proprietary product sales and progress payments from contracts. The difference must be made up from external sources—namely profits, loans from private investors, sales of stock, lines of credit from financial institutions, and short term trade credit.

The financial and market plans become the basis for a formal presentation to the financial community—including individuals, venture capital firms, SBIC's and other financial institutions. A well prepared presentation emphasizing a marketable product, financial control, and management depth usually enables the entrepreneur to obtain the financing needed to assure a successful start for the business. Experienced entrepreneurs are typically able to secure the necessary financing prior to starting business. The first generation entrepreneur is often in business a year or more before he begins to perceive the need for additional funds. The failure to prepare a financial plan usually means that the firm will be undercapitalized and highly susceptible to a cash flow crisis.

A Balanced Management Team. First-time entrepreneurs admit that technical experience alone is not sufficient to manage and develop a new business. Weaknesses in marketing and management and inexperience in the methods of conducting business spell failure for many new firms. In putting together a management team, the experienced entrepreneur usually recognizes the importance of business experience and the need to interact with the business community. Multiple founders are typically used to provide a balance of business skills and part of the financing. Operating management is hired with emphasis on selecting individuals experienced in project and production management. The experienced entrepreneur surrounds himself with good people and

259

delegates authority. The first generation entrepreneur too often tries to manage everything himself and is labeled as a poor manager.

Interaction with the business community is made possible by having outside members on the board of directors or an executive committe made up of corporate management and outside advisors such as a C.P.A., lawyer, venture capitalist, consultant, etc. This latter technique works well as a method of bringing outside expertise to bear on the company's problems because the committee can meet informally and with greater frequency than a board. Some venture capital firms are making the establishment of an executive committee a requirement in all firms they finance. Most entrepreneurs welcome the idea because the outside individuals provide an excellent sounding board for new ideas.

CONCLUSIONS

Learning is a property of almost all business activity. Applied to technical entrepreneurship it means that experienced entrepreneurs exhibit substantial learning when they form a second technology-based enterprise. Usually their experience is reflected in a business having a product orientation, substantial initial financing and a balance of essential business skills.

Market and financial planning are key factors in the experienced entrepreneurs' performance. Entrepreneurs should strive to begin business with a market plan that focuses the technical activity and gives the firm a head start on the required product development. Careful financial planning is also necessary. Investors are reluctant to provide capital for a business venture when the requirements are uncertain. When these tools are combined with an experienced management team, the business has a sense of direction and a high probability of success.

EIGHT

The Entrepreneur's Philosophy

The entrepreneur differs from the salaried professional manager in that he cannot live within the framework of occupational behavior set by others. In their lead-off article, *The Enterprising Man and the Business Executive,* Orvis Collins and David Moore examine the roles played by entrepreneurs and business hierarchs and discuss the essential differences in their viewpoints and philosophical outlooks. For the prospective entrepreneur who has an innovative idea, situational factors may influence his decision actually to start the business venture. Germane to the situation are the risks in divulging the idea to another company, the employability of the individual (health problems), the relationship of the intended business to a previous hobby, prior specialized experience, and the need for money. The organization man, on the other hand, is usually preconditioned by his social environment—family and social contacts—or interested only in a specific field, and therefore is not as affected by such factors. These comparisons were made on the basis of data collected by Collins and Moore via in-depth interviews with 150 small manufacturers, supplemented by Thematic Apperception Tests administered to a group of 40 selected entrepreneurs, and on published data collected by other researchers on executives in large organizations.

Collins and Moore discuss certain personal traits that further differentiate the entrepreneur from the organization man. Interestingly, entrepreneurs are seen as rebels, self-made, highly driven, and creative, whereas organization men are generally more role directed. "The typical big business executive, when he first enters a company, is not concerned with running a business as much as he is with occupying a job. His interest lies in finding a niche where there is a potential for advancement; to him, ultimate success is the top of the ladder, to be climbed rung by rung. Entrepreneurs, on the other hand, enter business without much more than a yearning for a place of their own and an overwhelming compulsion to be on their own."

What is particularly significant in describing the entrpreneur's philosophy are the data on the entrepreneur's perception of his place in the environment. Essentially he sees himself as an integrator of talented people to aid in furthering the exploitation of his idea. The executive is more a user of men to aid in his rise up the corporate ladder.

A business does not get started by itself. It is the entrepreneur who takes the risks and is willing to face devastating failure. Failure to the company executive may mean little more than locating a new job, perhaps even at a higher salary.

In *The Enterprising Man,* some of the entrepreneur's traits, personality characteristics and philosophy have been discussed and differentiated from those of the organization man. In the second reading, *Executive Self Selection in Small Business,* Louis Allen further clarifies the differences by examining the personal qualities needed in small business management if success in a new-founded business is to be expected. These factors in small business success further define the entrepreneur and his philosophy. Specifically, Allen anticipates a greater chance of success if the individual has a high degree of commitment, is willing to make significant sacrifices, has personal experience in the planned business, and is willing to accept personal inconvenience.

In addition to these personal success qualities, the author of the *Forbes* article, *The Entrepreneurs: Luck and Pluck—and a Strong Succession,* emphasizes the need for self-confidence, leadership, and just plain "guts." The article takes a look at the companies that climbed onto *Forbes'* "Top 100" list since 1917, and at the extraordinary men who built them.

The concluding article by Robert L. Bendit, *Working With the Entrepreneur,* offers advice to employees of entrepreneurial concerns. Because entrepreneurs work harder and longer, they seldom expect less than full commitment from their employees. Bendit suggests a philosophy for employees who must learn to cope with the entrepreneur's philosophy. Adopting this view, according to this author, can make the entrepreneurial concern a better place to work for everyone.

In summary, then, the entrepreneur has his own, unique philosophy. He integrates resources and technologies into profitable business ventures for the exploitation of his idea. Unlike the organization man, the entrepreneur is adaptive and flexible in the direction of his business career. Situational factors, rather than tradition, will influence his decisions. Once committed, the successful entrepreneur wil make personal sacrifices to ensure attainment of his goals.

The schematic models shown in Fig. 9 depict the entrepreneurial and managerial iterative processes and illustrates the differences in the entrepreneur-manager roles. In the entrepreneur system model, the entrepreneur functions as an integrator of resources. He interacts directly with his staff and is cognizant of the environment in which his firm operates (defined as the consumer market and influencing economic, political, cultural, and competitive forces). His staff is committed to the venture's goals and the establishment of informal and efficient intradepartmental communication channels; thus they are shown in the illustration as being contained in one box. The decisions the entrepreneur makes are likely to be very responsive to environmental conditions.

The manager, on the other hand, is depicted as a *controller* of resources. Because of this role, he relies on information about the environment from his subordinates who, because of the bureaucratic hierarchy and political struc-

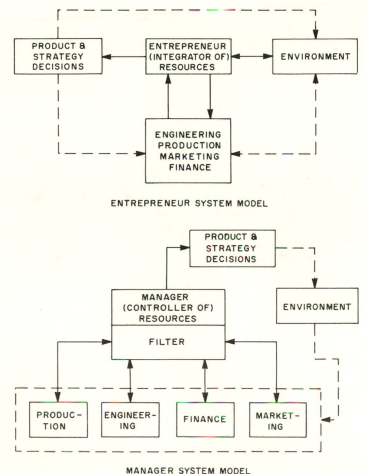

ENTREPRENEUR SYSTEM MODEL

MANAGER SYSTEM MODEL

FIGURE 9 Entrepreneur and Manager System Models

ture of the large company, are likely to communicate mostly with the manager rather than among themselves. These subordinates, however, are likely to perceive the marketplace in terms of their own specific needs, rather than in terms of the total needs of the corporation. This indirect and often biased flow of information to the manager is schematically shown as passing through a filtering process that alters the true state of the environment. The manager's own perceptive framework will also cause a filtering or false interpretation of incoming data. Thus, the manager makes product and strategy decisions that may often be poorly related to the needs of the consumer and other forces acting in the environment.

THE ENTERPRISING MAN

AND THE BUSINESS EXECUTIVE*

ORVIS F. COLLINS / DAVID G. MOORE /
with *DARAB UNWALLA*

The word *entrepreneur* evokes conflicting images for Americans. In one heroic theme in American thought, the entrepreneur is a risk-taker—a man who braves uncertainty, strikes out on his own, and, through native wit, devotion to duty, and singleness of purpose, somehow creates business and industrial activity where none existed before. Viewed in this way, the entrepreneur is a folklore figure akin to Davy Crockett and other truly indigenous epic types—stalwart independents who hewed forests, ran trapping expeditions into unknown country, built new communities, rose from impoverished beginnings to positions of prestige, and did all those things American heroes must have done to build a great nation.

In a sharply contradictory tradition, the word entrepreneur engenders negative emotions. It has an accompanying connotation of manipulation, greed and avarice, and grasping acquisitiveness. While it is believed that the entrepreneurial hero built railroads, canals, industries, and great systems of trade, there is also the belief that in the process he befouled nature, sullied valleys, denuded forests, muddied and contaminated the rivers and streams, and generally ravished the natural order.

Thus, the entrepreneur is the heroic representation of the American theme of building and constructive effort and at the same time is the destroyer of nature and the exploiter of his fellow man. Even the formal historians cannot make up their minds—sometimes viewing the entrepreneur as a builder and at other times seeing him as a robber and pirate.

For most Americans the entrepreneur, on balance, probably emerges as essentially heroic, and in the long run more constructive than destructive. Like him or not, he is fascinating. His values and activities have become integral to the character of America and intimately related to its ideas of personal freedom, success, and—above all—individualism. He represents the rags to riches theme in its purest form. He rises on his own by solid achievement, not by social climbing. He gets there by what he knows, not who he knows. His resources are all inside, not outside. The story or, if you wish, the myth of the entrepreneur is a drama in which the protagonist challenges the established order and forges ahead toward the glowing light called success using only native wit, skill, and hard work—with perhaps a bit of luck and Calvinistic fate thrown in for good measure. He is successful because he sticks to the simple and obvious American virtues. He builds a better mouse trap or provides a better service, and he does these things in the best way he knows. He is resolute, disciplined, and utterly devoted.

*From *MSU Business Topics* (Winter, 1964), pp. 19-34. Reprinted by permission of the publisher, Division of Research Graduate School of Business Administration, Michigan State University.

The Entrepreneurial Dream

The entrepreneurial dream is still today the haven for the common man—the dream of escape from an established and overly complicated social order and dream of the opportunity to build a place for himself. The American worker today, trapped in dead-end production jobs, still dreams of getting off the assembly line and into his own business. This ambition, whether it is dream or reality, serves as an effective safety valve in our society. It is in a sense a kind of permanent revolution, which does not call for direct atack on the established citadels of power. It represents for the ambitious man an acceptable route for advancement and one which places upon him and his own efforts the responsibility for his success or failure.[1]

Many Americans, at least once in their lives, dream the dream of owning a business that they have created. Many also make at least one attempt to transform the dream to reality. For many, again, the transformation takes place when they have set up a restaurant, cleaning establishment, or repair shop. For such people a dream has come true when a small service establishment has achieved sufficient size and stability to support its creator and his family.

But some Americans dream on a grander scale. For these the dream can only come true when the business they have established has grown into a sizeable enterprise employing personnel and making an industrial product. These are the ones who strive to achieve a foothold in the world of manufacturing enterprise. This dream is closer to the heart of the entrepreneurial myth, for Americans have always regarded themselves as a nation of producers rather than of shopkeepers.

BUSINESS HIERARCHS AND ENTREPRENEURS

Throughout this article we will call men who have created their own businesses *entrepreneurs*. We are making a distinction between the independent entrepreneur and the bureaucratic entrepreneur. While the functions performed may be the same once the business has been well established, nonetheless there is a world of difference between the creation of a new business enterprise and the entrepreneurial functions as performed while climbing a hierarcnical ladder within an existing structure.

Situational Differences

There are certain obvious characteristics that differentiate entrepreneurs who create their own businesses, from executives in large-scale, established companies. First, there is the difference in contexts in which entrepreneurial tasks are performed. Men in established organizations have the resources of an existing business on which to build. They have capital and credit to draw upon; but, even more important, they have high-talent manpower organized around the key entrepreneurial activities. They have well-trained management personnel who can move in and take over new developments. They have research and development laboratories, marketing organizations for launching new products,

---

[1]For careful documentation, see: Eli Chinoy, *Automobile Workers and the American Dream* (Garden City, New York: Doubleday & Company, Inc., 1955).

and existing production facilities which considerably reduce the expense and risk encountered in developing new product-lines.

Second, the typical big business executive, when he first enters a company, is not concerned with running a business as much as he is with occupying a job. His interest lies in finding a niche where there is a potential for advancement. To him, ultimate success is the top of the ladder, to be climbed rung by rung. Each step up the ladder represents not only effort on his part but the willingness of those higher on the ladder to allow him, and even help him, to move up. He quickly becomes aware that he is operating within a system where job performance, to be sure, pays off, but also where acceptance by those above him is of crucial importance. More than this, he learns that the climb is not just a matter of acquiring new job skills but also of developing social skills associated with higher status and organization power.

It is quite different with entrepreneurs starting from scratch. Many of them enter business without much more than a yearning for a place of their own and an overwhelming compulsion to be on their own. Typically, they have a craft, some tools, sometimes a few thousand dollars saved, and that is about all. With such meager resources, entrepreneurs choose to strike out on their own. The choice of setting up their own business implies, in effect, that they have turned their backs on the large-scale organization with all its available supportive apparatus.

Questions of Motivation

Why do these men reject the world of big enterprise? We do not usually ask such a question about men who pursue success in large organizations. The question does not occur to us simply because success in our society today typically is conceived as mobility in an established hierarchy. With the entrepreneur, however, it is appropriate to ask why he rejected the current and increasingly traditional route to success. Why did he turn away from the seeming security and, one might say, clarity and simplicity of existing mobility paths to strike off on his own into a frequently disorganized and irrational economic wilderness? Had we the answer to this question, we would still have the problem of explaining the success of the entrepreneur and especially his success in operating effectively "in the open." With the established business executive, we only have to explain his effectiveness in hierarchical structures.

Because of the heroic figure which the entrepreneur cuts in American symbolic life, we might readily assume that those who enter this role are attracted into it by the glittering possibilities for symbolic as well as material rewards and satisfactions. We might suppose that all red-blooded American boys dream of having their own businesses but are thwarted in their ambitions and, as a consequence, finally take a job in someone else's business because of inadequacies and the basic inability to succeed on their own. In this view, those who go on to achieve success in entrepreneurial activities are the ones with the fired-up imagination, the ambition, and the fundamental intelligence, knowhow, and social skills needed to gain positions of prominence and leadership.

Certainly the American symbolic dream of entrepreneurial success plays an important part in motivating many who start their own businesses. It is also true that those who succeed have a unique ability and drive. Nonetheless, under close examination the glittering possibilities of the entrepreneurial way dissolve into quite different realities. The image of the entrepreneur as the great promoter, or the great and daring risk-taker simply doesn't square with the facts. The reality is far less spectacular than this. Setting up a new business is hard. A competitive economy does not welcome newcomers. In fact, in the beginning, entrepreneurship turns out to be mundane and not at all heroic. There is the entrepreneur without capital resources, without apparent social skills, and without even a good idea. No respectable element in the community is even aware of him, let alone ready to help him.

Studies of the Executive Role

Up to this point, we have known much less about the character of the enterprising man than about that of his opposite number, the business hierarch. In recent years, books like *The Organization Man*[2] and *Industrial Man*[3], together with a number of other reports, both popular and academic, have dealt with executives in established organizations. Some of these reports on executive life have been supported by extensive research. Of particular interest is the work of W. Lloyd Warner and associates, who have studied the social backgrounds, patterns of mobility, and personalities of successful executives in big business and the federal government.[4] These studies offer considerable insight into the origins and behavior of executives who have moved up to the very pinnacle of success and power in well-established organizations. They furnish important information regarding the governing elite—those who direct and control the established network of relationships in major organized activities in our society. At the same time, these reports provide a point of reference, or a standard against which to compare other leadership groups. Executives in big business and big government are not the only elite in a complex industrial society. There is, for example, a scientific and technological elite; there is an elite of the "free" professions like medicine and law; and there is, as we have pointed out, a little understood but vital entrepreneurial elite—enterprising men who, refusing to stay put in established organizations, move out on their own to create new enterprises.

In order to gain an understanding of this latter group, we made a study of a selected sample of men who have successfully created their own business enterprises. We wanted to acquire more intimate and subtle knowledge than questionnaire-type research could afford. We wanted to know about the character formation, the role performance, and the technical skills of men who had accomplished the formidable task of turning the entrepreneurial dream into reality by establishing a manufacturing enterprise of their own. This objective dictated the design of our research and the choice of techniques employed.

[2]William H. Whyte, Jr., *The Organization Man* (New York: Simon and Schuster, Inc., 1956).

[3]W. Lloyd Warner and Norman H. Martin, *Industrial Man* (New York: Harper & Brothers, 1959).

[4]W. Lloyd Warner and James C. Abegglen, *Occupational Mobility in American Business and Industry* (Minneapolis: University of Minnesota Press, 1955); W. Lloyd Warner and James C. Abegglen, *Big Business Leaders in America* (New York: Harper & Brothers, 1955); W. Lloyd Warner, Paul P. Van Riper, Norman H. Martin, Orvis F. Collins, *The American Federal Executive* (New Haven: Yale University Press, 1963).

DESIGN OF THE RESEARCH

Selection of a research sample is inevitably a compromise between optimum coverage and practical considerations. The size of the sample depends primarily on the research technique. If questionnaires are used, mass survey is possible. If, however, intensive techniques like depth interviewing and projective instruments are used, the size of the sample must be sharply curtailed. Curtailment is required not only because it takes longer to gather the data but, *more important,* because it takes much greater labor to analyze such data once they have been collected.

Depth Interviews and Projective Techniques. We decided on a small sample and intensive information secured through depth interviews and projective techniques. This decision was dictated by several factors. First, we could not identify in advance the person in each firm who was the "actual" entrepreneur. Identification of this figure was therefore a function of the field work itself. Further, review of the literature suggested that differences in social backgrounds between entrepreneurs and big business and federal executives were so great that it was hardly necessary to do a massive survey to refine the statistics of such gross differences.

A final, and by far the most important factor, was our interest in the subtler aspects of entrepreneurial behavior. The influences \of early childhood, the personality configurations, and the adult social roles of entrepreneurs were intriguing to us. As the research advanced, however, we began to see that this more intimate data on the entepreneur gave us understanding of life patterns which, taken in the aggregate, accounted for the gross differences between entrepreneurs and executives in large organizations as these differences are measured by such indices as occupations of fathers, levels of education achieved, and ethnic backgrounds.

In this article we will present some of the percentage differences found to exist between these two groups along such dimensions, and then briefly indicate some of the situational and psychological factors which can be seen to account for these differences.

The Sample. However, the reader should know several additional facts about the sample. In selecting it, we imposed several rules to insure initial homogeneity. First, we selected only manufacturing enterprises, thereby eliminating the firms in trade, service, transportation, construction, and so on. Within the manufacturing sector, we further eliminated such enterprises as those in food and textiles, restricting our sample primarily to manufacturing establishments. Second, we chose enterprises established within a fairly narrow segment of time: between 1945 and 1958. By concentrating on the postwar period, we were able to examine entrepreneurship during a time when the social and economic climate was somewhat homogeneous. Furthermore, by concentrating on recently established enterprises, there was considerably more likelihood of finding the original entrepreneur. In this connection also, it should be noted that our cut-off date of 1958 meant that these enterprises were "successful," at least in the sense that they had survived the first trying years and were still functioning at the time of the field work in 1960 and 1961. A third rule limited our research to Michigan firms. The heavily industrialized lower one-third of the state was divided into quarters. In addition, we ranked the various cities by population. One city in each quadrant was selected with both population and the character of the community in mind.

The firms included were selected from *The Directory of Michigan Manufacturers 1960.*[5] We tried to select businesses which were of sufficient size and scope to be more than marginally stable. We were most concerned with successful entrepreneurs and felt that size of organization was one measure of success. In our initial sampling, then, we chose firms with twenty or more employees. The actual sample obtained includes some firms (about one-fifth) with less than twenty employees. This was in part because of ups and downs in employment and in part because of the difficulties in some cities of finding a sufficient number of cases in the "twenty or more" group. The total number of firms finally included in our sample is 110. Because of the need to interview more than one individual in many companies, and the necessity for repeat interviews in other cases, the total number of depth interviews was 150.

Methods. The research methods used in this study have been developed by many researchers through repeated use in problems of this type. The method was non-structured interviewing supplemented by projective tests. The interviewing was conducted by trained interviewers, all of whom not only had a knowledge of the techniques of depth interviewing but also a knowledge of business. Business background was important in understanding the "business culture" of the entrepreneur, and was also necessary to identify areas of interest along which to shape the interview.

The 150 depth interviews were supplemented by Thematic Apperception Tests of 40 selected entrepreneurs.[6] The TAT interviews were directly recorded on tape. Typescripts were then given to a clinical psychologist[7] with extensive experience in the use of projective tests in studies of this sort. This psychologist had not participated otherwise in the study, and did not have access to any of the interview materials. He worked "blind" in abstracting the interpretation of the TAT protocols.

On the basis of these data collected from our own research, and on data collected by other researchers on executives in large organizations, some broad comparisons can be made.

BROAD COMPARISONS

The social and psychological processes which lead to men going into established organizations on one hand, and striking out for themselves on the other, begin early in life and have a cumulative effect. This is to say that no one element or event can be said to be decisive. There is, rather, a subtle interplay of events leading to the crisis in a man's life during which he elects to cut free from the world of establishments and try it on his own.

This interplay might be pictured as consisting of forces of rejection and attraction. The forces do not, however, all work in one direction. It is not only that large organizations reject the entrepreneur, but that the entrepreneur rejects the world of large organizations. The interplay is dynamic.

In the aggregate, this dynamic interplay leads to gross differences between

[5]*The Directory of Michigan Manufacturers 1960* (Detroit: Manufacturer Publishing Company, 1959).

[6]For those who are concerned with technicalities, the numbers of the cards used in the TAT analysis were 1, 2, 4, 6BM, 7BM, 17BM, and 19 from the "official" collection published by Harvard University Press, plus two special cards used by Social Research, Inc., Chicago, Illinois.

[7]Roger Coup, Social Research, Inc., Chicago, Illinois.

entrepreneurs and executives which can be expressed in statistical terms. Interpretation of the causal factors behind the statistics is, at the interpersonal and psychological level, extremely complex. Within the confines of this paper we can only outline some of the broader patterns.

A Statistical Profile

A few words of caution are in order before examining the statistics. In making comparisons, we will use data from several sources, including the Warner and Abegglen study of big business executives previously mentioned.[8] Their study was conducted in 1952; accordingly, these data are approximately nine years older than ours. Furthermore, the Warner and Abegglen study is truly extensive, covering more than 8,000 executives throughout the United States. Our study, in contrast, covers only slightly more than 100 entrepreneurs, all living in Michigan. Most of our tables include less than 100 respondents because the information sought is not always included in the interview protocols. Fortunately, however, there is the O'Donovan study which directly concerns executives and lower management groups in large-scale business primarily in the Michigan area.[9] Where necessary, we can use data from this research. In addition, we can draw some comparisons with the study of Mabel Newcomer of the "little businessman" in Poughkeepsie, New York.[10]

Age and Sex. Our sample of entrepreneurs is composed almost entirely of men. There are two women in our sample, one of whom is clearly an entrepreneur. The other might be classified as quasi-entrepreneurial, since her late husband had before his death played a very active role in the business. Mabel Newcomer found a larger number of female proprietors of manufacturing businesses in her Poughkeepsie sample, but she indicates that these were businesses mainly inherited from deceased husbands. Our sample includes a smaller proportion of entrepreneurial widows, no doubt because we were looking for true entrepreneurs. Certainly, we would judge that entrepreneurship in the manufacturing segment of our economy is almost exclusively a male game.

The average age of our respondents at the time of the interviewing was 52. However, ages as shown in Table 1 ranged from 30 to over 70. The definite concentration of ages in the 50 to 54 bracket may be explained by the large number of businesses in our sample established right after World War II. Incidentally, this age level is close to that of the big business executives at the time of the Warner and Abegglen study. The executives were slightly over 53.[11] In Professor O'Donovan's sample, the executives and lower managers were 46,[12] somewhat younger than our group.

[8]From *Occupational Mobility in American Business and Industry, 1928-1952,* by W. Lloyd Warner and James C. Abegglen, University of Minnesota Press, Minneapolis. Copyright 1955 by the University of Minnesota. Used by permission.

[9]Thomas R. O'Donovan, "Contrasting Orientations and Career Patterns of Executives and Lower Managers" (Unpublished Ph.D. dissertation, Michigan State University, 1961).

[10]From "The Little Businessman: A Study of Business Proprietors in Poughkeepsie, New York," by Mabel Newcomer, *Business History Review,* Harvard Graduate School of Business Administration, Vol. 35, No. 4, Winter 1961, p. 477. Copyright 1961. Used by permission.

[11]Warner and Abegglen, *Occupational Mobility in American Business and Industry, op. cit.,* p. 131.

[12]O'Donovan, *op. cit.,* p. 146.

TABLE 1   Age of Entrepreneurs at Time of
Study

Age	Number	Percentage
30 to 34 years	1	1.2
35 to 39 years	6	7.3
40 to 44 years	10	12.2
45 to 49 years	18	22.0
50 to 54 years	24	29.3
55 to 59 years	12	14.6
60 to 64 years	4	4.9
65 to 69 years	5	6.1
70 and over	2	2.4
Total	82	100.0

Ethnicity and Race.   There were no Negroes in our sample. Considering once again that our sample, within certain limits, was randomly drawn, we must conclude that Negroes are not active as entrepreneurs in the manufacturing segment of the economy, at least in Michigan, and most probably elsewhere.

However, there was a large percentage of foreign born. Twenty percent of the entrepreneurs, as indicated in Table 2, were immigrants to this country. In addition, 35 percent were the sons of immigrants. Thus, 55 percent, or more than half of our sample, were either themselves foreign born or first generation Americans. Only about 5 percent of the big business leaders were foreign born and an additional 20 percent were U.S.-born sons of foreign-born fathers. Our figures of 20 and 35 percent are disproportionately large. There are almost three times as many foreign born as would be expected from the general population figures, and twice as many sons of foreign born.

TABLE 2   Comparison of Nativity of Entrepreneurs and Business Leaders with Nativity of U.S.A. White Population in 1950

Nativity	Percentage of Entrepreneurs	Percentage of Business Leaders*	Percentage of U.S.A. White Population in 1960
Foreign-born	19.8**	5.3	5.9
U.S.-born with foreign-born fathers	35.0†	19.7	15.0
Total	54.8	25.0	20.9

*Business leader data adapted from Table 34 in Warner and Abegglen, *Occupational Mobility in American Business and Industry,* p. 90. Number of business leaders was approximately 7,500.
**Number of entrepreneurs reporting nativity, 86.
†Number of entrepreneurs reporting father's nativity, 40.
‡Computed from data appearing in U.S. Bureau of the Census, *U.S. Census of Population: 1960.*

Clearly, ethnicity is no barrier to entrepreneurship. In fact, if anything it may be a motivational factor. Mabel Newcomer found in the Poughkeepsie group that almost 23 percent of the proprietors of manufacturing establishments were foreign born.[13] When we consider that her sample covers a longer period than ours, chances are that her figures and ours are comparable. About the foreign born, Professor Newcomer says:[14]

> The number of foreign-born proprietors is out of proportion to the foreign born in the total population. . . . In view of the fact that the native born are likely to have a wider range of choice of occupations than the foreign born, this suggests that the native born regard small business as a relatively unsatisfactory channel of advancement, but that the foreign born, with more limited opportunities, still regard this as one of the most promising ways of getting ahead.

There are, however, other considerations which Professor Newcomer does not mention. We are referring to the impact of immigration itself, the separation from culture, home, and father, and the release that comes from a break with tradition. Margaret Mead has said:[15]

> The immigrant who comes to America from a small European country in which the possibilities of building anew are all defined by the, to him, irrevocable past—as each new road must follow, in effect, a prehistoric path—finds the unpatterned plains of Kansas an exciting challenge upon which anything can be built.

Even deeper than this is the fundamental rejection of the past which not only influences the foreign born but their sons as well. Immigration involves a kind of rebellion. It is typically accompanied by a rejection of old-country ways—the beliefs and manners of one's fathers. Just as the foreign born acted out their rebellion against their fathers through the act of immigration, so their own sons rejected them because of their broken accents and their old-country ways, which clung to them in spite of their efforts to get rid of them. The rebellion against country and father, more than any other consideration, may explain the patterns of occupational adjustment of foreign born and first-generation U.S.A.-born.

Place of Birth. Do entrepreneurs in Michigan tend to be "home-grown"? Table 3 shows that almost two-thirds of our respondents came either from Michigan or surrounding areas. Somewhat better than one-third represent "imported" talent. Of the imports, about 60 percent were born outside the United States. These figures suggest that, if you want entrepreneurs, you either grow your own or try to attract immigrants. Certainly, very few are going to come into your region from other parts of the country.

We do not have enough entrepreneurs in our sample who are sufficiently specific about their places of birth to say very much about the size of their communities of origin. Table 4, for what it is worth, suggests that a disproportionate number of entrepreneurs came from the cities rather than the farms. Warner and Abegglen found also that a disproportionate number of business leaders came from the cities. This is not unexpected in both cases since business is essentially an urban activity and more likely to attract those on the scene.

[13]Newcomer, *op. cit.*, p. 514.

[14]*Ibid.*, p. 480.

[15]From *Male and Female*, by Margaret Mead, p. 181. Copyright 1949. William Morrow &. Company. Used by permission.

TABLE 3 "Home-Grown"
Entrepreneurs
Versus "Imports"

Place of Birth	Percentage of Entrepreneurs*
Michigan	43 ⎫ 64
Great Lakes Region	21 ⎭
Elsewhere U.S.A.	15
Foreign-born	21**
Total	100

*Number of entrepreneurs reporting place of birth with sufficient specificity for this table was 75.
**Figure slightly higher than Table 2 because of smaller number of entrepreneurs included in this table.

Educational Level. There are sharp differences in the educational level of entrepreneurs and big business executives. Only about 20 percent of our respondents were college graduates, while 57 percent of the big business executives were. The contrast with the Michigan area executives in O'Donovan's study is even sharper. In this study, 69 percent of the executives were college graduates.[16] The manufacturing proprietors in the Newcomer study in Poughkeepsie,

TABLE 4 Size of Place of Birth in 1910 of
U.S.-Born Entrepreneurs
Compared with Distribution of
U.S. Population in 1910

Size of Place of Birth in 1910	Percentage of Entrepreneurs*	Percentage of General Population in 1910
100,000 or more	32	22
2,500 to 100,000	33	24
Less than 2,500	35	54
Total	100	100

*Total U.S.-born entrepreneurs reporting, 59.

however, were very close to our sample—19.4 percent.[17] Furthermore, the so-called lower managers in the O'Donovan study seem to be similar to our group.[18] Twenty-five percent of them were college educated.

The number in our sample who had not graduated from high school was, as

[16]O'Donovan, *op. cit.*, p. 59.
[17]Newcomer, *op. cit.*, p. 518.
[18]O'Donovan, *op. cit.*, p. 59.

might be expected, proportionately higher than the big business executives. There were almost 36 percent in our sample, as compared with 13 percent among Warner and Abegglen's big business leaders, and 3 percent of O'Donovan's Michigan area executives. The Newcomer figure of almost 40 percent is probably comparable to ours since her sample is broader and includes an older group.

While our entrepreneurs do not compare favorably with business executives in educational achievement, they do not look quite so bad compared with the general population in Michigan. Three times as many entrepreneurs were college graduates as the adult population (25 years or more) of Michigan in 1960. Considerably fewer of our entrepreneurs than Michigan adults generally had less than a high school education. Altogether, our sample seems to be an in-between group. (See Table 5.)

When we consider the great significance of education to upward mobility in the business heirarchy, we can begin to understand the obstacles which our entrepreneurs faced, particularly in Michigan, in their efforts to rise in established organizations. Certainly, more than half of our entire group had little chance to rise to executive positions in major business organizations. Only one-fifth had anything approaching a good chance to rise. It is clear that, for most, the opportunities in established enterprises were limited to the foreman level.

An additional consideration is the failure of these men, who seem otherwise quite capable, to achieve in established educational organizations. The school is an organized structure replete with age-grading, status hierarchy, and established authority, not unlike any other structured human activity. We might at first assume that these men had no chance to get a complete education but made the best of it by going into their own businesses. On the other hand, it is very possible that their failure to achieve in the educational sector may be related to their rejection of established organizations at a more general level.

TABLE 5   Educational Level: Entrepreneurs Compared with Business Leaders and General Population in Michigan

Educational Level	Percentage of Entrepreneurs*	Percentage of Business Leaders**	Michigan Percentage of Population 25 Years Old and Older in 1960†
Less than High School ...	17	4	37
Some High School	19	9	22
High School Graduate ...	25	11	26
Some College..........	19	19	8
College Graduate	20	57	7
Total	100	100	100

*Number of entrepreneurs reporting level of education, 84.
**From Table 39 in Warner and Abegglen, *Occupational Mobility in American Business and Industry*, p. 96.
†Computed from data appearing in U.S. Bureau of the Census, *U.S. Census of Population: 1960*.

274

Economic and Social Level of Family. One way of evaluating the economic and social level of the family from which the entrepreneur originated is by looking at the occupation of his father. In the Warner and Abegglen study, 15 percent of the big business leaders were the sons of successful major executives. No single entrepreneur in our sample was the son of a major executive. Successful bureaucrats apparently beget more successful bureaucrats but do not produce entrepreneurs, at least in the manufacturing segment of the economy. Eleven percent of the big business leaders are the sons of minor executives, a category including foremen. Only 2 percent of the entrepreneurs about whom we have information are the sons of minor executives. Nine percent of the big executives are the sons of owners of large businesses. Only 1 percent of our entrepreneurs are sons of owners of large businesses. (See Table 6.)

TABLE 6   Fathers' Principal Occupations: Entrepreneurs
Compared with Business Leaders

Father's Principal Occupation	Percentage of Entrepreneurs*	Percentage of Business Leaders**
Unskilled or Semi-Skilled Laborer	18	5
Skilled Laborer	12	10
Farmer	19	9
Clerk or Salesman	6	8
Minor Executive (including foreman)	2	11
Owner of Small Business	25	17
Major Executive	—	15
Owner of Large Business	1	9
Professional Man	10	14
Other	6	2
Total	99	100

*Number of entrepreneurs reporting, 80.
**From Table 5, Warner and Abegglen, *Occupational Mobility in Ameri can Business and Industry.* p. 45.

Twice as many entrepreneurs' fathers were unskilled or skilled blue collar workers (30 percent) compared with the business leaders' fathers. But most significant was the fact that 25 percent of the entrepreneurs' fathers were the owners of small businesses, often entrepreneurs themselves on a smaller scale. Seventeen percent of the big business leaders' fathers fell into this category. Another large segment of entrepreneurs' fathers were farmers—19 percent, or more than twice as many as big business executives. The number of sons of professional men among entrepreneurs was 10 percent, as compared with 14 percent among big business executives. This is surprisingly high, however, considering the social level of a great number of entrepreneurs. If we consider

275

farmers and most professional men to be owners of small businesses, fully 54 percent of our sample came from entrepreneurial families. This compares with 40 percent of the big business leaders. Professor Newcomer found even stronger tendencies in this direction, suggesting the possibility that entrepreneurial patterns can become a way of life for some families.[19]

The occupational level of the fathers of entrepreneurs indicated working class origins. However, in addition, we assessed the economic level of the families of origin from the entrepreneurs' interviews. Almost two-thirds of them described their early family life as poor or even underprivileged. Twenty-nine percent were well-off, and 6 percent were affluent. Most of them have clearly moved a long way from the somewhat impoverished economic level of their childhoods.

In about 15 percent of the families of our sample of entrepreneurs either the father or mother or both were dead. In addition, about 6 percent were divorced or separated. In short, one-fifth of our group of entrepreneurs clearly came from broken homes. In addition, there were a number of families in which the father was away, detached through drunkeness, illness, or travel.

Comparisons of Action Patterns

These statistical figures paint in broad stroke some major differences between the backgrounds of entrepreneurs and of executives in established organizations. To leave the matter thus, however, is to say very little about other and perhaps more significant differences between the two groups of men. Using the statistical material as a point of reference, we can, as space allows within the confines of this article, make some more meaningful comparisons.

The statistical evidence suggests that men who become entrepreneurs have as part of their family heritage a history of being "detached" from well-established institutional and organizational frameworks. The high proportion of entrepreneurs who are immigrants and the sons of immigrants reflects families on the move and already cut off from deeply imbedded roots. Over half of all the entrepreneurs for whom we have data came from families which had migrated across international boundaries.

Coupled with these data on ethnic backgrounds are the figures for occupations of the fathers of entrepreneurs. Here, again, we find that entrepreneurs do not come from families where the roots are firmly down in the world of large organizational and institutional activity. Entrepreneurs grow up in families either of the skilled and unskilled laborers, or in the world of small enterprise. Those entrepreneurs whose fathers were farmers necessarily at some point had to undergo mobility from the farm to the city.

Finally, entrepreneurs tended to leave formal education more rapidly than did the men in large organizations. Only 20 percent of the entrepreneurs graduated from college, compared with 57 percent of the Warner and Abegglen, and 69 percent of the O'Donovan, sample. Although the statistical sample for our own study is small, analysis shows that it corresponds quite closely to the Newcomer study of entrepreneurs.

Background Factors. What lies behind these figures? In seeking an answer to this question, we must necessarily enter into the world of the personal dynamics of the entrepreneur and into his patterns of interpersonal relations.

[19]See especially the data on pages 516 and 517 of Newcomer, *op. cit.*

This is the world revealed by the entrepreneurs in our interviews with them. Careful analysis of the interview and TAT materials suggests something of the following.

First, the act of creating a new and successful business is not an isolated incident in the life of an individual. It is, rather, a further development of a life-way which may in some aspects go back before the actual birth of the entrepreneur. Men establish new businesses not as an isolated career strategy, but as a learned response to their total social, emotional, and economic environment. We may only briefly mention here some of the background factors which lead to a man's creating a business as response to pressures placed on him by his environment.

Cultural Heritage. The first of these, and perhaps the most crucial and fundamental, is the cultural heritage of men who grow up in the United States. To say that the entrepreneurial figure is part of the "mythology" of America is not to say that for people growing up in this country the figure does not have objective reality. The values, dreams, and ideals of a culture are as objectively real as are its physical objects such as spears, castles, and television antenna.

All American children are more or less exposed to this cultural heritage. Why is it that for some of them the tradition "takes," entering into their very bloodstream and becoming part of their make-up? Why is it that others may play with the tradition in fantasy, but firmly reject it and choose to follow the well demarcated pathways to be found in large organizations?

The statistical data suggest that men who become entrepreneurs tend to be men who were from an early age "detached" from the well-established systems. The interview and TAT material, going deeper than the statistical data, furnish us with understanding of dynamics at play one upon the other.

Personal Dynamics. Entrepreneurs look back upon their childhoods as periods of impoverishment and stress. In their interviews they tell highly stereotyped tales of economic deprivation, of dead or drunken fathers, and of being forced to be on their own at an early age. In one sense, this self-portrait is a necessary step in identifying oneself as part of the entrepreneurial tradition. The orphaned waif is necessary to the first scene in the drama, just as the two-fisted captain of industry is a necessary figure in the last scene of the final act. The drama, of course, tells how the orphaned waif grew to be the captain of industry.

That the statistical and other "objective" evidence so shows that entrepreneurs, more often than not, do come from such impoverished backgrounds is not beside the point. It is, however, further necessary that the actor identify himself as being a figure in the entrepreneurial story.

A necessary corollary to making this self-identification is the discernment of the adult figures in the childhood scene as basically threatening, non-supportive, and disgusting. The interview data are replete with such appraisals of the parental figures in the worlds of entrepreneurs. Such ideas square, once again, with the myth in American culture. The presence of such untrustworthy figures in the childhoods of entrepreneurs serve, however, a further function: It is out of these original figures that the entrepreneur shapes his perceptions of the figures he encounters in the formal institutional world he has to cope with, initially as a child, and then later as an adult.

Entrepreneurs who did not finish formal schooling often explain this by talking in vivid terms about the poverty that forced them to leave school. Equally often, however, in a more relaxed mood later in the interview they will tell about "troubles" they had with a teacher. Further, time spent in formal education is very often viewed by them as time "wasted" in not getting ahead with the true business of life—that of earning a living.

Attitudinal Differences. Here, again, the attitudes toward formal schooling are only a foreshadowing and preparation for attitudes toward work situations which entrepreneurs typically show in their young adult years. The career executive may enter a firm or a government agency with firmly developed plans that his career will be worked out within the confines of that organization. Entrepreneurs, as a group, are never able to achieve such commitment to any organization for which they may work.

In their formative work years entrepreneurs tend either to drift from job to job, or to form ties with older men who stand in the relation of teacher and sponsor. Executives coming up through the ranks of established organizations may also form such ties as part of their career development, but for such executives the ties may be relatively unemotional and continuing. The interviews suggest that such is not the case for the entrepreneurial type. The entrepreneur may form such ties for immediately exploitive purposes, or he may enter into them because of strong emotional compulsions. In either case, the ties tend to be short-lived and to terminate in a crisis of anger and disgust. The entrepreneur learns that he can live neither within the restrictions of large organizations nor within the restrictions of protege-sponsor relations. He rebels. The rebellion often takes the form of identifying the sponsor with the untrustworthy figures from childhood.

Skills and Techniques. The rejection of large organizations and of sponsoring figures is, again, not enough. The preparation of the entrepreneur requires the positive learning of skills and techniques. It is probably here that the American mythology about entrepreneurship most widely differs from the situational reality. The myth states that in America anyone can succeed in business. The interviews show that this is not the case. For most entrepreneurs, success in business was preceded by a long period of training and trial, often marked by periods of broken dreams and of bankruptcy. It is in this crucible of experience that the entrepreneur develops his skills and learns his trade.

Simple technical skill is, again, not enough. The act of bringing into being a new business is a creative act of the highest order. Like most creative acts it requires in the beginning a certain intuition and a certain imagination. Like other creative acts, however, the intuitive insight must be worked through by a process of sheer drudgery if the original dream is to become a reality. Entrepreneurs who succeed must be able to discipline themselves to such drudgery during the early and formative years of the new firm. If they do not have the capacity for such discipline, their dreams come to nothing and their years are wasted.[20]

CONCLUSION

Entrepreneurs, then, are typically marginal to large-scale organizations. They are not necessarily, however, ambitious men who have found their drives

[20] In these pages we can only outline some of the factors involved in the success of an entrepreneur. The reader interested in further exploration is referred to *The Enterprising Man,* published by the Bureau of Business and Economic Research, Graduate School of Business Administration, Michigan State University, which reports fully on the study.

for success blocked in established organizations. They are instead, in many cases, the antithesis of the "organization man"; they don't stay on in established organizations because they can't stand them. They are often driven men who have deliberately placed themselves in "open" positions because they would rather face the impersonal forces of the economy than cope with interpersonal relations of the established organization.

The essential difference between the entrepreneur and the business hierarch lies in the area of their mode of approach to the world around them. The negative way of putting this is to say that entrepreneurs are men who have failed in the traditional and highly structured roles available to them in society. In this, entrepreneurs are not unique. What is unique about them is that they found an outlet for their creativity by making out of an undifferentiated mass of circumstance a creation uniquely their own: a business firm.

EXECUTIVE SELF SELECTION

IN SMALL BUSINESSES*

LOUIS L. ALLEN

No book about personnel management, to my knowledge, devotes any significant amount of space to the selection of people for small business ownership. Unlike the giant firm which has recruiting and selection experts to screen the wheat from the chaff, the small business firm, which comprises the most common economic unit in our business system, cannot afford to employ a personnel manager. The end result is that in the 11 million businesses in this country, the vast majority of which are small, the vast majority of the top managers have been through a rather unsystematic personnel selection process in terms of conventional personnel theory. More than that, there's something very special about the selection of the owners:

They have selected themselves.

Study a dozen texts in employment and selection, and you'll find none have a chapter or even a paragraph to cover the problem of the man who must screen himself for top management in his own small firm.

In this article I propose to fill this gap in the literature—not completely, but in a few key ingredients that have impressed me as essential in your own self selection process if you're toying with the idea of starting your own business.

Please note that these observations are subjective and aren't based on any of the newest findings of behavioral research. I am essentially a banker. My bank is a rather specialized kind, a SBIC (Small Business Investment Company)

*From *Management of Personnel Quarterly* (Summer, 1965), pp. 3-6. Reprinted by permission.

which is limited to making loans to people who have selected themselves to be owners, presidents or managers of small firms, and also seek some financial backing. As I face self-selected top managers across my desk, or visit them in their plants or offices, I become more and more impressed with the fact that his self-selection process is far more important to the success or failure of the company the man is starting than the monetary aspects of our negotiations.

What's proposed here isn't a complete guide to self-selection—or self-elimination—for top management of the small firm. I'll stick to being a banker, and let the professors write such a book. When they do, however, I'd like to suggest a few key points which they should include that have impressed me as germinal in the top management self-selection process.

Perhaps, if you are going into small business, or have been thinking about it, you can't await the complete guide. If this is the case, perhaps, this stop-gap article will help.

GUIDE NUMBER ONE

About 18 months ago, in the course of one day, I had an appointment with two different groups. One group consisted of three engineers from a national electronics firm who wanted to start a business of their own. The other group comprised an engineer with an electro-mechanical background and a CPA who wanted to start their small business. The story of what happened to these two groups illustrates the point which this article will attempt to make, i.e., a small businessman's success will be measured in direct proportion to the sacrifices he will be willing to make in order that his small business succeeds.

The three engineers sat across my table and outlined their background. Each was making over $35,000 a year, married and had several children. Their program was to start a business of their own in a line of products directly related to the work they were doing for their present employer. Their program was beautifully presented in an impressive binding with five-year forecasts and a complete analysis of all the salient facts. Naturally, I was quite impressed. They needed $350,000, and when I asked the question "how much can you come up with as a group?" the spokesman for them said "just a minimal amount, perhaps $25,000." I next asked them what salaries they were willing to work for and explained that it was certainly no crime this day and age to be poor. I also said I was not impressed with the savings that they were able to accumulate, so, I naturally assumed all they had to put into this business was their time, and thus, I was interested in the charges they would levy for their efforts. After a brief consultation between them, the consensus was that they might be able to reduce their salaries to $25,000 apiece. At that point, it was completely obvious they had no idea what self selection into a small business meant, in spite of the fact that their brochure is still one of the most complete that I have ever seen.

The other group that I talked to that day was just two men, the engineer and the accountant. And, like the first group, this second group started off by telling me that the engineer was now making $18,000 a year and that the CPA had a practice which he and his wife ran in which they had a gross draw of $15,000 after expenses. Their first statement was that they had, jointly, been able to save $15,000 and that this amount was completely committed to the program. Furthermore, the engineer went into some detail with me to show how it would be possible to keep his family together and meet minimum expenses on $8,500 a year, a reduction in pay of $9,500 from the $18,000 he was currectly earning.

Also, the CPA stated flatly that he was willing to give up two days a week of his own time and a day a week of his wife's time to work directly for the company at no charge. This group then presented me with a program of projected sales and income which was broken down in such a way that the investment could be made step by step with a review at each period. This program showed an ultimate need of $200,000 from the investor. The profit potential as outlined by the second group was roughly similar to that of the first although the product line was technically different.

I recommended to my loan committee that we make an investment in the second group and, of course, we gave a complete turn-down to the three engineers in the first group. Eighteen months later the situation is this: the first group of engineers found investors to put up the $350,000, and when that turned out to be insufficient got another $150,000 from the same investors. The company that they formed is bankrupt, and all of the invested capital has been lost. Ostensibly, it was salary costs that ate them up. Actually, they had selected people (themselves) who wouldn't pay a present price for future success.

The second group now has a sales volume running at an average of $45,000 a month, and their profit is just a little better than 27% on sales before depreciation and taxes. The president of the second group is now drawing $12,000 a year salary, and the accountant, although he is no longer associated with the company because of a new situation that presented itself, has been paid a fair price for the original cash investment which he made. It is the contention of the writer that given a half decent idea for a needed product or service, the first essential in a small business is selection of the man or men who are running the business. I have never seen a small businessman go broke if he was willing to make the necessary sacrifices. On the other hand, nearly every small business failure which I have seen is a direct result of a lack of willingness to make the appropriate sacrifices on the part of the one or more of the principals.

A few well known ideas: "bread cast upon the waters," or perhaps "ask not what your business can do for you, but . . ." apply in the early years and formative periods. This does not mean to say that great personal sacrifices always have to accompany the successful growth of a small business, because sometimes good fortune and other events work towards the situation in which the progress is made without the attending sacrifices. Nor will self-sacrifice replace a hopeless product or service nobody wants. Hence, the first guide is:

Be willing to pay the price.

I would like to touch just briefly on several of the other important areas of personal sacrifices which seem to me fundamental in terms of the commitment that a man must make before he goes out on his own.

One area requiring major sacrifice is well documented by a conversation I had several weeks ago. A gentleman who was very highly recommended came into my office. In his opening remarks he said the following, "I like the idea of forming my own sales representative organization." There are two things that are basically wrong with this statement, and they are among *the most common of the mistakes* I have observed on the part of self-selected small businessmen. The first mistake is that a man, and particularly a small businessman, cannot afford the luxury of indulging himself in an avocation that he "likes." If you pick yourself for top man in your own firm because you think in so doing you'll avoid the menial or unpleasant jobs, your selection is weak. The world is full of very capable individuals who are doing an excellent job at their assigned tasks. Therefore, my first comment to this young man was that he spend some time learning what he must do to make his business succeed and then forcing himself to learn to like it. Hopefully, he might prove most competent as a salesman, but the proof was needed. He selected himself as head of his own sales organization because he disliked his recent job.

The second major fallacy with his opening remark is somewhat similar. No one who has taken the trouble to look into the problems and the attendant sacrifices which have to be made by small businessmen, could possibly say that "he would like to be a small businessman," that is, unless he is a glutton for punishment. The reason why a man selects himself to head his own small business is because he *must* do it. The American dream is made up of such urges. The drives which force him to do this are as old as capitalism itself. A man may have complete security as somebody else's employee where he is fed, clothed, housed, where his medical needs are taken care of, but he has fewer prerogatives of his own. On the other hand, the individual who wishes to accept the responsibility for providing his own security has complete freedom of choice in selecting the means for providing the security he wishes. Thus, in return for abdicating his individual prerogatives, one individual may choose the security which some rather facetiously have termed being in jail, while the other individual may choose to be hungry or cold or sick or any combination of these conditions merely for the privilege of determining his own future. Thinking that "owning my own business is all rosy" is an illusion.

GUIDE NUMBER TWO

Some time ago, I was asked to appear as a guest lecturer at a well-known graduate school of business administration and to talk there to the class which was dealing particularly with the problems of small business. By way of some material for preparation, I presented the students with the following situation:

Assume you are thinking of purchasing control of a manufacturing concern. In descending order of importance, rank the following results of your investigation:

1. The plant and equipment are old and need attention.
2. After deducting the purchase price, you have left what you consider to be barely adequate funds to supplement working capital.
3. The existing management you will inherit is old in age but has many years' experience in this field.
4. You, personally, have less than three years actual working experience in this industry.
5. The company's product or products meet the needs of a broad class of customers, and well-established distribution methods exist in this industry.

Based on these assumptions, would you go ahead or not?

An amazing compilation of answers were given to this simple question. Not one of the 198 students ranked first in importance Item No. 4 which had to do with personal working experience in the industry being reviewed. To the writer this was a shock. There is no more important aspect of self-selection for small business ownership than facing sacrifices which a man must make, especially spending his personal time learning completely about an industry before making the commitment to get into it on his own. In the writer's experience, over half of the small businessmen who have failed have had a real blank in their own personal experience in the business which they were trying to run.

Don't choose yourself as a candidate to run your own business
if you don't know that business extremely well.

Let's look back at the situation described in the first few paragraphs of this article. One of the first things that a self-selected small businessman needs is money. Yet, it is this writer's firm conviction that a worthwhile program presented by a man who knows his business is *capable of being adequately financed.* If his small business venture is to have any chance for success, he must couple his own time and effort with cash; by time, I mean up to 15 hours a day, 7 days a week, for as long as it takes the company to cross the first major plateau where it is established in the eyes of its customers. If your self-selection system shows you to be a confirmed 9 to 5 type, better stay out of small business!

There are always a great many reasons why small businessmen say they need money. In the writer's experience, the infusion of money never cures a problem of poor self-selection, and this had lead the writer to come to the conclusion that money cannot be the main problem.

GUIDE NUMBER THREE

Can you accept personal inconvenience?

Some areas in which the small businessman is frequently unwilling to make the necessary sacrifices are: (1) he could not reduce his living standards and had to draw a larger salary than the company could afford; (2) he could not control himself in his desire to acquire more machinery or other fixed investment than he needed and could get by without, provided he was willing to sacrifice some effort and be willing to accept, possibly, a product that does not have the same quality as could be made on more expensive equipment; (3) he was unwilling to live where his business had the best chance of success; or (4) he insists upon hiring people to do jobs he should be doing himself.

A man I had known and liked for nearly 10 years stopped in to see me several months ago and said that he desperately needed some financing for his business. Upon examination he indeed appeared to have a cash problem. When he came in, he brought his papers, and the facts showed that he had been drawing some $3,500 a month salary out of his business because that was the amount required to continue the living standard which he and his wife had adopted while this man had been employed in a very large national concern in a top executive post. My friend had left his business in order to go into business for himself, and he had done quite well at the start. A cash problem? On the surface it seemed so, but it was more than money.

283

I was much distressed to have to tell my friend that before I could help him, he would have to reduce his draw to not more than $1,500 a month. This was a very unacceptable proposition to him, and he left in somewhat of a huff. Several weeks later, he came back saying that he had found that other bankers with whom he had talked had adopted an attitude like mine, and since he was going to have to cut back on his living standards, he would prefer to do it with an old friend rather than with a stranger, and would I still do it? The answer was "yes." My friend then did the following things. He sold his house, which was a beautiful place and was on the cover of a magazine, and moved into a small modest home which he rented. He put the proceeds of the sale into his business. He let his maid go. And in other ways he reduced his requirements so he could keep his family going on the $1,500 a month. Very happily his business looks very bright indeed. Was it the cash alone that tipped the scale? Hardly. It was the eased pressure and determination to place his long run goals ahead of immediate income.

One of the first prospects who came into my bank for financing was a man in the millwork and woodworking business. He was doing a considerable volume and seemed to be making a profit, yet he was continually pressed for cash. The situation was sufficiently interesting to warrant a visit to his plant which I made very shortly thereafter. Having once been in the sawmill and logging business myself, I can state without fear of contradiction, that this man had the most beautifully equipped shop I had ever seen. I admired his plant immensely. Here was his problem: he could not control himself in the acquisition of machinery. This man eventually ended up in bankruptcy, and his machinery account which had a book value of over $600,000 was sold at auction for $92,000.

A different problem was presented to me by a young engineer who had started a company in a very specialized product line with which he was completely familiar. His initial success was very encouraging, and on the strength of this good history he decided to expand into other lines. To do this, it was necessary for him to hire other engineers. The problem that he faced when he came to talk to me was that in order to keep his expanded product line from becoming technologically superannuated, he had to hire more and more engineering talent. And this direct payroll expansion had to be incurred substantially in advance of any product sales and profits which might accrue. After he had outlined the problem to me, he said with a half smile on his face that what he really wanted to do was to continue his program of deficit financing. Quite obviously, this type of program was a zero incentive for an investor, and my bank declined the risk. One of his problems was that so long as his product line was one which he personally could develop, he could keep himself in the forefront of the technology. In his zeal for technical achievement, he lost sight of his business goals. When he hired other engineers, these men could not provide the same drive in their areas and had little concern for where the money would come from. When I suggested that he start making a profit *soon*, even if it meant deferring some technical schemes which intrigued him, he left in a cold mood.

CONCLUSION

In this article I have tried to suggest a few key points which those thinking of starting their own business might well consider. They are based, of course, only on my own personal experiences and observations as a banker. Take them for what they are worth, and realize that when thinking of starting your own business, you are really selecting yourself to be a top executive. In summary, remember: (1) there is nothing to be obtained without paying the price; (2) self select only experienced men to start a new enterprise; and (3) ask yourself whether you can accept personal inconvenience? If you're with me up to here, maybe my bank, or somebody else's, will be more willing to consider you as a good loan prospect.

THE ENTREPRENEURS: LUCK AND PLUCK—

AND A STRONG SUCCESSION*

Sitting in his Beverly Hills office, the former MCA Corp. mansion, Litton Industries Chairman Charles B. (Tex) Thornton was telling how he started his company and pushed it from nothing to assets of $743 million in just 14 years. Litton, as he explained it, was born of his personal frustration. Said he, choosing his words carefully, "I saw opportunities I was unable to follow up working for other men."

Other people learn to live with the frustrations they meet in daily life. But men like Thornton are different. They balk at taking orders they do not respect. They see opportunities that others overlook. His great energy and driving ambitions blocked, first at Ford Motor and later at Hughes Aircraft, Thornton had to start his own company to try out his ideas.

In a way, Litton's story is typical of many of the new names on the 1967 list of the Top 100 industrial corporations. Almost every one of them—General Tire & Rubber, Lockheed, Georgia-Pacific—is a monument to the drive, talent and energy of a single man or of a small group of men. Existing companies couldn't hold them. Nor were they satisfied with small successes. They started companies, or took over small and faltering ones, infused them with their own zeal and enthusiasm and attracted like-minded men.

TOO MANY DU PONTS

A close observer of the business scene puts it like this: "There are two kinds of companies in the U.S.: Those run by any tradition, by old-school ties, by the rules; and those run by abnormal men." By "abnormal," he means abnormally ambitious, abnormally strong in motivation, in drive. These men would most likely agree with Joseph Wilson of Xerox when he says, "You have to be very naive so as not to see how deep a risk you're taking." Such are the men who run most of the companies that outpace industry as a whole.

It's true of the recent newcomers, but it's an old story in American

*From *Forbes* (September 15, 1967), pp. 200, 202, 204, 209, 210, 212, 214, 216.

285

industry. Take Sears, Roebuck, now one of the great business organizations in the world. Sears is the lengthened shadow of two exceptional men: Julius Rosenwald, a Chicago apparel manufacturer who made Sears king of mail-order business; and General Robert E. Wood who made it the world's greatest department store chain. Wood is the kind of man Tex Thornton could appreciate. Before World War I, Wood went to work for du Pont. "He stayed there awhile," recalls Sears' ex-Chairman Charles Kellstadt, "looked around, saw a lot of du Ponts in the place and figured there wasn't much chance for him. So he got into (Montgomery) Ward where they made him a vice president. But he was a vigorous fellow and he had strong ideas on merchandising and they wouldn't listen. Someone told Rosenwald to grab Wood and he did.

"Rosenwald didn't have too much confidence in Wood's idea of getting into stores, but he did have a great deal of confidence in the General," added Kellstadt. Rosenwald gave Wood the go-ahead to open the first Sears store (on Chicago's West Side; it's still there), and the rest is history. Wood never learned 'to live with his frustrations. He met them head on. In so doing he made business history.

In much the same way, the great Kaiser companies were created, not by money or monopoly, but by the will and talent of Henry J. Kaiser. Radio Corp. of America would have remained a relatively small company without David Sarnoff's visionary leadership. International Telephone & Telegraph was built by the great Sosthenes Behn; it was revived by the hard-driving Harold S. Geneen.

Geneen was cut from the same mold as the others. He never stayed long in any one place, partly because he was hard to get along with, partly because he was constantly in a hurry—in a hurry to be his own boss. He started with the New York accounting firm of Lybrand, Ross, then was chief accountant at American Can, controller at Bell & Howell and assistant to the vice president at Jones & Laughlin Steel. At Raytheon, as executive vice president, he was second in command, but he started looking around when he tired—after a scant three years—of waiting for a crack at the top job. Donald C. Power was an immensely successful attorney, but money and comfort weren't enough for him. He took the presidency of General Telephone, remade the company in his own image as GT&E. He took only eight years to make this once-sleepy telephone company into one of the great billion-dollar corporations.

NO SOFT JOBS WANTED

The true entrepreneur is a man who, when faced with the choice between security and a challenge, will pick the latter every time. After World War II, Continental Oil had a chance to break out of its regional, domestic boundaries by joining the industry's exploration rush. But aging, ailing President Dan Moran was not equal to the task, and succession was wanting within the company. Conoco's directors went after Leonard F. McCollum, who was making a name for himself at Jersey Standard, and negotiated two years to get him. "I was happy as a possum at Standard," said McCollum later, as he accepted plaudits for having built Continental into a middle-sized international giant. McCollum had been poor as a youth, and the chance of the top job at Jersey must have had its appeal for him. But the greater lure to his entrepreneurial temperament proved to be the challenge of building Continental. Conoco ranked 16th among oil companies on *Forbes'* 1945 list, 9th on the 1967 list. The value of management? Conoco's stock price has appreciated sevenfold since McCollum took over.

The impressive thing about these entrepreneurs is that they don't necessarily need a growth industry like telephone or electronics to operate in. The late J. Spencer Love built a great enterprise, which is among today's Top 100 companies, in, of all places, the textile industry. Like the others, Love was possessed of monumental self-confidence. Everyone told him debt was dangerous, especially in a cyclical business like textiles. "Dangerous!" he sneered. "Why shouldn't I borrow when I get money at 5% and it's tax deductible and I can make 10% on it? I believe in borrowing all I can." Today, Burlington Industries' debt-to-equity ratio of 34% is among the highest in the industry.

To get borrowed capital to leverage his equity, Love used every trick in the book. He set up some 30 different operating companies, using the credit of the stronger ones to support and expand the weaker ones that had trouble borrowing on their own. Caught in a storm of technological change, he didn't try to fight it. Using his borrowed money, he kept his plants as up-to-date and modern as was humanly possible. The result is that Burlington gets more sales per employee than all but one or two of the major companies in the industry.

Change the name and the industry, throw in an even greater dose of daring and you have the same story with Owen Cheatham of Georgia-Pacific. In the mid-Fifties, some of his shrewd, conservative competitors were convinced that little Georgia-Pacific was going broke. As against $47 million in equity capital (in 1956), it had $126 million in debt. And paying fancy prices for timber reserves! What would happen to G-P when prices dropped!

But Cheatham, one of the original financial minds of this generation, was not just indulging in wild gambling. He was simply placing all the bets he could get on what he regarded as a sure thing: that growing demand and growing utilization of the entire tree were going to make timber an increasingly valuable asset. He got the Prudential and Metropolitan insurance companies, more venturesome than most, to lend him the money, using the timber itself as self-liquidating collateral. The results? Georgia-Pacific is among the more recent arrivals to today's Top 100 list whose stock market performance has led all the rest. From 1945 to 1967, a $1,000 investment in its common stock has grown to almost $95,000.

FIND 'EM & TRUST 'EM

Being human, these entrepreneurs can make mistakes. One of the most common is an egotistical failure to develop a strong successor. This is why the list of dropouts from the Top 100 includes companies built by great entrepreneurs, companies like Curtiss-Wright, American Standard and Koppers. And that is why the truly great entrepreneur is not just a risk-taker; he is also a great leader.

A case in point is Monsanto. Edgar Monsanto Queeny took over the presidency in 1928 from his father John F. Queeny, who had built the business by breaking the German stranglehold in artificial sweeteners. To son Edgar fell the challenge to make the company greater, in fact, to build it into the giant it has become today. And he did it by acquisitions, made in a way that reveals his ability.

Queeny saw that what Maytag and others were doing to home laundering had great implications for the chemical industry. He realized that automatic washing machines would require more powerful cleaning compounds than the old elbow-grease-powered washboards. Therefore he acquired a small Alabama-based chemical company that was doing research in phosphate cleaning compounds, built a huge plant to turn out the compounds, and made Monsanto the great supplier of the basic cleaning stuff to the detergent industry.

Good leader that he was, Queeny realized he needed talent for his company; ordinary men wouldn't do. In 1963 he brought Dr. Charles Allen Thomas to Monsanto by buying Thomas' small company. Salary alone wouldn't have attracted Thomas; indeed, larger companies than Monsanto had been trying to lure Dr. Thomas and his partner, Carroll Hochwalt. So Queeny did something unusual for the time: He gave Thomas stock in Monsanto. Thomas put Monsanto into plastics and later into synthetic fibers, which, more than anything else, pushed Monsanto into the billion-dollar class.

MEN LIKE THEMSELVES

Herbert Dow was another who combined impatience with an understanding of the human factor. As general manager of Midland Chemical in Midland, Mich., he used that town's great brine deposits to break the German monopoly on bromides. But he wanted to go beyond that, using the brine for a whole family of chemicals. The stockholders and the board turned him down; they wanted dividends, not pie in the sky. Dow left his safe job in 1895 and started Dow Process Co. Five years later Dow took over the faltering Midland company, and Dow was well on its way to becoming the fourth-biggest chemical company in the U.S.

Like Thornton today, Wood and Dow yesterday were impatient men. If the companies they worked for wouldn't give them what they wanted, they started their own. But they were more than merely impatient. Once in control of their own destinies, they tried to create an atmosphere in which men like themselves could flourish.

Like other successful entrepreneurs, Dow succeeded in instilling his successors with his own spirit. In the late 1930s Dow pioneered in petro-chemicals, being among the first to build in the now-booming Texas Louisiana Gulf Coast area.

It was at that time that Dow chemists came up with two promising discoveries, styrene and acrylonitrile; the former a basic plastic, the latter an element in plastics and synthetic fibers. Dow chose to develop styrene and therefore benefited from the demand for butadiene-styrene synthetic rubber during the war. But, having limited resources, it let acrylonitrile pass it by; and as a result, says President Ted Doan today: "We never got off the ground, we never made money in fibers." Monsanto developed acrylonitrile, formed Chemstrand Corp., and with the growth of fibers since the war is ahead of Dow today in assets and revenues . . .

This much is clear: An entrepreneur, if his work is to last, must be a kind of Pied Piper of talent. Take William L. McKnight, who built Minnesota Mining & Manufacturing. Chairman Bert Cross says, "The best thing he ever did was to hire Richard P. Carlton [president from 1949 to 1953]. He was an electrical engineer by training. He was great with technical people; they gravitated to him. He got us a lot of good men." Their inventions and innovations opened up market after market. Cross gives this example: "In 1929 we bought a company that owned a hill of quartz. Dick Carlton asked our technical people, 'What do we do with it?' The ideas flowed in: Use it as chicken feed, use it in bird cages. The one that clicked was to make permanently colored roofing granules of it. Today," Cross says, "we own four quartz quarries." Because 3M challenges its people, Cross adds, "If a man can't find anything to interest him in this company, nothing interests him. He must be dead."

Again and again, in talking with the great entrepreneurs and with the men who know them, there is a recurring note: Find the right people and trust them. Julius Rosenwald trusted General Wood, even though he distrusted Wood's idea. Ernest Breech's job at North American Aviation in 1934 was to convert it from a holding company to a manufacturing company. He got the best man he knew, Dutch Kindelberger, chief engineer at Douglas Aircraft, and let him use his head. The planes Kindelberger designed and built soon had the company flourishing. In recalling the turning points in his own career, General David Sarnoff recalls a similar experience when RCA was jointly owned by General Electric and Westinghouse. "General Electric was interested in manufacturing mass items, so I began to propagandize my music box with Owen Young [GE's chairman]. They called in an efficiency engineer and he reported to Young. His advice was: "What's this young fellow talking about music in the home for? He's supposed to be running a communications business; make him stick to it!' Young read the report and threw it in the wastebox, and RCA as we know it today was born."

The aircraft industry has been an entrepreneurial business if ever there was one. But as the industry grew, so did the need for men who could not only build but could put their imprint on a whole organization.

This is where William Boeing of Boeing succeeded and Donald Douglas of Douglas failed. Like Douglas, Boeing was an aircraft pioneer. Quitting Yale a year before he was to have graduated, he caught the then-prevalent flying bug and started one of the two dozen or so companies then hand-building planes in the U.S. In 1927 Boeing made his big gamble: He put in a bid to fly the mail from Chicago to San Francisco. He got the contract but at a price that everyone was convinced would break him: $2.89 a pound *vs.* a bid of $5.09 from his closest rival.

But Boeing had no intention of committing economic suicide. He was convinced he could *build* a plane that could carry mail at $2.89 a pound and make money on it. He set about designing a plane around Pratt & Whitney's new Wasp engine. He bought 25 engines and built 25 model 40-B biplanes. It was a highly efficient plane, but that wasn't Boeing's only ace. He designed his craft to carry passengers, something no other mail plane did. It carried only two of them, but the fare was $200 one way. With the aid of passenger fares, he figured he could come out ahead on each flight. He was right.

In similar fashion, Boeing was ahead of the pack in 1934. The U.S. Army Air Corps invited bids on a new multiengine production bomber. In those days "multiengine" meant *two* engines, but Boeing came up with a four-engine job, the B-17. Douglas, with a more conventional plane, got the contract, but the Army Air Corps decided to encourage Boeing's bold experiment. The company got a contract for 14 of its B-17s for flight testing.

When World War II came, the Boeing Flying Fortress, as the big plane was known, dropped the bombs that weakened Germany. Out of it, too, came the far bigger B-29 and, eventually, the B-47 and B-52 jet bombers and their refueling tanker, the KC-135. That, in turn, led to the family of jet airliners that has made Boeing the No. One commercial plane manufacturer. Its great success had been reflected in the price of its stock: $1,000 invested in 1945 is now worth [1967] nearly $56,000.

Bill Boeing dropped out of the company in 1933, but the management in depth that he built continued under his successors, including current President William M. Allen. That was where Boeing's bitter rival, Donald Douglas, went wrong.

In the Thirties Douglas captured first place from Boeing in the air-transport market with the series that culminated in the handy and efficient DC-3. Douglas was lulled into complacency when its big DC-6, successor to the DC-3, led the postwar market for piston planes. It hung back on jets, hoping that the DC-7 would constitute a new generation of piston planes. But the jets began sweeping the market and Douglas came late with its DC-8.

Worst of all, when Donald Douglas Sr. passed the presidency on to his son in 1957, he failed to provide the kind of in-depth management that Boeing had. The new team failed to cope with losses on the DC-8 and the financial problems growing out of the DC-9. The Top 100 tables tell the story: In 1945, Douglas ranked 80th among the industrial firms, Boeing 114th. On the 1967 list, however, the positions are drastically changed: Boeing is 40th, while Douglas before its recent merger with McDonnel, was only 83rd. This year [1967] Douglas was taken over by McDonnel Aircraft Co., headed by James McDonnel who ran a St. Louis aircraft company that had done a volume of only $21 million at the height of World War II when Douglas' revenues were well over $1 billion. McDonnell is able to give Douglas the management depth Douglas had not built for itself.

BIG FLOPS, BIG SUCCESSES

The great entrepreneurs are certainly not infallible. Boeing suffered several serious setbacks, one of which, involving the big Stratocruiser in the late Forties, plunged it into the red. But the important point is that Boeing had the management flexibility and ingenuity to survive the blow and come back. So did Lockheed, which was badly hurt by heavy losses on its big Electra turboprop, a serious marketing miscalculation. Douglas lacked that resiliency.

Henry Kaiser avoided Douglas' mistake. Kaiser, flushed with his shipbuilding successes in World War II, decided he could crack the auto business. His Kaiser-Frazer Corp. lost $114 million before throwing in the sponge (it survives in the fast-growing Kaiser Jeep Corp. today). But Henry Kaiser did not have all his eggs in one basket. Between 1939 and 1946, he plunged into cement, magnesium, ship-building, steel and aluminum as well, borrowing freely to do so. Though heavy interest payments often held down their profits, his companies grew so rapidly that today they rank second in aluminum, fourth in gypsum, ninth in cement and tenth in steel.

Why was Kaiser so successful? True to his rugged, confident self, he adopted an all-or-nothing attitude while breaking into these industries. He scoffed at those who predicted that a recession would follow the war. He expected a boom in autos, in housing, in consumer goods. He wasn't one to hedge his bets by building tiny steel or cement mills. He built big, and therefore very efficient, ones. The great demand that did in fact follow the war's end proved the soundness of his plan. And what if the pessimists had been right? What if there had been a major recession? Kaiser might have lost control but he would still have founded some great companies—as did William C. Durant, the man who founded General Motors, only to lose control to the du Ponts in the recession of 1920. Kaiser, who died this year [1967] at 85, left the empire in the hands of his son, Edgar, and a brilliant management team.

Royal Little's Textron was taking it on the chin in the late Forties, when the textile business went into the doldrums. A less flexible man would simply have ridden out the hard times. But Little was too impatient for that. Where other great entrepreneurs switch jobs when frustrated, Little did them one better: he switched industries. "I didn't see how the textile business would ever be good again in my lifetime," he says. He gradually sold off the textile properties and reinvested the money where he could get a better return. To help him, he called in banker Rupert Thompson, who pushed the company into watchbands, power saws, helicopters and more.

It was Royal Little who put Textron together: it was Rupert Thompson who made it work. Thompson realized sooner than most that the nature of the corporation was changing, and he molded Textron to the changes. "I think," he told *Forbes*, "that the lesson of our company is not to try to be restricted by products, but rather to be motivated by the use of capital. I don't think this type of company existed years ago." The Textron-type company, devoted not to making any particular products but to keeping capital gainfully employed, has this big advantage, according to Thompson: It protects against technological obsolescence. Steel or railroads or shoe-leather or printing may become obsolete, and product-oriented companies decline: but a Textron is in so many product lines that some are always gaining ground at least as fast as others are losing. As for the losers, they can be shucked off and the capital reinvested in growing businesses.

Thus stated, the idea seems sensible enough, but it was radical when Textron first tried to practice it. It took courage. "How could one company run so many different businesses?" the conservatives wanted to know. Textron, like Litton and others, has shown that it *can*—given the tools of modern management.

With assets of $501 million, Textron didn't quite make the Top 100 list this year, [1967] but at the pace it is growing it will almost certainly make the next one. Moreover, its success has influenced many another company to adopt a less rigid approach.

Tenneco Inc. didn't go quite as far as Textron in diversification, but it did shift the whole emphasis of its growth. Gardiner Symonds had the vision to foresee the dynamic growth of gas pipelining in the Forties and Fifties—and then its gradual slowing down. Over the last ten years, he successfully diversified into oil, chemicals and packaging, and this year [1967] arranged to buy Kern County Land. Pipelines now provide only 40% of Tenneco's revenues. And Tenneco, which was just a few years old in 1945, has shot up to the 17th position in *Forbes* 1967 list of the Top 100 companies.

How could Symonds move so fast without stumbling? "We buy companies with good management," he says. "Many people are willing to sell us their companies so they can retire to Florida. But this isn't what we look for. We want companies with young executives who will stay and run them for us. I can't run the company myself; I have to depend on others."

YOU'VE GOT TO LET GO

Kaiser, Little and Symonds had learned a lesson. Let Tex Thornton, speaking from his own experience, tell what it was:

"You wonder why we don't have more multibillion-dollar companies around. There are so many that start with promise, but what happens? I think it's because one, two or three men build the company to the extent of their capacity and don't let go. They feel insecure if they don't make all the decisions. Yet the company's growth has saturated their capabilities. Three times I've started small, and as the companies grew, I've had to discipline myself to decentralize. It wasn't easy the first time, but you've got to do it or you can't grow."

And it works both ways: "If you don't grow," says Xerox' Joseph Wilson, "you won't attract the kind of people you need. If the growth of copying should slow down and we were content to grow at, say, 5%, our best people would lose interest; they'd leave in droves. We *have* to diversify."

In other words you need a leader, but the leader can't do it alone. He must attract others like himself.

Another great company-builder, Dr. Henry Singleton of Teledyne, Inc., says the same thing in another way: "A great corporation never has to go outside for its president."

It's no different in a family-run company. General Tire & Rubber's founder, William F. O'Neil, had three ambitious sons in the company. "He didn't give us responsibility," says Michael G. (Jerry) O'Neil, General's 45-year-old president. "We took it. I grabbed a lot of it, the stuff he didn't want to do."

ITT was in bad shape in 1957 and had to create a committee of the board to look elsewhere for a new president. That was a sign of weakness, but an attempt was made to correct it—and they did find the right man. After Harold Geneen quit the second spot at Raytheon to take the top spot at ITT, things started to happen. Since Geneen took over, the company's sales have tripled, earnings per share have more than doubled.

About the same time ITT was going downhill, National Steel fell on bad times. The brilliant but cantankerous Ernest Weir, whose Weirton Steel was the key element in the 1929 merger that formed National, presided over its swift rise, based on its concentration on the lighter steels. But Weir stayed too long at the helm. Says President George Stinson discreetly. "Towards the end of Mr. Weir's tenure, he was not as aggressive in planning the company's growth as he had been." When Weir finally retired in 1957 at age 81, George Humphrey and Thomas Millsop got the company back on track, then brought in lawyer Stinson to manage its resurgence. Yet despite the work of the last decade, National's 1967 rank among the Top 100 is 12 places below its 1945 rank.

WHO'S IN CHARGE?

Almost as bad as having to go outside is the case of the company that has a succession that can't measure up to the man who created the company.

That is what befell General Dynamics, the creation of hard-driving John Jay Hopkins. Starting with tiny Electric Boat Co. and merging with much bigger companies like Canadair and Consolidated-Vultee, Hopkins had by 1957 pulled together a company with sales of $1.6 billion. He died before the nearly autonomous divisions could be brought under good managerial controls, however. While he was alive, only his dominating personality made the company hang together. The man who got the top spot when Hopkins died, leaving an uncertain line of succession, was Frank Pace. But Pace was no match for the task of whipping this sprawling company into shape. It ran aground on its biggest project, the Convair 880/990, which eventually lost $490 million. Today, under Chairman Roger Lewis, GD is well along on the road back to recovery. But it was a close call and it took Lewis, an outsider (he had been executive vice president at Pan American World Airways), to save the day.

There are interesting parallels between the near-disaster at General Dynamics and the near-disaster at Chrysler. On the surface they were different: GD's was a dramatic throw of the dice that came out wrong; in Chrysler's case, it was a slow downward drift. Both were companies that came up fast under a great entrepreneur but failed to develop depth of leadership. And both came back smartly when they got it—with the result that the work of the entrepreneur was salvaged and both stayed in the big time.

Walter Chrysler built his company from 4% of the market in 1925 to 26% in 1933; this at a time when the Hudsons, the Auburns, the Graham-Paiges were declining.

In a 1929 interview with *Forbes's* founder B. C. Forbes, Walter Chrysler told his own story. It was a story different in its details but not in its essentials from that of Tex Thornton or Robert E. Wood. It was the story of a mechanically minded boy who worked his way up to a responsible job with the Chicago & Great Western Railroad at 33, then quit because he realized that few men with his background ever got to the top in railroading. Besides, he had already decided that the future belonged not to the railroad, but to individual transportation as represented by the motor car.

Chrysler later cured a sick Buick operation, making a fortune in General Motors stock in the process and ending up as executive vice president. He moved on to take over and restore to health an ailing Willys-Overland at an annual compensation of over $1 million a year. That didn't hold him, either. In 1921 investment bankers brought Chrysler a moribund auto company, Maxwell Motors. Four years later, he changed its name to Chrysler and made it such a force in the industry that it was able to absorb the big Dodge Brothers company in 1928. By 1929 $1,000 worth of the old Maxwell stock purchased in 1923 had grown to $33,800.

But whereas Alfred Sloan built General Motors into an organization that could carry on, Chrysler did not. In 1935 he made K.T. Keller president, and Keller ran the company until 1950. Recalls Ernest Breech, a man who knows well what happened in the auto business at that time: "Chrysler didn't have modern financial management. K.T. Keller wouldn't let you have an organization chart. I don't want to blame Keller, but it sure went downhill." It did indeed. By 1950 its market share was just 18%. Under Lester Colbert, it fell still further, to 13% in 1954, barely half its peak share, and the company made only $18.5 million on sales of $2 billion.

UNFLINCHING

Adds Breech: "Look what they did later when they got good management again." One of the men who gave Chrysler its good management was able George Love, now chairman of the executive committee. Says Love: "Chrysler started to fail because it didn't see that marketing was becoming more important than manufacturing. It should have seen it; General Motors and Ford did.

"A company needs the type of fellow who can find a way to meet circumstances whatever they may be. He has to have commercial ingenuity, the ability to see things that are changing for his industry, and move ahead of his competitors to meet it. He doesn't necessarily need knowledge of the industry. What he does need is a combinstion of mental toughness and a willingness to take a risk." In Love's view, Chrysler just didn't have that kind of man in a leadership position when it needed him. But Love found such a man in Lynn Townsend. Love says: "Spotting this type of fellow is the tough part. That's where the judgment comes in. In fact, if you limited your *investments* to companies that had that sort of management, you'd have done quite well."

The kind of man who can do everything, the board chairman who delights in tinkering in the plant, is a familiar figure in American business. But he can be a danger to a big corporation by suffocating the initiative of other men. This may not happen, however, if the man is a real leader. Consider the case of Harold W. Sweatt who took over the presidency of Minneapolis-Honeywell in 1934 when it did a $5-million volume and ran it until 1961 and a $470-million volume. Sweatt, now honorary chairman, was a real "tinkerer" and a despiser of organization charts. All the decisions were centralized with him. But Sweatt, fortunately for his company, was a great leader.

YOU FIGURE IT OUT

He had about him a wry, deprecating humor. He liked to tell stories about secretaries sassing him back. Rather than killing initiative, Sweatt nourished it in his men—and he developed good men. Paul B. Wishart, who succeeded Sweatt as president in 1953, then as chairman, was head of production when Sweatt came to him, said Honeywell needed financing, that he was "tired" of doing that sort of thing and told Wishart to do it. Taken aback, Wishart protested, but asked how much money was needed. "You figure it out," said Sweatt. Wishart toiled away and came up with a $16-million figure which he took to Sweatt.

Sweatt, unimpressed, just said, "I'd figured $16 million myself. Now go and get it." Sweatt, in short, was a man who poked into everything, but he was no tyrant, no smotherer of initiative, no inspirer of uniformity. Thus, when Wishart stepped up to chairman, he was succeeded as president by James Binger, a man as different from Wishart as the latter was from Sweatt. And this continuing vitality accounts more than anything else for the good performance of the company stock. . . .

It's clear from these cases that truly great companies are not simply built by men who had the guts to pioneer. The builders must also be leaders. Like great politicians and great generals, great businessmen know how to make others rise above their normal limitations, know how to inspire, cajole or bribe dedication from ordinary men.

Listen again to Ernest Breech. Here's what he says it takes: "You've got to inspire men; you've got to give them goals." This General Motors graduate reorganized Ford Motor, helped build North American Aviation and Bendix and pulled TWA back from the brink of bankruptcy. Though he never founded a major company, his was the spark of inspiration that built or rebuilt a half dozen giant corporations. Concurs Arjay Miller, president of Ford Motor, "You are dealing with people, and you have to know how to motivate them and to lead them."

Perhaps, above all, the great leaders must have the self-discipline to rise above the illusion of omnipotence. They must be willing, even anxious, to pass decision-making responsibility on to others.

Tex Thornton, who has thought a good deal about the subject, puts it this way: "We stimulate people to do things and we're willing to gamble on their making a few mistakes."

What of writers, like John Kenneth Galbraith, who think that the day of the great individual entrepreneur is past? The facts simply prove him wrong. What Galbraith overlooks is this: Even a highly organized, diverse modern corporation needs leadership. It needs someone to call the tune. All the system and the organization in the world are worthless without leadership.

Will the Cheathams, the Thorntons, the McDonnells, the O'Neils be the last of the great American entrepreneurs? Not likely. There are new ones coming along every day. James Ling of Ling-Temco-Vought, Charles Bluhdorn of Gulf & Western Industries, Henry Singleton of Teledyne are creating huge new corporations right before our eyes. Not all of them will go on to greatness, but some will. And there will be new names and faces in the Seventies.

GO WEST . . .

Gardiner Symonds, the soft-spoken, courtly Chicagoan who founded Tenneco, tells a story that nicely illustrates the whole entrepreneurial principle. "Back when I was studying at the Harvard Business School in the Twenties, Dean Wallace B. Donham used to give a lecture to graduating seniors on the theory of Horace Greeley: 'If you stay around in one of the fine old New England companies, that would be good and it would be comfortable. But it will take you quite a while to climb up the business structure. If you go West or South, on the other hand, you only have to be right three times out of five, not three times out of three.' That is because the growth of the country and industry allows for mistakes and for the possibility of correcting them."

The entrepreneurs today don't necessarily have to move geographically— the "Souths" and "Wests" are all around them. But they still follow the spirit of Horace Greeley: By looking for new ways to do things; by trying to create industries rather than waiting for them to come in on their own; by taking tired old, uninspired companies and turning them into lean, tough, young ones again.

WORKING WITH THE ENTREPRENEUR*

ROBERT L. BENDIT

To the man looking for a job the climate or style of an organization he considers joining becomes an important factor. The consultant, because he works with many companies, becomes similarly aware of the differences between organizations so that he, too, thinks in terms of their maturity, their stage of development from their entrepreneurial beginning to the structure of the old and complex organization. From the outside viewpoint of either applicant or consultant, companies differ almost as individuals differ, and the story of their lives contains fascination and romance.

There is excitement in being asked to join a new company. It is an opportunity to participate in what you believe will be successful, a chance to "get in on the ground floor", and there is the hope that because the enterprise is new it will not make the mistakes we see around us in older companies. There is a unique fascination in the prospect of being a principal participant in the forming of a new company.

It does not take long for anyone associated with the average new company to see that these expectations had in them some wishful thinking, and that these hopes were something less than realistic. Smooth running systems do not spring full-blown into being, and the pressures and confusions of human inter-dynamics foul the hopes and delay the progress of most newly formed companies. Usually the principal organizers have brought in all of their own background and knowledge, but they have also brought in their biases and prejudices. The product may be a new one or a variation of some old product, but the people are the "same old people."

Among the personalities undertaking to run a new corporation, the entrepreneur, usually a self-appointed leader of the group, is the predominant figure. He is usually a man of intelligence, strength and vitality, a man whose important contribution seems to be to push many ideas ahead. It is this rare quality which has made it possible for him to form a new company and which may make it possible for him to carry it through to maturity. This does not mean that he has the administrative capability needed to mediate conflicts and harmonize the purposes of the diverse human beings he brings together. He usually works long, hard, irregular hours, and because, like everyone else, he gets tired at times, he is likely to disappear at intervals when his energy is spent.

Some of the very qualities which make a man able to start a new enterprise are likely to cause distress in those attempting to work with him. Stubborness to the point of bull-headedness, independence, sullenness, argumentativeness, peevishness, periods of elation and depression, anxiety and insecurity—all go into making up his total behavior. His insecurities in this high-risk situation are heightened by the uncertainties he faces in the early days of his business. He

*From *Periodic Report No. 47* (August, 1970), The Vernon Psychological Laboratory, pp. 2-5. Reprinted by permission.

lives under extraordinary pressures, and for this reason he is likely to over-react. He wants desperately to succeed.

His drive to be different and to have his company different becomes a compulsion. This drive can make problems, for there is the danger that the entrepreneur may automatically reject techniques which have been successfully practiced in other companies. He may insist on re-inventing the wheel, or he may insist on practices which have a history of failure in other companies, convinced that *he* can make them work. The resulting scene is a continual flow of problems and actions centering around the special interests and desires of the founder.

Among the men who join entrepreneurs at the inception of new businesses there is a fair number of casualties. After a man has made his original contribution, a role may be outlined for him where he can continue to serve, or he may lose his usefulnesss to the group. In a new company the demands change rapidly. If he does not make the adjustments involved in becoming a member of an ever-growing management family or if a neutral assignment cannot be created for him, a clean-cut separation may be the only solution, and the old adage that "founders make poor managers" may be the only explanation. The climate resulting in this kind of scrappy, hectic, confused, emotionally charged atmosphere sometimes seems to promote rather than inhibit the growth of a company, and if the undertaking succeeds, it seems to succeed in spite of all the political byplay that goes on.

As a new company is born and staggers to its feet, all of the personnel problems that plague older companies make their appearance, and the solutions or failures to arrive at solutions emerge and become part of the habit systems of management. There is the critical need for good selection of people; the necessity to train inexperienced managers functioning in key assignments for the first time; the importance of open, clear channels of communication; and at the same time, there are ad hoc systems produced in desperation, fire-fighting behaviors and the hiring of any immediately available personnel (sometimes friends and relatives).

The natural tendency makes its appearance to simply hide the expense of hiring caused by turnover rather than to take the time necessary for careful interviewing, reference checking and psychological testing. The entrepreneur is likely to be grateful that he is in business at all, he may be a little pleased because people want to work for him, and too impatient to support the involved and costly procedures necessary for adequate selection. To round out the picture, he often attributes to himself a gift of perception and intuition in judging people, so that tools in this area do not seem to him to be of major importance.

New companies usually come into being because of the possibility of making and marketing some new product, and the men who start new companies are likely to be product-oriented men. "If the product is not developed to a salable stage, there will be no company." This makes a difficult atmosphere in which to develop programs concerned with the selection of people, with the motivation of men, with human relations and all the necessities of effective teamwork. The need for prompt production of a salable product is often used as an excuse to delay badly needed work in selection and training, and the result is an illogical situation in which everybody is too busy to take the time for programs that would ultimately relieve their work load.

After the excitement of initial success has subsided, the entrepreneur gradually awakens to a feeling of new power and new security. He may now become an "expert" in all facets of business, and if, during the earlier chapters of insecurity he learned to be a manipulator of people, he may now embark upon elaborate games of personnel checkers, moving and removing people with great authority. He may also expand his horizons into a world of mergers and acquisitions which usually have to be carried on without the knowledge of the rest of the organization. Lower-level managers are then required to work in an information vacuum, and the feeling grows that they do not know or understand the company's goals and policies. Key employees still hope there will be a "special" place for them in the company's future, but at lower levels anxiety will increase, there will be a high turnover, and the ground will be prepared for unionization.

As a company becomes large and successful the entrepreneur and other original employees tend to fade into the bigness of the organization. Job assignments at all levels become more sharply defined and firmly established and top management has to learn that it is not free to do anything it wants to in any department. If problems at the top are fewer, they are also bigger; and absenteeism from decision making begins to appear. Trips abroad become popular and there is increased attention to new cultural pleasures. Concern about the welfare of the company, so intense at the beginning, may now evolve into concern for expansion of the "empire", a pursuit that can go on forever.

The entrepreneur is a man whose idea of success was to create and run a successful company. As it grows, he may also grow, or he may fail to do so. The man who is big enough to run a large company successfully will usually display early in his career an awareness of and a concern for the fundamentals of good administration, and a large part of that concern will be for the selection, development, motivation and training of people. He will have shown that interest from the very beginning of the enterprise.

ADDENDUM

Minority Business Enterprise

Increasingly in recent years, members of minority groups have looked upon business ownership as a means of self-fulfillment or increased economic well being. However, their opportunities for business ownership have long been severely restricted. Though comprising approximately 17 per cent of the population, minorities own fewer than 3 percent of the nation's businesses; furthermore, these minority-owned enterprises represent less than ½ of 1 percent of the nation's industrial and business capital. Some observers have suggested the reason is that minority group members generally have a low *n* Ach, and that their entrepreneurial inclination and performance can be increased by increasing their achievement motivation. They point to the "success" of David McClelland's experimental achievement motivation courses for businessmen and potential entrepreneurs among the black population of Washington D.C.[1]

Other sources, on the other hand, have suggested that members of minority racial groups are unable to establish their own businesses almost solely because they are unable to obtain financing and proper training and advice. To surmount these obstacles and generate economic opportunities for disadvantaged minority groups on a par with those available to the general population, President Nixon in March, 1969 established the Office of Minority Business Enterprise (OMBE) as an agency of the Department of Commerce.

The concept of "black capitalism," however, has its opponents as well as its proponents. Some authorities insist that it is not enough to change a man's motivation, or to provide him with generous amounts of capital and management training and assistance if the environment in which he lives doesn't support his entrepreneurial efforts. Bernard Booms and James Ward in *the Cons of Black Capitalism,* for example, state that the ghetto is not the best place to start a business if the entrepreneur has the alternative of starting at some other location. They maintain that the risks of black capitalism are greater than those of white capitalism, and that the only really

[1]"Black Is Beautiful, But Is It Bountiful?" Jeff A. Timmons, *Harvard Business Review,* November 1971, 49:81-94.

promising path to equal opportunity for blacks in business lies in an integrated national economy.

Though admitting that black capitalism programs will not go far in revitalizing the inner city, Richard Farmer asserts that the idea is not without merit. In his rebuttal article, *The Pros of Black Capitalism,* he highlights misconceptions about the idea and describes a feasible program for encouraging black entrepreneurship.

THE CONS OF BLACK CAPITALISM*

BERNARD H. BOOMS / JAMES E. WARD, JR.

From the 1880's on, the Negro masses, urged by their leaders, were led to place increasing faith in business and property as a means of escaping poverty and achieving economic independence. Although ostensibly sponsored as the means of self-help or racial cooperation, as it was sometimes called, through which the masses were to be economically emancipated, Negro business enterprise was motivated primarily by the desire for private profit and looked toward the establishment of a Negro capitalism employer class. One of the clearest expressions of the growing tendency to look upon the development as the basis of racial economic advancement is found in the proceedings of the Fourth Atlanta University Conference (1898) on "The Negro in Business." In his paper, "The Meaning of Business," John Hope, the late president of the new Atlanta University, called upon the Negro to escape the wage-earning class and to become his own employer. [1]

There is no new thing under the sun. (Ecclesiastes 1:9)

Black capitalism has recently become the most popular and widely discussed remedy for ghetto ills. Its present popularity seems to have sprung up almost overnight. This blossoming was fostered in large part by President Nixon during his campaign for the presidency when his speech writers coined the phrase "black capitalism," which soon became a political idiom.

Black capitalism has a certain appeal to both Negro radicals and white conservatives because "each group can bring its own particular meaning to the term and still agree on tactics. What appears to the white group as the simple extension of the private enterprise system to the nation's ghettos is to Negroes a fairly radical proposal for the community to assume ownership of the means of

*From *Business Horizons* (October, 1969), pp. 17-26. Reprinted with permission.

[1] Abram L. Harris, *The Negro as Capitalist* (Philadelphia: American Academy of Political and Social Science, 1936), pp. 49-50.

production." It has also been noted that "black capitalism seems to appeal to white conservatives more than to white liberals, since it amounts to a drastic shift away from traditional liberal approaches and goals."[2] Nevertheless, conservatives and liberals, blacks and whites, militants and moderates, President Nixon and the man on the street, all lend support to the idea—a rather amazing fact which seems to substantiate the conclusion that there are many different interpretations given to the meaning of black capitalism.

The political popularity that has been accorded black capitalism has made it a potentially important tool of public policy. There has been much favorable discussion regarding the potential worth of a policy promoting minority ownership of business. On the other hand, there has been very little comment concerning the potential disadvantages of such a public policy. The favorable promotion has included many promises, both implicit and explicit, that the multitude of problems inherent within our urban centers will be corrected but it has omitted any potential drawbacks which might be linked to such a program. Since so much attention has been devoted to extolling black capitalism and its promised rewards, an examination of the cons of black capitalism and its limitations seems to be in order. The purpose of this article is to present and discuss some of the possible disadvantages that black capitalism might entail.

This article was not written to show that the black capitalism movement is without merit. We feel that it offers certain favorable outcomes. Some jobs might be opened; some incomes could increase; and the path to restoration of minority pride and independence could be initiated. Perhaps even further insight into the real problems confronting our cities would be uncovered. However, we feel that while some benefits may exist, they will not be sufficient to improve the living condition of many urban residents. In addition, there are strong reasons to believe that the promised benefits will be overshadowed by the potential drawbacks that have hitherto received little attention.

WHAT IS BLACK CAPITALISM?

Any definition of black capitalism is likely to be somewhat arbitrary, but it is important to understand what we mean by the term. The most common meaning attributed to black capitalism is ownership or the encouragement of ownership of the means of production by Negroes and other minorities. Richard Nixon, in his speech "Bridges to Human Dignity," said:

> . . .This is precisely what the Federal central target of the new approach ought to be. It ought to be oriented toward more black ownership. . .an expansion of black ownership of black capitalism. We need more black employers, more black businesses.

In the language of the economist a capitalist need not be an entrepreneur, but in the popular sense these terms take on identical meanings. In this article, ownership and entrepreneurship will be used interchangeably. Thus, black capitalism or black entrepreneurship means black ownership of businesses with the residual rewards going to the black owners. Black capitalism implies government promotion of black ownership, supplemented by private programs.

[2]"Is Black Capitalism the Answer?" *Business Week* (August 3, 1968), p. 60.

Most advocates of minority entrepreneurship feel that the efforts of these programs should be directed toward the establishment of minority businesses in the *ghetto areas* where most of the minorities reside.[3] The implication is that the benefits to be derived from a minority-owned business would also accrue to the ghetto area, for example modernization and revitalization of the inner cities. Interestingly, one seldom hears discussion about placing minority entrepreneurs outside the ghetto area. A more complete definition of black capitalism, then, is that it is a policy for the promotion of black ownership of businesses within the urban ghetto.

WHY BLACK CAPITALISM?

"What does black entrepreneurship hope to accomplish?" In other words, what goals are sought; what benefits are to be expected; and what problems are to be overcome? Once the objectives are brought to light, it will then be possible to evaluate their potential for achievement critically and to investigate the side effects of pursuing a program of minority business ownership.

The concerns of the promoters of minority enterprise can be divided into two broad categories: *place* improvement and *people* improvement. Each is linked to the ultimate goal of helping to solve the multifaceted social problem of urban crisis. Only a few individuals think that minority entrepreneurship is a panacea for the problems within the urban crisis.[4] Despite the divergence in opinion as to what constitutes the urban crisis and as to which elements of the crisis black capitalism can be applied successfully, it is possible to list place and people goals that are generally accepted.

Place Goals

The most widely discussed of the place goals is the revitalization and modernization of the decaying inner city. Revitalization is more difficult than simple renovation. It is an unending task because it requires a change in the residents of the ghetto, not just in the decrepit structures. It is reasoned that minority entrepreneurs will see the need for improvement in their environment and will act as catalysts to bring about such improvements. It is also felt that only members of the minority group can understand and work with the other residents in the area; and that white businessmen in the ghetto have neither the interest nor the capability to gain the support of the ghetto community. In modernizing the ghetto, the objective is not so much revitalizing the decaying area as it is improving its appearance. It is felt that if minority entrepreneurs are encouraged to establish themselves in the ghetto, they would repair old, de-

---

[3]For example, President Richard Nixon has said in a speech that "The third bridge is the development of black capitalism. . .we can help Negroes to start new businesses *in the ghetto* [italics added] and to expand existing ones." "Bridges to Human Dignity," p. 5.

[4]One such person is Ross Davis, assistant secretary of commerce for economic development. He has said, "When ghetto residents have substantial full-time jobs in businesses managed and owned by black people, I believe that many of the social, as well as economic, problems of our cities will be solved." From "EDA Helps Launch Black Capitalism," *Economic Development,* VI (February, 1969), p. 8.

crepit, run-down, often vacant stores; add a few coats of paint and possibly a new store front; sweep the sidewalk; and, all in all, provide a clean, nice-looking area in which their customers might shop comfortably.

A second place-oriented goal is the desire to generate tax revenues within the ghetto. It is hoped that the tax base will be lifted as operations become successful and that a rise in property values and tax revenues will ensue. In this way, each section of the city will be paying for its own development. Although place-oriented goals for minority enterprises are part of the overall group of programs designed to promote minority entrepreneurship, greatest emphasis has been placed on people goals.

People Goals

Perhaps the primary objective of minority enterprise programs is economic improvement for persons of minority races. As minority members are encouraged to establish and run their own businesses, they will gain a greater share in the general economic system, and thus poverty will be reduced or, hopefully, eliminated. It is felt that the owners of the new businesses will be integrated into the economic system, and, through a multiplier effect, that others will rise from the ranks of poverty. (The multiplier is based on the notion that minority entrepreneurs will hire members of their own race, whereas absentee owners of ghetto businesses have not.)

Social integration is closely tied to economic integration. If minorities benefit economically from the minority entrepreneurship programs, they may be in a better position to move out of the ghetto into an integrated neighborhood. If black capitalism succeeds in creating a significant middle class among minorities, it is argued that social integration might be easier.

Conversely, some of the proponents of black capitalism see it as a means of establishing a separatist society that would enable the minority group to live and educate its people as it would like and to provide its own jobs and opportunities without dependence on the white man and his institutions.[5] This goal envisions two societies, one white and one black, with relations carried on at the level of foreign countries.

Another people goal is that of greater economic and social self-determination. This proposal would not create a separate society but would give minorities a greater voice in affairs affecting their lives. Minority businessmen are expected to provide a sense of self-determination because they will be more attuned to the needs of their people and will provide alternatives to whites who are charged with overpricing and selling inferior merchandise.

These are some of the general goals that various proponents of black capitalism hope will be achieved through minority enterprise programs. What is the probability of actual attainment of these objectives? What unforeseen consequences might develop? In the following section we will explore the potential undesirable aspects of black capitalism as a government policy.

[5]See, for example, Robert Sherrill, "We want Georgia, South Carolina, Louisiana, Mississippi, and Alabama—Right Away. . .We Also Want Four Hundred Billion Dollars Back Pay," *Esquire* (January, 1969), pp. 70-76, 142-46.

CONS OF BLACK CAPITALISM APPROACH

There are two major limitations of black capitalism, the inherent short-comings of minority enterprise proposals and the indirect negative consequences that could arise from a minority enterprise campaign. Some of the inherent shortcomings will now be discussed.

Before the government or any private organization can speculate about establishing minority-owned businesses in ghetto areas, it must understand the ghetto economy and community and obtain facts concerning existing minority-owned businesses. There is almost a total lack of any kind of data on minority-owned enterprises either inside or outside the ghetto.[6] This lack of information is certain to hamper efforts to assist Negro entrepreneurs. In addition, we know of only one economic study of the needs of the ghetto and the type of businesses it might support. From these few known facts we can deduce that proportionately Negroes are tremendously underrepresented in business ownership. In New York City, for example, 1 out of every 40 whites is a proprietor, but only 1 out of every 1,000 blacks is a proprietor. Although New York has a Negro population of over 1,100,000, there are less than 30 black-owned enterprises employing as many as 10 persons.[7] In Harlem, 15 percent of the commercial establishments are owned by blacks. The New York experience is apparently representative of other parts of America. For instance, in 1966 the population of Washington, D.C. was two-thirds nonwhite; yet blacks owned only 13 percent of the businesses. Also, the number of Negro-owned businesses has been declining since 1950.[8] The reason for these disparities is unknown.

Why is there so little information concerning minority enterprises? Why does a smaller percentage of blacks become small businessmen? Why does the relative number of black businesses decrease as the number of white businesses increases? What does it take to operate a business successfully in the ghetto? What types of businesses seem to have a chance of surviving in the ghetto? Answers to these questions and many others are desperately needed to gain some insight into how best to establish new minority enterprises in the ghetto. Although the answers are not available, many offer black capitalism as at least a partial solution to the urban crisis. However, what good is a tool if one does not know how to use it? Some Negroes scoff at the idea of whites attempting to implement their programs in ghetto communities because of this lack of knowledge and understanding. They say, "White folks don't know anything about us." Actually, *no one* really knows how to initiate a program of minority

---

[6]One rather extensive study of Negro businesses has been published. See *An Analysis of the Little Businessman in Philadelphia,* I (Philadelphia: Drexel Institute of Technology, 1964); *The Census of Negro-Owned Businesses* (Philadelphia: Drexel Institute of Technology, 1964). Also there is a study on the Negro businessman in Harlem included in the *Hearings on the Role of the Federal Government in the Development of Small Enterprises in the Urban Ghetto,* May-June, 1968, Select Committee on Small Business, 90th Cong., U.S. Senate, 2nd sess. (Washington: U.S. Govt. Printing Office, 1968). In addition, the authors know of only one economic study of the needs of the ghetto and the type of businesses it might support. See *Retail Locations Analysis Manual and Retailing in Low Income Areas,* prepared for the Chicago Small Business Opportunities Corp. (Chicago: Real Estate Research Corporation, 1968).

[7]*Hearings on the Role of the Federal Government in the Development of Small Business Enterprises in the Urban Ghetto,* May-June, 1968.

[8]Dan Cordtz, "The Negro Middle Class Is Right in the Middle," *Fortune* (November, 1966), p. 228.

entrepreneurship successfully. This uncertainty contrasts sharply with the glowing picture that has been presented by proponents of black capitalism.

Another shortcoming is that little is known about what makes a successful entrepreneur, or how to identify a potential entrepreneur.[9] Also, a special problem may exist in relation to minority entrepreneurs since they may not be *naturally* forthcoming. If minority groups wish to increase their percentage of businessmen, they will probably have to take the initiative to instill the entrepreneurial spirit. This has not been necessary in the development of white entrepreneurs because of free opportunity, tradition, and example. Without this effort there may not be "potential" ghetto entrepreneurs to receive aid. This is probably one of the greatest obstacles to a program calling for more minority-owned businesses.

In addition, managerial competence is lacking. Some minimum education is necessary, especially for today's market. But can managerial competence be taught? If so, how does the government or private institution train persons to become business owners? How can potential entrepreneurs be identified or selected for training? Even if these two shortcomings are surmounted through time and research, others remain. Programs aimed toward establishing new minority-owned businesses probably will be limited to small, retail businesses. Limited financial resources for minority development lead to low loan ceilings for any given venture, effectively excluding development of businesses with large capital requirements. One example of low loan ceilings is the $25,000 limit placed on loans through the Small Business Administration's Economic Opportunity Loan Program. [Editor's note: This ceiling has since been raised to $50,000.] The low ceiling limits are designed to spread limited capital over many clients. A lack of business experience and training on the part of the budding entrepreneur also restricts the size of an initial business venture.

If it is true that black capitalism programs will focus on attempts to establish small, mainly retail businesses in slums or low-income areas, it is important to analyze what has happened to such firms, particularly to those in ghetto areas. Facts about small business in general are readily obtainable, but much less is known about low-income area businesses and even less about minority-owned businesses that are usually located in low-income areas. The following picture from the few existing studies emerges.

GHETTO EXPERIENCE

Retail Business

The number of small businesses in central cities or socially changing neighborhoods has been declining. Brian Berry found that the average annual drop in

[9]"An analysis of occupational position of 55 Wesleyan graduates some 14 years after graduation indicated that significantly more of those originally scoring high in need Achievement (n Ach) than those low in n Ach were found in entrepreneurial occupations. A cross-validation study...confirmed the finding that males with high n Ach gravitated toward business occupations of an entrepreneurial nature." Even if n Ach can identify potential entrepreneurs, the problem of how to create more n Ach people among minorities might have to be solved. David C. McClelland, "N—Achievement and Entrepreneurship: a Longitudinal Study," *Journal of Personality and Social Psychology,* I (1965), p. 389. See also "As I See It, Entrepreneurs are Made, Not Born," an interview with David C. McClelland, *Forbes* (June 1, 1969), pp. 53-57.

the number of retail establishments was about 15 percent in areas of Chicago undergoing transition to low-income neighborhoods.[10] Over a ten-year period 60 percent of all the businesses studied had liquidated. On the average, 33 percent of these businesses ceased operation after less than two years. In addition to numerous failures there was also a high rate of turnover. These figures illustrate the great instability of small retail businesses in low-income, racially changed or changing, older, inner-city areas. Berry states, in fact, that the situation is most critical in areas undergoing racial change and nearly as severe in stabilized Negro areas. Thus, the few facts available about the very areas where black capitalism programs might be expected to be put into operation, and about the types of firms that can be expected to be established, seem to predict that the fight for success will be a tough one. Despite these dismal statistics, some black capitalism programs will probably be instituted. Therefore, it is interesting to investigate successfully established black firms.

In general, these retail businesses are very marginal. Often they are one-man operations with help from family members. The owners work long hours, many reporting 16- to 18-hour workdays.[11] Many ghetto businesses are operated in addition to regular full-time employment (the exact percentage is unknown). Few concrete figures are available for the important matter of the rate of return on capital and labor obtained from these firms. The *Real Estate Research Report* states ". . .generally, such enterprises do not earn enough return to provide both a competitive return on the investment in them and standard wage rates for the people who run them." When Eugene P. Foley was director of the Small Business Administration, he testified that, for 45,000 Negro enterprises in depressed urban areas, ". . .the annual profits of such concerns average $3,300. This figure, 43 percent below the white level, illustrates the tenuous hold they have on life." Mr. Foley also stated, "with rare exceptions the small businessman in decayed urban areas has no discernible prospects for growth."

This picture of the average small retailer does not show much economic promise. Perhaps black capitalism programs will only create a set of marginal firms and eventually bring the owners into a worse position. An essential goal is the establishment of *viable* business enterprises, rather than merely increasing the number of black businesses. Additionally, given the probability that the type of enterprises to be established will be of the retail variety, the multiplier effect (mentioned previously) is not likely to be very large since most retail organizations do not hire many employees.

It should also be noted that a change of face does not necessarily constitute a change in business practices. This point has been well made by Negro author E. Franklin Frazier, who said, "When the opportunity has been present, the black bourgeoisie has exploited the Negro masses as ruthlessly as have whites." More minority members may be hired, but without competition, an improved environment, and managerial competence, operating costs will be high—and so will prices.

[10]Brian Berry and others, *The Impact of Urban Renewal on Small Business* (Chicago: University of Chicago, Center for Urban Studies, 1968), p. 116.

[11]These characteristics were discovered in a survey of Negro businesses in Gary, Ind. The facts reported here are based on unpublished material from this study. For a report on the Gary, Ind. study see Richard N. Farmer, "Black Businessmen in Indiana," *Indiana Business Review,* XLIII (November—December, 1968), pp. 11-16.

Demand and supply forces underlie both the decline in the number of small retailers and their high turnover rates. Many of the problems of minority businesses are also experienced by whites. Although we do not support separate standards, we do feel that there are additional problems encountered by new businesses in ghettos that hinder their chances for success. Changes in the aggregate income and tastes of the customers account for much of the decline in the total number. Middle-income whites are replaced by low-income minorities, mostly blacks. As the racial balance changes, the willingness of whites to shop in the area drops. For example, in one Chicago area that underwent racial change the percentage of white patrons dropped from 88 percent to 54 percent. Another demand factor that has worked against the small retailer is a rise in mobility, which generally results in greater interbusiness-district competition and a decrease in the locational monopoly of any one district. Marginal businesses already in trouble feel this increased competition most keenly.

On the supply side, the forces of technological change have weakened small retail outlets. For example, given the heavy use of cars today, shopping centers, which provide easy access and free parking, have an advantage over the older business areas. Another example is the change in merchandising techniques to the emphasis on a wide range of goods and self-service. These methods require more footage and display areas than usually are available in the older districts. One other supply factor connected with declining numbers of small retailers is urban renewal. By 1966, 60,000 businesses had been displaced by urban renewal; it is likely that somewhere between 100,000 and 120,000 businesses will have been displaced by 1972.[12] In his study of the impact of urban renewal on small businesses, Brian Berry points out:

> . . .since race of owner is usually correlated with a variety of other variables such as level of education, skills, capital resources, general business know-how, site preference, type of business, income, profit, and attitude toward business as a profit-making enterprise or as a way of life, and since Negroes make up the largest percentage of persons in the low-income levels, Negro-owned businesses in Negro communities undergoing urban renewal generally have high liquidation rates.[13]

A differential liquidation rate between black and white businesses in an urban renewal area was found in a recent study. In the Elmwood section of Detroit, 57 percent of the Negro-owned businesses failed to survive urban renewal, compared to a 35 percent liquidation rate for white-owned businesses in the same area. Hence, supply forces, which include urban renewal, may work against the success of black capitalism programs.

In the short run, urban renewal is probably bad for all small businessmen in a renewal area. But over the long run, urban renewal may be beneficial to the *remaining* businessmen. If the government establishes black capitalism programs, it could be in the position of conducting two major projects, one of which (urban renewal) works against the goals of the other (minority enterprise)!

[12]W. Kinnard and Z. Malinowski, *The Impact of Dislocation from Urban Renewal Areas on Small Business* (Storrs, Conn.: University of Connecticut, 1960), p. 86.

[13]Brian Berry, *Commercial Structure and Commercial Blight: Retail Patterns and Processes in the City of Chicago* (Department of Geography Research Paper No. 85; Chicago: University of Chicago, 1963).

So on the demand side, the inner-city small businessman finds his market shrinking due to the change in the socioeconomic level of the residents in his neighborhood. In addition, since the total number of potential customers might be reduced by the actions of urban renewal, his market becomes limited. On the supply side, his lack of business experience, the shortage of modern retailing facilities and methods, and the absence of capital prevent him from being efficient, and thus his costs are high. The interaction and combination of these forces result in the lower returns observed for small businessmen and explain why the outlook for ghetto businesses seldom brightens despite valiant family efforts and long hours of drudgery. In view of the long-run trends adverse to small-scale retailing in decaying urban areas, the marginal nature of most small retail operations, and the strong forces working to continue these trends and characteristics, the outlook for a black capitalism plan appears very unrewarding.

Wholesale and Manufacturing Businesses

Let us suppose that black capitalism programs will not be limited to establishing retail outlets and that wholesale and manufacturing companies will also be encouraged. Suppose, too, that the large capital requirements and the highly trained minority entrepreneurs needed for such operations are available. (Again, we argue that these are unlikely assumptions.) Given these assumptions, will these firms take root in inner-city areas?

The ghetto or inner-city area represents an environment in which the development of many of these types of business organizations would be impossible. This fact goes a long way toward explaining the migration of wholesale, service, and light manufacturing to the suburbs. The ghetto presently is simply not an economically feasible place in which most businesses can be sustained. But, most of the proponents of black capitalism advocate establishing businesses there! Although forming Negro businesses outside the ghetto area would probably offer greater chances for success, the discrimination barrier looms large there. The economic obstacles of the ghetto and the discriminatory barriers facing Negro businesses desiring to locate elsewhere may combine to eliminate most business opportunities for Negro entrepreneurs. Promotion of black capitalism may be virtually an impossible task without a prior attack on the discrimination faced by Negroes.

What environmental conditions in the inner city create disadvantages for businesses? The existing commercial buildings are usually dilapidated. Many are multistory and thus inefficient for many of today's production processes. High crime and fire potential are a disadvantage and make insurance unobtainable or prohibitively expensive. Inability to obtain insurance may cause ineligibility for a bank loan, always a critical factor in starting and operating a small business. Many small businesses must be located near other businesses to obtain necessary support and services. Examples of these support services are businesses specializing in printing, machine repair, drafting, industrial photography, and janitorial services. Generally, small firms rely on agglomeration economies connected with close physical location to other small- and medium-sized businesses in order to obtain these necessary services. Most small businesses cannot support their own service departments, but a number of small firms in close proximity can provide the demand to justify the existence of support and service firms. However, more and more of the existing medium-sized firms are moving to the suburbs and building internal support service departments at their new locations.[14] This leaves the inner city without the necessary agglomeration base for smaller firms that cannot afford an internal service department. The climate of the inner city has become less suitable for business development as more and more businesses leave. As the agglomeration economies are lost, the traditional role of the central city as an incubator for fledgling businesses is being destroyed. In addition, the entry scale for new non-retailing business is becoming larger because new firms must now establish their own support departments. The odds for success from a modest beginning are decreasing; a firm must be born big.

Also, communication devices such as the telephone and their widespread use have made face-to-face interaction less important. In fact, AT&T expects to promote a combination telephone and television system commercially within the next two years. This means that one of the forces, the need for face-to-face contact, helping to create the agglomeration economies traditionally found in the city center will tend to disappear.

The prevalence of car and truck ownership in America today has drastically changed the relative industrial locational advantages of the inner city and the suburbs and has affected location decisions of firms. Readily available public transportation is no longer necessary to attract a sufficient labor force. Free parking, which can be provided easily in the suburbs, may be more important than ready mass transit. Therefore, a ghetto location can be a disadvantage in attracting workers. Even resident ghetto workers, who are supposedly to be employed as a result of black capitalism, require transportation since not all can walk to work, and public transportation is often inadequate. The increase in the number of cars has been paralleled by the growth in the number of trucks. Trucks, too, have affected the trend toward decentralization. Industrial firms were once restricted to inner-city locations because of their need for easy access to freight terminals, rail lines, and ports, all traditionally found at the city center. With the advent of trucks, transportation costs for firms may be lower in the suburbs near freeway interchanges than in the central city. Trucks have a difficult time getting through crowded, narrow, deteriorating city streets, and it is awkward for firms to deliver or receive goods. Thus high transportation costs are another obstacle to the success of firms planning to locate in the ghetto.

Corporations

Some evidence that the drawbacks enumerated here are influential can be found in the experience, admittedly limited, of major corporations which attempted to establish black manufacturing plants in inner-city ghettoes. After studying the record of recently established ghetto subsidiaries of large American corporations, Sar A. Levitan and Robert Taggart, III of the George Washington University Center for Manpower Policy Studies state, ". . .the experience generally has not been favorable and the business environment of ghetto areas does not seem to be profitable." Note that this is a statement about

[14]For evidence that firms are moving to the suburbs see John Kain, "The Distribution and Movement of Jobs and Industry," in James Q. Wilson, ed., *The Metropolitan Enigma* (Washington, D.C.: Chamber of Commerce of the United States), pp. 1-31.

the experience of black capitalism efforts initiated by large corporations, which have an ample supply of managerial talent, experience, and financial resources to be used in the effort.

The Levitan-Taggart report gives detailed information on three of the most widely publicized corporate black capitalism projects, Aerojet-General's efforts in Watts, EG&G's Roxburg plant, and IBM's plant in the Bedford-Stuyvesant area of New York City. In the Aerojet case, "despite a $1,300 per man training subsidy . . . and $1.5 million in Department of Defense set-aside contracts, Aerojet has lost several hundred thousand dollars." Recently the work force in the Watts plants has been cut from 500 to 300. The authors state that the Aerojet problems are "clear-cut: in the first year 1,200 had to be hired to maintain a work force of 500; and the company estimates that its training costs were closer to $5,000 per man than to the $1,300 paid by the Labor Department." The EG&G experience is similar. Again, $575,000 of government aid notwithstanding, the plant was $75,000 in the red in 1968, and a $250,000 loss is forecast for this year [1969]. IBM claims to have had better results, but admits that absenteeism in this plant has been twice as high as for the company as a whole. In addition, IBM estimated that renovation costs for the black capitalism plant were 10 percent higher because of the inner-city location. The study concludes that "no doubt some of the recent corporate efforts have suffered from birth pains and ghetto plants may prove more profitable in the future. But it is also probable that if these plants do not get out of the red soon, some plants will be abandoned, thereby discouraging other ghetto locations."

These black capitalism efforts are apparently proving to be unsuccessful, as hypothesized in this article, and the efforts are costly. Levitan and Taggart claim that the Bedford-Stuyvesant Restoration Corporation spent an average of approximately $42,000 in assistance to establish 22 firms ($35,000 per firm in direct funding—not loans—and $7,000 per firm on management assistance). Thus, creation of 22 firms with an average work force of 16 cost nearly $1,000,000. These figures tend to support our contention that there are prohibitively costly problems, if not insurmountable drawbacks, in carrying out a national policy of black capitalism.

INHERENT RISKS OF BLACK CAPITALISM

Statistics for small business failures in America certainly reveal that extensive risk is involved in operating a business enterprise, notwithstanding additional risks incurred by minority-owned ghetto firms. These failures are a function of a multitude of factors, including lack of managerial competence and lack of capital. These problems must be solved if a program of minority enterprise is to attain any degree of success. Yet, the programs would place those who are *least capable* of accepting risk in the position of bearing *large risks.* Potential minority entrepreneurs must be acquainted with the hazards involved but must not be prohibited from assuming it if they desire. No false views should be presented, and no legitimate opportunities hidden. Individuals who would be set up as owners of small businesses by minority enterprise programs should have at least some degree of skill and work experience. For them, operating a business would probably mean giving up a job, risking their reserves, and signing loan notes, with no guarantee of a secure and successful future. For many people, this route might prove disastrous, rather than fortuitous. Of the businessmen displaced by urban renewal in four areas of Chicago who subsequently liquidated, 20 percent reported incomes greater after liquidation than before, and only 10 percent reported decreased incomes—most of these were persons who chose to retire or those with health problems. Fifteen percent said they preferred to be out of business.

SEPARATISM

For many persons, both white and black, the goal of separatism is of dubious worth. Rev. Leon Sullivan, a Negro minister who has achieved some success in developing black enterprise in Philadelphia, feels that, "Separatism in any form offers no future. What a lot of people are talking about, really, when they talk about 'black capitalism' is a separate economy, and that would be no different from the way things are in the Republic of South Africa."

Although the desirability of separatism is debatable in many ways, the question of the feasibility of a viable separate black economy is more concrete. Could blacks organize into a separate economy or group of economies that would result in economic improvements? Can the noneconomic gains of a separate society, such as the minimization of racial discrimination, be obtained under separatism without damaging the economic condition of blacks? There are some economic arguments that tend to indicate that these goals cannot be achieved through separatism. Separatism entails separate markets. Blacks would own plants in the black communities, hire only blacks, and sell only to blacks. Although limited trade with white society would be allowed, the minority economy would have to be nearly self-sufficient. It is doubtful that any minority group has the necessary skills and technology, let alone the capital, to establish and operate all the production facilities needed. Even if the necessary factors of production existed, it is still doubtful that efficient operations could be conducted because many production activities rely on scale economies to make them economically feasible. By arbitrarily limiting the market to minority communities, the potential for reaching the necessary production scale is lost. Automobiles, for example, cannot be economically produced on a small scale.

NEGATIVE SIDE EFFECTS

There is a danger that any potential benefits of black capitalism will be overstated. Its wide press coverage and the support by diverse groups may elevate minorities' hopes, only to later crush them by reality. This end result can only lead to frustration, resentment, and mistrust on the part of the disappointed groups.

It should be obvious that minority entrepreneurship is at best a limited solution to our urban problems because very few persons can be owners of businesses. For the nation as a whole, only 10 percent of the labor force are entrepreneurs. Although entrepreneurship is one means of gaining a slice of the economic pie, by far the most predominant means is by becoming a wage earner. Therefore, most of the population, including racial minorities, cannot expect to become owners and will have to be content as wage earners. The probable impact of minority enterprise programs is further limited since existing white competition will not disappear. For minority entrepreneurs to reach the national figure of about 10 percent, total demand must expand to support new businesses, or existing white owners must be encouraged to sell businesses to blacks at an accelerated rate. It appears likely that net additions to the number of minority-owned businesses will occur slowly, if at all. These limitations on the possible benefits of minority enterprises must be considered and explained to the public to avoid raising the ghetto's hopes falsely.

Another possible side effect is that the promotion of black capitalism could reinforce the tendency in this country toward two separate societies. Encouraging Negro ownership of businesses in the ghetto will limit the amount of white-black interaction. This will shrink an already weak communications link, and whites and blacks will be even more segregated. Since promotion of minority enterprises in the ghetto will perpetuate the ghetto, the best policy for integration would seem to be dispersion, not concentration.

Finally, there is the danger that, by devoting so much time, energy, and money to minority entrepreneurship, the govenment may be overlooking other more efficient alternatives. Before minority enterprise is fully established as a program of the government, the plan must be evaluated critically, and this analysis must be compared with similar evaluations of other proposed alternatives. To date there has been insufficient analysis of *both* the pros and the cons of the black capitalism policy. Surely it is a proper goal of government to ensure that all persons willing to attempt the establishment of a business have an equal opportunity to do so. But to ensure such a condition does not require the promotion of black capitalism. All that is necessary is that discriminatory barriers along racial or other noneconomic lines be removed or offset by government action. (Of course, this is easier said than done!) It is one thing to remove discriminatory barriers to *all* embryonic entrepreneurs and then let the market work to determine the resulting number of minority-owned firms, and quite another to interfere with the market by creating additional minority-owned businesses. We have seen that the potential hazards accompanying the latter policy are not to be taken lightly.

THE PROS OF BLACK CAPITALISM*

RICHARD N. FARMER

Some observers of the American scene take a gloomy view of the future of black capitalism. In their judgment, there is not much hope in this concept as a cure for urban ills, given all the problems associated with developing new entrepreneurs among our Negro population.[1] Basically, their arguments are well-founded; it is highly unlikely that any black capitalism program, however de-

---

*From *Business Horizons* (February, 1970), pp. 37-40. Reprinted by permission.

[1]See, for example, Bernard H. Booms and James E. Ward, Jr., "The Cons of Black Capitalism," *Business Horizons*, XII (October, 1969), pp. 17-26.

veloped and financed, will ever make much of a dent in our overwhelming urban problems. Those who expect that a few billion dollars poured into this area will transform the ghetto are likely to be disillusioned.

However, black capitalism should not be written off as a total failure. If one considers the modest gains that might be made by a realistic approach, it is possible that some support for such a program would pay big dividends—although not in the short run. There is no magic here, nor even a faint hope that the results will revitalize the inner city. But a modest effort, built on a realistic set of assumptions, could have positive impact. These conclusions are based on a program now in operation at Indiana University, which sends students to consult with black small-businessmen in Indianapolis, and on data developed in Indianapolis and Gary by survey work in the black business community.[2]

PRESENT MISCONCEPTIONS

The types of programs envisioned by government planners for black business are unlikely to work for much the same reasons that so many foregin aid programs are relatively unsuccessful. The wrong model has been applied to the problem, and, as a result, all the wrong variables are dealt with. The really important variables rarely get tackled in a systematic manner. Federal programs tend to have several erroneous characteristics.

They Are Far Too Ambitious. Work with small businessmen has driven home to us the real difficulty of moving rapidly toward business improvements. It is not uncommon for a team of rather sophisticated M.B.A. consultants to spend a hundred man-days working with a small businessman and succeed in raising his net profits by only 10 percent. Moving from perhaps $3,000 in net income this year to $3,300 next year represents an improvement, but such gains are not likely to shake the world. These gains are also diminished by an economic consideration. The consultants this year are likely to be highly paid business consultants, staff men, and junior managers next year. If they are worth $100 per day then, they may be worth at least $50 per day now. Students willingly give their time, but providing perhaps $5,000 of free consulting for a $300 gain suggests the economic impracticality of such large-scale projects.

To expect a marginal small businessman (black or white) to move from two employees and $20,000 in sales this year to perhaps a hundred employees and $1 million in sales next year is totally unrealistic. Booms and Ward mentioned some of the major reasons (see footnote 1), but did not note that smaller businessmen have great difficulty in making such a managerial leap; typically, they just do not know enough to do the job.

The Programs Raise All the Wrong Hopes. The expectations are strikingly similar to those related to aid programs in poor countries. Miracles seem about to happen: incomes will jump and everybody will have well-paying jobs. But they do not happen. Hopes are destroyed as reality slowly sinks in, and big-ticket programs are wrecked along with more modest workable ones.

The Programs Assume That the Key to the Problem is a Shortage of Capital. This is totally wrong. The real problem is the shortage of skill, ability, and the kinds of behavioral characteristics that would make a successful large capitalist. We have never been unable to obtain a reasonable loan from a

<hr/>

[2]R. N. Farmer, "Black Businessmen in Indiana," *Indiana Business Review,* LXIII (November-December, 1968), pp. 11-16.

variety of public and private sources if the small firm is sound and deserving. Clearly, there has been discrimination in the past, but now, if anything, there appears to be "reverse" discrimination. We have obtained loans for rather shaky and unbankable types of black operations, which, if white-owned, would probably be denied capital by lending agencies.

The real problem is that so few small businessmen are able to use capital wisely. Most of them are good technicians; this is how they got into business in the first place. But they tend to be bad managers. Their books (if any) are in poor shape; planning is often absent completely; and control systems leak like sieves. Money loaned to such entrepreneurs would be quickly lost.

As already noted, training men to utilize capital efficiently is a labor intensive, time-consuming process. The labor required is exactly that in most short supply—namely, highly trained business consultants and managers.

BLACK BUSINESS THE RIGHT WAY

It is possible to build a modest program for black entrepreneurship that might pay some long-term dividends, as well as complement more realistic efforts in other sectors. Such a plan would have four major characteristics.

It Would be Modest. Perhaps a few hundred million dollars spent correctly is about all that could be absorbed in the entire United States. This more modest approach, incidentally, might also achieve one very real objective: to keep the fast buck boys out of the game. Whenever government money is being doled out in big chunks, the possibilities of con jobs in the program are very real.

One major reason for not needing a great deal of money is that if we can figure out how to produce a group of good potential black entrepreneurs, the normal small business capital markets can easily handle their needs (mainly through banks and SBICs). People with sound businesses and good plans can find capital.

It Would be Focussed Largely on Practical Business Training for Existing and Potential Small Businessmen. Our own Indianapolis work suggests that existing small firms and those who are thinking of starting firms all want help. These are far more than any set of existing or potential trained human resources can handle at present . . .

Clients . . . are not hard to generate. Already a whole set of institutions exists that can cooperate by passing the word, screening potential firms, and finding existing firms in trouble. The Urban League, C.A.P., the National Alliance of Businessmen, and many others are ready to do the job.

The Program Would Utilize Largely the Existing Pool of Trained, High Skill Manpower Available for Such Training. There is only one of these: students in schools of business. Many of these young people are willing to help out with smaller firms if asked, often for small fees or none at all.

Anyone who starts a big aid program for small struggling firms by hiring existing manpower to train such people is going to be disillusioned. The right kinds of people can easily find good jobs elsewhere, and they already have. What is available are students, and they tend to be overtrained for the job at hand. Quite a few B-schools have had small programs of this sort (Indiana, Stanford, Harvard, and Columbia, to name a few), and their experiences should

314

be looked at closely.[3] If these young people cannot do the job, it is unlikely to be done at all.

The Program Should Zero in on the Innumerable Entry Controls Prevalent in Many Businesses. Personal entry controls fill a good sized book just to list;[4] firm entry controls are particularly vicious in motor freight and passenger transportation, where late arrivals are excluded from any activity. If you were not in the game in 1926 or 1935, you are forever excluded.

If we are serious about black capitalism, or, for that matter, capitalism in general, it is about time that we started to act like it. It is time for the successful manager to stop complaining pompously that young men just do not want to get into business for themselves any more; he should realize that two-thirds of the feasible alternatives are partially or totally blocked from entry. We could start 400 small taxi firms in Indianapolis alone next year if the entry control law were changed. None of these would become a gold mine, but they would provide a reasonable living for a lot of people now unemployed or underemployed. In addition, these firms would do a better job for consumers than the present system; service would improve and would cost less.

It is highly unlikely that anything of this sort will happen. We preach the virtues of free enterprise, we encourage blacks and other to enter business, and then we make quite sure that all our upper middle-class subsidies are preserved and protected, even if in the process some of the more interesting possibilities are ruined. No wonder blacks question our real motives. To put it bluntly, we are quite cynical, and a lot of the talk about helping blacks is a fraud. They know it too.

Modest programs, even if successful, are not likely to change the world. What they may do is to contribute toward the economic development of some of the poorer segments of our population. With some luck, a few of the more capable black capitalists will grow enough, become efficient enough, and perhaps even brave enough to become capitalists—not black capitalists. The real business opportunities are out in the mainstream, not in some decaying ghetto. But a shrewd black businessman, who has done his homework and struggled for years against overwhelming odds, might make it. He should not be surrendered so casually. What he needs is knowledge and confidence, not cash. A program of the sort suggested above might do this for a few outstanding men.

And the rest? Not much will happen. A few small firms might become a bit better, and their increased efficiency may help both them and their clients. A man netting $3,000 a year, after a lot of work and worry by students, may get up to netting $5,000 a year. The only ones who will really care will be his consultants and his own family. But such gains, in a part of America where any gain is extremely hard to come by, could in the end represent something worthwhile.

Another argument in favor of black capitalism has little to do with blacks, but may in the end be most important of all. I encourage my white and black students to work with small, marginal black firms in the ghetto. I have no trouble finding volunteers; we pay nothing, yet plenty of young men are willing

[3]Joel Glasser, "Student Consultant—Ghetto Client: a Developing Rapport," *The MBA* (October, 1969), pp. 30-33.

[4]U.S. Department of Labor/Manpower Administration, *Occupational Licensing and the Supply of Professional Manpower* (Washington: U.S. Govt. Printing Office, 1969), pp. 19-50. Also see R. N. Farmer and H. H. Kassarjian, "The Right to Compete," *California Management Review*, VI (Fall, 1963), pp. 61-68.

to go. As one might expect in a volunteer program run and managed by students, we end up with the truly marginal and submarginal small firms. Modestly successful black-owned firms have their own professional sources of support. One outcome of this program is that an immature, white middle-class student will grow up in about five weeks while he works with his firm. The client may be a submarginal, one-man retail operation with a negative net worth, but, for the first time in his life, the student finds out what it is like to do a man's work in a world which he never really knew existed.

Such young men will go on to big corporations as junior managers and staff men, and they take with them an experience that will make them a bit different forevermore in their business careers. This sort of consulting work creates in most of the young people working with it a sensitivity to social problems that they otherwise might never have developed.

Of course, and as usual, this is one more black man's subsidy to the white man. But in the end, it may end up being worthwhile. The submarginal client becomes marginal, which is no big deal for the world but is important to the client. The student grows up and discovers that what he has been learning is not all that well known, even in business circles. And, perhaps most important of all, we whites have had an opportunity to conduct a relevant dialogue with our hard-working black counterparts in business. In a world of racial tension, this alone may make black capitalism worthwhile.

APPENDIX A

Sources of Help and Venture Capital Lists

1. The SBA publishes on a quarterly basis a complete listing of SBICs (Small Business Investment Companies) listing name, address, and size category. Write:

   SBA Investments Divisions
   1441 2nd Street, N.W.
   Washington, D.C. 20416

2. Stanley M. Rubel publishes "A Guide to Venture Capital"—plus newsletters and other material on venture capital (SBIC/Venture Capital monthly newsletter). Write:

   Capital Publishing Company
   10 South LaSalle Street
   Chicago, Ill. 60603

3. A 134 page study by the Management Department at Boston College entitled "Venture Capital—A Guidebook for New Enterprise" published in March, 1972 is especially good for northeastern United States businesses. Write:

   U.S. Government Printing Office
   Re: Committee Print #75-292
   Washington, D.C. 20416

4. Leroy W. Sinclair publishes a hardcover book entitled "Venture Capital," which offers details on all venture capital firms across the United States. In addition, he also publishes a spiral-bound book entitled "The Business Plan," which is a practical guide on how to write a business plan. Write:

   Technimetrics, Inc.
   919 3rd Avenue
   New York, N.Y. 10022

5. Donald Dible has written a 300 page how-to-do-it book entitled "Up Your Own Organization." Especially helpful are the appendixes, which offer reviews of many forms of help including excellent bibliographies and venture capital lists. Write:

The Entrepreneur Press
Mission Station Drawer 2759T
Santa Clara, Cal. 95051

6. John Komives, the director of the not-for-profit Center for Venture Management, offers many valuable services for entrepreneurs, not the least of which is a bibliography of articles and a monthly newsletter. Write:

Center for Venture Management
811 East Wisconsin Avenue
Milwaukee, Wisconsin 53202

7. Dun & Bradstreet produces an excellent booklet of 50 pages that identifies many of the good articles and books on small business. This is especially valuable for specific industries as reports on special opportunities are numerous. Write:

Dun & Bradstreet
99 Church Street
New York, N.Y. 10007

8. A list of publications and committee memberships of the Select Committee on Small Business of the House of Representatives, 77th-92d Congress, Jan. 1973, is available from:

Government Printing Office
#87-842 Pamphlet
Washington, D.C.

9. Pamphlets and books published by U.S. Government agencies, such as the Small Business Administration, should be purchased from the Superintendent of Documents, Government Printing Office, Washington, D.C. 20401.

Free SBA pamphlets (and they are numerous) may be obtained from the SBA, Washington, D.C. 20416 or from local SBA branch offices.

10. A newsletter is published for small businessmen that offers items of interest to all small businessmen and is especially relevant to small business and the government. Write:

Newsletter Small Business
1225 19th Street, N.W.
Washington, D.C. 20036

11. A group of New England small businessmen have formed an organization for their mutual benefit known as Smaller Business Association of New England (SBANE). They hold seminars and offer a newsletter. Write:

Mr. Lew Shattuck
SBANE
69 Hickory Drive
Waltham, Mass. 02154

12. An excellent monthly brochure is offered free by the Bank of America entitled *The Small Business Reporter.* Write:

Small Business Reporter
Bank of America
Box 37000
San Francisco, Cal. 94137

13. Joseph Mancuso, Worcester Polytechic Institute, has written *Fun 'n' Guts—The Entrepreneur's Philosophy* (Addison-Wesley 1973). A combination of telling it like it is, humor, and advice along with a good bibliography is available in the 203 pages.

14. Besides the low cost pamphlets offered by the Small Business Administration, they also offer numerous services and seminars. Inquire about Service Corps of Retired Executives (SCORE) and the teams of the Small Business Institute (SBI). Each may be of value to you.

15. "How to Form Your Own Corporation Without a Lawyer for Under $50.00," written by Ted Nicholas, is published by Enterprise Publishing Company, Wilmington, Delaware, 1973. 103 pages.

16. A free 15-page booklet is published by the U.S. Department of Commerce entitled, "Publications for Business." It provides an extensive list of government literature in business. Available from Superintendent of Documents, Government Printing Office, Washington, D.C. 20401.

APPENDIX B

National Associations of Value to Small Business

American Management Association
135 W. 50th Street
New York, N.Y. 10020

Association of Management Consultants
811 E. Wisconsin Avenue
Milwaukee, Wisc. 53202

Presidents Association
135 West 50th Street
New York, N.Y. 10020

National Small Business Association
301-1225 15th St. N.W.
Washington, D.C. 20036

National Federation of Independent Business
150 West 20th Avenue
San Mateo, Cal. 94402

The Executive Committee (TEC)
1201 North Prospect Avenue
Milwaukee, Wisc. 53202

The Young Presidents' Organization (YPO)
375 Park Avenue
New York, N.Y. 10022

Sons of Bosses (SOBs)
53 East Main Street
Moorestown, N.J. 08057

National Council for Small Business Management Development
c/o University of Wisconsin—Extension
Civic Center Campus
600 West Kilbourn Avenue
Milwaukee, Wisc. 53203

APPENDIX C

Periodicals of Value to Small Businesses

Administrative Science Quarterly
Cornell University
Graduate School of Business and
  Public Administration
Ithaca, N.Y. 14850

Advanced Management Journal
Society for Advancement of Management
135 West 50th Street
New York, N.Y. 10020

American Legion Magazine
P.O. Box 1954
Indianapolis, Ind. 46206

The Bankers Magazine
89 Beach Street
Boston, Mass. 02111

Business Horizons
Indiana University Graduate School of
  Business
Bloomington, Ind. 47401

Business Week
330 W. 42nd Street
New York, N.Y. 10036

California Management Review
University of California
Berkeley, Cal. 94720

Dun's
Dun & Bradstreet Publications Corp.
466 Lexington Avenue
New York, N.Y. 10017

Electronic News
Fairchild Publications, Inc.
7 E. 12th Street
New York, N.Y. 10003

Financial Analysts Journal
Financial Analysts Federation
219 E. 42nd Street
New York, N.Y. 10016

Forbes
Forbes, Inc.
60 Fifth Avenue
New York, N.Y. 10011

Fortune
Rocketeller Center
New York, N.Y. 10020

Harvard Business Review
Harvard University
Graduate School of Business Admini-
  stration
Soldiers Field Road
Boston, Mass. 02163

Industrial Research
Industrial Research Blvd.
Beverly Shores, Ind. 46301

Industrial Research & Development
UNIDO
United Nations Publications
New York, N.Y. 10017

International Management
330 W. 42nd Street
New York, N.Y. 10036

Journal of Applied Psychology
American Psychological Assn., Inc.
1200 17th Street N.W.
Washington, D.C. 20036

Journal of Small Business Management
Editor Stanley J. Kloc, Jr.
Bureau of Business Research
West Virginia University
Morgantown, W. Va. 20506

Management Accounting
National Association of Accountants
919 Third Avenue
New York, N.Y. 10022

Management of Personnel Quarterly
University of Michigan, Bureau of Industrial Relations
Graduate School of Business Administration
Ann Arbor, Mich. 48104

Management Review
American Management Association, Inc.
135 W. 50th Street
New York, N.Y. 10020

Marquette Business Review
Marquette University
College of Business Administration
Milwaukee, Wis. 53233

The MBA
MBA Communications
555 Madison Avenue
New York, N.Y. 10022

Monthly Review of Management & Research
(Formerly: (Management Research)
Box 4
Dolton, Ill. 60419

MSU Business Topics
Michigan State University
Bureau of Business and Economic Research
East Lansing, Mich. 48823

Nation's Business
Chamber of Commerce of U.S.
1615 1st Street, N.W.
Washington, D.C. 20006

Personnel Psychology
Box 6565, College Station
Durham, N.C. 27708

Research & Development Management
108 Cowley Road
Oxford, OX4, IJF, ENGLAND

Texas
Commerce Clearing House, Inc.
4025 W. Pereson Avenue
Chicago, Ill. 60646

Wall Street Journal
30 Broad Street
New York, N.Y. 10004

APPENDIX D

Selected Books on Entrepreneurship and Small Business

A Guide to Managerial Accounting in Small Companies
Jack W. Still
Prentice-Hall, Inc.
Englewood Cliffs, N.J. 1969

American Small Businessman
John M. Benzel
Alfred A. Knopf, Inc.
New York, N.Y. 1962

Business Policy in Growing Firms
Robert B. Buchele
Chandler Publishing Co.
New York, N.Y. 1967

Data Processing for the Small Business
Byron L. Carter
Macfadden-Bartell Corp., 1966
New York, N.Y.

Effective R & D for the Smaller Company
Russell W. Henke
Gulf Publishing Co.
Houston, Tex. 1963

Entrepreneurial Dimensions of Management
G. Jay Anyon
Livingston Publishing Company
18 Hampstead Circle
Wynnewood, Pa. 19096

Entrepreneurship and Venture Management
A readings book
Clifford R. Baumback
and Joseph Mancuso
Prentice-Hall, Inc.
Englewood Cliffs, N.J., 1974

Financing for Small and Medium Sized Businesses
Harry Gross
Prentice-Hall, Inc.
Englewood Cliffs, N.J., 1969

Financing the Dynamic Small Firm
Roland I. Robinson
Wadsworth Publishing Company
Belmont, Cal. 1968

Fun & Guts—The Entrepreneur's Philosophy
Joseph Mancuso
Addison-Wesley
Reading, Mass. 1973

How to Make Money in Your Own Business
Ernest R. Field
Prentice-Hall, Inc.
Englewood Cliffs, N.J., 1965

How to Organize and Operate a Small Business
5th Ed.
C.M. Baumback, K. Lawyer, and P.D. Kelley
Prentice-Hall, Inc.
Englewood Cliffs, N.J., 1973

How to Run A Small Business
J.K. Lasser
McGraw-Hill Book Co.
New York, N.Y., 1963

Management of Small Enterprises, Cases and Readings
William Rotch
University Press of Virginia
Charlottesville, Va., 1967

Managing the Dynamic Small Firm
Lawrence Klatt
Wadsworth Publishing Co.
Belmont, Cal., 94002

Managing for Profits
H.C. Krentzman
Small Business Administration
Washington, D.C., 1968

Managing the Small Business
L. L. Steinmetz, John B. Kline ana D.P. Stegall
Richard D. Irwin, Inc.
Homewood, Ill. 1968

Managing the Smaller Company
Russell Banks, ed.
Management Association, Inc.
New York, N.Y., 1969

Portfolio of Accounting Systems for Small and Medium-Sized Businesses
Marjorie D. James
Prentice-Hall, Inc.
Englewood Cliffs, N.J., 1968

Small Business Bibliography
John K. Chance
Center for Small Business
Urbana, Ohio
Summer 1972

Small Business Management, 3rd Ed.
H.N. Broom and J.G. Longenecker
South-Western Publishing Co.
Burlingame, Cal. 1971

Small Business Management: A Casebook
Hosmer, Tucker, and Cooper
Richard D. Irwin
Homewood, Ill., 1966

Social Responsibility and the Smaller Company
James Brown
National Industrial
Conference Board, 1972
New York, N.Y.

Starting and Succeeding in Your Own Small Business
Louis L. Allen
Grosset & Dunlap
New York, N.Y., 1968

Strengthening Small Business Management
Joseph Schabacker
Small Business Administration, 1972
Washington, D.C.

Technology and Change
Schon, D.
Dell, N.Y., 1967

The Enterprising Man
Collins, O., and D. Moore
University of Michigan
Ann Arbor, Mich., 1964

The Entrepreneur's Handbooks
Joseph Mancuso
Starting, financing, and managing a technical firm
Artech House
610 Washington Street
Dedham, Mass., 02026
1974—2 volumes

The Future of Small Business
Edward D. Hollander
Frederick A. Praeger, Inc.
New York, N.Y., 1967

The Organization Makers
O. Collins and D. Moore
University of Michigan
Ann Arbor, Mich., 1970

*The Young Businessman—Small
  Company or Large?*
Ronald E. Herinton
Hobbs, 1967

The R & D Game
MIT Press
Cambridge, Mass., 1969

Up Your Own Organization
Donald Dible
Entrepreneur Press
Santa Clara, Cal., 1971

*What You Should Know About Small
  Business Management*
Donald Grunewald
Oceana, 1966
New York, N.Y.

Subject Index

Growth (*cont.*)
  problems of, 151-60, 180-84, 196-226, 292
  raising capital for, 81, 133, 196

I

Incubator organizations (*see* Entrepreneurail environment)
Industrial Research Institute, 72
Initial capital (*see* Start-up capital)
Innovation (*see* Product innovation)
Invention, significant sources of, 59-61 (*see also* Product innovation)
Insurance and risk management, 91
International Franchise Association, 85, 86
Inventory control, 80, 93

K

Kuder Occupational Interest Survey, 12, 13, 14, 16, 17, 20, 21

L

Lawyer, consulting a, 38, 88, 89, 90, 91
Leadership in business (*see* Management and leadership)
Loans (*see* Capital, sources of)
Location, selecting a, 49-50, 80, 90
Long-range planning, 151, 160-79
  analytical steps, 164-65
  break-even analysis, 170-72
  in decentralized companies, 178
  master planning form, 166-68
  the planning gap, 169-70
  return-on-investment approach, 170, 171
  selecting key objectives, 169-70
  strategic factors, 165-66
  structure and process of planning, 162-64
  use of check-off lists, 166
  use of standard accounting statements, 172-74

M

Management consultants, use of, 37-38, 83
Management and leadership, 38, 79, 91, 102, 151-52, 155, 156-58, 180-84, 227, 251, 279-98, 305 (*see also* Personnel and employee relations; and Subordinates, recruiting and motivating)
Management succession, 227, 229-36, 286-95
  in the family business, 228, 233, 235, 244, 247-48, 292
  reasons for lack of succession planning, 233-35, 235-36
  succession planning and subsequent profitability, 232-33, 235
Marketing plan, 102-105
Maturity crisis, 196-226
Mergers, 196, 197-98, 203-209
  benefits of, 196, 197, 205-206
  governmental requirements, 207
  picking the right buyer, 207-208
  role of the intermediary, 208-209
Minority business enterprise, 129-30, 299-316
Minority Enterprise Small Business Investment Companies (MESBICs), 129-30

N

N-Ach, 2, 3-10, 11-14, 16, 18 (*table*),20, 21, 26-29, 33-34, 36, 228, 299
  measurement problems and techniques, 6-7, 11-14, 21, 28, 29
  relationship to regional economic development, 6-9, 27
National Alliance of Businessmen, 314
National Association of Securities Dealers, 213, 216, 217, 219
National Better Business Bureau, Inc., 86
National Inventors Council, 59, 60
National Quotations Bureau, 213, 216
Navy China Lake Laboratory, 63
New businesses (*see also* Entrepreneurship):

Index of Names

335